Fighting Words

Fighting Words

**A Tale of How Liberals Created
Neo-Conservatism**

Ben J. Wattenberg

THOMAS DUNNE BOOKS
St. Martin's Press ⧳ New York

THOMAS DUNNE BOOKS.
An imprint of St. Martin's Press.

FIGHTING WORDS. Copyright © 2008 by Ben J. Wattenberg. All rights reserved. Printed in the United States of America. For information, address St. Martin's Press, 175 Fifth Avenue, New York, N.Y. 10010.

www.thomasdunnebooks.com
www.stmartins.com

Book design by Meryl Sussman Lerari

Library of Congress Cataloging-in-Publication Data

Wattenberg, Ben J.
  Fighting words : a tale of how liberals created neo-conservatism / Ben
J. Wattenberg. — 1st ed.
        p.   cm.
  ISBN-13: 978-0-312-38299-5
  ISBN-10: 0-312-38299-5
  1. Wattenberg, Ben J.   2. Conservatives—United States—Biography.
3. Conservatism—United States.   4. United States—Politics and government—
1989– I. Title.
  JC573.2.U6W38   2008
  320.52092—dc22
  [B]   2008010393

First Edition: July 2008

10 9 8 7 6 5 4 3 2 1

To my grandchildren,
Maisie, Lylah, Michael, and Emma . . .
may our tribe increase.

And to Richard M. Scammon.

Contents

Acknowledgments

IN THEORY, A book like this personal narrative should require a relatively brief set of acknowledgments. After all, it is a political yarn of what happened to *me* and, I hope, how that reveals something about America, and the world, in recent decades—and perhaps in decades to come. The principal acknowledgment should therefore be to *me*, as it must be with any memoirist.

But I fancy myself as someone who has farmed the fields of "data journalism" and, in fact, I think I have done it in a way that has not quite been done in such manner before. So what the reader finds here are not just recollections, but also serried ranks of fact upon fact in the attempt to paint a political portrait that is both readable and realistic. (I do not shield my light under a basket, nor do I ever use clichés.)

I came to this notion of numerical storytelling after reading a mind-bending book of political narration, *The Making of the President, 1960*, by Theodore H. White. I describe how that came about in chapter 8 of this chronicle. You will see there why I regard Teddy as a most unusual man. I once had a dinner with Pat and Liz Moynihan, Teddy, and Diane, my wife-to-be. The spirits flowed freely, and we all learned a lot.

So my first debt of gratitude goes to the not-so-small army of data-mongers—public and private, economic, sociological, climatological, geographical, psephological (look it up), criminal, and so very many more. The fruits of their labor can be found in one of the world's great annual volumes, *The Statistical Abstract of the United States*. I used to read its 1,000 pages of tables like a novel.

That book is produced by the U.S. Bureau of the Census. I began going out to their main offices in Suitland, Maryland, in 1962. I met the Census director, Richard Scammon. We became collaborators and began writing. A couple of years later, *This U.S.A.* was published. That book led to a job in President Lyndon Johnson's White House in mid-1966. I thought that I would return home to Stamford, Connecticut, after my two-year tour was up—but I am still in Washington. It is a marvelous place to live and work.

I can name only a few of the hundreds of people who went out of their way to introduce a neophyte to their arcane mathematical world, and then left me alone to draw my own conclusions. These include Richard Scammon (of whom much more later), Conrad Taeuber, Herman Miller, Stephanie Ventura, Ed Goldfield, Joe Chamie and Larry Heligman (both of the United Nations), Dan Levine, Ross Eckler, Meyer Zitter, Roger Herriot, Gordon Green, and so very many more. Those are my names from the past. I went out to the Bureau in late 2007 to do research for an article and speech—again I was treated with cordiality by competent professionals. The Census Bureau is one reason I have never bought into the idea that "government is the problem not the solution."

If you can fairly accurately quantify something important that is going on, you have a leg up on trying to explain it (although, alas, as Mark Twain pointed out, "figures don't lie, but liars figure"). In our day, too many scientists endorse the pernicious idea of "lying for justice." This happens on both sides of the political spectrum, but I find it far more pronounced on the Left.

The next set of salutes goes to my colleagues at the quite remarkable array of think tanks in the Washington area, and beyond. Since 1978, I have been a senior fellow at what is surely the most important such institution anywhere: The American Enterprise Institute for Public Policy Research. The ideological range at AEI goes from conservative to libertarian, to moderate, to moderately liberal. The president of AEI, Chris DeMuth, is a most remarkable fellow and has been of steady help to me and my ventures. When I was writing a syndicated column and it didn't seem just right, I would e-mail him at 7:00 A.M. and within twenty minutes would receive a cogent reply, laying out what he thought was wrong. Sometimes I agreed, sometimes not, but the effort of a man running a complex 25-million-dollar enterprise to pay such attention stunned me then, and now. My colleague Karlyn Bowman, now the go-to gal on polling and survey research for a legion of hungry journalists, was often another recipient of my panicked early-morning messages.

Others at AEI who have been of particular help are Michael Novak, Norman Ornstein, the late Herbert Stein, Josh Muravchik, Doug Besharov, Leon Aron, Michael Barone, Walter Berns, Irving Kristol, Lynne Cheney, John Bolton, Nick Eberstadt, John Fortier, Newt Gingrich, Robert Goldwyn, Kevin Hassett, Anne Feng Shi, Steve Hayward, Rick Hess, Bob Bork, Larry Silberman, Antonin Scalia, Marvin Kosters, Jim Lilley, Jeane Kirkpatrick, Larry Lindsey, Michael Ledeen, John Makin, Allen Meltzer, Charles Murray, Richard Perle, Sally Satel, Christina Hoff Sommers, Paul Wolfowitz, and Bill Schneider.

Gertrude Himmelfarb and James Q. Wilson are two of the many outstanding scholars who serve on the AEI Board of Academic Advisors. Dick Cheney was a senior fellow and trustee. Notwithstanding the crazy portrait of him painted in the mainstream media, I have always found him to be calm, patient, and attentive, as well as conservative. I learned at AEI that very rich people can also be very nice people — in fact, that's probably one good reason they have succeeded.

I am now also a senior fellow at the Hudson Institute. I have been treated splendidly. President Herb London and CEO Ken Weinstein have shown great cordiality and understanding.

I helped form the Coalition for a Democratic Majority in 1972, described herein. The first executive director was Penn Kemble (described at some length later) who had a profound influence on me. Tragically, he died young.

At AEI, I started and served as the editor of *Public Opinion*, a magazine devoted to — public opinion. My deputy was David Gergen.

Karlyn and Bill Schambra rounded out my staff. We learned so much from our two consultants, Seymour Martin Lipset and Everett Carll Ladd. We argued about whether the socioeconomic data showed "continuity" or "change." We thought the answer was usually "continuity," although it's "change that always draws the headlines." We kidded a lot about whether we were seeing "the end of an era"—a political era, that is—and decided that we probably were. The Republicans are back in business.

I have been blessed by a (mostly) fine crew of AEI research assistants, some of whom later moved over to work with me on my PBS program *Think Tank with Ben Wattenberg*. Most have gone on to great things. Karl Zinsmeister was my first RA, and he is now the domestic policy czar at the White House. Tevi Troy was the second, and he is now the deputy secretary of the Department of Health and Human Services. Also, Jonah Goldberg (who has a number-one *New York Times* bestseller to his credit), Doug Anderson, Joe Manzari, Jeremy Kadden, Mark Mazzetti (now the chief reporter on national intelligence at *The New York Times*). The list could go on and on.

I started *Think Tank* in 1994. My executive producer then was Andrew Walworth; he still is. We have produced more than four hundred programs plus about a dozen specials. We are at work on two more as this is written, one about this book. The show has won many awards. A partial list of producers and helpers over the years includes John Sorensen, Andy Och, Adam Garber, Deborah Schull, Lynn Hoverman, Courtland Carter, Christina Mazzanti, Michael Sriqui, Wallace Cole, Iris Hernandez, Marina Malinec, Nick Schulz, and Scott McLucas. The team working on the documentary based on this book have worked furiously, fast, and with great skill: Roger Aronoff, Don Wilson, and Jack Harris. I know I am missing some.

My friend in California Judy Hanauer read parts of this book and provided invaluable assistance. She e-mails me constantly with items of interest and has helped set up a number of *Think Tank* programs.

Other names come to mind: Austin Hoyt, Gerry Lange, Bruce Shah, Elizabeth Deane (all of WGBH in Boston where I began doing PBS programs), Barbara Friedland, Michael Pack, Mel Elfin, Tom Foley, Andy Glass, Bill Cohen, Jay Winik, Janet Langhart

Cohen, Jacob Collins, Francis Collins, Tom Wolfe, Sam Vaughan, Harold Roth—and so many more.

I worked for more than a decade as vice chairman of the Board of Radio Free Europe and Radio Liberty. Frank Shakespeare and Steve Forbes were chairmen and taught me a great deal. Among the notable board members were Lane Kirkland, president of the AFL-CIO, and the bestselling historical novelist (and quite a liberal fellow) James Michener.

It has been a pleasure working with the team at St. Martin's Press, the publishers of this volume: Tom Dunne, Rob Kirkpatrick, Joe Rinaldi, Lorrie McCann, and John Schoenfelder. Karen Gantz-Zahler is a lawyer and my literary agent. She is always in my corner.

My final and most important debt of gratitude goes to my family: my four children, Ruth, Daniel, Sarah, and Rachel; my four grandchildren, Emma, Michael, Lylah, and Maisie. My son-in-law, David Kusnet, President Clinton's chief speechwriter for several years, and my daughter-in-law, Cindy Balmuth, are a joy to be with. I am proud of the work I do, but family comes first—and nothing is in second place.

—BEN WATTENBERG,
Chevy Chase, MD,
April 2008

Preface

IN THE COURSE of taping the public television special to accompany this narrative, I revisited the unique, all-Jewish little village in which I grew up in the 1940s. It brought to mind a splash of old personal memories that offer a context for this political yarn.

The village is in the middle of the New York City borough of The Bronx, which, when I lived there, had a population of about two million. The village had about a thousand souls. An all-Jewish sister village nearby, quite different in character, had about twice as many people. Small as the communities were, they proved to be very influential places that helped shape America over the course of the decades that followed. The villages in The Bronx were like small places everywhere: Everyone seemed to know most everyone else's business and looked around to see if the kids were getting into trouble. It takes a village to raise children right.

The director of the documentary crew was from Biloxi, Mississippi. He said my village reminded him of home. While the accent was different, some of the politics were eerily the same, even though there weren't a whole lot of professed Socialists in Biloxi, and hardly any publicly professed and proud Communists.

The building complex we lived in was called the Sholem Aleichem Houses, named for the famous East European Yiddish humorist. At the time it was the New World center of Yiddish culture. After the Holocaust, it is fair to say it was *the* center of Yiddish culture.

The other village was somewhat bigger: the Amalgamated Houses—a complex owned and operated by the Amalgamated Clothing Workers Union. It was a hotbed of union activity at a time when unions played a much more powerful role in American politics than they do now—and they are still potent today.

It was an all-Democratic neighborhood. I was seven in 1940 when Wendell Wilkie, the dark-horse Republican candidate, was nominated to run for president against Franklin D. Roosevelt, who was seeking an unprecedented third term. I found a Wilkie campaign button on the street. I showed it to one of my friends, who was not a stupid kid. He said, "What's a Wilkie?"

The Jewish community at the time was characterized—quite correctly, I think—as either moderate left, very left, or extremely left, and included some card-carrying Communists. My parents were of the moderate Left: My father read the more moderate of the three Yiddish daily newspapers (with huge circulations) as well as *The New York Times* (then a middle-of-the road newspaper) and the *New York Post* (then a liberal paper). Times change—a thought worth noting.

As I came to realize later, it was an intensely political environment. But for us kids, politics rarely came up. We were interested in basketball, punchball, stickball, softball, and—later—girls. Still, something political was going on in our young heads. We were four cousins: two children each of my mother and my uncle, who had come to America—and loved it—but each of whom intended to return to Palestine from where they had come.

We cousins were quite close until the death of my uncle at age fifty-four. A war came along, cousin David served in the merchant marine (eyesight too bad for the draft), then on some ships whose attempt to smuggle Holocaust survivors from Europe into British Palestine was deemed illegal, and then with the Haganah during the Israeli War of Independence. He later became a noted psychologist, specializing in gerontology.

We all got older. We got married and had children. My sister and I stayed in touch, but for a couple of decades contact with David and cousin Yona pretty well ceased. But when we four from that liberal ambience came together again, we noticed something quite remarkable: All of us, in varying degrees and in some mildly different ways, could be called neo-conservatives. And so too could some of our children (although some were quite liberal).

And it wasn't just our family. New York City is often deemed by pundits "the most liberal big city in America," with the possible exception of San Francisco. Strange things keep happening. That most liberal city was electing neo-conservatives to office! Of the last four mayors in Gotham, three can easily be described as neo-conservatives. Two of them would even describe themselves that way.

Ed Koch was a liberal Congressman representing Manhattan's artsy Greenwich Village who came to see the light. Crime and bizarre "nonnegotiable" leftist demands had disgusted New Yorkers. Koch responded with toughness. David Dinkins, a courtly black liberal career politician succeeded him, beating the abrasive Rudy Giuliani by a whisker in Giuliani's maiden run for elective office. Dinkins governed from the soft left—no bad boys, only bad societies. Giuliani scored his own narrow victory four years later. Upon taking office he set into motion a vigorous crime abatement plan, based in large measure on neo-con James Q. Wilson's theories on public safety. The crime rate plummeted, although Giuliani angered many New Yorkers, particularly blacks. Still, he was reelected by a landslide. When he retired he was succeeded by billionaire Mike Bloomberg, who continued Giuliani's successful policies, with one major difference: He didn't get many people angry.

Contrary to common belief, neo-conservatism first formed around domestic issues, not ones of foreign policy: How important was crime? In New York City, in my own family, my mother was mugged once and my father was mugged twice. My son was mugged twice, once in New York and once in Washington. In Philadelphia, my sister-in-law, a methadone nurse, was murdered—a crime that was never solved.

The early neo-cons were of an intellectual bent. But they did not sit down with their scholarly data and say, "My regression analysis demonstrates clearly that violent crime is a major issue in American cities." The public opinion polls showed that clearly. So did a conversation with most anyone on a bus or on a street corner.

There was a story making the rounds that, in a harsh way, captured some of the nature of what was going on: A liberal clergyman, of the sort who says there are no bad boys, only bad societies, was mugged. He was scheduled shortly thereafter to speak to a group of elderly citizens. He said, "I have gone through trauma. I have thought and rethought my views about crime. Despite the violence visited upon me, I hold fast to my liberal principles." The hall was silent. Then an elderly woman called out, "Mug him again!"

American politics are nothing if not *responsive*. The rise of the neo-conservative persuasion came from the bottom up, not from the top down.

The foreign policy issue—the issue that has led to a mindless and withering criticism of neo-cons, is different. You may rest assured that Americans don't go around saying, "America ought to noncoercively promote and purvey democratic views and values whenever and wherever we can if the price is not too high, and with armed force only as a last resort." But that's pretty much the way they feel—and public opinion polls and election results back up that view.

Most Americans understand full well the menace of totalitarian and dictatorial behavior. Their ancestors experienced it, so did their sons, fathers, grandfathers—and daughters. Many of them are buried overseas.

In my own family, my mother's family left Odessa for Palestine after the Kishinev pogroms. My father's older brother, Elya, was a committed Communist. In the early 1930s he was a lawyer for Amtorg, the Russian-American trading organization. He was invited to the Soviet Union to assume an important job. He did. In the early 1950s he and his wife were shot *in a courtroom* for the sin of "cosmopolitanism."

I had worked with hawkish President Lyndon B. Johnson, and former Vice President Hubert H. Humphrey, who was a tougher anti-Communist than most people knew. But I didn't realize just how much of a visceral anti-Communist I was until I started work on the presidential campaigns of my hero, Senator Henry M. "Scoop" Jackson, in the early 1970s. Scoop championed the cause of liberty in a way that marked him as one of America's most notable statesmen.

Today, the word *neo-conservative* has been poisoned—mostly by people who have little idea of what it stands for. And, alas, some neocons seem to have gone out of their way to further antagonize their enemies. By my lights, the major problem facing the neo-con idea today concerns a label change.

Things have changed in my old neighborhood in The Bronx, but perhaps not as much as you might think. It's true, there is (eek!) a Christmas tree in the center of the campus of the Sholem Aleichem Houses. Many of the elderly residents are Jewish. Most of the younger ones are blacks and Latinos. But crime is low. The kids get on school buses without much of a ruckus. I talked to some of them. I doubt that their views and values are quite akin to those of us Jewish kids. But they plan to be dental technicians or to major in business administration. Most of the Latino kids speak English with little trace of an accent. (Most neo-cons, as we shall see, are vigorously pro-immigration.)

My alma mater, DeWitt Clinton High School, went through a rough patch when The Bronx turned sour. Then it turned around, as the city did. The school went from all boys to coed. I received an alumni award one night, and a young Latina came up to me and said, "You know what saved Clinton? We did! Girls!" Women can do that sort of thing. Liberals are responsible for some very beneficial changes in America. Title IX, which encourages athletics for women, is one.

The boys I grew up with mostly moved up and out. Many of them moved up the Hudson to a place called New City (not New York City). Others are scattered across the country. Most have done very well. They have contributed a great deal to America and the world. There are Nobel Prize winners among the Clinton graduates, actor Burt Lancaster, author James Baldwin, and playwright Paddy Chayevsky. Bess Meyerson, the first Jewish Miss America, lived in my building complex.

Most American Jews are still liberals, probably more so than any group in America other than blacks. It used to be said in the Jewish community that if you voted Republican, your right hand would wither. Yet there have been years when the Jewish vote for the Republican candidate has topped one-third. I am not necessarily advocating such a vote, but it is a sign of political maturity and shrewdness. A smart group of voters does not want to be taken for granted.

Growing up not too far away from Yankee Stadium, where Joe DiMaggio was regarded as more than a minor deity, I was a fan of the faraway Brooklyn Dodgers. Perhaps I am countercyclical by nature. Perhaps that's what led me to neo-conservatism. But I think not. Most Americans believe roughly as I do: Be tough on where we have become permissive and generous in helping the unfortunate, understanding that we Americans have played—and will play—an important and beneficent role in world history.

Fighting Words

Introduction

NEO-CONS UNLEASHED

THERE HAS BEEN an explosive discussion of that body of political and policy ideas called neo-conservatism. Much of that commentary has been extremely harsh, or very wrong, or both. I can say this because I have been a neo-con for a long time, from the early 1970s by name, but for much longer than that without a label. I think I understand some unique aspects about neo-conservatism, in large measure because I came to it in a unique way.

In this book I relate what I know from those many years, but principally starting from my years as a speechwriter for President Lyndon B. Johnson, beginning in August 1966. Occasionally this volume rambles, but so does life. Strange and funny things happen. The narrative goes to the present and looks forward. It offers what I consider to be a somewhat startling view of the future. Samuel S. Vaughan, my first editor and later the editor in chief of Doubleday, had an interesting way of putting it: Everything is true and so is its opposite.

Perhaps. Although it may sometimes seem that way, neo-conservatism was not created out of whole cloth by the scholars we hear about: sociologists, political scientists (oxymoron!), economists, demographers, geopoliticians, historians, foreign policy experts, all-purpose policy wonks, theologians, and dedicated readers of *The Public Interest, Commentary,* and *The Weekly Standard.* (I should say at the outset that I have admiration for those publications and for most, not all, of those who came up along those academic tracks.)

I came to neo-conservatism differently. I am none of the above— although I have written on many of the topics mentioned, particularly demographics. But I am not even a demographer, although I have frequently been called one, and I have great regard for many of them.

So, I am not an academic. I have a B.A. from Hobart College, in Geneva, N.Y., with a major in English and a minor in drama. But if I don't have the experiences of most neo-cons who came along the more traditional ways, they don't have mine. In my own case, with no particular plan, over the course of forty years on the national scene, I stopped at many of the watering holes of neo-conservatism as they came about. I've even helped dig a couple of new ones.

It is a peculiar story. You will find here chapters *about* my life in the LBJ White House when the great new split in the Democratic party began, as exemplified by the hegira of Bill Moyers; *about* the post-Johnson Coalition for a Democratic Majority, a mischief-making "ginger group" trying to get the Democratic Party to shape up, and in which I played an important role; *about* how ex-Vice President Hubert Humphrey, allegedly a softie, "gave 'em hell" on "law 'n' order"; *about* Scoop Jackson's two seminal (and sometimes bitter) campaigns for the presidency in the 1970s; *about* some political machinations in the times of Presidents Carter, Reagan, Bush, Clinton, and Bush the Second; *about* some arguments I have had dealing with "facts" regarding global warming and homosexuality, among many other topics (it was Senator Daniel Patrick Moynihan who said each man is entitled to his own opinions but not his own facts, a precept regularly honored in its breach); *about* the great controversies about "values"; *about* my experience for more than twenty-five years at the American Enterprise Institute, a think tank and probably America's most influential such organization; *about* how think tanks have changed America, and consequently the world; *about* the early years of the twenty-first century; *about* the issue of "compassionate conservatism"; *about* Iraq; and *about* what comes next.

I write, too, about how my fascination with social demographics helped shape my neo-con political views. Something very strange is going on in the realm of births and fertility. It is not strange good, but strange bad, almost apocalyptic, even though it is good for America. I wrote a book as recently as 2004, *Fewer*. Even since then my foreboding has grown.

I THINK THE words "neo-conservative" and "ideologue" have gotten a bad rap in a variety of dictionaries. For example, *Merriam-Webster Online:* "neo-conservative—a former liberal espousing political conservatism." (Not anymore: the so-called baby-cons, mini-cons, and the second generation were *born* into it. Others have simply come to the conclusion that the neo-con principles make sense—whether they know the word or not.)

Webster's New World Dictionary (fourth edition) gets closer but is still off the mark: "Designating, or of, an intellectual, political movement that evolved in the late 1970s in reaction to liberal and leftist thought, advocating individualism, traditional moral standards, anti-Communist foreign policy, etc." (There is an error of omission here that will be discussed later.)

Merriam-Webster Online defines "ideologue" as an "impractical idealist," while the handy WordPerfect dictionary defines "ideologue" this way: "a person who follows an ideology in a dogmatic or uncompromising way." But neo-cons pride themselves as non-dogmatic and willing to compromise, choosing one from column A and one from column B as on a Chinese menu. That is a large part of what neo-conservatism is about. Suppose Iraq—a putative victim of such impractical idealism and dogmatism—becomes a more or less decent member of the community of nations, no longer drenched in blood—would it really be *impractical dogmatic idealism* that made it happen? And should the enterprise fail, wouldn't it still have been idealistic? And, by the way, where's the part, in any of these definitions, about the encouragement and promotion of the values of democracy and liberty in other countries?

Once upon a time, I thought of myself as a liberal; I was one, as the term was then used. It amazes me these days how card-carrying contemporary liberals can condemn neo-conservatism, *in its totality*, on the basis of one of its prime tenets, which calls for the peaceful extension of liberty, democracy, and freedom. In the good old days, that idea was a hallmark of liberalism.

SOME GROUND RULES: I try when possible to corroborate the events and language that appear here. A number of chapters have extended excerpts of single speeches that epitomize whole political themes. But no one but me knows what was going on in my mind. And there is no possible corroboration of conversations between me and a person now dead. When Scoop Jackson pulled me aside into a hotel bathroom in his campaign suite in Boston after his 1976 victory in the Massachusetts Democratic primary and said, "The nomination is ours," such words are not forgotten. In many other places I use quotation marks when I clearly remember the general thrust of a conversation (just like Bob Woodward).

With one exception, I have never used a tape recorder in an interview. (The exception concerned a meeting I had with President Ronald Reagan and three other op-ed types.) In such excerpts I have usually stricken the *uhs* and *aahs* and other language that breaks the flow.

I think my story can be of value. Because it is mostly a narrative, I hope this book simplifies complexity. I also hope that a narrative maintains interest in a topic that can be tangled and sometimes arcane. I am not accustomed to writing at length in the first person—I - I - I—and I hope this doesn't come off as a braggart's yarn. There are negatives here about me, too. But I do believe that my story is relevant and may help to explain aspects of what neo-conservatism is—and is not. I believe it is a healthy development. But it is not so simple, as I hope the reader will discover.

BEFORE GETTING INTO the meat of the journey, I offer a loose overview.

It was reported that President Reagan's favorite joke in 1980 went like this: A straightlaced member of one of his transition teams showed up one day at the Bureau of Indian Affairs. The aide was given a tour by a fast-talking bureau guide who concluded his tour in a huge bureaucratic bullpen. Suddenly, one of the bureaucrats hunched over his desk and began sobbing uncontrollably. "What's wrong?" asked the Reagan aide. "It's a sad story," said the bureau guide. "His Indian died."

Such a joke would never be a neo-con president's favorite. All government bureaucrats are not time-serving dunces. Many make real contributions to the well-being of the nation, although there are those who are rigid dopes.

And while Ronald Reagan talked big-time conservatism, his heart was also big and he knew that there were needy Americans who could only survive with help from their government. He also knew that Americans needed protection from the Soviet Union, a totalitarian, nuclear-tipped empire with an expansive vision. In the key words of *The Communist Manifesto*, Marx and Engels say "workers of the *world* unite." At the least, the Soviets posed a *threat* to America and its allies: It possessed roughly the same number of nuclear weapons and had many more ground troops. Since then, some observers have come to believe that Soviet might was overstated. We're not about to relive the Cold War here to seek a definitive answer. Suffice it to say that thirty thousand nuclear missiles aimed at you are many missiles indeed.

Some of the critiques of neo-conservatism have been nasty enough to qualify as hate crimes and some are plain stupid. There is one criticism about how neo-cons stole President George W. Bush's brain and made a liar of him so that he could militarize American foreign policy to the point of dragging America into an unwinnable war in Iraq that killed and wounded young Americans. Such language has taken its toll.

Although most recent attention has been paid to neo-con military, geopolitical, and diplomatic ideas, serious students of the matter know that neo-conservatism has a strong root in domestic matters, encompassing issues such as civil disruption, riots, a coarsening popular culture, political correctness, and crime—particularly violent crime, which had climbed to a point that made some areas of America close to unlivable. I believe that domestic issues, not matters of war and peace, were what initially energized neo-conservatism.

There was a time not that long ago when some liberals or "radic-libs" (a word marrying *radical* with *liberal* and not used in a compli-mentary way) would say *law 'n' order* is a code word for racism.

Why did the Left go over the edge? I'm not sure, although some speculation will be offered.

Most Americans, however, including liberal ones, never dis-missed criminality so cavalierly. Most know that a functioning and tough-minded legal system is needed to protect citizens from the bad guys who engage in violence for money, for drugs, or to make a political statement. For neo-cons, and most other Americans, law 'n' order was a code phrase for civilization itself.

Neo-conservatism mostly came about as a response to runaway liberalism, which in turn yielded new conditions and new atti-tudes. These mostly began in a faraway time called the sixties. In a democracy, when new conditions and attitudes are perceived as harmful, voters respond. In response to change deemed negative, neo-conservatism developed a mature, practical set of beliefs solidly in the American tradition. I believe it will be around for a long time to our benefit, albeit likely under a different label. The label has been tarnished, not the ideas.

After working on this project for about a year, I had a political epiphany of sorts. It dawned on me: so much of neo-conservatism is about personal safety. From what? From a soaring crime rate; from the Soviet "Evil Empire"; from terrorists who killed civilians in New York City, Washington, D.C., and rural Pennsylvania on 9/11, and later in Iraq, Madrid, London, and Bali; and in the future, safety from potential adversaries—possibly China.

Some say the neos are good for what ails us on both foreign and domestic fronts, while others are quick to debate that. Some argue that neo-conservative notions carved out new and unique territory on the political and geopolitical landscape, while alternatively we hear that they are little more than the bastard child of plain vanilla conservatism, or that conservatism simply became neo-conservatism. Many of those "some" and "others" will be identified in the pages to come.

NEO-CONS HAVE taken some big hits. They have been called racists, sexists, and environmental pigs. It is said as a matter of common knowledge that neo-cons are bought and paid for by big business. While the Iraq insurgency was in progress (during the presidential election campaign of 2004), former President Bill Clinton said that the situation was due to a neo-con "obsession," a strange word from a commander-in-chief who ordered the bombing of Iraq in 1998 and sustained no-fly zones for the entirety of his two terms, during which American jets were regularly fired upon. In addition, Clinton had authorized a four-day bombing of Iraq, *allegedly* aborted in a *Wag the Dog* scenario concerning the White House sex scandal involving Monica Lewinsky. (Alas, there are many "allegeds" in that story.)

That was piffle compared to what was emanating from the rank-and-file spinners of the 2004 presidential campaign of John Kerry: They bought the case that President George W. Bush looked to war as a first resort, not a last one, that Bush had purposefully neglected to seek allies in his Iraq caper, and that he purposefully lied about what he was up to. Of course, compared to President Bush, Vice President Dick Cheney has been regarded as a mad dog.

In a way, all that was small potatoes compared to what was coming in from the rest of the world, Europe in particular. Over there, neo-conservatism was regarded as a secret cabal, really a *Jewish* conspiracy that had taken over America and would bring tragedy to the world in the twenty-first century. But survey research showed that Jews in America were more likely than the population as a whole to oppose the war.

President Bush is not Jewish, nor is Vice President Cheney, nor is then–Secretary of State Colin Powell, nor former Secretary of Defense Donald Rumsfeld, nor then–National Security Council Director Condoleezza Rice, nor one of America's preeminent political scientists, James Q. Wilson, nor former CIA Director James Woolsey, to begin a long list.

To be sure, many of the Iraq hawks, in and out of government, were Jewish. Many were associated with the American Enterprise Institute. The most notable Iraq hawk was the deputy secretary of defense, Paul Wolfowitz, some of whose family was exterminated during the Holocaust. Wolfowitz believed that the United States, in its national interest, ought to try to help set up the conditions for a democratic state in Iraq. He believed that was the best way to establish peace in the Middle East, even if it involved the use of force. He wrote about it, not in classified memoranda, but in public literature, going back several decades. Some cabal.[1]

Neo-conservatism has become big time in America. A circulation pitch letter — an art form of its own — from *The American Conservative* in early 2005 devotes a paragraph to dividing Americans into liberals, conservatives, and neo-conservatives. Just think: Neo-cons have created a whole new philosophy of governance. The magazine is the mouthpiece of Pat Buchanan, who probably hates neo-cons even more than does *New York Times* columnist Paul Krugman.

In the political nomenclature, Buchanan is known as a paleo-con Republican, in a field that includes — as defined by their friends and opponents — classical liberals, democratic imperialists, crunchy cons (who vote for Bush and shop at Whole Foods), big business conservatives, country club Republicans, libertarians, supply-side Republicans, theo-cons, plain vanilla Republicans, K Street Republicans, Burkeans, eastern establishment Republicans, fiscally conservative Republicans, wing nuts, RINOs (Republicans in name only), Ripon Republicans, Rockefeller Republicans, Home School Republicans, and neo-conservative Republicans. And do not forget that some neo-cons — like me — are still registered Democrats. A few even vote that way.

There has been some serious work critical of neo-conservatism, particularly concerning Iraq. But there have also been books that can best be characterized as drivel. For one example, consider *Neo-*

---

1. *The Neoconservative Revolution: Jewish Intellectuals and the Shaping of Public Policy* by Murray Freedman makes the point that there is a very long history of Jewish conservatism. The Jewish concept of *tzedakah* — charity — involved giving to the poor, not giving to the government to give to the poor.

conservatism and the American Future (2004) by Stefan Halper and Jonathan Clarke, respectively of the Center for International Strategic Studies and the sometimes pacifist Cato Institute. Imagine! They claim, *as a pejorative,* that neo-cons think there is a difference between good and evil. For neo-cons everywhere, I plead guilty as charged.

But neo-conservatism, or something akin to it, has important backers. Governor George W. Bush's 2000 presidential campaign of compassionate conservatism can be seen as somewhat synonymous with neo-conservatism. Former Speaker of the House Newt Gingrich, a self-declared conservative, not a neo-con, talks these days of a "center-right progressive, natural majority." Norman Podhoretz theorizes that President Reagan, who believed himself to be a conservative, was a neo-con. After all, he hated Commies, and prior to becoming governor, was a liberal Democrat. I think in some very important ways President Johnson was a neo-con. And in 2006 many Republican candidates ran their races as "progressive conservatives."

I believe much of the criticism of neo-conservatism is a distortion of the first magnitude. What is neo-conservatism? After all, there is no neo-con manifesto, nor a neo-con membership card. What do neo-conservatives believe?

Many neo-cons say it is not a movement at all. Irving Kristol, the putative godfather of neo-conservatism, calls it a persuasion. It has been called a tendency, an orientation, a mind-set, and a sensibility. Kristol has also endorsed the idea of a "conservative welfare state," which may well be where neo-cons, and America, now stand—not such a bad place.

Indeed, the abandonment of that lionized landmark piece of Democratic legislation going back to President Franklin D. Roosevelt's New Deal was just what President Bill Clinton signed into law in 1996. It came about after great pressure from Republicans and neo-cons, and it backed up one of Clinton's 1992 campaign slogans: "End welfare as we know it." I believe in his heart Clinton is a mildly soft liberal, but he ran for president on some neo-conservative notions, including the one I liked best: "No more something for nothing."

Neo-con columnist David Brooks of *The New York Times* has pointed out that when a sentence begins, "Neo-conservatives believe . . . ," what follows is almost surely wrong. But part of this story is that neo-conservatives disagree among themselves, let alone others. Kristol says neo-conservatism seeks to "convert the Republican Party, and American conservatism in general, against their respective wills, into a kind of conservative politics suitable for governing a modern society." I wonder only about that part about "against their respective wills." I have found that converting thoughtful people to a neo-con view is often like pushing on an open door. Kristol also notes that neo-cons are at home with modernity but "even the secular among them want to work with religious traditionalists to uphold decency and democratic culture." I agree. He says neo-cons support a muscular role for the state, and for America in particular. Yes.

Neo-cons, says Kristol, see the national interest in broad terms and want to defend democracy everywhere whenever and wherever plausible and encourage patriotism while clearly working to defeat America's enemies. Amen to that, although Kristol himself has backslid a couple of times. Finally, he says neo-conservatives do not favor world government because it could lead to global tyranny. Again, amen. How would you like to be governed by the one-country-one-vote system of the corrupt United Nations General Assembly?

Foreign policy scholar Francis Fukuyama takes little note of those elections in Iraq, with women courageously waving their purple fingers in the air after casting their first-ever ballots. He minimizes Freedom House's statistics showing the sharply accelerating number of true full-bodied democracies. He ignores other Arab countries that started moving—haltingly—toward democracy and human liberty after the Iraq war began. He seems not to care that America's legacy twenty-five or fifty years from now may well be that we helped to broadly expand liberty in the world. His notion that terrorism can't really hurt us is bizarre: One dirty bomb, a better anthrax delivery system, a purposeful smallpox plague could obviously cause enormous damage.

Did America make mistakes in Iraq? Certainly.

Fukuyama wants a new American foreign policy: "Wilsonian Realism." It sounds like neo-conservatism to me. I hope he will be back among us when we come up with a better label. *Wilsonian Realism* won't cut it, though. Woodrow Wilson was a racist.

I do not think Midge Decter will be back. She was once the

earth mother of neo-conservatism, and as warm, smart, loyal, and decent a woman as I have ever met and a great American patriot. In tough language she says she is now off the wagon.

I e-mailed her, asking why. There were some personal reasons, but in the nut graph she wrote: "The Democratic Party is the enemy. The labor movement is the enemy. The Republican Party is better only by comparison. The people I rely on are my own particular crowd of conservatives, who are for the war [Iraq II], loyal to the interests of the state of Israel, and concerned about the moral component of Western culture. If I were truly passionate about economics, which I'm not, I'm completely on their side, too." She added: "Anyway, how long is 'neo'? Twenty years? Thirty? Thirty-five?" Midge writes with a stiletto. She is married to Norman Podhoretz, a brilliant, if somewhat abrasive, man, whom I like, but who sometimes seems to live in a bitter Norman-centric world (to be discussed).

Perhaps the word *neo-con* entered popular boost phase on September 6, 2005, when Mick Jagger and the Rolling Stones released an album entitled *A Bigger Bang,* addressed principally to President George W. Bush. The key track is titled "Sweet Neo-Con." The lyrics go: "It's liberty for all 'cause democracy's our style. Unless you are against us. Then it's prison without trial . . ."

My own strand of neo-conservatism would regard the song's "liberty for all" as the greatest contemporary human political goal, centuries in the making. Only when historians of the future gauge what has happened will we know whether freedom has advanced as far as it now seems it has. I think the verdict will be remarkably positive.

As Senator John McCain pointed out to crowds during the 2000 election campaign, "We need a cause greater than ourselves." When serving as the U.S. ambassador to the United Nations in the mid-1970s, it was Pat Moynihan who reminded Americans that they belong to the "Liberty Party." That's one big neo-con cause, and it's larger than ourselves. My kind of neo-con was for the Bush doctrine before there was one. We were for the Reagan doctrine before there was one.

The Stones notwithstanding, we should never underestimate either the core intelligence of voters, even if they lack knowledge of specific political nomenclature. There is the hoary anecdote of policemen breaking up a Communist rally turned violent. As one man is pummeled with a billy club, he says to the cop, "But officer, I'm an *anti*-Communist." To which the policeman responds, "I don't care what kind of Communist you are." Such may be the fate of neo-conservatism and of neo-cons like me: always confused with conservatism, with the key differences never quite understood. But differences there are, and those differences may well shape the lives of people who don't know the labels but know what they like, what they find repellent, and vote accordingly, often to the detriment of the Democrats.

I WROTE A weekly syndicated newspaper column with a neo-con point of view for twenty years, which adds up to about one thousand columns. For twelve years and counting I have also served as the "immoderator" of the PBS program *Think Tank with Ben Wattenberg*, which has run about four hundred original programs with many hundreds of panelists, principally authors and scholars drawn from think tanks and the academy, speaking in plain American English. Many of them were of a neo-conservative mind-set, although some definitely were not. The columns and television shows give me license to write here about an even wider variety of topics than I had originally envisioned, sometimes in short bites, sometimes at length.

The book tries to stay on message but does move tangentially to some stories partly for fun, but with a real relation to the topic at hand. Certain names surface again and again: Reverend Jesse Jackson, Governor George Wallace, Pat Moynihan. Each played an important role in shaping the nature of the country we live in today. All three were sharp and smart and have always treated me respectfully and amicably, although I only spoke face to face once to Governor Wallace, and ran like hell when he tried to recruit me. Notwithstanding all the talk about bitter partisanship, I have found that political Washington is generally a civil and cordial place.

Perforce, the book deals with politicians, activists, cause groupies, spinners, intellectuals, columnists, political bloggers, reporters biased in one direction or the other, public intellectuals, and action intellectuals. They're the ones in print and in the public eye. But although most Americans qualify as none of the above, I believe they have a good idea of what's going on. Over the years, a plurality of voters (40 percent) have regarded themselves as "moderates"; in second place were "conservatives" (about 30 percent); and last, "liberals" (about 20 percent). The word *neo-conservative* doesn't appear in those polls of general ideology but I think a "moderate conservative" pretty well fits the bill, and a blended total yields 70 percent of the electorate.

There have been times I have felt like the title character in Woody Allen's *Zelig,* popping up at times and places at just about the right moment and wondering how I wandered into the frame. And yet, as I think it through now, I sense there is a pattern of sorts. There is one thing I do know about the widely held view that neo-conservatism is a movement that suddenly seems to have dominated American public and political life: It wasn't so sudden.

My political hero, Scoop Jackson, might have coined the best definition for neo-conservatism—though he never actually used the term. His campaign slogan in the 1972 Democratic presidential primaries was "Common sense, for a change."

CHAPTER ONE

White House Speech Writing

THE DEMOCRATIC SPLIT EMERGES

NEO-CONSERVATISM IS A somewhat new word. It is not a new concept.

I learned a great deal about what would come to be called neo-conservatism through my work with President Lyndon B. Johnson during the two and a half years I worked with him from mid-1966 to just a few weeks shy of the end of his term on January 20, 1969.

My political journey began early in the afternoon in the summer of 1966 at my home in Stamford, Connecticut. I was working as a freelance writer and editor—not an easy way to make ends meet, especially with a wife and three small children. I had just returned from lunch and my son Danny, then seven, said, "Mr. House called." I asked for more information. He stared at me blankly.

The phone rang again. A White *House* operator asked me to hold for Mr. Redmon. In a moment Hayes Redmon came on the line and identified himself as assistant to Bill Moyers at the White House. Redmon asked if I could come down to Washington to meet with Moyers. They needed a speechwriter for President Johnson.

Moyers had been reading, and liking, *This U.S.A.*, an optimistic book based on census data that I had coauthored with former U.S. Census Bureau Director Richard Scammon.

Incumbent politicians tend to point with pride; challengers usually view with alarm. In 1966 President Lyndon Johnson was the leader of the incumbent point-with-pride Democratic congressional team. And who would be better as a speechwriter than the coauthor of such an optimistic book?

A few days later, I was having lunch in the White House Mess with Moyers, a man my age whose picture had already been on the cover of *Time* with the cover line, "The Young Man Next to the President." He seemed to be in charge of everything at the White House, including speech writing.

As we ate, Hubert Humphrey, then the vice president, came into the dining room. Moyers caught his eye, waved him over, and introduced me, "Ben's going to come here as a speechwriter." (I was?) Humphrey was delighted. "I've been reading your book," he effused. "It's terrific. We need some optimism around this place. Dick Scammon's an old friend of mine." I responded shrewdly: "Thank you."

Walt Rostow, the director of LBJ's National Security Council (certainly a neo-con by today's standards) stopped by the table. He said, "Wonderful book; my wife's teaching a course from it." *Whoa!* What was I doing here? This was high cotton (not a phrase I knew until I later met White House staffers from the South and Southwest).

Moyers and I chatted. I told him that Johnson should start giving some optimistic speeches. I argued that everything coming out of the White House was about a crisis: a crisis in the cities, a crisis in the environment, a crisis in poverty, a crisis in race relations. Yet there were plenty of census statistics showing that while there were indeed lots of problems, there had also been much progress he could take credit for in America during the five-plus years of the Kennedy-Johnson administration. Crisis-mongering was an oft-used political weapon of both sides in Washington, but liberals—who have suffered at the polls for their relentless gloom—employ it with much greater intensity. Wouldn't it be better to say: "Look how far we have come; let us continue."

After a while Moyers said, "Let's go. There's someone I want you to meet." We walked through a maze of corridors to a tiny elevator. Moyers, slick black hair, black horn-rimmed glasses, taller and broader than he looked in his photos, smiled at me gently. He did not tell me whom we were going to visit.

In a moment we entered Lyndon B. Johnson's bedroom and faced two men, one of whom was in blue pajamas. That was the president, getting ready for his midday nap. Moyers introduced me and I said, "Hello, sir," just the way I addressed officers during my stint in the Air Force. I sensed this was not quite enough. "Hello . . . sir . . . Mr. President," I went on, almost sure that "Mr. President" was what one called a president.

Moyers then said, "Hello, Henry," and introduced me to Henry Ford II ("Hank Deuce"), who was in a blue suit, not blue pajamas. LBJ and Henry had just had a private lunch in LBJ's bedroom. (Who says only Republicans cavort with fat cats?) After a moment my new friend Hank took his leave.

Johnson sat down, looked at Moyers, looked at me, and began talking. "I've been reading your book," he said, gesturing to a built-in bookshelf behind him in a way that made me suspect that perhaps he might not have been reading much of it.

"It's a great privilege to work in a White House," Johnson said.

"Yes, it surely must be," I countered.

"But it requires selflessness," LBJ went on, "and even more than selflessness. Old Tommy Corcoran said that a good White House aide had to have 'a passion for anonymity.'"

I countered, sagely, "I'm sure it does." I did not know who Old Tommy Corcoran was.[1] Several years later, as I was preparing to leave the White House, I recounted Johnson's remarks about a passion for anonymity in an interview for an oral history by Professor Harri Baker from the University of Tennessee. I expressed my ongoing bewilderment about it: Why was LBJ telling that to me, an unknown kid? Baker said, "Did it ever occur to you that he was lecturing Moyers, not you?"

The president went on nonstop for about ten minutes. I was too petrified to interrupt. Moyers at last found an opening and said,

---

1. Corcoran was a member of President Franklin D. Roosevelt's "Brain Trust" during the New Deal days of the 1930s.

"Ben, why don't you go ahead and tell the president what you were telling me at lunch about his speeches?" Why? Because I couldn't believe where I was, and who I was with. Terrified, though with surprising vigor, I advanced my anti-crisis-mongering view. Johnson grunted affirmatively several times.

(After some time on the job I was able to talk to the president almost normally. But not before one Saturday morning; I was still in bed, and the phone rang. It was LBJ. It concerned a matter of little consequence, and the conversation seemed to go on and on: five minutes, ten minutes, twelve minutes. Then I heard my six-year-old daughter Sarah scamper down the stairs saying, "Mommy, Mommy, Daddy's on the phone with Mr. Yes-Sir.")

The conversation in LBJ's bedroom lasted about twenty minutes. Moyers and I left. Back in his office, Moyers said he wanted me to work at the White House as a speechwriter. He explained that Johnson's plan was to fly around the country and give "a hundred speeches in ten weeks" in order to reelect the "great Eighty-ninth Congress," the one that had passed most of Johnson's near-revolutionary Great Society programs into law. Moyers emphasized that the hundred-speeches idea was a huge project and that he would need help.

Moyers said the Executive Office of the President could pay me a couple of thousand dollars more than I had made in the previous year in the private sector. I accepted. By (legitimately) adding in every conceivable source of income, I got the number up to about $28,000, which included teaching Sunday school in two temples, and so my starting salary was $30,000 per year, then the very top of the scale for U.S. government political appointees. I was one new appointee who could not claim he was making a sacrifice to work for his government.

Before heading back to Stamford I walked around the perimeter of the White House grounds. It was midsummer and sweat soaked through my cheap cord suit. I said to myself, *Don't be silly. You're not Jimmy Stewart, and this isn't* Mr. Smith Goes to Washington. But I took the whole walk, hardly believing that I would really be coming to work at the White House; me, a kid from The Bronx who had never before even worked regularly in Washington.

A couple of weeks later, on August 11, 1966, I arrived. Within a few days I was staying up until one and two A.M. in Moyers's office, with Bill[2] and a bottle of bourbon, editing, writing, and rewriting the campaign texts that had been submitted as part of the hundred-speeches program.

I believe the LBJ White House was the last where the key aides on the staff wrote the big speeches concerning the topics they dealt with: S. Douglass Cater on health, education, and welfare; National Security Director Walt Rostow on foreign policy, particularly Vietnam; and Harry McPherson Jr. and John P. Roche on both foreign and domestic issues.

Joseph Califano, a protégé of Secretary of Defense Robert MacNamara, ran the White House legislative program shop and had brought over some subalterns from the Department of Defense. Under LBJ's general guidance, they and others wrote the Great Society's legislative messages by the bushel, many of which would be transmogrified into law on Capitol Hill. That legislation, mostly useful by my lights, changed America, changed the Democratic Party, and in many ways set into motion the stance now called neo-conservatism.

Speeches on lesser matters, like those made at campaign stops, were mostly written by speechwriters who composed what was unkindly and unfairly called "Rose Garden Rubbish." That team worked under the putative direction of Robert Kintner, an old Johnson buddy and former newspaper columnist who drank a lot.

The "rubbish" was typically for delivery on the political trail by the president during weekend morning campaign swings. Moyers and I did not think highly of the product. We believed the draft speeches were the products of "wordsmiths," not people with serious policy interests. That judgment was unfair. There were some very good writers there, but Moyers and I had to work very long and very late during the hundred-speeches project. The speeches typically came in at the end of the day, making necessary some late, hectic Friday-night work. That surely colored our view.

Later on, I worked on some pomp-and-fanfare rubbish. Unlike the president's domestic speeches, draft remarks for toasts and arrival

---

2. Moyers was then, officially, the Reverend Billy Don Moyers.

statements for foreign heads of state or prime ministers were made available by State Department officials many days before the actual event. That, thankfully, allowed time for rewriting. Talk about going native! If the visitor were, say, the president of Ghana, the draft from the State Department—had it ever been delivered by LBJ—would have drawn headlines in Ghana about the effects of coffee tariffs on Ghana, and next to nothing in the United States. Speechwriters for the president should be writing speeches for the president, not for Ghanaians. So I would ask State to send me over a package of background material and work from it. I redid the Ghana toast on civil rights progress in America. We got good coverage (*and* we included the coffee tariffs).

When the Italian president visited on Columbus Day, the line in the toast I wrote for LBJ was: "We Americans are not so proud that one Italian came to the New World but that five million did so."

I also wrote a number of major speeches and participated tangentially in some policy matters. Working on LBJ's speeches was very gratifying. Like many neo-cons, I never thought that the federal government was—as President Ronald Reagan put it years later—"the problem, not the solution." Of course, the "law of unintended consequences," popularized by neo-cons, was always lurking, but that should be dealt with case by case. The federal government wasn't the problem but rather what it did, for good or for ill.

There would be plenty of examples of both. Indeed, at a symposium called "The Great Society Remembered" at the Lyndon Baines Johnson Library and Museum in 1985, there was (justified) glorification of the boss, as well as acknowledgment by some ex-LBJ aides that some mistakes had been made, by him and others. And Moyers told a lovely story about LBJ and civil rights. A reporter asked LBJ why he was doing so much for civil rights, when his record in Congress had been less than sterling. Moyers watched LBJ, thinking he would look for a way to duck or divert the question, not uncommon for the man who many journalists thought was the father of "the credibility gap." But LBJ played his candor card: "Some people get a chance late in life to correct the sins of their youth, and very few get a chance as big as the White House."

At the time, I don't think that Moyers and I disagreed about a word in those speeches we worked on together. And yet, we ended up walking very different political paths, which reflect the subsequent neo-conservative vs. liberal/progressive/radical split in the Democratic Party.

Johnson's campaign for the 1966 congressional elections didn't work out well. I traveled on several of the campaign trips. We were often met by demonstrators with black balloons, already highly displeased with America's role in Vietnam.

I knew little about Vietnam then. One day I walked through the White House press lobby. Hugh Sidey (*Time*) and Peter Lisagor (Washington bureau chief of *The Chicago Daily News*) mentioned to me the grave problems in the DMZ, the demilitarized zone separating North Vietnam and South Vietnam, about which I knew not. I muttered, "Yeah, that's a hell of a problem."

Months later at a meeting, I suggested to the president that he would be helped politically by mixing it up with demonstrators (as Nixon later did, to his benefit). He stared me down. He did not want to sully the office with cheap theatrics.

SOON, LBJ's LET-A-HUNDRED-SPEECHES-BLOOM strategy had been dumped as a loser. And so President Johnson, and I (thanks to Moyers) ended up taking a trip of state for a summit conference in Manila with America's allies in the war in Vietnam. On the way to and from Manila, the presidential cavalcade stopped off at the home turf of those allies in New Zealand, Australia, Thailand, and South Korea, as well as the U.S. base in Cam Ranh Bay in Vietnam. Each stop required speeches.

Traveling around the world with a presidential entourage was an eye-opener. The traveling party moved about in four 707s: Air Force One, two press planes, and a back-up Air Force One, commonly called "Air Force Two" but often referred to as the "zoo plane," because of its alcoholic, informal, and boisterous reputation. (There were also several C-141s involved sporadically.)

I almost didn't make the trip. Moyers and McPherson had traveled for two weeks advancing the trip for Johnson. When Moyers returned he asked to look at the twenty or so speeches that the "rubbish" speech team had prepared for the journey. He had read through them and asked me for an assessment. I told him I thought that some were adequate but that many were condescending: "You should be so proud of your progress on trichinosis. . . ." Moyers asked me to write him a straightforward memo telling him what I thought. I did. He decided to pass it on to LBJ, who told him to get me on the trip, pronto. In a few days, I took all my vaccination shots at one time, got feverish, and headed west to the Far East.

Few things with Johnson were simple. I was a published author. But Johnson told Moyers that he didn't want me visible lest the press think that presidential speeches were written by presidential speech-writers (Flash!). He said I should travel on the back-up zoo plane and stay hidden at Air Force bases along the way.

I heard myself telling Moyers I wouldn't do that (and was astonished by my courage). I was either on the president's staff or not, but I wasn't going to travel hidden away like a second-class citizen. LBJ apparently relented; it was agreed that I would travel on the press plane (of all places), as an aide to Deputy Press Secretary George Christian, a wonderful human being. In fact, I ended up bouncing around from one plane to another as the trip progressed. It turned out the zoo plane had its advantages. During the long flight from American Samoa to New Zealand, I participated in a big-money poker game with high table stakes and pot limits. The participants included the deputy undersecretary of state for administration (the number four man in the department), LBJ's marine assistant to the White House, a master sergeant from the White House communications office, a Filipino-American mess steward, a few in-and-outers, and me. RHIP—rank has its privileges—but not at this meritocratic game—quite in tune with neo-con, anyone-can-play beliefs.

Money moved quickly. At a crucial moment in a big pot the marine assistant—a major—shoved in his stack in a head-to-head confrontation with the sergeant, who worked for him. Faced with a matching bet of several hundred dollars, the sergeant folded his hand. Unforgivably, the major turned up his cards—he didn't even have a pair—and breaking poker protocol happily announced, "I bluffed you out."

The sergeant, neck veins bulging, screamed at him: "You mother-fucking, lily-livered, yellow-bellied piece of shit! *Sir.*"

The cards were running for me in an almost unbelievable way. I won about a thousand dollars. I carried the money in my back pocket all through the trip. When I returned home, we bought a piano. My son still plays it.

An interesting vignette played itself out in Bangkok. I was asked by Harry McPherson to write the president's speech slated for delivery at Chulalongkorn University, Thailand's finest. It was to be an important address, and I wrote into the small hours. The night before the speech, Harry and I met with the president after his nap in the quarters provided for him in Bangkok. It was the old palace of the King of Siam, the very one where the king had laid down the law to Anna, the tutor who educated the king's children, and where she confronted the king in the cause of individual liberty and modernism, perhaps an early version of neo-conservatism.

As he read the draft, Johnson, stone-faced, nodded with approval a few times. While he was reading he was being dressed in formal wear by his valet, who handled the cuff links and stud buttons, adjusting the suspender lengths—nasty tasks that mortals struggle with for themselves. Lady Bird Johnson (one of my favorite people) then came in dressed in a flowing formal gown, a vision of elegance. She said to LBJ, "Dear, we have to be at the head of the grand staircase at *exactly* 6:00 P.M. to start the state dinner. That's ten minutes from now. The king will be at the bottom of the stairs, waiting to greet us." Johnson grunted and kept reading the draft. In a few minutes Lady Bird came back and said, "Dear, five minutes. . . ." No response. Then a couple of minutes later, "We're going to be late." Finally, Johnson responded grumpily, "What are they going to do about it?"

A neo-con moment. Americans were *primus inter pares*. Johnson was not being disrespectful to the king; he and Lady Bird showed up with several seconds to spare at the top of the gilded staircase.

But the question *What are they going to do about it?* rattled around in my head afterward. True enough, the Cold War was going on, and we were terribly entangled in Vietnam—but there seemed to me some grand accuracy to Johnson's question. Along with most neo-conservatives then and now, I believed that America was number one. True, the Soviets were a nuclear superpower. But America led the world by far in science, education, economics, cultural reach, technology, diplomacy, and military might. Its language, English (or "American," if you prefer), had become nearly universally spoken. It was the most admired nation in the world. Never had a country achieved such influence.

Twenty years later historian Paul Kennedy would write *The Rise and Fall of the Great Powers*, claiming that America was going the way of other once-great powers—down—the victim of what he called "imperial overstretch." Other "declinists" echoed the theme with different variations. The thesis of decline never resonated with me or most neo-cons. I think Kennedy, an ex-Brit, consciously or subconsciously wanted America to go through the dissolution of empire that Great Britain had experienced. The United States, in the years following the publication of Kennedy's book, did not decline: It became more influential.

Many years later, after the fall of the Soviet Union, I ran a contest in my newspaper column asking for better names than the oft-stated "sole superpower" then in use. These are some of the answers I received: hyperpower, magnapower, omnipower, maxipower, megapower, multipower, semperpower, suprapower, ultrapower, and unipower. No accident, all those words had Latin roots: The Romans had an empire, too. The winner, declared solely by me, was omnipower as in, according to my dictionary, "denoting a quality of unrestricted or universal range." Unlike Rome's or England's, however, America's empire is one of ideas that defies the physical limits of treasure and territory.

The speech at Chulalongkorn spoke of the universality of mankind, streams of Christians, Jews, Muslims, Buddhists, and Hindus forming a single mighty river. It was a global neo-con theme, somewhat utopian but tempered with a realism that stressed the predominance of national sovereignty. Power and passion were required to maintain great civilizations. I was proud of the speech I had drafted. That evening I shared a cab with Peregrine Worsthorne, a well-known conservative Brit writer with attitude. "What drivel," he said. I said not a word, proud of my discipline.

I learned a lot about speech writing at the White House. It's just writing, but some writers do it well almost instinctively, getting into the rhythm, vocabulary, and political essence of the speaker—and some never do get the hang of it. Almost every morning I would walk with a very attractive research assistant/secretary over to the East Room to hear LBJ hold forth on one matter or another. I didn't know LBJ well and wanted to hear him talk as much as possible, and wanted her to as well. I also learned that in speech writing you must believe what you are writing—and that your boss would write it himself if he had the time. It is very easy to fall into the dangerous trap that your boss is only mouthing your ideas. I think that Richard Goodwin, who was a very important LBJ speechwriter before I arrived, sometimes believed that LBJ was mostly parroting his thoughts.[3]

MANY NEO-CONS CAME to understand that being number one carries a burden with it, but that there is glory and greatness there as well. There was not much Americans could not do if we set our minds to it. Such rich patriotism and pride is an easy position to parody, and it is easy to show how history does not back it up. But I think Ronald Reagan had it right. When aides told him something couldn't be done, he often said, "But we're Americans."

Such a view tended to help form the neo-con agenda over the years—which included noncoercively promoting democracy around the world. Nor was it an accident that most every foreign leader visiting America made the point that America was the global leader, that American sacrifice and risk were indispensable to making a better world.

In fact, *indispensable* was invariably the word that the somewhat soft Clinton foreign policy team used to describe America's role in

---

3. During LBJ's term, only one writer was ever actually demoted and moved off the White House staff. But Peter Benchley later went on to write a minor novel about a killer shark named *Jaws* and made far more per word than any other former speechwriter in history.

foreign affairs. Bearing the burden of leadership is better than just sitting around acting like a run-of-the-mill country. (Although Jeane Kirkpatrick wrote after the Cold War that America should start behaving like a "normal nation." It's not going to happen.)

For me, that view was bolstered as we stopped at each of the five countries on the seventeen-day presidential trip in 1966. The news lead of each page-one story was nearly identical: "Lyndon Johnson, the most powerful man in the world, today arrived in (Canberra) (Bangkok) (Manila) etc. . . ." And America wouldn't get any lasting diplomatic bad marks if the president showed up late for a state dinner in Bangkok.

I did a lot of thinking during the summit trip. LBJ was a ferocious anti-Communist. I don't recall if the "war of ideas" was a common phrase then, but it was certainly what Johnson believed in and what he frequently talked about.

The reason we were in Vietnam was that Ho Chi Minh's North Vietnam was a Communist state armed and supported by both the Soviet Union and Red China—hence the geopolitical axiom "the friend of my adversary is my adversary," typical neo-con language. Conservatives would likely say, "The friend of my enemy is my enemy," which was probably more accurate, given what was at stake.

This idea is a sorry fact of geopolitics. But when the adversary is strong and the stakes global, so it must be. It would be nice to look at things case by case, humanistically, and historically. But the stakes were then the plausible threat of America's nuclear destruction, and these days, mass terrorism with potentially horrific results. We needed a strong defense. But most neo-cons believe that the West (led by America) *won* the Cold War because it won the war of ideas, and it will probably prevail again in the same way.

Johnson was a defense hawk because he believed that American ideas, and global democratic ideas, were under threat from Soviet steel. The policy was the long-standing one of containment. He also knew that the cost was extra high because ill-tempered voters could undermine his Great Society babies.

Such views are much easier for a geopolitical analyst to hold than for a president who listened to the chant *"Hey, hey, LBJ, how many kids did you kill today?"* and who met the parents of soldiers killed in action. All that took a great personal toll on Johnson. After he left office in early 1969 he went back to his ranch and resumed smoking, drinking, and heavy eating at a near-suicidal pace. He died just four years after his term ended, a morose and despondent man. In any event, I learned what the DMZ was. I learned the rationale of America's involvement in Vietnam.

Because of my census background, most of the speeches I wrote concerned domestic issues. Still, I came to be a true believer and defender of Johnson's international policy. I often wondered: Suppose, after reflection and study, I had come out the other way on Vietnam, as so many of my friends had? Suppose I came to believe that it was the wrong war at the wrong time in the wrong place for the wrong reasons? Would I have resigned from the White House in an act of conscience?

Unless I felt that the North Vietnamese were really the good guys or that America was committing genocide, I don't think so. As a matter of policy, the North Vietnamese and their Viet Cong surrogates often behaved like barbarians. American troops were far better, but also had innocent blood on their hands, at My Lai and other places. But these were aberrations. Still, war is horrible.

In the 1970s, after my White House years, I coauthored a novel entitled *Against All Enemies* with Ervin Duggan, my good friend and a splendid writer.[4] The critical theme was that the president deserved the whole-hearted commitment of his staff, with very few ifs, ands, or buts, even if they harbored some doubts. There were also a few gentle sex scenes. Ervin wrote them.

All in all, I came to feel a great admiration for Johnson. Most of the Great Society programs had been passed before I was hired, but in general the ideas they espoused made sense, even the small stuff. For example: Seat belts save lives. And unlike some other recent legislation, which drives conservatives to distraction, it does indeed have Constitutional backing through the Interstate Commerce Clause.

---

4. Duggan was Douglass Cater's White House assistant and later became president of PBS, the Public Broadcasting Service.

We should (reasonably) protect the environment. And poor people should get health care.

Many of the programs were much overdone, and that became a central neo-con theme. In his very important book *Losing Ground*, Charles Murray, who later became my colleague at the American Enterprise Institute, claimed that the Johnson programs were among the principal culprits that were driving America down. I do not think the programs were the villains. I do think that some of them were taken overboard by mostly unelected officials: the courts, regulatory agencies, burgeoning congressional staffs, cause groups, and some members of Congress. On balance, the Great Society has helped the American people. How far would an elected official get today if he ran on a platform of eliminating Medicare?

Withal, LBJ knew in advance that he was taking on two of the most incendiary issues in American politics—a land war in Asia and desegregation at home. There are phone tapes to prove it.

The LBJ White House was a meritocracy. It was sufficiently disorganized to greatly benefit even midlevel functionaries such as me. For example, I was encouraged to write memos directly to the president. One day I idly mentioned an idea to Cater about some ideas for a speech about the War on Poverty. He told me to write up a memo and send it to LBJ. So here I was, a smart-ass kid writing directly to the president, and not always about speeches. LBJ usually answered the next morning, sometimes by ticking the yes or no box. When Moyers left the White House staff a few months after I arrived, I worked under the aegis of Cater and McPherson, and was occasionally asked to help out Joe Califano, Walt Rostow, John Roche, and others. R. Sargent Shriver, the capable and hyperkinetic head of the controversial Office of Economic Opportunity, had a pretty good idea of how things worked. When he finished whatever other business he had at the White House, he would frequently drop by my office unannounced, to sell me a bill of goods, and sometimes I bought. "If you want something done here," he would say, "ask a speechwriter." Not quite (better to ask LBJ).

So to a surprising degree I was left alone to gin up my own projects. After the race riots I put together a briefing of the entire cabinet about the status of what the Census Bureau still called Negroes, which I delivered together with my White House colleague Cliff Alexander, the one black man on the staff.[5]

Along with other staff members I was sent around the country to get firsthand impressions of what was going on in the black community. In my case I did so with the help of Louis Martin of the Democratic National Committee, an unsung hero of the civil rights movement. My modus operandi was original: I got Census Bureau credentials and went along on house visits with enumerators, asking respondents questions for the Current Population Survey, taken monthly. The locale? The South Side of Chicago, not such a safe place.

Johnson was highly displeased by the famous report of the Kerner Commission, whose chairman was Illinois Governor Otto Kerner. LBJ had created the commission in 1967 after several years of summer riots culminating in a monstrous display of death and destruction in Detroit. The report's most famous passage warned that the United States was "moving toward two societies, one black, one white—separate and unequal." It presented a list of demands and recommendations. Johnson said he had already proposed or implemented what the commission wanted.

New policy comes about in many ways. Every couple of months or so I would invite Dick Scammon to a brown bag lunch with a few of the president's domestic aides. Scammon would offer his political views as we peppered him with questions about the current political climate. It was a rough time: race riots, Vietnam, crime in the streets, and much more. I would then write up a memo with Scammon's views for the president. Since then, they have been examined by scholars of the Left and described as hard-line on the social issues, usually with a lead-in to the effect that tough ideas

---

5. Johnson, of course, thought very highly of Martin Luther King Jr.—in the early days of the civil rights movement. But when King broke with LBJ on the Vietnam War there was a change. A major King advisor was Stanley Levison, an important member of the Communist Party USA during the 1950s. Accordingly, LBJ asked FBI head J. Edgar Hoover to bug King's calls and his rooms, which were replete with bedroom talk with many women to whom he was not married. As the tapes circulated to some of the higher-ups there were giggles and gasps. Among the gigglers were some who later became outspoken civil rights and feminist leaders. (Lucky me, I never heard the tapes, only the talk about them.)

often described as neo-conservative were at work even back in 1967 in a liberal clime.

Indeed the ideas were tough, but they were not driven by Scammon, nor the LBJ aides who would attend the meetings, nor LBJ. They were driven by events. When there are riots, a soaring violent crime rate, draft dodging, value-busting feminism, anti-war demonstrations, and a counterculture advising people to "turn on, tune in, drop out," there was going to be a political reaction from American voters. Many of the thoughts in those memos would later be refined, augmented, and revamped in the next book Scammon and I coauthored, *The Real Majority*. I don't recall ever receiving a direct response from LBJ on these memos, but I know he read them and believe he agreed with them. He was a good politician who knew what was going on.

I HAD WRITTEN a couple of speeches that included some pointed gags. Apparently that was not a frequent occurrence, and I heard that LBJ loved them. McPherson called me in one day in the spring of 1968 and asked me to do a speech for the White House Press Correspondents Dinner, an annual high-alcohol-content black-tie affair. The president had skipped it a few times in a row (probably because he didn't think Vietnam was a laughing matter), much to the dismay of the press corps. The formula at these affairs, Harry explained, was for the president to speak humorously, often in a self-deprecating way, and then take the high ground at the end, asking all in attendance to pull for America. It is a formula that has been used to great effect by other presidents, before and after LBJ. Ronald Reagan (and wife, Nancy) were supreme. President George W. Bush (and wife, Laura) were almost as good.

Johnson was not what one might describe as a self-deprecating man. I had already learned that it was nerve-racking listening to the president give a serious speech that you had written. Was the audience showing interest? Was the president showing interest? Was the press showing interest? But I was about to learn that listening to the president of the United States trying to be funny in front of a thousand journalists and their bosses was scary enough to soak my cheap tuxedo in sweat. Suppose no one laughed? LBJ would go on being president but my stock at the White House would surely plunge. Boldly I marched forward, with the help of a few wiseguys and wisegals I called in for help in gag writing. One was a very good friend and a college fraternity brother, Jeff Stansbury, working then at the United States Information Agency. Jeff ultimately did what more people in Washington should do: He quit. He believed the Vietnam War was abysmal and just walked away.

I had been invited to the dinner by Marty Schramm, then the very young White House correspondent for Long Island's *Newsday* who later wrote for *The Washington Post*. LBJ gave the speech splendidly and received a roaring reception from the very journalists who had been giving him grief in large doses. I was smiling so broadly and was so relieved that Schramm asked if I had written the speech. I didn't break the then-extant tradition of omertà and claim credit for the president's words, but my broad grin of relief probably gave the game away. Schramm, Mike Waldman, who wrote features for *Newsday* (and who had been a member of my high school newspaper, *The Clinton News*, in The Bronx), and I hit some of the private parties after the dinner. It seemed as if the whole press corps was in on the big secret. It didn't help any when McPherson came up to me and congratulated me for the speech, although I much appreciated it.

As we made the rounds of the parties, I felt as if I was being congratulated by every political scribe in town. That felt grand for a while—until I realized that one of these drunken sots might publish some item about who wrote the speech and the president might see it and think I was not showing a "passion for anonymity." But I went home that night, half in the bag and feeling I had done a day's work for my country and my president, who had seemed to come out of his rhetorical shell, at least for an evening.

In early June 1967, a Saturday, at around noon, I got a call informing me that I was on the manifest for the president's flight to New York City, leaving in a few hours. The agenda was three pre-election year fund-raising dinners in rapid succession and a return flight late that night. I was told that the president wanted jokes and humor for the beginning of the speech. I did my duty, tearing my hair out and writing on the plane. I was excited: The president had asked for my services *by name*. In the White House, that's big time.

Robert F. Kennedy, then the junior senator from New York, was speeding across the Atlantic from an engagement in England to get to New York City in time to introduce the president at some of the fund-raising events. He arrived late. Here are some excerpts of what Kennedy said. Given that the two men disliked each other deeply (a feud that would play a role in shaping American policy and politics for years), they are quite remarkable:

> I have just returned from England. I had hoped to have the opportunity to introduce President Johnson to you, my fellow New Yorkers. I would like to say some of the things that I had hoped to say prior to the time that he spoke.
>
> *Webster* defines greatness as "largeness in size, being much above the average in magnitude, intensity and importance."
>
> That definition could have been written for the man who just spoke to you. The height of his aim, the breadth of his achievements, the record of his past, and the promises of his future, all these bespeak the largeness of size, that magnitude of effort, that intensity of devotion, and that importance of accomplishment. He came to lead this nation at a time of uncertainty and danger, pouring out his own strength to renew the strength and the purpose of all of the people of this nation, and of the nation itself.

Something tells me RFK's remarks were prepared by a professional speechwriter, not penned on a cocktail napkin as he crossed the ocean. *The Washington Post* reported the next day that Kennedy had "praised the president so effusively that party members wondered whether the Johnson-Kennedy feud had ended." (It hadn't.) But politics is politics. Robert Kennedy had some neo-conservative tendencies. When he came to run in the presidential primaries in 1968, he was particularly tough on crime and saluted for that stance by some of the same journalists who had criticized LBJ for it.

At about midnight, on the plane on the way back to Washington, President Johnson came up to me and said, "*Bain*, I want you to git a box with index cards in it and put a hundred jokes in it. Then whenever I need a joke I could just fish into the box and git a joke." I didn't tell him that's not quite the way political humor works and anyway, I think he knew that better than I. LBJ spoke with a Texas twang but knew how to use language and was as articulate as any man I've known.

The idea is to get a laugh *and* make a point—not always easy. Johnson also wanted the speechwriters to give him speeches that were "four-word sentences, four paragraphs long," the way a local columnist of his youth had done. We checked it out; the columnist had done no such thing. But every politician—with no exceptions that I know of—wants his points crafted short and sweet. The idea of a one-page memo is not so stupid if you understand that a president may get scores of very important ones each day.

LBJ raised a great deal of money for his political party that night. We returned early on June 4, 1967. It was a grand night. If LBJ was happy, I was happy. I had come to admire and love the man, for all his flaws.

REALITY INTRUDES. THE next day news came in that the Israelis had preemptively lashed out at Egypt after President Gamal Abdel Nasser had blockaded the Straits of Tiran. That, the Israelis maintained, was an act of war.

The Egyptians were military clients of the USSR, which issued a bellicose statement to the United States to stand back. Israel was attacked by Syria and Jordan. A major power confrontation between nuclear states was suddenly on the table. Jokes and fund-raising were long forgotten. The Israelis were overpowering their Arab enemies. The State Department spokesman, Robert J. McCloskey, issued a statement that the United States was "neutral in word, thought, and deed." The well-organized Jewish organizations in America went ballistic. LBJ neutral? Impossible! They quickly organized national demonstrations, the most important of which was in Washington's Lafayette Park, across from the White House. Johnson decided not to go out and talk to the crowd.

The protests went on for several days. I had always been a pretty ardent Zionist and was by then a pretty strong hawk on Vietnam. I sat down with Larry Levinson, deputy to Joe Califano. Johnson had been catching hell from Jewish liberals and radicals about Vietnam, many of whom at the same time were more than prepared to ask for more military aid from the United States for Israel. (On occasion LBJ had referred to them as "Kosher hawks.") At my suggestion, Larry and I dispatched a memo to the president regarding a mass meeting of American Jews scheduled for the next day. We urged him to go speak. The last paragraph read:

> Events are moving very rapidly—but as of this hour, from a domestic political point of view, it seems to us that this would be a highly desirable action for you to attend and speak. It would neutralize the "neutrality" statement and could lead to a great domestic political bonus—and not only from Jews. Generally speaking, it would seem that the Mid-East crisis can turn around a lot of anti-Viet Nam, anti-Johnson sentiment.

Johnson was furious when he got the memo. He saw Levinson in the hall of the West Wing and chewed him out ferociously. How dare we play domestic politics when great powers with nuclear weapons were in play? Who was this Wartenberry [sic] anyway? Levinson told me later he had never been so scared in his life. The incident is recorded in Califano's memoirs. Rereading the memo, I think the point I made was generally sound. Many of the leading anti-Vietnam War doves were Jewish. Like many activists, they wanted it both ways. The point I thought he should make was relevant—to be stated with some subtlety and exceptions—that freedom was indivisible. If America was in the freedom business it ought to be as universal a business as we could make it, in Israel as well as in Vietnam. Most neo-cons then (and now) tended to vigorously endorse America's encouragement of liberty with force only as a last option and only when American interests were threatened.

Johnson used to talk about Vietnam most every day—to grieving parents assembled in the East Room, in policy statements, in remarks to visiting heads of state. Some evenings I would be on the cocktail circuit or at a dinner. I remember one when I was asked, "How can you work for a maniac?" I mouthed off, explaining the rationale of LBJ's war policy and echoing his remarks. And the response was: "Why doesn't Johnson ever explain it that way?" It was a clear case of selective perception: People hear what they want to hear.

During Iraq II, a similar charge was made against President George W. Bush. He talks and talks about the Iraq war. And critics and supporters alike say: Why doesn't he explain it to the American people? (Bush's second inaugural address in 2004 was an astonishing speech that explained his rationale for his administration's policy in Iraq. The whole speech, except for one paragraph, was about foreign policy. Yet, the cogniscenti keep saying Bush doesn't explain why we are in Iraq.)

The memo on Israel called forth the big freeze, a not unfamiliar Johnson technique. It seemed to me as if I had become a nonperson. (After all, when Moyers left I became known as "a Moyers man," and the parting of the ways between Moyers and Johnson had not been wholly amicable, although over the years LBJ surely appreciated Bill's many talents.) Then, about a month later, the social thaw came. I received an invitation to a state luncheon. As my wife headed through the receiving line, the president said, "Miz Wattenberg, I just don't know how this White House could run without Bain; he's wonderful." All bullshit, but the point was made.

Most of the time a White House staffer senses his status indirectly. I had written some tough Republican-bashing speeches for Johnson that he liked. A line from one of them even made the quote of the day in *The New York Times*.[6] Sometime later, McPherson told me that the president said that I "really hated Republicans" and wanted me on his campaign plane for the 1968 reelection campaign. That was before Johnson decided not to run. Years later, I would be referred to as "Reagan's favorite Democrat." Strange world.

John Roche, an LBJ assistant, professor of political science at Brandeis University, and former president of the Americans for

---

6. In early October 1966, *The New York Times* quote of the day was "Afraid, afraid, afraid. Republicans are afraid of their own shadows and the shadow of progress. But the only thing that most Americans are afraid of are Republicans."

Democratic Action (before it went way Left) worked closely with McPherson. One day John asked me to write a tough partisan speech for John Bailey, the chairman of the Democratic National Committee. I was rattled. I had been active in some local Stamford (Connecticut) politics in the early 1960s. I had run for low-level office there two times and had lost twice. (I found out that by looking at the back of one voting machine in a district whose patterns you know, you can determine whether you are a winner or a loser, a good exercise for a pundit-in-training.) At the time, Bailey was the political boss of Connecticut and was regarded as a near-mythical political deity, at least to those of us near the bottom of the Connecticut political food chain. How could I deal with John Bailey *himself*?

I wrote the speech and hand-delivered it to Bailey at the Democratic National Committee. Bailey read it, peering over his bifocals. After about ten minutes, just when I thought he would start picking the draft to ribbons, he asked plaintively: "Mr. Wattenberg, would it be all right if I changed this word?" Any affiliation with the White House can intimidate people you deal with. It's a nice feeling.

But when I came to write a column, I loved it. I was writing in my own name. In particular, I loved encouraging politicians to run for president. I think I did so on three separate occasions with Senator Joe Lieberman. Other beneficiaries of my political largesse included Senator Charles Robb and Republican Dave McCurdy. Once I privately visited with Pat Moynihan to suggest that he run.

By THE 1960s the Democrats were beginning to change; that change yielded a major change in American politics. Neoconservatism was being born all over America. As I see it now, the change often concerned what was *not* said rather than what *was* said.

From my White House perch I could sense some of what was going on. The White House Mess was an elegant dining room, albeit somewhat small. It was for the exclusive use of upper- and midlevel White House aides, who were served by a staff of all-Filipino U.S. Navy stewards—a situation that could never survive in today's quota-heavy, PC ambience. Moyers had me put on the mess list when I started at the White House. All the tables were reserved except for a large circular one at the rear of the room, which was open to staff on a first-come, first-served basis. Most days I would head for the group table and order a New York strip steak at a ridiculously low price. Working journalists were not allowed in the mess.[7]

When a reporter seeking information wanted to talk to a White House aide, the conversation took place outside of the White House. Yuri Barsakov, a KGB agent posing as a journalist for the Soviet newspaper *Izvestia*, invited me out to lunch about once a month, and I would tell him what I thought was on Johnson's mind, and give him my own views as well. But before lunching with him for the first time, I asked Walt Rostow if talking to an enemy agent was appropriate. He said absolutely—if I wrote him a brief report of what Barsakov's questions were. He explained that by examining several such reports the National Security Council could get a sense of what the Soviets wanted to know.

At the group table I would mostly listen, or ask questions of the great and the near-great of the White House firmament—economists, foreign policy mavens, political tacticians, a few assistants. In the almost two and a half years I worked at the White House, I never heard Vietnam discussed seriously, not even once! Not even in praise. That sounds impossible, but such is my recollection. Accordingly, I assumed that all the White House staff shared Johnson's basically hawkish stance on the war, which I saw principally as a message that America would not return to isolationism when the going got tough.

In Washington it is said that you never write the letters you sign, and never sign the letters you write. My first political employer was Congressman Donald J. Irwin, a Democrat representing Connecticut's Fairfield County. He was a devout Catholic and a hawk on Vietnam. In 1968 the peaceniks had their way and Irwin was defeated. A losing congressional candidate might normally expect a pro forma letter of regret from the president of his own party. I decided Don deserved something special and drafted a letter from LBJ:

---

7. Years later, I was writing a newspaper column. I was lunching in the Reagan Mess at the invitation of Jim Pinkerton, Lee Atwater's assistant. I was rather nastily told to leave immediately by Karna Small, the deputy press secretary.

November 9, 1968
Dear Don:

I was sad indeed to hear of your defeat in your campaign for re-election.

I know of no man in Congress who served his district, his party and his nation more steadfastly or ably than you. I know, too, of the strong personal support you gave me at a time when that was not necessarily the "political" thing for you to do. Be assured, Don, that I have deeply appreciated that support.

You have, of course, my best wishes for whatever you plan to do now. I do know, however, that sooner or later you will again be doing what you have been doing so well: helping build a better nation and a more secure world.

Sincerely,
Lyndon B. Johnson

Honorable Donald J. Irwin
House of Representatives
Washington, D.C.
LBJ:BW:rks

The letter meant a great deal to Don. Years later, at his house, he called me into his bedroom where a framed copy of the letter was proudly displayed, and Don preened a bit and said how special it was that the president understood his unique political bravery. I did not say I wrote it and I don't think the thought ever occurred to him, although there was that "BW" subscript. Don returned home, became the mayor of Norwalk, and later taught American studies at Yale. I haven't seen him in years, but if I do I will execute a hand salute.

CURIOUS. WHEN LBJ announced on March 31, 1968, just as the presidential primaries were beginning, that he would not run for reelection, most of the White House minions who supported LBJ all the way were suddenly prepared to denounce the war and work for or support Senators Robert Kennedy's or Eugene McCarthy's campaigns for the Democratic presidential nomination. And less than a year after his obsequious comments about LBJ, Robert Kennedy was denouncing the Johnson administration's policies as "bankrupt" and noted that those policies had "removed themselves from the American tradition, from the enduring and generous impulses that are the soul of this nation." He added that Johnson was appealing to the "dark side" of the American character.

McCarthy entered the fray early and challenged LBJ in New Hampshire. Early polls in New Hampshire showed McCarthy getting only about 15 percent of the vote against Johnson. After he left politics—pushed out in 1970 by Hubert Humphrey's run for the Senate in Minnesota—McCarthy told me he had known right off the bat that he'd do a whole lot better than that in New Hampshire. "You get more than 15 percent," he said, "just from the palsy vote, from people hitting the wrong lever." (Nasty, and not sayable these days. Whatever your opinion of McCarthy, the man had as coruscating a wit as could be found in American politics.) In the complex New Hampshire primary, McCarthy ran very well. LBJ did not file a single delegate slot in the state, nor did he travel there—he drew his voters as a write-in candidate. Still, Johnson got a majority of the popular vote. But because of better organization, McCarthy won more delegates.

To show you how much most of us on staff knew about Johnson's eventual decision not to actively campaign in New Hampshire: Duggan and I were in Cater's office a few days before the LBJ announcement preparing campaign material. One involved a full-page endorsement by actor Gregory Peck.

Johnson had some good reasons for his decision not to run for a second full term. Principally, he felt that *he*, not *the war*, had become the issue, and no positive purpose would be served if he stayed on. Those New Hampshire results, and LBJ's announcement, liberated many elected Democrats to run as doves. It also brought Vice President Hubert Humphrey into the race. It was said that Humphrey would be free at last from the subservient role of LBJ's vice president, and he was indeed sometimes treated in a humiliating fashion by LBJ in his darkest moments.

The received wisdom is that Johnson was driven out of the race by the anti-war movement and that had he run, he would have lost. I am dubious on both counts. Johnson had talked to General William Westmoreland, to Press Secretary George Christian, and others as early as the fall of 1967 about not running for a fresh term in 1968. LBJ would have been a somewhat better vote-getter than Humphrey, who lost a very tight race against Richard Nixon in 1968, and probably would have won reelection. But had segregationist Governor George Wallace not run as a third-party candidate in 1968, taking many conservative votes, Nixon would have beaten either Johnson or Humphrey by a solid margin, although not a landslide. Dick Scammon, America's premier psephologist, believed that, and so do I.

There were rumors afloat that LBJ would show up in Chicago and try to stampede the convention into nominating him. I had been asked, along with Larry Levinson, to go down to the LBJ ranch in the Hill Country of Texas during the convention week and write a draft speech for LBJ should he decide to do so. I wrote a draft that didn't have a single plausible boo-line in it.

I was very proud of such verbal gymnastics, proud too that LBJ had designated me to be the man on the ground at the ranch to work on it. Years later I learned that a number of others had sent in drafts for what could have been a very important address. But LBJ never went to the convention. When carnage erupted in the Chicago streets in 1968, the Secret Service informed him that it could not guarantee his safety and the venture was dropped. Some critics have said that LBJ was a coward. Certainly not politically.

A JOURNALISTIC AVIARY formed. Among others, there were "ostriches," "turkeys," "chickens," and, of course, "doves," and "hawks." I was and am a hawk. But there was more to it than labels about one tragic war in Vietnam. We lost it—more accurately, our South Vietnamese allies lost it two and a half years after American combat troops disengaged.

Remember what happened in Vietnam: It was part of the Cold War. And at the end of the day, decades later, the free nations of the West—under American leadership—prevailed in that conflict and the Soviet Union was no longer on the map. That's how wars often work: You win some battles and you lose some. You prevail if you win the last one. If you believe that the course of history has something to do with the advance of human liberty, then the Cold War triumph stands as one of the great milestones of human history. After the Soviet implosion in the late 1980s, a label was affixed to those who believed that the triumph was indeed a triumph. They were labeled "triumphalists," among whom most neo-conservatives counted themselves. In the dominant liberal press the word was often used in a smug and pejorative context. I suspect that if we said that the free nations had merely "prevailed" in the Cold War the same commentator would have smugly labeled us "prevailists."

The Vietnam War is generally acknowledged to have split the Democratic party, with pro-war Democratic neo-cons often cast in the role of super-splitters. Indeed, there were competing mind-sets at work that would play themselves out in the years to come (although many hawks thought it was the wrong war in the wrong place).

A wedge phrase that hangs in my mind is "the arrogance of power." That was the way William Fulbright, chairman of the Senate Foreign Relations Committee, characterized the U.S. position in Vietnam, and the world. LBJ, who, as Senate majority leader, had appointed him to the committee, sometimes referred to him as "Senator Halfbright."

I thought it was Fulbright who was arrogant. I remember watching one of the many famous Fulbright hearings, televised live, just as the Senate was voting on the third of LBJ's transformative civil rights bills, the Fair Housing Act of 1968. Fulbright, the liberal darling *du jour* and a long-term segregationist, stepped out of the Vietnam hearing room to vote *nay* on fair housing. Before the civil rights acts were passed the Southern politicians tended to fall into at least three identifiable groups. There were those who were against segregation and could occasionally see their way to vote that way. Tennessee senator Albert Gore was one. Senator Ralph Yarborough of Texas and Senator Estes Kefauver of Tennessee were even more outspoken. As Senate majority leader, LBJ had pushed forward a mild civil rights bill in the 1950s.

There were others who opposed segregation but understood that if they came out that way in public, or by a vote, they would be soundly beaten in the next election. Jimmy Carter ran for governor of Georgia as a relative racial liberal and lost; the next time he ran as a segregationist and won. The same scenario, in more dramatic fashion, played itself out with Alabama's governor George Wallace. But there were also those who truly believed in segregation. Fulbright was of the latter group. In *Fulbright: A Biography*, University of Arkansas Distinguished Professor of History Randall Bennett Woods bluntly asserts that Fulbright was a racist.

President Bill Clinton (often called "the first black president") was surely a racial liberal as president. But he awarded Fulbright the Presidential Medal of Freedom. And according to biographer David Maraniss, when Clinton worked on Fulbright's staff as a young man he regarded Fulbright as "his first political role model."

If there is one thing most neo-conservatives do not believe, it is that America is too arrogant in trying to purvey its message. Indeed, the more plausible pejorative word associated with neo-conservatism is "messianic." The Fulbrightians and their present-day counterparts believe that America is a suspect power. Most neo-cons believe that America can lead the world to a better place. Certainly a mindful eye must be kept on American activity around the world. But the homespun New York–North Carolina pundit and philosopher Harry Golden said, "America ain't what's wrong with the world."

If neo-conservatism came about as a response to changing situations, the case of Bill Moyers is instructive. I should stress, although it has been implied here in many places already, that Moyers was nothing but kind, courteous, and helpful to me during my time in the White House. For many years on August 11, I used to call him and thank him for the 1966 anniversary of helping me get my job at the White House, which led to my role on the national scene. Before this, I don't believe I have ever before written a public word against him. Over the years he has shown an excellent television presence on PBS and for a while as a commentator on CBS. At one point we even thought of doing a joint PBS television program. He has, similarly, said some nice things about some of my PBS work, although after we went our separate ways I did hear periodically that

he told others ruefully that he was responsible for getting me involved in public life. That was true in a way; but it was a book I had
written that brought me to the attention of the White House.

But Moyers, by my lights, has moved from Johnson moderate
liberal Democrat, to liberal, to very liberal, to mildly radical. He calls
himself a progressive. In 2002 Moyers was made editor in chief of a
new one-hour weekly PBS program called *Now*. (He then left the
program, after being half-pushed out the door.) Its topics touched
every radical base, with almost no "balance." His 2004 book, *Moyers
on America: A Journalist and His Times,* is in a similar cast. In addition, the Schuman Foundation, of which Moyers is president, funds
ads in *The New York Times* that also offer somewhat radical fare.

Moyers, an ordained Baptist minister, comes across today as a
man who thinks that millions of Christian fundamentalists believe
that environmental destruction is not only to be disregarded but actually welcomed, even hastened, as a sign of the coming apocalypse—
that such Christian views are "delusional" and "no longer marginal,"
but coming from "the seat of power in the Oval Office and in Congress. [That] for the first time in our history, ideology and theology
hold a monopoly of power in Washington." Moyers believes American
media is controlled by right-wing journalism in the service of big
business. He believes that conservative think tanks do the same thing.
He writes that big corporate money runs our politics and our media,
although he regularly takes corporate money for some of his television programs, a practice that is unavoidable. I have been told that he
says he spends about 50 percent of his time raising money, although
I cannot verify this; I'd guess I spend about 20 percent of my time
raising funds for *Think Tank*.

Speaking on *Now*, apparently not from a written text, he said that
"the ruling ideology, the ruling religion of America, has been free
market. Its God is profit. Its heaven is the corporate boardroom. Its
hell is regulation. Its bible is *The Wall Street Journal*. Its choir of angels is the corporate media." Moyers believes that Democrats over-
reached, became intellectually bankrupt, which allowed "a resurgent
conservatism" to resurrect "social Darwinism as a moral philosophy,
multinational corporations as a governing class, and the theology of
markets as a transcendental belief system." I have never heard him

say that market economics makes ordinary people richer, sometimes at a slower rate than the wealthy, sometimes more quickly, depending how you measure.

During coverage of the 2004 presidential election, Moyers stated, "I think that if Kerry were to win this in a tight race, I think that there would be an effort to mount a coup. The right-wing is not going to accept it." (Talk about delusional.) In a letter to the editor of *The New York Times* in August 2005, Moyers wrote: "I served in the Johnson administration when we circled the wagons and clung, at great cost, to the United States and Vietnam, to the official view of reality."

I gather he is now, finally, writing a book about his Johnson years in which he states he was against the Vietnam War early on. But if that was his belief, forty years is a long time to wait to put it out publicly. But, in a way, he hadn't waited. A few years ago a grizzled old high-ranking Washington journalist during Moyers's White House years told me that Hayes Redmond, at Moyers's direction, was leaking such thoughts off the record to the press. Moyers was very well known. Had he broken with the president early and denounced Vietnam publicly, might it have made a difference? It gets worse and funnier in the more popular media. In July 2005 Moyers was asked this question by MSNBC's *Hardball* host Chris Matthews:

> MATTHEWS: There's a highly successful conservative cable network called Fox. Why isn't there a highly successful liberal network?

> MOYERS: I don't understand it. I think the people who run television think that liberals and progressives don't get worked up about anything. I think that they think that they're too subtle, too complex, too erudite but the people out in the country who listen to Fox News, who listen to Rush Limbaugh, they like red meat. And, you know, by nature, it's very hard for a liberal to throw red meat simply because the issues are more complex than you can reduce down to a soundbite.

So, nonliberals are not only wrongheaded in Moyers's world, but they simply can't handle complex ideas. In short, they are not very smart. You can almost always tell who's a liberal in a political context when you hear the words "It's very complex." Conservatives tend to say, "It's all quite simple." My own view is that it's often simpler than it seems. Are you for desegregation, or against it? Do you want a cleaner environment? Do you want women to get a fair break? Do you believe in (noncoercively) spreading liberty in the world?

Moyers's observation is interesting given the view expressed by Senator Daniel P. Moynihan, a Democrat and a complex neo-con hero with a generally liberal voting record widely regarded as one of the most intellectually acute men ever to serve in the U.S. Senate. Some years before Moyers's remark, Moynihan wrote: "The Republicans simply left us [Democrats] behind. They became the party of ideas and we were left, in Lord Macaulay's phrase, as 'the stupid party.'"

If Moyers's view is representative of *nouveau* liberalism in the recent era, and a good deal of it is, then neo-conservatism can be easily seen to have come about as a response to changed conditions and attitudes. That radicalism-progressivism comes in at least two forms. There are those who want to help America, albeit in ways I think would be most unhelpful. I would put Bill in that number.

There is a second class—linear descendants of Vietnam activists who not only wished that America would leave but wanted it to happen in a humiliating way: shamed before the world, never to do damage again. That view is held by a relative handful of people, but it was not often denounced by more sensible anti-war people. That attitude did as much as anything to weaken the *sensible* anti-war movement in Vietnam and the anti-war movement in Iraq. It loses huge numbers of votes for the party seen to endorse it—in recent years the Democrats.

Americans generally believe we are the good guys of history.

CHAPTER TWO

The Real Majority

THE SOCIAL ISSUE SURFACES

THERE IS NO specific chapter in this book on politics, although the book is suffused with politics most everywhere, even when chapters deal with policy, or media, or values, or sex. But this chapter on *The Real Majority* (TRM) is as close as you will get to straight politics.

The Real Majority, which I coauthored with Dick Scammon in 1970, got it right the first time. Scammon and I believed it was still right when it was republished in 1992 with a new introduction. Scammon died in 2001 after a very long incapacitation, but I have no doubt that from wherever Unitarian neo-cons go when they pass away, he still believes it is still right today.

It was a neo-conservative book, although the word is not mentioned in *TRM*. Many of the themes form a backdrop to much of the substance that follows in this book. A primary theme: Elections matter.

Shortly after Richard Nixon's election in late 1968, Scammon called me to ask if we could have lunch. We ate at the White House Mess and he suggested that we collaborate on another book, this one about elections. It emerged less than eighteen months later as *The*

*Real Majority: An Extraordinary Examination of the American Elec-
torate.*

I thought Scammon and I had helped influence the national debate with *This U.S.A.,* our earlier collaboration about the 1960
census—the one that had brought me to the attention of the White
House. But *The Real Majority,* published in 1970, hit the jackpot.
The book made *The New York Times* Best Seller List and managed to
alienate most every liberal in America—except those it converted. It
was regarded as a neo-con lodestar.

It was said to be "the bible" of the 1970 elections, for both political parties. There must have been fifty (really) nationally syndicated
newspaper columns about it, pro and con. To this day members of
Congress, of both parties, tell me that not only have they read it, but
many of their predecessors had, and that they still insist that all
newly hired staff members read it. In 1992 a new paperback edition
was published by the small Donald I. Fine firm. Fine told me he
thought it deserved republication because it was a classic. Neither
Scammon nor I argued about that. Don Fine was a liberal, an ec-
centric, and a canny publisher. *TRM* was my breakout book. Almost
forty years later it is still regularly quoted to prove one point or another. It was the best collaboration in which I have been involved.
Scammon and I each brought very different skills and experiences to
the table. It was a joy to work with him.

Modestly, *TRM* set out to establish "a general theory" of elections in a field that is not generally amenable to grand Keynesian or
Einsteinian theorizing. I find that most of those who do analyze
election data use it to get where they want to go instead of letting
the data lead them. I don't believe that *TRM* did that.

TRM had three basic themes, all contradicting established
liberal political wisdom. First, Scammon and I looked at the demographic nature of the electorate, and noted that a majority of voters
were "*un*-young, *un*-poor, *un*-black." We specifically wrote that did
not mean "anti-young, anti-poor, or anti-black." It was elemental demographic data, but liberals did not like to hear it at a time when the
New Left was glorifying all three groups and claiming that a direct
appeal to those votes could elect a Democratic national ticket. Fred
Dutton, a McGovern guru, regularly made the point that 80 percent

of young people would vote and 80 percent would vote for McGovern. The election exit polls of 1972 showed 30 percent of young people voting, with 25 percent voting for McGovern. Remarkably, young people were more likely to favor segregationist George Wallace than were their elders.

I had a rip-snorting argument with our editor. Notwithstanding our use of the word "un-black," the census data we used was still labeled "Negro" or "Negroes," and we were using census data. President Johnson's famous civil rights speech at Howard University referred frequently to "Negroes." The courageous cadres of the civil rights revolution of the 1950s were called "the New Negro." It was not a pejorative term. The editor, of course, knew better. The word "Negro" would have to be changed to "black." They were hip up there in New York. We would get in trouble using "Negro."

I told him to stuff it. Scammon agreed. I went back and forth with the editor. I won. He agreed we were the writers and ultimately it was our book and our call. But when the finished books came in, every "Negro" (except in direct quotation) had unilaterally been turned into "black." Polite usage has changed in a relatively short span of years from "colored" to "Negro" to "black" to "Afro-American" (a brief run) to "person of color" to "African American" today. But there is an unresolved problem: What about recently arrived American immigrants, some of them citizens, from sub-Saharan Africa? Aren't they also "African Americans"? Of course, in general usage everyone knows that "African American" refers to American blacks of slave descent. My preference would be to use whatever the group in question wants. But what do you do when that doesn't make sense?

Ironically the Yiddish word for black is "shvartz," but it is an insult to describe blacks as "shvartzes" (with some merit). And have you ever noticed how rarely the word "Jew" is used? A person can be "Jewish," but to call him a "Jew" is often regarded as insulting. I've seen writers use "a member of the Jewish community" or even "a person of the Jewish peruasion" to avoid using "Jew." "American Jew" works fine for me: Neo-cons don't like PC.

Second, we wrote that the power position in an election *was the center*—again, elemental. The idea in a winner-take-all democracy

(also called first past the post) is to get one more vote than your opponent whether that be in a primary, or a general election—unlike
in a proportional parliamentary system. (This method was later
changed for American presidential primary contests.) By definition,
the winning vote was in the center of the ideological spectrum.
Every vote can count in a big way in such a system where, in the race
for the White House, a *one-vote* plurality can yield *all* the electoral
votes of a state. We carefully noted that the center was moving and
could (and did) certainly change over time. We further noted that
most voters in a presidential election often vote on the basis of the
candidates' attitudes, not just the issues.

The third theme was the most controversial. We called it "The
Social Issue," a constellation of concerns with crime the most important. We said it had achieved *coequal* status with "The Economic
Issue" that had achieved primacy after the financial breakdown during the Depression of the 1930s. We noted nautically that many
American presidential elections could be likened to an ocean, sometimes calm, sometimes choppy, and sometimes yielding electoral
tidal waves. Our contention was that the Social Issue was such a tidal
issue. What did the Social Issue consist of? We looked at Barry
Goldwater's acceptance speech in 1964:

> Tonight there is violence in our streets, corruption in our
> highest offices, anxiety among our elderly, and there's vir-
> tual despair among the many who look beyond material
> success toward the inner meaning of their lives.

Sound familiar? Of course, it inflamed liberals that we used Goldwater's rhetoric as an example, but it was also the type of ominous
matter so many on the Left often embraced.

We looked at a series of Gallup polls over a dozen years concentrating on "the most important problem" or "the most important issue." We saw it move from keeping out of war and unemployment
(1958) to civil rights, integration, crime, crime, and more crime,
with the Vietnam War interspersed.

But Vietnam was hard to survey: Voters generally took a win-it-
or-get-out position. What Americans could not stomach were the

demonstrators who publicly rooted for the North Vietnamese to win or those who dodged the draft. And they did not like it when sensible doves opted for the radical doctrine: "No enemies on the Left," an idea that has haunted the Democratic party for decades.

Regarding "un-black": The continuing conflation of race and crime is not just racism, although that is surely an important component. Over the years blacks have been convicted of violent crime at a rate about five times that of whites, most typically black-on-black violence. (Once, in an unguarded moment, Reverend Jesse Jackson said that if he saw young blacks walking behind him on the street he was much more afraid than if he saw young whites.) The violent crime that people were talking about, in FBI language, were "crimes against persons": murder, rape, robbery, and aggravated assault. We noted that much of the crime in the 1960s could be attributed to the advent of huge numbers of male Baby Boomers reaching their teen years, which are years of prime crime time.

Scammon and I noted that people were buying guns for their own protection, often illegally. Many years later my colleague at the American Enterprise Institute, John Lott, wrote a book entitled *More Guns, Less Crime*, making the case that those states with right-to-carry laws—which permit law-abiding citizens to own concealed handguns—had lower crime rates. (A majority of states in 2005 had such laws.) Why? Because the bad guys feared they might get killed.

In describing the Social Issue, we went beyond the backlash of Wallace and Goldwater and the "frontlash" that Lyndon Johnson had talked of, and looked at "kidlash," listing some items that were troubling most voters, including long hair, short skirts, foul language, and mind-bending drugs. To this combustible mix, we added another element of the Social Issue—values. We noted that pornography was blossoming with legal sanction, sexual mores were becoming permissive and promiscuous, Catholic priests were getting married, and sex education in public schools was sometimes instilling views that parents did not want taught to their children. The underpinnings of a moral code were being shredded, or so it was perceived. (Sound familiar?) We speculated as to which party would best respond to the social turbulence. The Democrats were in second place.

We wrote that the national electorate was "middle-class, middle-aged, and middle-minded." But we also noted that the Social Issue could involve "progressivism on economic issues. . . . Clean up the slums, clean up the environment. Clean out the criminals, clean out the drugs." That could be a statement easily made by a neo-conservative today. Listen to Bill Cosby and you hear something pretty close to that.

Scammon and I believed that patriotism was elemental in American politics, and that while foreign policy did not usually show up as the number one issue, it best told voters that the candidate in question was, or was not, a stand-up, take-charge guy. That, we believed, was likely the characteristic that counted most when voters chose a president.

The book was about the study of elections or *psephology*, a word regularly used in the United Kingdom but that has never caught on in America. *Psephos* means "pebble" in Greek and refers to voting Athenian-style: by casting either a white or black pebble into their equivalent of a ballot box. *TRM* identified three tidal shifts in relatively recent American psephology. One was the now-quaint issue of Free Silver that blossomed in the late 1800s and was used by Republicans to label Democrats the party of radicalism and social disorder. (Sound familiar?) The second tidal issue began during the Great Depression and let President Franklin D. Roosevelt call Republicans "economic royalists." (Sound familiar?) And the third, we maintained, was the Social Issue that reached shore in the 1960s, with its core values still very much with us.

Some liberals called Scammon and me sellouts. But one reason that so-called crime in the streets is such a potent issue is that it was real on an everyday, personal level for so many people, engendering fear that distorts and trumps both the quality of life and economic issues that inspire liberals.

As in *This U.S.A.*, Scammon and I used hard data—this time including a variety of public opinion polls, academic survey research, and election returns—to make our points. We said that Democrats should be as tough on "law 'n' order" as Republicans. After all, we noted, wasn't it blacks who were disproportionately getting mugged and murdered?

Wallace knew how to play the Social Issue fiddle, fingers dancing on the strings, bowing furiously. Here is one of his riffs that I used later in a television special called *The Democrats*. Wallace was being hassled by demonstrators:

> Come up here after I've completed my speech and I'll autograph your sandals for you. There's not anything wrong with you that a good haircut wouldn't cure. You're not a 'she' are you? You're a 'he'?
>
> We've got some folks out here who know a lot of four letter words, but there are two four-letter words they don't know: w-o-r-k and s-o-a-p.
>
> You who want a passport to Hanoi? The day after I go into office you just check with me and I'll give it to you, and you go on over there. And you anarchists better have your day now, because you're through after November 5th in this country. You lie down in front of my automobile and you won't want to lie down in front of it anymore.

Wallace is a pivotal figure in American political life. His "send 'em a message" is the classic slogan of a third-party candidate, or a candidate far from the mainstream of his own party. (Wallace ran both as a Democrat and as an independent.) He not only racked up huge votes in the segregationist South but also scored very well and won in some non-Southern primaries as well. In the midst of a "busing" crisis he carried *Boston* in the 1976 Democratic primary! His famous "stand in the schoolhouse door" forced President Johnson to federalize the Alabama National Guard to enforce the law.

But ultimately Johnson's three major civil rights laws wore down most all of the recalcitrant Southern segregationists. And Wallace changed his ways. He reverted from racial populism to the economic populism from whence he came. In his last years he drew large numbers of African-American votes but was still tough enough so that voters knew this was no social issue softie. Famous blacks came to his funeral. There is a lesson here that neo-conservatives understand better than conservatives, who often say that "laws can't change the hearts of men." They can.

Scammon and I created a mythical "middle voter": a forty-seven-year-old housewife from the suburbs of Dayton, Ohio, whose husband was a machinist. She said she was afraid to walk the streets alone at night and had mixed views about blacks and civil rights because before moving to the suburbs she lived in a city neighborhood that had turned all black and where crime rates soared. Her brother-in-law was a policeman. She knew that she didn't have the money to move again if her new neighborhood deteriorated. She was concerned because LSD had been discovered on the campus of the local community college where her son was a student.

That composite "lady from Dayton," as she became known, was regarded as the typical voter—always a dangerous formulation. She was middle-age; her husband was a skilled worker who toiled with his hands, not in a more cerebral occupation. *Life* magazine, the leading weekly in America at the time, had a reporter track down a *real* woman who more or less fit the bill—Betty Lowery of Fairborn, Ohio. She tuned out to be a charming woman who also worked part-time in a bookstore.[1]

THE REAL MAJORITY was regarded as the Democratic rebuttal to the bestseller *The Emerging Republican Majority* by Kevin Phillips, a very young and very conservative fellow. Phillips posited that the votes of the future would more and more come from the Sunbelt states of the South and West (true) and that it was the Democrats who were particularly vulnerable to the constellation of issues that Scammon and I later called the Social Issue. He also stressed detailed historical ethnographic voting trends. We did some of that, but it gets tedious after a while. (By 1970, Phillips was working for Nixon's attorney general, John Mitchell, who would later resign in

---

1. Later, politicians would compete for her vote and seek her endorsement. I was told that one statewide Ohio candidate was asked at a press conference, "What about the lady from Dayton?" He turned beet red, probably because he hadn't read the book—leading to below-the-radar journalistic speculation that he had something going on with a woman who was not his wife. (Sound familiar?)

disgrace during the Watergate scandal and go to prison. [Sound familiar?]) Scammon and I did not wholly disagree with Phillips. We only noted that Democrats could indeed fall into the Phillips trap—but only if they continued to behave like damned fools.

We posited that a national election could be won by a candidate capturing the electoral votes of "Quadcali"—a *quadrangle* drawn from Massachusetts south to Washington, D.C., west to Illinois, and north to Wisconsin—with the addition of *California*. It still works, more or less, even after the great migration to the Sunbelt.

If in 2004, presidential candidate Senator John Kerry had carried Ohio, he would have been elected. He only lost by less than 120,000 votes out of 5,627,908 million cast; a switch of 2.1 percent there would have done it. A majority of the population in America is still east of the Mississippi River. After the decennial 2000 apportionment, Quadcali would still yield 267 of the 538 electoral votes: not quite enough to win, but almost (49.6 percent). But adding Maine (4 electoral votes) and Vermont (3 electoral votes) yields 274 electoral votes, a winning total. Today, probably the most important big states in the red-blue alignment—the so-called swing states—are in populous Florida, Illinois, Ohio, and Pennsylvania. The latter three are Quadcalinian.

During the elections of 2000 and 2004 there was much heated rhetoric about alleged voter disenfranchisement. But unmentioned has been that today the greatest numbers of true victims of disenfranchisement seeking to vote for president are those who live in "safe states," either "red" or "blue." If you are among the more than half of all Americans who don't live in a swing state, including Californians, New Yorkers, and Texans, you are effectively not voting for president. No wonder that by international standards we have low voter turnouts (although we have many more elections—for sewer commissioners, school board members, etc.).

There are massive constitutional and political barriers to the inherent problems with proportionalizing Electoral College voting, and it is not about to happen. I have at least a symbolic solution: Award *one* electoral vote to the winner of the popular vote. That would give every voter a stake in choosing a president and also make for an odd number of electoral seats, eliminating the possibility of a tie that would do away with the constitutional craziness that would result from the presidential election being thrown to the House of Representatives for a decision.

Kevin Phillips, over the course of time, moved left and then lefter (although probably not as far as Moyers). But given his early reputation as a conservative, his work has carried influence. Columnists and book reviewers write "as even Kevin Phillips says"; I wrote a column calling him "Even Kevin Phillips."

LET US GO through the years and see how the theme of *The Real Majority* stayed alive, and perhaps intensified.

In 1970, Republicans responded, with fear, to the theme of the book. I had the publisher send out bound page proofs of the book to a number of influential politicians and their aides. A young White House speechwriter named Pat Buchanan working for President Richard Nixon saw one of them. He sent a memo to Nixon that two Democrats were stealing their issues and that GOP congressional candidates had best be warned.

On November 1, 1970, just two days before the congressional elections, Nixon spoke out to most of the nation during time paid for by the Republican National Committee. The broadcast was aired during halftimes of regionally televised professional football games. The theme was said to have been inspired by one interpretation of *The Real Majority*. Press accounts of the speech said that Nixon sounded bellicose and almost wild. Here are some excerpts:

> When I was elected president two years ago, I promised that I would work to end the war in Vietnam and win a just peace in the world, and that I would work to stop the rise in crime in America.
>
> The president . . . can't do the job alone. Here at home I need the help of Congress, more help than I have had. . . . In the fight against crime, we need laws, we need judges, and we need men in the House and the Senate who will

speak out on this subject, not just at election time but all year round.

In recent weeks and in recent months you have seen on your television screens some of our young people engaging in violence, trying to shout down speakers, and engaging in activities that you disapprove of. Don't answer in kind. It is time for the great Silent Majority to stand up and be counted. The way you can be counted is by voting on November 3.

On November 2, 1970, the evening before the election, Senator Edmund Muskie spoke calmly from his home in Maine to respond for his party. His talk was based on another way of seeing *The Real Majority*:

In these elections of 1970, something has gone wrong. Honorable men have been slandered. Faithful servants of the country have had their motives questioned and their patriotism doubted.

Let me begin with those issues of law and order, of violence and unrest, which have pervaded the rhetoric of this campaign. I believe that any person who violates the law should be apprehended, prosecuted and punished if found guilty.

But we must also look for the deeper causes in the structure of our society. If one of your loved ones is sick, you do not think it is soft or undisciplined of a doctor to try to discover the agents of illness.

This is the "root causes" idea that conservatives always denounce— and then watch as Republicans join with Democrats to vote large sums in legislative attempts to rectify the problems that Democrats have often first identified. Neo-cons play a role all through the process and then try to make some sense of the new laws if they don't work out well.

Indeed, in 1970 many liberal Democrats responded directly to the thesis of *The Real Majority*. Senator John Tunney cruised Los Angeles in a police car, sirens blaring. Senator Adlai Stevenson III reminded Illinois voters that he had commanded a tank in combat during the Korean War. Most important was Muskie's speech, which in large measure led to the early success of his 1972 presidential candidacy.

In 1972, Democratic nominee George McGovern was trounced by Richard Nixon in a landslide. McGovern was seen to be on the wrong side of most every conceivable aspect of the social issue. I think it was the most important election of the last half of the twentieth century, and its meaning remains with us today.

Senator Hugh Scott, the Republican minority leader from Pennsylvania, said McGovern's campaign deserved to be characterized as one of "acid, amnesty, and abortion"—a harsh phrase that hit the political jackpot (columnist Bob Novak claims coinage). The amnesty refers to granting a free pass back to America to young anti-war Americans who fled the draft during the Vietnam War and were held in extremely low esteem by the public. Acid referred to LSD, as it still does. The polling on the abortion issue has yielded a very close call over the years, often dependent on how the question was phrased.

In 1976, running as an unknown candidate in the previously ignored Iowa caucuses, former Governor Jimmy Carter of Georgia captured a publicity bonanza when he won. As an unknown, he also gained a dream situation for a candidate: the ability to describe himself as he wished to be known. In this case, Carter and his people stressed that he was a nuclear engineer, a farmer, a submarine commander, and a family man with a remarkable mother and with a sister who was an evangelical Peace Corps volunteer—pretty good from a *Real Majority* standpoint. He also made it clear that in no way was he a softie on any social issue. (Only later did the shenanigans regarding his strange brother Billy come to public attention.) He said he would never tell a lie (a pledge broken as he said it).

At one point, as the racial issue boiled, Carter said he was for "ethnic purity" in neighborhoods and, even under journalistic pressure, would not retract the apparently racist remark. With all that, he received a scant 50.1 percent of the popular vote, and was the last Democrat to gain a majority in that category. When opponents like Scoop Jackson directed their pollsters to find out what people thought of Carter, many respondents echoed Carter's self-description. That's why money is so important in politics. It buys the ability, through travel, press conferences, and various forms of advertising, to paint a portrait of the candidate as he or she wants it painted.

But during his single term in office, Carter was pushed toward the soft Left, particularly so after he was challenged from within his own party by Senator Ted Kennedy. He also said that Americans had an "inordinate fear of Communism," which did not sit well with neo-cons and many other Americans. He later said his remarks were taken out of context. (Sound familiar?)

I think Carter was and is a strange man. After his presidency I did a speaking engagement with him—we were two of the four keynoters to a Young Presidents Organization international convention in Melbourne, Australia. The Young Presidents Organization is a fine international organization of CEOs under age forty whose membership is mostly American. In the course of his remarks Carter said, "The Soviet Union has never lied to us." Then I saw and heard something I could hardly believe. The great majority of this mostly American audience stood up and booed their former president, who was speaking on foreign soil.

In 1980, Ronald Reagan ran on a platform of "family, work, neighborhood, peace, and freedom," words that could have come straight from The Real Majority. Reagan had characterized many welfare recipients as hustlers or cheats and didn't buy the soft root causes ideas. His characterization was harsh and denounced by liberals. But when welfare procedures were changed in 1996 and beyond, amazing corruption and criminality was discovered.

A new economic situation had shown its face: "stagflation." It combined high unemployment with high inflation. Interest rates peaked at about 18 percent in 1981. It seemed that the United States was on its way toward becoming a banana republic. Inflation is routinely called the cruelest tax and has caused revolutions. The value of the German currency collapsed during the time of the Weimar

Republic, yielding a charismatic chancellor named Adolf Hitler. According to Theodore H. White, who was on the ground at the time, the Communists took over China because of inflation.

On the campaign trail, Reagan's tax-cutting goals involved his supply-side economic plan. Although widely mocked, the key aspects of supply-side economics made some good sense: A drop in the rate of marginal (top-rate) taxation has a favorable effect on how well the economy works because it leaves more money in the hands of investors, savers, and spenders. Of course, this requires "dynamic scoring" by various budget agencies, which reflects a reasonable view of how much incentive the tax cuts might yield. That, too, is ridiculed by those who want higher, not lower, taxes.

A major trouble with the way it was originally presented concerned the amount this reflow would show. Supply-side guru Arthur Laffer drew a diagram for some journalists on the back of a napkin that showed that the reflow would or could exceed 100 percent: If the government cut $1,000 through marginal tax rates, the yield in new revenues might well yield, say, $1,200 back to the government! The amount of the "reflow" is debateable—but there would be *some* amount. I do not know whether under some circumstances it could exceed the cut itself.

The supply-side plan was called "voodoo economics" by George H. W. Bush, the man whom Reagan would ultimately choose to be his vice president. The phrase, which achieved headline status, was allegedly written by David Gergen, who later went to work for Reagan. Toward the end of the campaign Reagan's economic advisors diluted the plan, although this was barely mentioned by the press.

Supply-side is often regarded as far-out, right-wing economics. But in moderate doses such thinking has the approval of many neocons as well, and intuitively, of most Americans. Its aim is economic growth across the board. What's wrong with that? It provides a policy to help Adam Smith's "invisible hand" work.

It is generally believed that Reagan was a goof-off, taking it easy, flying out to his ranch, suffering memory lapses, and so on. But Richard Reeves's wonderful book, *President Reagan: The Triumph of Imagination*, shows a different reality. He says Reagan got substantively involved in tax cuts and in Soviet relations, especially regarding the Strategic Defense Initiative (SDI, aka "Star Wars"). At an arms control meeting, Mikhail Gorbachev, the general secretary of the Soviet Union, was rather suddenly willing to sharply cut arms, much along the lines that the Americans had been proposing for years.

Most of Reagan's staff was beside itself with joy, but Reagan said no because Gorbachev linked the cuts to rolling back Star Wars. SDI may have been the most successful military program in history. For the cost of an announcement and a few billion dollars in start-up costs, a project unlikely to ever work, and unwise if it ever did, the Soviets flinched when they realized they could not match it. There is a lesson to be gleaned from SDI. A large part of the genesis of the idea was cultural: American kids felt free enough to tinker with computers without fear of state reprisal. Soviet kids did not have that liberty. That's why the Soviet leaders knew they couldn't compete. So the Soviets had to give in and cut deals on arms that they wouldn't have otherwise. Freedom matters. SDI played a role in ending the Cold War and the subsequent disappearance of the USSR.

When Gorbachev visited Washington in 1987 he had his limousine stop at a corner downtown. The crowd mobbed him, hugging him, shaking his hand, congratulating him for all that he was doing to try to straighten out what Reagan had called the "Evil Empire."

Reagan was strangely silent, saying only wait till he got to Moscow to say his piece. White House speechwriter Tony Dolan didn't like what was going on and convinced Reagan to host a press conference in the Oval Office with just four op-ed types: R. Emmett Tyrell of *The American Spectator*, syndicated columnist Georgie Anne Geyer, op-ed page editor Phil Geyelin of *The Washington Post*, and me, then writing a syndicated column. We went around the room seriatim, asking questions of Reagan. My first question was, roughly, "Mr. President, given the current situation, do you think the Soviet Union has lost the Cold War?" Reagan diplomatically ducked, saying roughly, "Well, I don't know who won or lost, or whether anyone did."

When my turn came for a second question, I apologized for going back to the same theme. I noted that Gorbachev was reaping all this glory. Wasn't it important to say who won? Reagan ducked again. On my third try I further excused myself to the president and asked the same question again. Reagan gave a long and rambling answer that ended with him saying, "Well, yes." This was the answer that neo-cons had waited to hear for many decades. It is the one interview that I ever taped. I wrote it up as a news story that appeared on the front page of *The Washington Times*. Tyrell wrote about it in his column, but I don't think Geyer or Geyelin appreciated how big it was.

Reagan's subsequent speeches at the Moscow summit delivered what he promised. He talked about American greatness, about the coming Soviet greatness, and about religion, and ended up throwing his arm around Gorby's shoulders "like a couple of guys coming off the field after a big game," as one witness described it. William Buckley went ballistic: He thought Reagan was getting soft, engaging in *détente*. George Will wrote a column saying we had just *lost* the Cold War. (Even George gets something wrong occasionally.)

Clare Booth Luce had a dictum that presidents are remembered by one sentence, if they are lucky: Washington was the father of his country, Lincoln freed the slaves—and two for Franklin D. Roosevelt: He ended the Depression (probably much overstated, although what he did do was of enormous significance), and he won the war.

When Reagan left office I wrote a column that used the Luce formulation and wrote "Reagan won the Cold War." I heard later that on the plane back to California Reagan was asked what he thought he accomplished, and he pulled out my column and said, "Well . . . it says here that . . ." It was poetically true, but in reality hundreds of millions of citizens of the free world paid taxes and sometimes put their lives on the line to achieve victory. Withal, it took forty years. Most neo-cons think *détente* slowed the process.

I feel so lucky to have been around when the Cold War ended victoriously, "without a shot being fired," as British Prime Minister Margaret Thatcher said (except for some spilled blood in Romania). When I think I played a very small role in that monumental event, I can cry.

REAGAN'S FIRST BIG supply-side cuts won with a big margin in Congress, but many Democrats added new cuts of their own,

"Christmas tree-ing" the bill to stratospheric levels. In the next years Reagan was forced to ask for a tax hike, giving Democrats a first-class "I-told-you-so."

To little effect. In 1984, Democrats were in convention in San Francisco waving plastic American flags, still trying to overcome McGovernism. But American flags didn't work and were often mocked by the commentators. The Reverend Jesse Jackson, a social apostle in the black community, had decided to move his work into the political fray. He ended up doing the Republican Party's work, defining Democrats as soft and radical—as if he were purposefully reading *The Real Majority* upside down and backward.

Reagan and his team had perfect pitch regarding the Cold War. His key commercial was entitled *The Bear and the Forest* and dealt with the ongoing Cold War threat from the Soviet Union. In the ad, a bear is prowling the forest—mean, angry, hungry—as the voice of a narrator is heard:

> There is a bear in the woods. For some people, the bear is easy to see. Others don't see it at all. Some people say the bear is tame. Others say it is vicious and dangerous. Since no one can really be sure who's right, isn't it smart to be as strong as the bear—if there is a bear?

A man appears, a rifle on his shoulder. The bear takes a slight step backward. And a simple written message is seen: "President Reagan. Prepared for Peace."

What label Reagan put on himself in his inner political soul I do not know. I do know that the meat of that key commercial was pure neo-conservative doctrine: The Soviet Union was expansionist, heavily armed and building up, a threat to the United States and to freedom everywhere. Not only neo-cons, but most all Americans believed that Communism was a global doctrine, and we'd better be ready to at least contain it, and do more if possible.

Meanwhile, Jesse Jackson was calling for massive defense cuts. In the long 1984 nominating process, no Democratic candidate challenged Jackson, not from the stump and not during the debates. Why not? Probably because no other candidate thought Jackson could win, and because all the Democratic primary candidates needed African-American votes to come close to winning in the general election. It was the same pernicious doctrine again: No enemies on the Left.

By never challenging Jackson's very soft and radical views, the Democrats became associated with them. Republicans feasted on this. At the 1984 Republican convention, the recently retired UN ambassador Jeane Kirkpatrick, one of the founders of the Coalition for the Democratic Majority and a former advisor to liberal Hubert Humphrey, was invited by the Reaganistas to deliver a major speech. She characterized her former party, in a widely repeated line, saying that Democrats always "blame America first." It was a charge that resonated ever since the radical opponents of the Vietnam War trashed the United States.

Reagan's 1984 opponent was Walter Mondale, Carter's former vice president. He had a different message. He said he would raise taxes.

Something weird happened. Jesse Jackson had broken the back of the idea that only politicians and generals could run for president. Penn Kemble—about whom there will be much more later—and I were walking up one of San Francisco's hills. He said, "You ought to think about doing that. I've talked to Midge [Decter] and she thinks it's an interesting idea." I thought about it briefly. There is no better place to surface ideas that in presidential primary debates, as Alan Keyes, Pat Buchanan, Pat Robertson, Ron Paul, and others later showed. No groundswell appeared for me, and that was a step too far, even for a man who preaches the purveying of ideas and has no problem with self-promotion for a cause.

In his 1988 convention acceptance speech, Vice President George H. W. Bush showed a clear understanding of political demography and went out of his way to salute the organizations where that lady from Dayton hung out:

> This is America: the Knights of Columbus, the Grange,
> Hadassah, the Disabled American Veterans, the Order of
> AHEPA [American Hellenic Educational Progressive
> Association], the Business and Professional Women of

America, the union hall, the bible study group, LULAC
[League of United Latin American Citizens], Holy Name—
a brilliant diversity spread like stars, like *a thousand points
of light* in a broad and peaceful sky.

Bush got plenty of kidding by journalists about the thousand points of
light, but the mainstream Americans who belonged to those organizations knew exactly what he was talking about. He soundly beat
Democratic candidate Massachusetts Governor Michael Dukakis.

During the campaign Bush drilled home the social issues. He
campaigned on the Pledge of Allegiance. He visited a flag factory—
and why not, if some Democrats were foolish enough to condemn
the pledge? Bush reminded voters that, as governor, Dukakis favored
weekend passes for murderers, like the infamous Willie Horton, who
were serving life sentences with no parole. It was an incredible idea;
such prisoners had nothing to lose. Horton got such a weekend pass:
He raped a woman in Maryland after incapacitating her husband.

Jesse Jackson had a strong primary campaign, and his caravan
rolled into Atlanta looking and sounding like a winner. The commentariat asked desperately, "What does Jackson want?" Again the
Democratic candidates refused to challenge Jackson, and again the
Democrats were associated with his radical views on both domestic
and foreign issues, causing great harm.

Professional Democratic politicians running against him would
not often challenge Jackson, but many columnists and commentators did. Over the years I squared off against Jackson a number of
times. Here is an excerpt from a 1988 edition of the *MacNeil/Lehrer
NewsHour* that aired after Jackson beat Dukakis solidly in the
Michigan primary:

> CHARLAYNE HUNTER-GAULT: Your victory seems to have
> caught a lot of people by surprise. Did it catch you by
> surprise?
>
> JACKSON (in a mélange of several responses): It did not.
> The Jackson message was: Stop economic violence
> against American farmers and workers. Stop drugs.

Invest in our children. Reinvest in America. That is the opposite of Reaganomics. The pundits are not present at the plant gates or at the farm auctions. I've been negotiating with foreign heads of state, I brought prisoners back home from foreign jails. We're shifting fundamentally from a racial background to economic common ground.

HUNTER-GAULT: [It was said before you came in] that if you were not black you would not be considered a serious candidate.

JACKSON: How could I not be black? How could Dukakis not be Greek? How could you not be female? I felt after the 1984 primary election that supporting the party was the right thing to do. If I win this nomination I expect the reciprocity.

ROBERT MACNEIL: Ben Wattenberg, in Tucson, you've been listening to this discussion, how do you think the results in Michigan changed the Democratic race?

WATTENBERG: I think it was an historic election. [I was puffing, having raced to the Tucson PBS station after giving a lunchtime speech somewhere not so nearby.] You had a candidate who was regarded as inevitable beaten by the candidate who was regarded as impossible. Reverend Jackson's a very unusual man, a political genius. But he kept talking about the *opportunity* to run, but no one has given him the opportunity to run *unchallenged*. I believe it fair to characterize his views as far-out, liberal-radical. I saw one of those debates in New Hampshire. There were seven people on the platform saying Paul said this, but Dick did a flip-flop, and Gary did that. And Jackson sat there and no one touched him. Here was a man way out on the political Left and no one said a word about Jesse Jackson.

MacNeil: Are you saying, Ben, [that Jackson is] too far-out liberal to get the nomination, too far-out liberal to be elected if he got the nomination?

Wattenberg: Any other candidate espousing those views would have been attacked early on, I do not think he would have come close to getting the nomination. He still has yet to break 10 percent of the white vote in an open primary. Somebody had better say, "Listen, what does Jesse Jackson stand for when he said 'Viva Che Guevara,' when he said that it was America's fault that Arabs were hijacking American airplanes? What does it mean when he has advisors from the Institute of Policy Studies, which describes itself as a center for radical scholarship?"

MacNeil: Reverend Jackson, how do you respond to Ben Wattenberg's feeling of the nature of your views, that they're so untested that people don't realize how liberal, in his words how far-out you are?

Jackson: I touched the heartstrings of America. . . .

Wattenberg: Reverend Jackson, you talked about Central America. You were on record as saying the Marxist-Leninist Sandinistas are the moral force in Nicaragua. On the Middle East I understand that you have taken contributions and supported the Libyan dictator Qadaffi.

Jackson: I've never met Mr. Qaddafi. All of us, Ben, may look alike, but we're not alike. I've never been to Libya . . . that's just a lie and you should not be telling that in public.

Wattenberg: It's been in the press that your organization has accepted such contributions. [I did not say he

had been to Libya or met Qaddafi, only that he had
accepted contributions.]

And so it went. There's more. Over the years Reverend Jackson has
been challenged for vastly overblowing his role in Martin Luther
King's organization. He was portrayed as a shakedown artist who
threatened corporations with demonstrations and boycotts. He has
been challenged as a race-monger, as a wordsmith who tarnished
words like *genocide*. He has been pro-quotas and in favor of set-
asides. He distanced himself from Louis Farrakhan at the height
of Farrakhan's campaign, which was both anti-Semitic and against
"white devils," but never repudiated him. He called for a 25 percent
defense cut during the Cold War—while 70 percent of Democrats
were either for raising defense spending or keeping it the same. He
appeared with the Vietnamese ambassador at a celebration that had
been dedicated to "the heroic victory of the people of Vietnam." He
is a man who called Jews "hymies" and New York City "Hymietown"
(for which he later apologized). He has called Zionism "a poisonous
weed." He has singled out certain Jewish organizations for opposing
preferential racial quotas, notwithstanding the fact that next to
blacks, Jews are the most liberal part of the American electorate and
were heavily penalized by quotas over the years. He has been both
anti- and pro-abortion. At times he sounds like a rhyming fool: "I'm
a tree-shaker, not a jelly maker"; "If you deal with the text out of context, you have a pretext"; "Super Tuesday is not superficial." Others
made more sense: "Choose the human race, not the nuclear race";
"From the slave ship to the championship."

Huff and puff. But there is another side. Jesse Jackson was born
out-of-wedlock into poverty, went to college, played varsity sports,
and became a sensational orator notwithstanding a harelip and a lisp.
When he first achieved fame in the 1970s he preached to black youth
that the doors were now open to young blacks, that they could make
it in America, that they shouldn't drop out of high school, that they
should work hard, that abortion was wrong, that drugs were wrong,
that "children having children" was wrong, that their mantra should
be "I am a man; I am somebody," and that the Ten Commandments
were right—just about what Bill Cosby would preach later. But at

some point Jackson went far Left on both domestic and foreign issues (running in direct contradiction to the Scammon-Wattenberg guidebook for center-left Democrats).

It is a mystery to me why he did not run again in 1992. He might have won. Big-name Democrats had opted out of the running because of Bush #41's popularity after the end of the first Iraq conflict. He might have beaten Bill Clinton, who had big drawbacks. But I think Jesse Jackson felt in his heart of hearts that, as a black man, he could not become president of the United States. I think otherwise: A man of his talents could indeed have become president—what a fantastic neo-con he could have been! (A Southern senator once said to me, only half in jest, and with more than a little cruelty, "Jesse just wants to be head nigger." I do not purport to understand the internal machinations of African-American politics, but they are very complicated.)

Jesse Jackson did not run in 1992. Some speculated that he feared "Stassenization" (after the wunderkind "boy governor" of Minnesota, Harold Stassen, who became a laughingstock for running for president again and again and again). There is also the issue of Jackson's health: He has a form of sickle-cell anemia that can put him in the hospital for a month at a time. Another African-American Democrat, Virginia governor Douglas Wilder, was considering a presidential bid. Ron Walters, a key Jackson advisor, says this: "[Running for president] takes a lot out of you, and Jesse and his family just felt he wasn't up to it." (That's what they all say.)

Because he would no longer be an active political candidate, Reverend Jackson made a big deal of his new weekly talk show on CNN. It started after his 1988 defeat and lasted until January of 2001. He did not have editorial control; his panelists were chosen by producers to make sure there was balance. Even I appeared a few times. He was very cordial to me. But he was not a good panel show host, reading from the prompter for questions, conducting halting conversations. A slot on cable television news or a program on PBS can be a fairly big deal. But this was a man who could have been elected president of the United States had his politics not gone wild.

We may find out about the possibility of a black president. But Caribbean-black former Secretary of State General Colin Powell once ran *first* in the "horse-race" polls for the *Republican* nomination.

(He opted not to run.) In late 2005, despite denials of interest, an African-American woman who had never held elected office was also in *first place* on some survey lists (Secretary of State Condoleezza Rice, also a *Republican*). Several other African Americans have shown up periodically on the list of ten most admired Americans: Oprah, Michael Jordan, Cosby, and Jackson himself. My sense is the Americans would love to have a black president (think about how much Barack Obama's support in 2008 reflects on racial progress in America)—if he or she were moderate.

In the early 1970s, the publication of *The Real Majority* caused a political sensation. Whitney Young, then the president of the Urban League, asked to meet with Scammon and me. We met in Young's suite in the Mayflower Hotel in D.C. After pleasantries, Young asked us, "What would you think of a black man running for vice president?" My, we were so smart: We quickly explained that a black man wouldn't really bring anything of electoral value to a Democratic ticket. Blacks already voted in overwhelming numbers for Democrats. Young paused silently, as if he were thinking profound thoughts. Then he asked: "Did I say Democrat?"

There is a lot of media buzz about African Americans moving to the GOP. After all, many blacks are deeply religious and deeply concerned about crime. But every four years polls show that the GOP share of the black vote is only about 10 percent. If that changed—if a black American were on a *Republican* ticket and led to 15 or 20 percent of blacks voting Republican—it would be tantamount to an electoral earthquake.

When the 1992 edition of *The Real Majority* came out in the spring, Don Fine sent me to Disneyland, to the American Booksellers Association to meet booksellers and give them a free autographed copy. About two hundred members stood in line patiently as I scribbled my name and a message. As they came by I asked them whom they were supporting in the presidential race, Governor Bill Clinton, President George H. W. Bush, or H. Ross Perot, the Dallas tycoon running as an independent. I couldn't believe what I heard: About 80 percent of the ABA members—probably mostly mild liberals—answered "Perot." Later, because he's a strange fellow, Perot—a businessman populist, certainly no garden-variety liberal—pulled out of the race, claiming a conspiracy to disrupt his daughter's wedding. Then, even more oddly, he reentered the race. But he still received an astonishing 19 percent of the vote, despite the classic third-party he-can't-win syndrome. Since then, I have never easily dismissed the notion of a serious third-party candidacy. Perot was an oddball billionaire entrepreneur, tough on crime and a plausible, if nutty, neo-con.

Arkansas Governor Bill Clinton understood *Real Majority* politics. He ran on a centrist platform of "personal responsibility" and "no more something for nothing" and said that he would "end welfare as we know it." But Clinton had social issue problems as well: extramarital behavior (Gennifer Flowers) and, most important, the allegation of illegal draft evasion at the time of the Vietnam War. I interviewed Clinton in his New Hampshire hotel room along with two fellows from *U.S. News & World Report,* Matt Cooper and my former American Enterprise Institute colleague and friend David Gergen, who had developed a close personal relationship with Clinton over many years. It was at the peak of Clinton's draft-status media firestorm. (Gergen served for four years in the navy during Vietnam and was privately less than ecstatic about Clinton's draft dodging.) Clinton was rattled but had answers for everything. The issues became sensations in the press. On the trail, candidate Democratic Senator Bob Kerrey of Nebraska—who was backed by Pat Moynihan—said that if Clinton became the Democratic nominee the Republicans "would open him up like a soft peanut."

Probably the best neo-con line in 1992 was delivered by former Senator Paul Tsongas who, in his standard stump speech, explained that government spending cost money, and said, "I'm not Santa Claus." That is not normal Democratic primary rhetoric; in fact, it would be a good line from a common-sense neo-con.

Tsongas left Congress when he was diagnosed with cancer, but said that his doctors had given him a clean bill of health. He also said that he didn't want to go to his Maker thinking that he had worked too long and too hard at the expense of his family. Good point to be sure. But how many people go to their Maker saying, "I wish I had the courage to go for the main chance"? Tsongas, from neighboring Massachusetts, won the New Hampshire primary. I went to one of his meetings at the home of a supporter. He was very good. I had a chance to chat with his doctor. He said that what was said in the press about Tsongas's health was absolutely so; Tsongas had indeed recovered. Gergen and I went swimming with him. He was very good. He died in 1997. You can't trust anyone in this game.

Meanwhile, the economy had faltered and Clinton consultant James Carville had a sign on the Clinton war room in Little Rock reading "It's the economy, stupid." Clinton's chief speechwriter during the 1992 campaign was David Kusnet, author of *Speaking American*, in which this line appears: "Americans like America." Kusnet would later write the basic draft of Clinton's 1993 inaugural address. By my lights the best line of the speech was: "There is nothing wrong with America that cannot be cured by what is right with America." David is a fine writer, with roots and an ongoing professional and ideological interest in the union movement. He can perhaps be best characterized as a left-liberal willing to acknowledge the potency and validity of the social issue concerns. If there were more Democrats like him, they would win more elections. (Most important, he is my son-in-law and the father of two of my grandchildren. He cooks very well.)

Pat Buchanan's primal scream at the 1992 Republican convention in Houston attacked Democrats on "the culture war." He had "won" in New Hampshire, where he received about 37 percent of the vote, while Bush got 53 percent. But that a challenger could get that close was treated as big news. Bush later creamed him everywhere. The Republicans, for unexplained reasons, gave him a spot during prime time, notwithstanding the fact that he had lost all fifty states to President George H. W. Bush in the course of his aborted presidential campaign.

Pat's text at the Houston convention was actually somewhat moderate by his standards, but the press went after him as if he were Hitler. In his moment of glory he denounced Bush's National Endowment for the Arts for funding an artist's portrayal of a crucifix in urine. Bush had had years to fire NEA Chairman John Frohnmayer. Buchanan ran one television commercial about homoerotic blasphemy, and Frohnmayer was toast. Before you ask: No, I don't think Buchanan is anti-Semitic, not at all. He is, however, vigorously anti-Latino, seeing an evil Mexican wetback in every bathtub.

The Democrats should learn one lesson from modern psephology that fits nicely into the neo-conservative ideology. Every time they nominate a perceived tough guy they win: Roosevelt, Truman, Kennedy, Johnson, Carter the first time, Clinton twice running as putative social hawk, the first time flying back to Arkansas to sign the papers of execution for a mentally retarded black murderer. But when they go with someone perceived as soft—Adlai Stevenson, George McGovern, Carter the second time, Walter Mondale, Michael Dukakis—they lose. But in the first two years of Clinton's first term he turned left. The Republicans gained a majority in the House in 1994 for only the second time in fifty years, led by Newt Gingrich's Contract With America, which "nationalized" House elections, not a normal course of events. Clinton veered back to the Social Issue center under the guidance of Dick Morris, stressing mini-issues like school uniforms, which are a pretty good idea.

By 1996 Clinton had moved back toward the center and was re-elected, beating Senator Bob Dole, with Clinton getting just a shade under 50 percent of the national vote. (My, how he wanted to break 50 percent!) At an American Enterprise Institute meeting in Vail, Colorado, in June that year, with Distinguished Fellow Gerald Ford presiding, I predicted that Dole would win. (Scammon, where were you when I needed you?)

In his 1996 State of the Union address Clinton famously declared that "the era of big government is over" (not going to happen). But with the help of the Gingrich Congress, Clinton also eliminated welfare (Aid to Families with Dependent Children, or AFDC) as an entitlement. (Entitlement spending doesn't require regular approval from Congress to keep growing.) The change reformed a basic 1930s Roosevelt program and it passed only over the vehement objections of Hillary's left-wing pal Marian Wright Edelman, head of the Children's Defense Fund, and Pat Moynihan, a true welfare expert. But AFDC was an extremely unpopular program. Not only did Clinton support the termination of the program but so did Vice President Al Gore and Hillary Clinton—a woman who recognizes a good opportunity when it presents itself.

And in 2000, George W. Bush ran as a "compassionate conservative," which is, at its essence, neo-con phraseology. But he was no

strong internationalist, coming out against "nation building"—code
for an America that ought not to be as involved internationally as it
had been. He beat Clinton's vice president, Al Gore, in a highly
controversial election decided by the Supreme Court on a vote of
5 to 4.

I was invited to the inaugural by Dick Cheney, and some of the
signs on the ceremonial ride from the Capitol to the White House
were obscene. Why? Perhaps because Gore ran ahead of George W.
Bush 48.4 to 47.9 percent, but did not carry an electoral vote majority, quite probably due to Ralph Nader's third-party candidacy. There
is an interesting twist on that one. *Before* the election it was *Gore's*
spinners who were saying that it was *electoral* votes that counted, not
popular votes. Afterward, it was *Bush's* spinners who said *electoral*
votes counted, not *popular* votes. The Bush people, meanwhile,
complain that they could have amassed more of a popular vote had
they done a get-out-the-vote campaign in Bush's home state of Texas.

After the 9/11 attack on the American homeland, Bush dramatically changed his views. Late in 2000 I was invited to a meeting
of alleged movers and shakers at the Department of Defense, with
Secretary Don Rumsfeld presiding and Undersecretary Paul Wolfowitz in attendance. It was there that I first heard the phrase *pre-
emptive war.*

In 2004, for the first time in recent electoral history, Democrats
had as much money to spend as Republicans. But after the awful
events of 9/11, Bush was a freedom fighter such as America had
never seen, as well as a compassionate conservative running up big
federal deficits. That is, he continued policies that were in play at
least since Reagan's time. A freedom-fighting hawk willing to spend
government monies on useful domestic programs is often called a
neo-conservative. In May 2006 I heard him speak to the American
Jewish Committee and repeat his Iraq mantra, "I will not lose my
nerve." At another meeting geopolitician Eliot Cohen called Bush
the most important agent of radical change since Lenin.

For his reelection in 2004 Dubya didn't need the Supreme
Court to declare in his favor; he beat John Kerry in the popular vote
51 to 48 percent, a long way from a landslide but not a bad showing.
Still, the vagaries of the Electoral College almost worked in Kerry's

favor. Kerry would have won had he carried Ohio, home of that lady from Dayton.

The liberal Democrats thought they were in clover when Michael Moore's anti-Iraq war documentary *Fahrenheit 9/11* drew huge crowds. It was not a good movie, even by Moore's standards as a documentary filmmaker, which I do not regard as high. The film was a vicious and stupid attack on America's Iraq policy. I think Moore is not just a radical but an anti-American, not a term I use loosely. The Democrats in charge of convention arrangements sat Moore in a front-row box seat of honor for a night, right next to ex-President Carter. They may well deserve each other. Once again, the Dems didn't get it: Associating with and honoring a radical personality creates an image that is hard to rub off.

Throughout much of 2005 and on into 2006 surveys showed Republicans in trouble. It is customary for the party in power to lose seats in the first congressional election after a second-term presidential victory, and the Iraq war was going poorly and getting even worse publicity. The Republicans lost seats, but actually somewhat fewer than historical averages for off-year elections in a second-term presidency.

Many on the Democratic Left say they *hate* President Bush — not just oppose him or disagree with him or dislike him, but *hate* him. By my lights, there has been too much hatred expressed of presidents in recent years. Each one has tried his best given the constraints he has operated under. So have the vice presidents, although it is hard to forgive Spiro Agnew, who accepted a huge *cash* bribe while vice president for services rendered while governor of Maryland. They have all been patriots.

CHAPTER THREE

The Center Strikes Back

THE 1970 HUMPHREY SENATE CAMPAIGN

IN 1970 I learned that smart liberals and moderates, like LBJ's former vice president Hubert H. Humphrey, understood the validity of The Social Issue, the domestic heart of neo-conservatism. I learned afresh that New Left liberals could go into gloomy verbal excess. I learned that campaigns were fun but that tawdriness and silliness is everpresent. I learned that patriots are not afraid to talk about patriotism. And I learned that politics can be uproariously funny.

I had come to know the vice president and some of his staff people during the course of my work at LBJ's White House. Because we were on the federal payroll, President Johnson had told White House staffers that assisting Humphrey's presidential run in 1968 was illegal. Still, many of us did what we could, when we could, to help the vice president become president. Humphrey's office was in the Old Executive Building, just across an alley from the West Wing of the White House. My office was close by, two suites away.

But Humphrey was narrowly defeated by Nixon in the 1968 election. The Democratic Convention in Chicago had turned violent; anti-war demonstrators tried to break through police lines and threw bags of feces at the police. The police fought back. The American Civil Liberties Union supported the protesters. I thought that a civil liberties organization ought to have condemned demonstrators who were trying to break up a convention of the oldest free political party in the world.

During the convention and after, the protesters dogged Humphrey with chants of "Dump the Hump." His rallies were often disrupted. Anti-war demonstrators had earlier mocked his announcement speech, which talked of "the politics of joy." Too many liberals think politics has to be about how terrible everything is.

Humphrey had been the liberal's liberal. He was the man who, at the 1948 Democratic Convention, famously told this to a party with an important stronghold in the "Solid South" of segregationist Southerners:

> To those who say this civil rights program is an infringe-
> ment on states' rights I say this: The time has arrived in
> America for the Democratic Party to get out of the
> shadow of states' rights and walk forthrightly into the
> bright sunshine of human rights!

He wondered: How could the people whose battles he had fought turn on him so?

In 1970, Humphrey decided to run (again) for the Senate from Minnesota. That meant pushing aside the incumbent Senator Gene McCarthy, who had been late and darkly unenthusiastic in his support of the Humphrey-Muskie ticket in 1968. (McCarthy opted not to campaign for his own Minnesota Senate seat when he saw state polls showing Humphrey beating him by 80-to-20 percent margins.)

In early 1970 I was asked to be the speechwriter on Humphrey's Senate campaign, which ran under the flag of the Democratic-Farmer-Labor Party (DFL), Minnesota's rough equivalent of the Democratic Party. (Humphrey had not yet determined whether he planned to run for president again in 1972.) The offer was tendered to me by Norman Sherman, one of the funniest men in American politics, who had worked for Humphrey as his press secretary and in his 1968 presidential campaign. I accepted the job, and with a family cottage on beautiful Gull Lake as part of the deal, I went to work in stunningly beautiful Minnesota. On weekends I would commute from the Humphrey campaign offices in Minneapolis to the cottage, about 130 miles away. My family and I learned to water ski.

IT IS USEFUL and important to understand the frame of mind of the Democratic political establishment and the media mainstream of the time. I was thinking of writing another book and I was squirreling away the published remarks of some very prominent people and publications. They show the political ambience that led moderates away from the Democratic Party.

In 1972, with most all American troops out of Vietnam, we heard from the somewhat flaky political philosopher Shirley MacLaine: "Right now the social soul of America is so sick that even the overthrow of a political regime may be insufficient." Ms. MacLaine is a good actress, and drew attention when she spoke.

The New Republic magazine was never flaky nor extremist. But in 1971 its editorial read: "We seem to be in one of those long periods when civilization is in decline."

Nor did anyone ever accuse John Gardner of extremism. A nominal Republican, but LBJ's former secretary of health, education, and welfare, Gardner was later the founder of the do-good Common Cause. He was a nice man and a media golden boy. His view, in 1969: "And while each of us pursues his selfish interests and comforts himself by blaming others, the nation disintegrates. I use the phrase soberly: The nation disintegrates."

Nor was Norman Cousins any kind of extremist, as editor of *The Saturday Review*, earlier known as *The Saturday Review of Literature*—under either title a prestigious, albeit boring publication. His view in 1970: "The evidence is strong that human society is in a stage of comprehensive breakdown."

What evidence of breakdown? War? There are about fifty wars going on around the world at most times, and they do not appear to have led to the comprehensive breakdown of human society. Those of us in the neo-con camp were always looking for evidence, and discovering none found it increasingly difficult to respect the views of those whom we thought spoke without evidence.

Famously, the very-liberal literary doyenne Susan Sontag wrote in the winter 1967 issue of *Partisan Review*:

> The white race is the cancer of human history; it is the white race and it alone—its ideologies and inventions— which eradicates autonomous civilizations wherever it spreads, which has upset the ecological balance of the planet, which now threatens the very existence of life itself.

Imagine the uproar and outrage if a distinguished person put forth a statement promulgating that the black race, or the yellow race were the cancer of history. I will grant you that Susan Sontag never had a mainstream audience for her reverse racism, but *Time* magazine did and does. It pronounced: "There is a vague anxiety that the machine of the twentieth century is beginning to run out of control."

In 1972, the distinguished and soft-spoken political scientist James MacGregor Burns gloomed along with the rest: "The nation is essentially evil and the evil can be exorcized only by turning the system upside down."

Of course, the despair mongering was not only a phenomenon of the Left. Way back in 1964 the very conservative Republican presidential candidate Barry Goldwater had this to say: "Something basic and dangerous is eating away at the morality, dignity, and respect of our citizens."

In 1972 former LBJ speechwriter Richard Goodwin, writing in *Newsweek*, had this to say: "Material well-being is only an instrument for the pursuit of more fulfilling, freer lives. Yet wealth has not brought liberation, but increasing confinement."

This from the man who drafted President Johnson's famous Great Society speech at the University of Michigan. The poverty rate had declined from 22 to 12 percent in the first years of the Johnson presidency—and actually lower than that according to new methodologies. Did the new un-poor feel more confined? Did their automobiles not give them the liberation of mobility? Did their air conditioners not liberate them from oppressive heat?

Another former member of the LBJ team put an international spin on the new wealth. Here is what Stuart Udall, secretary of the interior from 1961 to 1969, had to say in 1973: "We've become a gluttonous, greedy nation, acquiring wealth we do not need, and as we do this, we extinguish the hopes of other, poorer nations."

What didn't we need? Houses? New medicines? Automobiles? The next question in this progression is: Is it any wonder that Republicans always score points for optimism?

So much of the above concerns raw economic ignorance, or an excess of guilt, or both. The polymath Herman Kahn, first with the Rand Corporation and then the founder of the Hudson Institute, was famous for his views regarding nuclear warfare (*Thinking the Unthinkable*). But later Kahn (who was surely a neo-con and would without doubt have been an ever-greater intellectual leader of the neo-conservative persuasion had he not died prematurely in 1983 at age sixty-one) turned his thoughts toward international economics. He noted that *the best thing going for poor nations is the presence of rich nations.* Only the rich have the wherewithal to buy goods and services from the poor, making the poor nations richer—which has happened, starting from very low economic levels. The process is called international trade, or globalization. I am a strong supporter and so are most neo-cons. Many liberals and traditional conservatives are likely to be a lot more nervous about it.

The madness in the air was not confined to rarefied quarters of the bicoastal liberal commentariat. Here is what then-Minnesota Senator Walter Mondale had to say in 1971:

> The sickening truth is that this country is rapidly coming
> to resemble South Africa. Our native reserves and Bantus-
> tans are the inner cities. And our apartheid is all the more
> disgusting for being insidious and unproclaimed.

Unproclaimed? It was hard to read anything concerning public policy that did not concern the problems of the inner cities. Over the years many neo-cons lost faith in the grand LBJ-style urban renewal and thought that market forces, if given protection from violent crime, would do a better job of building healthy urban neighborhoods. But Mondale's view was characteristic of the liberal gloom of the time. Not many years later, in 1984, Mondale would capture the Democratic nomination for the presidency—and lose in a landslide to Ronald Reagan, the perennial optimist. I came to know Mondale during Humphrey's 1970 Minnesota campaign. I thought he was a decent and smart man, as were many of the other men and women who had lost faith in what was happening and blamed America first. Is it any wonder that the bubbling, hopeful Hubert Humphrey, apostle of progress, was deemed out of touch with his despondent Democratic colleagues?

The political jib of Ronald Reagan was quite different. His opponents underestimated him. Democratic wise man Clark Clifford called Reagan an "amiable dunce." He had to fight the State Department to call the Soviet Union the Evil Empire, but the phrase bolstered those who were subjugated by that empire. Despite the cautious détentists at State, he gave public advice to his superpower adversary in the Cold War conflict: "Mr. Gorbachev, tear down this wall." Neo-cons, and most all speechwriters, believe that rhetoric, when backed by reality, can yield results. Reagan personified this notion and understood that it was important to state the obvious.

Politics was on the agenda at Gull Lake as it was in much of Minnesota, believed to be one of the most responsible and politically active states in America. One of our neighbors on the lake was the daughter of the mythic former governor of Minnesota Floyd B. Olson, the self-described radical and Socialist who had opposed President Franklin D. Roosevelt from the left when FDR sought reelection in 1936. (Olson died of cancer that year.) Kids have big ears. One weekend, Humphrey spoke near Gull Lake and I took the family to hear him. In the car on the way over my eight-year-old daughter asked, "Will we see Mr. Humphrey talk out of both sides of his mouth?"

Humphrey was a political genius—maybe too much of one. He was so good and so smart he really could almost be all things to all men, a charge periodically leveled at him. Our official slogan was "Humphrey: You know he cares." (At times I said to myself, "Humphrey: You know he cares enough to tell you what you want to hear.") That is not an uncommon political stance. But that was not what was at Humphrey's taproot. This was:

> The moral test of government is how that government treats those who are in the dawn of life, the children; those who are in the twilight of life, the elderly; and those who are in the shadows of life, the sick, the needy and the handicapped.

Such was the real political liberalism, and it meant not just saying the pretty words but putting them into law and trying to make the laws work. For that the nation owes Hubert Humphrey a good deal. Most neo-cons are not opposed to a social safety net, but want those aspects that are not productive, or that are counterproductive, changed so that they come closer to doing what they were supposed to do.

Hubert Horatio Humphrey was one of the few political men of high rank in the contemporary era who could deliver a written speech as if it were his own, a skill that brought great joy to speechwriters. (I would count Adlai Stevenson, Ronald Reagan, and Bill Clinton among them.) But to the dismay of Humphrey speechwriters he would often follow their golden prose that had been worked on together with Humphrey—with the equivalent of a second speech, delivered off the cuff, typically of equal length and at least of equal quality. Humphrey had a graduate degree in political science from Louisiana State University, and taught the subject both there and at the University of Minnesota. Part of his reputation for loquaciousness was based on that habit—two speeches for the price of one.

Strange, that: Humphrey was of Norwegian extraction—allegedly strong, silent types. Of his verbosity, Humphrey said, "Some guys drink, some chase women, I like to talk." Fair enough.

Humphrey would often end his speeches with a riff about the Pledge of Allegiance. It went something like this:

The Pledge of Allegiance has real meaning. There isn't a
person in this room that at sometime has not said, as his
own son or daughter has said, those very important words,
which portray what America should stand for and what its
hope is.

Some Humphrey staffers at the back of the hall would exchange
glances that said, "Uh-oh . . . there he goes again!"

I've talked to students about it, even though it seems old
hat. But it's not old. It's the newest thing in the world. Because it speaks of what mankind cries out for. We make
that Pledge of Allegiance to the flag of the United States
and the republic—not the dictatorship, not the police
state, but the republic—representative government, the
republic for which it stands.

We must make our commitment, as the founding fathers
of this republic made their commitment for their lives,
their fortune, and their sacred honor.

And what is that commitment—one nation, not two separate and unequal, but one. Yes, under God, which is the
one phrase that gives real meaning to human dignity and
humanity and soul and spirit. [Humphrey, running as a liberal in a Midwestern traditionalist state, had been instrumental in inserting "under God" into the pledge in 1954.]

Indivisible—not black, not white, not North, not South,
not urban, not rural—but one nation indivisible—not
unanimous, but united—and with liberty. Not license,
just liberty—which means respect for the rights of others
so that you can have rights for yourself, which means the
willingness to fulfill the obligations of responsibility and
duty as well as to expect the privileges that come with cit-
izenship.

With liberty and justice for *all*—not justice for the rich
and the powerful only. Not justice even for a selected

minority, but justice for *all*. Then we understand that
there is no conflict between liberals and conservatives on
the issue of law and order.

The sophisticated staffers would look around the room and see eyes
glistening in the audience. And sometimes our eyes would glisten
too—at least mine would. And sometimes so did Humphrey's. It was
a pleasure working with a political man who believed that there was
nothing wrong with an avowal of patriotism, particularly when it
was under attack from the harsh left.

Most neo-cons believe that a feeling of patriotism is not only valid
but that it helps the nation do great things. For many decades following
World War II transnational polls showed that the three nations with
the lowest patriotism levels among their citizenry were the three Axis
powers of World War II: Germany, Japan and Italy. They hadn't much
to be patriotic about. The U.S. always ranked first in those surveys.

HUMPHREY'S OPPONENT IN the general election was Congressman Clark MacGregor, a popular figure in Minnesota. It was a
hard-fought campaign. There are things that go on in campaigns
that a book dealing with politics should try to explain in order to provide some background.

Our media man was D. J. Leary, a hyperactive professional political man who would later publish a much-respected Minnesota
political newsletter. One day he called in several senior staffers. He
had heard that MacGregor would be running a new set of campaign
commercials. He proposed to go to one of the television stations, an-
nounce that he was from the MacGregor campaign, and ask for the
tapes for a couple of hours to see that everything was in order. He
wanted to bring the tapes back to our office so we could view them
in advance. Sherman and I and whoever else was in the room all told
D. J. that it was a crazy plan. We would see the tapes very soon in any
event, and the risk was nowhere near the reward. Suppose he got
caught? D. J. went ahead anyway. We watched the tapes, which
probably made us accessories to something.

At about that time, a young man named Donald Segretti was

plotting "dirty tricks" for the forthcoming 1972 presidential campaign of Richard Nixon, as part of what was subsequently called "Watergate." Segretti's were not serious crimes, although they were surely more serious than what D. J. was hatching. Segretti was sent to prison for four months. Let me state for the record: Pushing political rules beyond their legal limit is wrong. Such actions can happen in either party. But the press regularly makes them the big story even when they are trivial. This crowds out items of greater political import.

It was revealed in *The Washington Post* in 1975 that what had long been rumored was true: J. Edgar Hoover, the director of the Federal Bureau of Investigation, kept scurrilous secret and confidential files to use as blackmail against public officials. Shortly before the 1964 election, top LBJ aide Walter Jenkins was arrested for a homosexual incident in a Washington men's room. Bill Moyers was told by LBJ to ask Hoover to check out Goldwater's staff to see if he could dig up countervailing evidence of homosexuality. Writing in *The Wall Street Journal* in 2005, former Deputy Attorney General Larry Silberman explained how things worked:

> Mr. Moyers's memo to the FBI was in one of the files. When the press reported this, I received a call in my office from Mr. Moyers. Several of my assistants were with me. He [Moyers] was outraged; he claimed that this was another example of the Bureau salting its files with phony CIA memos. I offered to conduct an investigation, which if his contention was correct, would lead me to publicly exonerate him. There was a pause on the line and then he said, "I was very young. How will I explain this to my children?" . . . I thought to myself that a number of the Watergate figures, some of whom the Department was prosecuting, were very young, too.

I wonder how *I* would have responded had LBJ asked *me* to make the request of Hoover. Today, after the scandal-gating we've lived through, I surely would have said no. Back then I probably would have done what Moyers did, although, if caught, I hope I would not have subsequently begged for forgiveness the way Moyers did. But I might have; I too had young children at the time.

There were other political acts that crossed the line in the Humphrey campaign. The head of the Humphrey campaign was Jack Chestnut, a Minneapolis lawyer. He was fined $5,000 and sentenced to prison for four months for knowingly accepting illegal corporate campaign contributions from the Associated Milk Producers Inc. He later resumed his law career and went on to become a respected local civic leader. Sherman and his political partner John Valentine were also marginally involved. They had simply received bad advice from Chestnut. Norman Sherman was never deposed or called to testify. Nonetheless, he pleaded guilty to a non-willful misdemeanor for unwittingly depositing a corporate check and paid a $500 fine. Sherman is a thoroughly decent man and I find it inconceivable that he would intentionally do anything wrong. The Associated Milk Producers Incorporated pleaded guilty to one count of conspiracy and five counts of violating campaign contribution laws and was fined $35,000.[1] Luckily, campaign finance laws are incredibly complex and beyond my ken. I have never been indicted or even investigated. Sherman and Leary went on to distinguished public and private careers.

HUMPHREY HAD ACCEPTED a speaking engagement in St. Louis before the American Bar Association for early August 1970, and it was decided to make it a major effort. I had several days to work on the speech, a rare luxury. I even put a title on it—"Liberalism and Law and Order." The theme was the obvious one: liberalism as a humane political philosophy could not survive unless it showed voters that law and order was essential to keeping a society from plunging into chaos.

Humphrey was nervous about it. I was told that the night before the talk Humphrey paced his office, toning it down with the help of another advisor, Paul Tchita, a former FBI agent.

Humphrey didn't like being characterized as tough. I'd put the T-word in a speech; he'd take it out. But Humphrey knew that

---

1. All reported in Watergate prosecutor Leon Jaworski's book, *The Right and the Power.*

politically he needed one well-publicized tough speech; he also knew it was the right thing to bring up in a country plagued by violent crime. Here are excerpts (as delivered) from the address, whose title was changed from a statement to a question: "Liberalism and Law and Order: Must There Be a Conflict?" It ended up as a long Humphrey-style disquisition, but thanks to his nervousness, it ended up even tougher than written! Still, it was applicable then, and much of it is now.

> The problem centers to quite an extent around the phrase *law and order*, a phrase which conjures up different images to various minds. To some it means racial and social oppression; to some it means suppression of rightful and necessary and legitimate dissent; to some it means a slow, bureaucratic, unsatisfactory machine working ineffectively to right civil and criminal wrongs. On the other hand, to some the phrase *law and order* means the ability to walk safely in a city park on a summer evening.

> The political conflict that rages over this law-and-order issue is usually described as involving two groups. These groups have generally been called the liberals and the hardhats.

> We've seen some pictures of the conflict and the confrontation between hardhats and the peace demonstrators up in Wall Street. They met head on, and it looked as if there might be an explosion. But all that the hardhats were chanting on that day was, "All the way with the USA."

> Look for a moment at that cluster of clichés that surround the so-called hardhats. To read some accounts, one would assume that the American middle class is racist, anti-student, anti-intellectual, hawkish, disdainful of civil liberties, incipiently fascist, and anxious for a crackdown of law and order, even if it means repression. It isn't a very nice picture. And frankly, it's not at all accurate.

But the so-called liberal fares little better. He's often described as permissive, elitist, and wealthy. He is pictured as concerned primarily about the welfare of the poor black man that he seldom sees—but not about the poor or the lower-middle income white man. He is identified with dissent and disruption. He's perceived as "soft" on law and order. Both sets of descriptions are far from the truth.

Look at those so-called hardhats. [Consider] the American labor movement. With all of its limitations it is very hard to make the nasty rhetoric stick. For the labor movement in the last forty years has been the point of the spear for every major liberal and progressive program enacted in the Congress. That includes obvious pro-labor measures, but it also includes aid to education, job training, Job Corps, the War on Poverty, Medicare, aid to cities, medical research, and more dramatically, a concerted effort in support of a series of major civil rights measures and civil liberties protections.

In fact, while the critical pundits were sipping their martinis at Georgetown cocktail parties, and while a new breed of self-proclaimed militants were condemning the labor movement, that labor movement was actively peacefully helping to revamp the American social and economic fabric—for the better! [Humphrey's words: I would not have had the guts to go after the Georgetowners like that!]

The charge has been made that the rank and file of the union membership sits around in their undershirts drinking beer, looking at TV, cursing hippies, and voting for George Wallace. But in America political deeds are enacted most significantly in the voting booth, not at the bar stool. Old Sam Rayburn [former Speaker of the House] used to say, "There's no sense in feeling ignorant and weak when for one drink you can get smart and strong." And the voting boxes in the so-called hardhat labor districts the American workingmen are voting liberal. [But only by about 60 to 40 percent.]

Are they really the ivory-tower elitists that the critics say they are? There are admittedly a few dilettantes within the current ranks of liberals, but most of the liberals in the 1960's were willing to do tough, courageous work. The civil rights workers that went into the South were as courageous a group as this nation has ever seen. I can also tell you that those liberals, young and old, who have sincerely protested the war in Vietnam and its extension into Cambodia, who have protested hunger in America, who have condemned pollution, who have dramatized the plight of the migratory workers—are tough-minded idealists. No panty-waists, these people.

What's the problem? It's the code-phrase *law and order.* In 1968 there was a cliché afloat that said *law and order* is a code word for racism. Well, *law and order* may indeed sometimes and in some places be a code phrase for racism, but it is also a code phrase for domestic tranquility. Americans are deeply upset about crime, about riots, about violent disruption, about drugs, about all facets of law and order, and they rightly should be.

Liberals don't favor crime, or mugging, or riots in the ghetto or on the campus. Nor do they burn the flag or ransack draft boards. Extremists do that. Violent militant radicals may do that. Revolutionaries. But not liberals. Americans scorn extremists of the left as well as the extremists of the right—the black extremists with guns and the white extremists with sheets and guns. [His formulations, not mine.]

(The italics below are mine, indicating which statements drew substantial news coverage.)

The nub of the law-and-order issue was raised first as a national concern in the elections of 1964 by Senator Goldwater and Governor Wallace. The liberals recoiled. *And when finally they did begin to speak out, they spoke out too softly and apologetically and in the judgment of the electorate, they lacked credibility.*

Black militants, burning and shooting, may well have set back the cause of civil rights for a decade. White radicals rampaging on campuses may well have spawned an antiuniversity backlash. Draft resisters who took the law into their own hands have served neither the cause of peace nor of draft reform.

And when some liberals, seeing all of this, responded by saying "I don't agree with it, of course, but they are well-meaning," then the cherished goals of liberalism were set back.

What liberals must do now is an ironical imperative: *they must show the courage to take on a popular position when the cause is right.*

Liberals must let the hardhats, Mr. and Mrs. Middle America, know that they understand what is bugging them, and they must let America know that they, too, condemn crime and riots and violence and extreme social turbulence.

What about hardhats? Sometimes we talk about alienation as if it were the exclusive province of people who write introspective novels. Well, it's not. What about the American who is angry because he feels that no one knows or wants to know what he feels?

The time has come for liberals to let America know in the most emphatic terms that they share these concerns. I do not believe that the only solution to our problems is the so-called long-range solution. I do believe that is clearly one important approach. We must get off the dime and re-order our social and economic priorities. *But in the short run violence and crime are rapidly becoming a barrier to*

> *the attainment of these long-run goals. You can't play*
> *Hamlet with crime. You can't play Hamlet with violence.*
> Get a good look at some of the injustices of justice and
> you get fighting mad. The answer is more efficient sys-
> tems of justice. *It is surely not the coddling of the crimi-*
> *nals of any age, background, or race, or the condoning*
> *of violence in the name of sympathy.*

This was neo-con stuff with extra verbal flourishes. And then
Humphrey ended with his Pledge of Allegiance riff. I wasn't there
but I suspect there were some glistening eyes in the sophisticated
audience of the American Bar Association.

To be sure, Humphrey "talked out of both sides of his mouth,"
paying obeisance to both the soft and tough sides of the political argument. Some (much? most?) of the language was put in by
Humphrey on the spot; I know I didn't write that tough Hamlet line,
nor the near-demagogic one about coddling criminals.

Sometimes a speech can be judged by who gives it and who de-
nounces it. In this case the giver was the former vice president of the
United States, a professed liberal. The denouncers came from both
the Left and the Right. The radical Earl Craig—who ran in token opposition to Humphey in the DFL primary—claimed that the speech
represented Humphrey selling out to the law-and-order tough guys
and showed not courage but cowardice. Humphrey's Republican opponent, Clark MacGregor, said Humphrey was really mushy on
crime and the speech was just a trick from a well-known softie.

The speech gained national attention. Soon, press clips flowed
into the office. After the speech, Sherman came up to me and said,
"Congratulations. We just won the election. MacGregor had only
one way out—calling us soft and making it stick. You just closed it
off." Which is only one of the reasons I love Norman. Later, I got a
gift from the staff—a hardhat. I also received an autographed picture
from Humphrey calling me a "realist and an idealist." It is on my
wall as I write this.

Humphrey was reelected to the Senate with solid numbers. I saw it as a victory for more than just Humphrey, a grand human being with flaws. It was a national win for the neo-conservative notion that a candidate could be liberal, kind, tough on domestic issues, *and a winner*. Humphrey was also an up-front anti-Communist, having fought them when he was mayor of Minneapolis.

Bound galley proofs of *The Real Majority* were in circulation. I believe the St. Louis speech was the first public endorsement by a major liberal Democratic candidate for high office to follow the common sense precepts laid out in the book. The wages of fame: *The Real Majority* became known as "the bible of the 1970 elections." One evening, on our way to some campaign speechifying, I was riding an elevator with Humphrey and a visiting national correspondent. The reporter kept asking me questions about the book, paying little attention to Humphrey. Embarrassed, I grunted monosyllabic answers. But the reporter continued. Finally, Humphrey erupted: "Wattenberg! Wattenberg! That's all you want to talk about! Who am I, Mortimer Snerd?" (Snerd had been ventriloquist Edgar Bergen's dummy some decades earlier.) By 1970 Humphrey had dyed his hair—"prematurely orange," it was said—and taken to mod, wide-lapel suits in an attempt to be seen as a hip fellow who knew what the sixties were about. He had been accused of being a practitioner of "the old politics"—which had elected a couple of generations of Democrats to major office. Neo-cons didn't have much of a problem with the old politics.

I left the campaign a few weeks before the election to go to New York. I had been invited to appear on *The Johnny Carson Show* along with the demographic doomsayer Paul Ehrlich, who had appeared solo with Carson about twenty times. Some viewers were asking for "balance" (sound familiar?). Ehrlich and I followed the slob comic Buddy Hackett, whom the producers thought was uproariously funny.

Ehrlich and I each did our shtick. We each drew applause. In the green room after the program I said to him, "Paul, you know, you exaggerated some things." He said, "Well, you have to exaggerate things to get attention."

I took a walk around the block, wondering what was going on. The Ph.D. in biology was exaggerating and I, not a scientist, was trying to stick to facts. It was a phenomenon that would occur again and again. It was a tactic some on the Left called "lying for justice."

It's not nice, but opposing it kept me and many other neo-cons in business for decades.

CHAPTER FOUR

Scoop's Troops

NOT-SO-CIVIL WAR

THE LESSON HERE is to go where your beating neo-con heart
tells you to go. It happened to me during the seminal presidential primaries of 1972, which became the splitting wedge in the
Democratic Party and in America's public culture. That split remains
in play today, to the Democrats' detriment. The 1972 elections are
worthy of study for everyone interested in politics and public policy,
no matter their spot on the ideological spectrum.

Senator Edmund Muskie had been Humphrey's choice for his
vice presidential running mate in 1968. After Humphrey lost narrowly to Richard Nixon, many "great mentioners" in the media noted
that Muskie had been a more attractive national candidate than
Humphrey or Nixon and would make an excellent national presidential candidate in 1972. (Poor Nixon: His policies are now recognized
as far more moderate than those of run-of-the mill Republicans of the
time. But the man couldn't recite a breakfast menu without sounding
smarmy.) Muskie had indeed been a good vice presidential candidate
in 1968. He had one other advantage over Humphrey in the putatively
more-dovish-than-thou Democratic primaries: He was unsullied by
any close political relationship with LBJ.

Muskie announced his decision to run for president early in the process. Soon he was not only the front-running Democrat, but was ahead of President Nixon in some of the hypothetical 1972 presidential "head-to-head horserace" polls. It was a situation that left Nixon and the "Re-Elect Nixon" team worried, and allegedly a central reason for the Watergate break-in, cover-up, and all the associated lawlessness that led to Nixon's resignation. His vice president, Spiro Agnew, was also forced to resign over an issue of personal financial corruption. Once regarded as a moderate, he had antagonized many liberals, serving as "Nixon's Nixon" with the help of sharp, witty speechwriters like Pat Buchanan and William Safire (who condemned "limousine liberals" as "nattering nabobs of negativism").

I never thought Watergate was such a big deal, although it was surely an impeachable offense for which Nixon could have been convicted if Congress had chosen to do so, which they did. I did not believe it was a great constitutional threat to the republic. What drove me crazy then (and now) was the conflation of Vietnam and Watergate to evince America's bad times. America's military action in Vietnam killed 58,000 Americans and injured 153,000. Troops of our allies and the number of killed and wounded from South and North Vietnam added vastly to that total. And this was supposed to equate with a third-rate crime at the Watergate Hotel that turned into a second-rate crime? (Every decade or so I make a mistake. When I went to work for Senator Scoop Jackson, I once counseled him to come out against Nixon's impeachment before the actual process even began.)

By the time the 1972 campaign began in 1971, the number of American troops in Vietnam had diminished substantially—it was actually close to zero under Nixon's policy of Vietnamization, for which he received little credit. The demonstrations continued, and anti-war passions remained intense. The economy had been down but was picking up.

The smart Democrats were lining up behind Muskie. One day I got a call from a Muskie aide asking me to meet with the senator. In his Senate office, he asked me if I would join his campaign as a speechwriter. I told him I was honored to be asked (I was) and said I would get back to him. The more I thought about it, the less I liked the idea. Muskie was already articulating some of the very ideas Scammon and I had criticized in *The Real Majority*.

Some of his already announced staff were fairly well to the left; in their hearts I suspected some were probably for McGovern. Their idea, I assume, was that Muskie would be the candidate-vessel of the mainstream Democratic Party, that Muskie would win; and that they would then pour their views into the vessel and be able to influence a Muskie administration. Politics often works that way.

In my innocence I thought first that Muskie's reaching out to someone from the neo-con ranks was a good sign of a balanced Democratic Party. But the more I thought about it I felt my neo-conservative views would not be well accommodated in a Muskie campaign. I have a big mouth—*"argumento" ergo sum*—and I quickly came to realize that I might be either a troublemaker or window dressing, but not much more.

Moreover, Muskie was not simply an empty vessel. He had bought into the liberal rhetoric of despair. Consider: In 1971, at Attica Correctional Facility in upstate New York, 1,300 prisoners staged a rebellion against their guards, took over the facility, held 40 guards hostage, and presented a list of demands for better living conditions. Under intense media scrutiny, negotiations between the prisoners and the state government authorities lasted for a week, under the direction of Governor Nelson Rockefeller. Then the National Guard and state police seized the prison, killing 43 people, including 10 hostages.

Here is what Muskie had to say about it: "The Attica tragedy is more stark proof that something is terribly wrong in America. We have reached the point where men would rather die than live another day in America."

Who wanted to die? The hostages? I think not. The prisoners? They were only doing what they had seen anti-war students doing— taking over the dean's office and presenting "nonnegotiable demands" (the rhetoric of the time). It was the kind of hot overstated political language of doom that I wanted to work against, not for.

Republicans and neo-cons do their own share of public political trashing and thrashing, but I generally don't find it nearly as nasty as the liberals' anti-American screeds. (Whoever would have believed that the principal instrument of anti-Semitism and anti-Israeli sentiment would come from the Far Left of the Democratic Party?)

Democrats, alas, have come to be known as a party of pessimism, which goes against the American grain. On the other side, the idea of "National Greatness" was presented in the neo-conservative *Weekly Standard,* edited by neo-cons Bill Kristol and Robert Kagan in the late 1990s, *before* 9/11. They called for grand projects to reinstill national pride, just as President John F. Kennedy had pledged to put an American on the moon during the 1960s.

But going to the moon was essentially a military response to the Soviets' early and surprising lead in the space race. America does not have to go out of its way to look for great projects. They come along quite regularly. Moreover, the private sector is doing great projects all the time: in medicine, in high-tech, in agriculture. (And there is immigration and assimilation, which America does better than anyone else, albeit imperfectly.) A big one did, indeed, come along: September 11, 2001. The terrorists had struck American buildings on American soil. We responded.

DELIVERANCE FROM MY ambivalence soon arrived. The day after I visited with Muskie, I received another call. This one was from Sterling Munro, the administrative assistant for Senator Henry "Scoop" Jackson, a Democrat from Washington State. Sterling asked me to meet with Jackson about working on speeches and communications for the senator's 1972 presidential campaign.

I had never met Jackson before and didn't know much about him other than that he was regarded as one of the very few Democratic legislators who paid a great deal of attention to matters regarding defense, that he was a hawk, that he supported Johnson and Nixon on the Vietnam War (almost, but not quite to the very end), that he was tough on the Soviets, and that he was a strong supporter of Israel. He played an important domestic role about which I didn't know much until later.

I met him the day after I received Munro's call in Scoop's Senate office. Scoop was a low-key, pleasant man. He was very complimentary about the ideas Scammon and I had set forth in *The Real Majority* which, recall, was a book mostly about *domestic* matters, not *foreign policy* issues. Unlike LBJ, it was clear that he had read the book carefully.

Those on the foreign policy team of his Senate staff, Dorothy Emerson Fosdick—"Dickie," the daughter of the famed pastor Reverend Harry Emerson Fosdick—Richard Perle, Elliott Abrams, and Charles Horner among them, were very much in tune with my thinking at the time. I didn't know much about what Scoop's top domestic aides Grenville Garside, Bill Van Ness, and Howard Feldman were up to but they were obviously smart straight shooters. His core supporters from the state seemed solid. At our meeting, Jackson asked me to sign on as his speech and communications man for the 1972 campaign. I said yes on the spot. In his 1976 run for the presidency I had neither a formal nor salaried role but was very active in the campaign nonetheless.

I had run and lost for low local office twice in Stamford before I came to the White House in 1966. I worked as a speechwriter for a Congressional seat. I had worked in the White House for President Johnson, coming into a functioning staff. I had worked in a senatorial campaign for Humphrey. But I learned with Scoop's campaign that setting up a *national* presidential political campaign is different. It is perhaps best seen as starting a major new business with many new branches simultaneously. A campaign needs fund-raisers, advertising experts, television gurus, pollsters, speechwriters, office managers, secretaries, schedulers, accountants, office help, and political operatives to set up popular delegate slates and make deals. This has to be accomplished quickly, from scratch, often using volunteers acting all across America. Moreover, a public officeholder like Scoop needed a full Senate staff that was willing and able to work substantively, smoothly, smartly, and legally with the new campaign staff.

Most important, a campaign needs a "horse"—political lingo for a good candidate with good ideas about which he is passionate. And the horse had best be physically fit. I recall seeing Scoop in a hotel suite, drenched in sweat after delivering one major speech, changing into a fresh shirt and underwear to get ready to give another one. Adrenaline was still dropping off from the first speech, while booting up for the next one.

The 1972 Democratic presidential primaries were central to the emergence of modern politics and contemporary life. I think it was the most important set of electoral contests in the second half of the twentieth century and beyond. Tragically, it moved the Democratic mainstream toward the Far Left.

Those primaries were also the first that applied the so-called McGovern rules to choose Democratic convention delegates; they involved a maddeningly complex mix of primary states, caucus states, and convention states, and later required race and sex quotas for delegates and proportional representation of the delegates, rather than the customary "winner-takes-all" system then in place. The new rules had been adopted by a commission instituted at the violent 1968 Chicago Democratic Convention as a concession to anti-war delegates who claimed they had been cheated. The chairman of the commission was Senator George McGovern.

As it turned out, the McGovern staff's intimate knowledge of the new rules was of great advantage to him. George Wallace, Hubert Humphrey, and George McGovern each drew about one-third of the popular vote, but McGovern ended up with the nomination.

In meetings in his office, Scoop would call us "leader," as in, "Leader, what do we do about Florida?" He studied his issues and knew them cold. Because he hired people who believed in his ideas, he would compliment them publicly even if they were not present. He gave them wide leeway to speak their mind in quotable situations. He backed them up even if they goofed. More than one staffer regarded him as a father. He was best man at Richard Perle's marriage at Howard Feldman's house.

The first chapter of *A Certain Democrat*, a book about Scoop published in 1972 by Seattle journalists William Prochnau and Richard Larsen, is entitled "The Last Cold War Liberal." But Jackson certainly was not. Who repealed the Cold War? In 1972, the Soviets were backing "wars of national liberation" as well as squashing their Eastern European satellite conquests whenever they showed restlessness. Prochnau and Larsen supported the notion that Americans hated the Vietnam War, but that was not quite the way it was. Both the polls and the fellow on the street corner expressed a commonly held view: win it or get out.

That sounds good, but LBJ and Nixon believed that winning meant risking a major conflagration with either the USSR or mainland China. Could that have happened? We will never know. Getting out (as Nixon put it) meant that America was a "pitiful, helpless giant." That is a mostly valid notion. It is what led Osama bin Laden to think there would be little reprisal for 9/11. It was not a good situation and America's elected leaders understood it, as the once-secret Johnson and Nixon phone tapes reveal. Vietnam may have been unpopular, but the public gave at least plurality support on the war to every president from Kennedy to Johnson to Nixon, even as their positions changed.

And who repealed liberalism? The Democratic Congress and President Nixon supported and expanded efforts to help the poor and the needy. Today, it is said that the country has moved to the conservative Right, but governments controlled completely by Republicans routinely run deficits to increase domestic spending, much to the chagrin of conservatives and some neo-cons. But unlike most conservatives, many neo-cons have no visceral dislike for moderately high big-government spending provided the programs can be shown to work and can be changed if they don't. I extend that to most of the so-called pork-barrel and earmarked spending. The nation needs an infrastructure. Investigative journalists offer a running narrative about how our bridges are ready to collapse, about how tunnels will flood, how the interstate highway system is eroding, and so on. But the same journalists cry scandal when a congressman puts a little pork in the various infrastructure bills, which amounts to a tiny portion of the total appropriated. It is true such spending does not go through the rigorous cost-benefit examinations by the dedicated folks at the U.S. Army Corps of Engineers—the same ones who gave you the levees in New Orleans. Might it not be that a member of the House might know something about his or her district and what it needs?

Jackson, at that time, was a man of the political Left. Scoop's disciple, Congressman Tom Foley of Spokane, came from the eastern, much more conservative, part of Washington, definitely not liberal in its voting proclivities. Foley later became Speaker of the House. He says that for quite a time, "Scoop was the closest one in the

Congress I can remember to a European Social Democrat . . . voting for all the social programs." Today (and even then) that would be
too much for me. (These days, it would be a bit much for many
European Social Democrats.) But by the time of his death Scoop
was changing substantially even on domestic issues.

Scoop was not regarded as a good speaker. (The line was "when
he gave a fireside chat, the fire went out.") But that needs more explaining. On the topic of national accomplishment he would invariably pause, then bellow out, "America is a great country," and snap
the crowd to a standing ovation. Simple? Yes. Potent? Yes. Good for
America? Indeed.

What I learned about Jackson I liked. As chairman of the Senate
Committee on Energy and Natural Resources and its predecessor,
the Committee on Interior and Insular Affairs, Jackson was an ardent
supporter of environmental causes. I had no problem on that score.
I had never given much thought to them, although I had experienced lovely times as a child in rural settings, fishing or climbing
trees to pick apples for a dime a bushel.

Scoop was the Senate author of the landmark National Environmental Protection Act, and the story making the rounds was that on
the way over to debate the legislation on the Senate subway he
scribbled out a one-sentence amendment calling for an environmental impact statement (EIS) that would set the conditions for
most federal legislation. In fact, according to Bill Van Ness, the subway story is apocryphal: Scoop had been working for years on putting together the act.

In any event, the EIS proved to be a decision he would live to regret. As Scoop explained it to me on PBS some years later, he had
expected the EIS to yield a simple two- or three-page declaration
that any damage to the environment had been considered during
the deliberations on most all proposed legislation. Instead, he said, it
brought forth *truckloads* of documentation in many legislative battles. In several celebrated incidents, an EIS showing only minor environmental impact had halted or substantially delayed construction
work, costing jobs and raising costs. Saving the snail darter landed
thousands of workers on unemployment rolls.

This was just the sort of thing that many neo-cons came to abhor:

going way too far on generally solid concepts. To me it was also an example that Scoop Jackson was seeing the situation differently and would have been a neo-con leader for several decades longer had he not died prematurely in 1983. That is conjecture. But judging from where most—not all—of his staff ended up, there is good cause to believe it. For political flavor, here is an enumeration of a very few. If you follow politics, the names should be familiar.

Richard Perle has held several high-level jobs at the Department of Defense and regularly makes the hawkish case on television interviews. He is very smart and has the rare capability of speaking on television in complete sentences, with the sentences organized into invisible paragraphs. As I researched this book I learned that some former members of the Jackson presidential staff did not appreciate Perle, or his views. (I understate.)

After working for Scoop, Elliott Abrams was on Senator Pat Moynihan's staff and then served as assistant secretary of state for Latin America in the Reagan administration. He was involved in a scandal concerning congressional testimony. At issue were the modalities of raising funds for the Nicaraguan Contras fighting the Sandinistas, Soviet-backed Communists trying to take over a country, and the whole Central American region, right on the North American landmass. It was not a trivial matter to neo-cons. Acting under explicit instructions from his boss, Secretary of State George Schultz, and by indirection from President Reagan, Abrams did not divulge a source of Contra funding—the Sultan of Brunei—to a Senate committee.

A special prosecutor with no budget constraints tried to break down Abrams, in more ways than one, particularly by using the leverage of huge legal expenses. Elliott was a young man of little means and with three young children. He vowed he wouldn't give in, but after a long fight, Elliott copped a plea to a noncriminal charge. I think he got a bum rap. He wrote a book about it called *Undue Process* that is very much worth reading. He was later pardoned by President George H. W. Bush. Elliott remains politically radioactive for a congressionally appointed position, but has recently served with distinction at the White House National Security Council, directing the global democracy campaign as well as overseeing

Middle East policy. Elliott is a good friend with a fine family, but when out of office, like Perle, he can speak with bitterness and sarcasm about opponents. It doesn't help the cause.

Howard Feldman has a thriving legal practice in Washington, D.C., dealing with many issues he worked on as a Jackson staffer. He is disgusted with what has happened to the Democratic Party and has switched his registration from Democrat to Independent, as have a number of Jackson alumni. His tart-tongued wife, Clarice—also a lawyer—makes Howard look like a mushy liberal.

Paul Wolfowitz, a principal architect of the Iraq II war, was not a full-time Jackson staffer, but worked with Perle for Jackson on several major documents regarding nuclear arms control. I find him to be a prince of a man.

Jackson brought into his hearings significant witnesses, many of whose thoughts were not well known in American public life. One was Albert Wohlstetter of the University of Chicago, a strategic analyst, mathematician, and logician whom Perle describes as the most rigorous man he ever met in terms of seeking facts behind his assumptions. Others included Robert Conquest, a great historian of the criminality of the Soviet Union, and Bernard Lewis of Princeton, a preeminent scholar of the Middle East.

By no means did all of Scoop's Troops end up in the neo-con camp. Jack Tanner, a black attorney from Tacoma, Washington, became a judge and issued a ruling about comparable worth pay scales for women that took quota hiring to a bizarre level. (The decision was overturned.) Many others became important activists in what turned out to be the new, lefter-leaning Democratic mainstream.

SCOOP WAS A consummate political professional of Norwegian descent, much like Hubert Humphrey. He practiced his trade. When asked, he campaigned in South Dakota for dovish Democrat George McGovern, who often needed a dose of credibility on national defense issues. But as Scoop patiently explained to me several times, he might need McGovern's vote on entirely other issues. Is that the right way to play the game? It is the way the political game is played.

Jackson was born in Everett, Washington, in 1912. He graduated from the University of Washington and in 1935 received his law degree there. He was in private practice for a few years and in 1938 was elected to the prosecutor's office at the age of 26. He remained in government office for the rest of his life. As a prosecuting attorney Jackson fought against the fascist Silver Shirts. He was elected to Congress in 1940, at age 28. At the beginning of World War II he served in the army as an enlisted man. Along with all other elected federal officials who were in the military, he was recalled to Congress by order of President Franklin D. Roosevelt. In 1945, Congressman Jackson visited the notorious Nazi death camp at Buchenwald a few days after it was liberated by American troops. He was traumatized by what he saw.

Jackson was reelected five times to the House of Representatives and in 1952 beat the incumbent Republican Senator Harry P. Cain 56 to 44 percent. His Senate margins became larger: 67 to 34 percent in 1958, rising to 72 to 27 percent in 1964 and to an astonishing 82 to 16 percent in 1970 despite (or because of) attacks on him by anti-war Democrats at the Democratic convention in a liberal state. (Before the admission of Alaska and Hawaii to the union, James Farley, President Roosevelt's political maestro, said that there were "forty-seven states and the Soviet of Washington.") Later, Scoop's majorities fell to mere landslide level: 72 to 24 percent in 1976 and 69 to 24 percent in 1980. Scoop really liked that 82 percent win in 1970. As is the front-runner's typical tactic, Jackson had declined to debate his opponent, a right-wing airline pilot named Charles W. Elicker. As the story has it, some years later Jackson was on a plane piloted by Elicker, who sent word that he would like Scoop to come up to the cabin to say hello. Scoop declined that invitation, too. Humphrey would have gone up and schmoozed.

In 1954, in the famous televised hearings that pitted demagogic Senator Joseph McCarthy against the U.S. Army, Jackson became a liberal hero by vigorously standing up to the senator from Wisconsin. Jackson always felt that the serious Communist threats to America came from *outside*, not *inside*, a typical liberal and neo-con view not generally held by conservatives, who were said to "find Commies under every bed." But Scoop didn't live to see the end of the Cold War or the release of Soviet Venona project

intelligence, cable traffic that revealed there had been far more spying than had been understood.

Scoop was a close friend of Senator John F. Kennedy. At the Los
Angeles convention, Scoop was the first choice of Robert F.
Kennedy (JFK's campaign manager) to be his brother's running
mate. But the nominee decided that a Southerner had to be on the
ticket, and Senate Majority Leader Lyndon B. Johnson was his
choice to help retain some of the conservative pro-segregation
Democratic South. But the tide was already changing in the Democratic South. Republican senator Barry Goldwater only carried five
states in his 1964 landslide loss for president: his home state of Arizona and four states in the deep South.

The results on election day seemed to bear out JFK's choice.
Kennedy beat Nixon by a thin whisker, carrying some distinctly non-
liberal Southern states. Jackson, as one of the most liberal Democrats in the Senate on domestic issues, could have hurt the ticket.
Pushing that view was JFK's conservative father, Joseph P. Kennedy,
the former isolationist U.S. ambassador to England prior to World
War II, who backed JFK's campaign with large infusions of cash, of
which much was legal. As a consolation prize, JFK named Scoop
chairman of the Democratic National Committee.

Not long before his own 1972 run for the presidency, in an informal survey taken among his Senate colleagues, Jackson was picked
as the senator best qualified to be president. Still, he was not known
to most Americans. His early campaign billboards in Florida simply
read, "Scoop?"—an idea of Gerry Hoeck, Scoop's long-time advertising counselor from Washington State. Scoop Jackson knew it was
so but he hated the idea that after all he had done over the years he
was not a national figure. But there are very few senators (today and
then) who are recognizable elected public figures of the sort who
will be stopped and surrounded in an airport. My short list runs out
after Ted Kennedy, Hillary Clinton, Barack Obama, John McCain,
and perhaps Joe Lieberman. That's the way it is; politicians use their
elbows to get in front of a TV camera (don't get in the way of New
York Senator Charles Schumer running to a bank of television cameras), and not many people pay attention. Full-bodied national po-

litical fame usually comes about by serving as president or vice president, or by leading an American military force to victory.

I was once approached about running for Congress from Montgomery County, Maryland. I thought about it for a while and couldn't figure out if I would vote for me or against me. A journalist, television personality, or think-tanker with some following probably has more influence on the way the world spins than do most of the 535 elected federal officeholders. Also, the pay of high-level journalists is vastly greater than that of an elective officeholder. It seems out of kilter that a handsome or beautiful newsreader who reports on air about Senator Jones earns far more money than Senator Jones. But if you payed everyone roughly the same amount of money you would have — my goodness! — socialism.

Scoop Jackson's most important political act was the introduction and ultimate passage of the Jackson-Vanik Amendment, which stipulated free emigration of Jews, Evangelicals, and Catholics from the Soviet Union as well as any other state that did not allow emigration. As it played out it was Soviet Jews who received the act's most publicized benefits. It became law in 1974 after a protracted fight with President Nixon and Secretary of State Henry Kissinger, both of whom believed that it would strike a harsh blow against *détente* with the Soviet Union.[1] Perle, a canny tactician, played a central role.

In order to curry favor without losing face, the Soviets started quietly letting out some Jews who had visas to Israel. I got a freelance assignment from *The Washington Post* to go to Israel and write the story. It was fascinating work and lasted about two weeks. I saw refuseniks landing at Ben-Gurion International Airport at two in the morning. I interviewed many of them who had been there for only a year or two, already speaking Hebrew, and involved in Israel's often-bitter politics. They explained to me what it meant to be a *Yid* in the USSR. At first, the Israelis were very cooperative in my quest for a story that had not yet really become public. Then, the day before I left, preparing to file the story, I was asked to pay a visit to an Israeli diplomat. He gave me a lecture about the glories of a free press, and

---

1. The definition of *détente*, originally a French word, is "relaxation of tensions."

told me that of course I could write what I wanted, but that he and his colleagues had decided that such a story at that time might embarrass the Soviets and possibly cut off Jewish emigration.

Hmm. Would I write the story with an Israeli dateline, which is what the Israelis did *not* want me to do? Or would I help Soviet Jewry? The final story began, "From listening posts around the world . . ." with no dateline. To salve my not-very-aching conscience, I stopped off in London on the way home and interviewed a couple of experts to make the article technically accurate. It's an old journalistic dilemma: get the story or save a life. For me, that one wasn't even a close call.

The Jackson-Vanik Amendment opens this way: "To assure the continued dedication of the United States to fundamental human rights. . . ." It was legislation that in effect mandated that U.S. foreign policy be linked directly to moral behavior. It again represented the opening of an old diplomatic struggle between the idealists and the realists, which was to become central during the second war in Iraq. Most of Scoop's Troops have maintained that for America, idealism is the best realism.

How important was Scoop's work? Some years later, here is what Soviet dissident Natan Sharansky had to say about Scoop's activity regarding the Soviet Union on a *Think Tank* program. It refers to Sharansky's "trial" and the massive documentation totalitarian societies compile in order to commit illegal, swinish acts:

> While reading all [fifty-one] volumes from my so-called case, I could find there the names of my fellow "official accomplices." But among those names there was one name mentioned not just one, not just dozens, but hundreds of times, the name of the man who was singled out at the head of this plot, as my closest and most important comrade in crime. It was the name of a person whom I never met, whom I never spoke with on the telephone, but whose very name symbolized for us the best that was in the West and all the peoples who came to our support when we needed it. It was the name of Senator Henry Jackson.

Was Scoop pro-Israel? Of course he was, as clearly reported in the book *Henry M. Jackson: A Life in Politics*, by Robert G. Kaufman. He did indeed get substantial campaign funds from pro-Israel American Jews. But what Democratic politician didn't? (And these days, most Republicans do as well.) I did not grow up in an atmosphere in which gentiles were philo-Semitic. Today, that feeling seems to be everywhere: Non-Jewish Americans often seek to move into significantly Jewish neighborhoods because schools are good and crime is low. I was somewhat startled when I first found that Richard Scammon, and later Jeane Kirkpatrick, were remarkably staunch in their pro-Israel views. Why? In large measure because they believed that Israel was a democratic state in an area of dictatorships, monarchies, and autocracies. As such, it deserved the firm support of America's democracy just as America had supported Western Europe and Taiwan. Such was also the cut of Scoop Jackson's jib.

Beyond the American Jewish community, Jackson had other major financial contributors, particularly among the military-industrial complex and the energy players: He was said to be "the Senator from Boeing." But what politician doesn't pay attention to the largest employer in his state? (Although Scoop sometimes opposed Boeing's plans for weapons systems.) In any event Scoop was a political pro: He wasn't about to be defeated in any election for lack of money.

At one speech at a synagogue Scoop told the audience that his mother had told him, "Love the Jews." I had never heard such a remark. I asked some synagogue members about it and they, too, were puzzled. Later, I suggested to Scoop that it wasn't doing him any good, and he dropped it from later speeches. It still mystifies me, although Christian Evangelicals take a firm pro-Israel stand to facilitate the coming of the Messiah.

SCOOP FORMALLY ANNOUNCED his run for the presidency in mid-November 1971. On August 11, 1971, he spoke to the New York State AFL-CIO Convention in New York City. I wrote his speech in collaboration with Tom Kahn, my deputy on the campaign. Scoop did some editing and revising. It reveals a lot about the neo-con frame of mind, although it was harsh by the standards of the time.

The text was released the evening prior to the speech. By the time Scoop entered the hall a story had already appeared in the *New York Post* that carried the headline "Radical Chic Assailed by Jackson." The *Post* writer noted that it was his third such speech "and by far the strongest attack against what [Jackson] sees as the threat to the [Democratic] party by radicals." The union audience had seen the article. As Scoop walked down the aisle to the podium to loud and rhythmic applause, labor skates were grabbing him and pounding on him, telling him right on, go get that radical chick.

Tom Kahn had been the "theoretician" of the Yipsels—the Young People's Socialist League. He was one of the best speechwriters I have ever worked with. His heroes were AFL-CIO President George Meany and AFL-CIO Secretary-Treasurer Lane Kirkland. Tom was a dazzlingly handsome man. Whenever he came to my office at the American Enterprise Institute the women in the shop stopped working and stared.

Beyond ideology, the speech served our tactical purposes: It let Scoop establish himself as someone quite different in a large, multi-candidate field. Let the others split up the liberal Democratic vote; Jackson would win pluralities and headlines by capturing the votes of moderates and moderate conservative Democrats. When the time came to nominate a candidate, leaders of other delegations would move to Jackson because of old political relationships and respect. (Frank Mankiewicz, McGovern's advisor and press spokesman, said he would have no problem supporting Scoop in the event that he was nominated.) Such was our strategy, which coincided with our beliefs. Most of Jackson's speeches were not of this style, and most were on wholly different topics—foreign policy and "Nixonomics" in particular.

It was a very tough time. And Scoop's references were accurate. The New Left, the hard Left, and some of the New Politics cadre were indeed calling cops pigs; demonstrators were waving Vietcong flags and some were publicly hoping not only for America's withdrawal but for a humiliating defeat. Labor leaders were publicly scorned as cigar-chomping racist retrogrades, and there was a demand to free

Communist Party member Angela Davis, who was on the FBI's most wanted list in 1970. Charged with conspiracy, kidnapping, and homicide, she had evaded police capture for two months and had then been tried. Eighteen months later she was acquitted of all charges. (How can you be innocent of all charges if you have evaded arrest?)

Note, too, that while some of the language is similar to Humphrey's "Law and Order" speech, Scoop's was tougher and cut a wider swath than Humphrey's did, even though it was Humphrey who was viciously condemned at the 1968 Chicago convention and on the campaign trail. Scoop didn't agonize about it or say that the topic ought to be in the form of a question.

Jackson began, as he did most all of his speeches, stressing President Nixon's failures:

> I believe that an assault has been mounted, from the Right and the Left, against the interests and the sensibilities of the working people of this country. The assault comes first of all from the Nixon administration. Can there still be any doubt but that the victim of this administration's economic policies has been the American worker and his family?

Jackson then listed Nixon's report card: high inflation, a recession, high unemployment, high interest rates, high mortgage rates, and rising poverty. And then he said, "I believe the time for this nonsense is over. The time has come for wage and price controls." Which, alas, in 1972 Nixon imposed, and which had the long-term effect of screwing up the economy even worse than it had already been screwed.

Nixon's chairman of the Council of Economic Advisors, Herbert Stein, probably best described as a soft neo-con, blanched—but went along. (Stein was a lovely human being, one of only two economists I knew of who wrote gracefully and with humor—John Kenneth Galbraith was the other.) Stein was a colleague of mine at the American Enterprise Institute. He was asked once by management if it would be OK to share a secretary with me. He said "sharing a secretary with Wattenberg is like sharing a canoe with an elephant."

Then Jackson prophetically turned on the other villain:

> I believe that working people are not only under attack
> from the Right. The working people are also under attack
> from the left fringes, by people who would like to take
> over the Democratic Party. If this takeover were to
> succeed the Democratic Party will lose in 1972 and be in
> deep trouble for years thereafter. . . . There are some
> people in the Democratic Party who have turned their
> backs on the working man. They are either indifferent to
> him or downright hostile. They mouth fashionable
> clichés about how workers have grown fat and conserva-
> tive with affluence, and how their unions are reactionary
> or racist.
>
> They ignore the fact that in the last two decades unions
> have been in the forefront of everything decent in this
> country—from civil rights to civil liberties to economic
> growth to education to national health insurance.
> Nonetheless, they sneer at labor—except perhaps at elec-
> tion time, when they want to use workers as voting fodder.
> Hence the new myth that elections will be decided by
> young people—as if millions of young people were not in
> unions. What most typifies the outlook of these absolutists
> on the Left is their attitude toward law and order. They
> seem to regard the whole issue as phony, demagogic, and
> unclean. . . . I am very sensitive to this word *repression*. I
> have what is perhaps the unique distinction of having
> been campaigned against by both McCarthys—Joe *and*
> Gene. Joe came into the state of Washington in 1952 and
> said I was soft on Communism. And Gene came in 1970
> and said I was too tough on it.
>
> But where is this repression today? I know that there is re-
> pression in many neighborhoods. Elderly people, poor
> people, black and Spanish-speaking people are afraid to
> walk out in the street at night—or during the day. These
> forms of repression do not arouse the indignation of the

chic radicals. They are too busy calling the cops pigs and romanticizing common criminals as political prisoners.

There are politicians in the Democratic Party—a small but vocal minority—who are pandering to these views. . . . They are alienating the very working people— black, white, and brown—who have traditionally provided the mass electoral base for liberal Democratic victories and programs. They are telling working people that liberals aren't interested in protecting them from crime and disorder, from disruption, from muggers and dope addicts. They are telling them to wait until all of our sociological and political problems are solved before they can expect personal safety and security. Well, I am a liberal Democrat. And I am not soft on law and order. Liberal Democrats have been the champions of the common man. And right now the common man sees two pocketbook issues: Nixon is draining his pocketbook and the muggers are swiping it. The rich are protected against crime—by their doormen, their closed-circuit TV cameras, their well-lighted streets, and their distance from the slums. But who protects the working man?

I am also very much disturbed by the way the absolutists on the Left are perverting the environment issue into an attack on working people. We are all disturbed by the sickening pollution of our air and water and land. But to the emotional absolutists of our day the way to do this comes out as mockery of what we believe. Stop economic growth, they say. Turn off technology. Shut down factories. Turn workers out. Turn back the clock to a simpler agrarian age. . . . Talk about ecology. What about human ecology? Don't we need to clean our environment of slums, of rats and roaches, of potholes and broken sidewalks, or broken-down subways and obsolete sewer systems, of dark and dangerous alleys, of honky-tonk streets where prostitution, pornography, and drugs flourish? Can we clean up our social and physical environment with a nineteenth-century technology and a dirt-farm economy?

I want to see an end to American combat operations in Vietnam by the end of the year. But I do not want to see the Democratic Party become a party which gives any comfort whatever to people who applaud Vietcong victories or wave Vietcong flags. Our party has room for hawks and doves, but not for the mockingbirds who chirp gleefully at those who are shooting at American boys. I do not want to see the Democratic Party become a haven for neo-isolationists of the Left or the Right—for those who believe that America is so corrupt that it can do only evil in the world. We must turn our backs on those who would make the Democratic Party the party of dejection and despair.

There is a great liberal impulse afoot in this land. It is a warm and generous impulse that seeks to build a still better America. We have yet to give a fair break to the black man or to the Spanish American. We still have hungry people in America. We have cities that are in grim shape. We have enormous historic responsibilities in a dangerous world.

I feel very deeply about these issues, and in the months ahead I shall be speaking out on them—speaking out as the labor movement speaks—loud and clear.

The campaign had begun. Scoop had great respect for the political acumen of Tom Foley, his protégé. Foley took an exploratory trip to New Hampshire, then as now the first primary election in the nation. It was a time when presidential candidates were not expected to run in every primary. John Kennedy ran in only four Democratic primaries in 1960—and was nominated. Foley reported back to Scoop that the state was not a good place politically for a conservative Democrat. Elsewhere audiences would ask about the economy, the Cold War, crime, and many other issues. In New Hampshire, Foley said, potential Jackson supporters asked about the evils of abortion. In short, Jackson might do well in New Hampshire but would likely get his support from far-out conservatives in a state where the views of the ultra–right wing newspaper *The Manchester Union Leader* got great national attention from political reporters from the rest the country. Foley said that was not how the campaign would want to define Jackson at the very beginning of a primary season.

I accompanied Foley on some of his visits to New Hampshire. His word on the politics of the matter prevailed, as it should have. But I thought this judgment was mistaken. Muskie, from neighboring Maine, received 46 percent of the vote, which was discounted for neighborliness. McGovern got 37 percent, giving him a sensational launch for what was to follow.

I learned a lot about America . . . and a lot about myself. I remember coming into some paper mill towns where the acrid smell of sulfur permeated the air. Scoop, who came from a paper mill area in Washington State, said back home they called the odor of rotten eggs "the smell of money." I also remember, early on, very specifically asking Sterling Munro how we would be traveling. "Campaign rule," he said, "two engines, two pilots." I discovered later that rule was for the candidate. Flying through the New Hampshire mountains in small single-engine planes, bouncing around with a sole pilot, was not my style.

Florida was our key state in 1972. If we could win there we thought we could prove something important. The political cliché is that northern Florida is like the South, southern Florida is like the North, and the middle of Florida is like the rest of America. We could show that we were the all-American candidate by campaigning intensely in just one state.

I traveled all over with Scoop, including the Florida Panhandle, along the Alabama border, together with the iconic local Florida congressman, Bob Sikes, known by all as the He-Coon, a reference to local raccoons. The area then was about as grubby, grimy, and poor as any area of the American southland, and to the untrained eye not that much different from the scenes one saw in some third-world countries. Racial attitudes were changing—but slowly. Scoop did not stress his brilliant civil rights record.

At the time of the 1972 election a big issue was "busing," or as it was often referred to, "crisscross busing to achieve racial balance." It was particularly salient in the South, but it was very unpopular by wide polling margins everywhere. Although there was a polling differential, most black parents, like white parents, did not want to put their young children on a bus for a long trip just to satisfy the call for racial balance. Horror stories surfaced describing cases where elementary school students were bused from their neighborhood school for an hour or longer *each way* from one end of a city to another, often from schools deemed safe (read white) to those deemed unsafe (read black). Many white parents who could afford to do so moved to the suburbs to avoid busing, further eroding the tax base of cities. But then the federal courts ruled that the suburbs, too, would be included in "balancing." There was no escape but private schools—often segregated "academies"—the exact opposite of what *Brown v. Board of Education* sought to accomplish. Yet one more example of how the new liberalism created neo-conservatism.

Scoop was a good constitutional lawyer. Because court-ordered busing came about through the Supreme Court, only a constitutional amendment could change it. Scoop introduced such an amendment shortly before the Florida primary. Jackson, of course, was denounced by liberals as pandering to racists to get votes. And surely presidential politics had plenty to do with it.

I have seen the busing amendment ascribed to the product of my evil genius. I caught hell in some later books written about it. In fact, I didn't even know of it until I saw the newspapers the next morning. I did support the amendment after it was announced. I still think it made sense.

I checked the *Congressional Record* to see what the proposed amendment said. Here it is:

> Section 1. No person shall be denied freedom of choice and the right to have his or her children attend their neighborhood public school.
>
> Sec. 2. Every person shall have the right to equal education opportunity in the Nation's public schools. This right

shall not be abridged by economic discrimination in the
allocation of the financial resources available to educational authorities.

Sec. 3. The Congress shall have the power to enforce this
article by appropriate legislation.

Of course, with busing in the headlines, it was Section 1 that received all the attention. But Section 2 was a very liberal proposal that
would help poor black children and all poor children—but it received no attention at all. Upon examination it means that schools in
most low-income neighborhoods generally receive relatively small
amounts of revenue per student, coming principally from state
school taxes, which are keyed to local property taxes and that the
same amount of educational resources should go to all public
schools. Jackson could and did introduce legislation to make reform
happen. Paying for it would have necessitated an increase in the federal share of local school budgets from what was then 7 percent to
33.3 percent, amounting at that time to an increase from $3.2 bil-
lion per year to $16 billion over a five-year period. In constant 2006
dollars, the gross five-year figure would have amounted to a shade
under $77 billion.

Since 1972, there have been a variety of ways promoted to accomplish what Scoop set out to do, always surrounded by controversy. Liberals have sought to equalize school funds for rich and poor
districts. Most neo-cons and some conservatives have been enthusiastic about a number of other means to achieve the goal of better education for less-privileged kids. Whether vouchers or charter schools,
these vehicles would allow poor children to do what many rich
students did—go to a private school. The idea is to link the money
directly to the kids, not to the schools. Although such programs
have been typically resisted by teachers' unions, as this book is put to
bed in 2008, vouchers are in effect in Milwaukee, Cleveland, Washington, D.C., all of Florida, and many other localities. A variety of
studies have been conducted on the efficacy of vouchers and—no
surprise—the unions and their allies say vouchers don't help, and the
neo-cons and conservatives maintain that they do.

Scoop's amendment turned to the civil rights acts of the 1960s, which said, in effect, thou *shall not* discriminate on the basis of race. He believed that the subsequent court rulings on busing were topsy-turvy, maintaining that thou *shall* discriminate on the basis of race. Some of Scoop's liberal supporters didn't like the amendment. Had they studied it and absorbed it I think they might well have understood that Jackson was in sync with the American mainstream. Neo-cons have been against "quotas" from the outset. If you quota someone in then by definition you quota someone out. In always seeking to capture the language—both sides do it—liberals called the quota process affirmative action with goals and timetables. Most all neo-cons have been very much for "merit" over the years. In chapter 10, Senator Moynihan offers his views.

There is a further irony. The so-called Philadelphia Plan proposed by Nixon after he was inaugurated in 1969 was a true quota scheme for construction unions. Working with Nixon to hatch the plan were Secretary of Labor George Schultz and Deputy Attorney General Laurence Silberman (now a super-neo-con), who hasn't stopped apologizing for that quota scheme for thirty-five years. There was allegedly a Nixonian political ploy involved: it would split pro-quota blacks from their putative allies, the (then) anti-quota AFL-CIO.

Later, during the administration of the first President Bush, the phrase *race-norming* was discovered in federal hiring guidelines. It was astonishing, eliminating any semblance of merit from the hiring process. Under its terms, all whites who took federal hiring tests were ranked from highest to lowest among the pool of white applicants. All blacks who took the same test were ranked among only blacks. Then, if twenty federal slots were to be filled, the top ten from each list would be chosen even though, say, the top seventeen whites might have scored higher than all but three blacks. Straight quotas, with taxpayer dollars.

AT ABOUT THIS time Scoop appeared on one of the national Sunday morning talk shows and was asked his opinion of the then-new *public* movement for homosexual rights. The Stonewall Riots, regarded as the beginning of the recent gay rights movement, had occurred in mid-1969, only a couple of years previously. Scoop responded in all innocence that homosexuals were sick people and ought to be treated. Indeed, until 1973, the Psychiatric Association of America listed homosexuality as an illness worthy of treatment by psychiatrists. The roof collapsed. Once again the liberals denounced Scoop as a sellout. The campaign staff didn't much like the position Scoop espoused, particularly since he had some quite important gay supporters. These included the great black civil rights leader Bayard Rustin.

I drew the short straw and was asked by staff members to inform the senator of our views. I phoned Scoop and we talked for a few minutes about his *Meet the Press* statement. I reminded him that he had always been a staunch civil libertarian. He didn't ask who his gay supporters were. After a moment of reflection he said he could see the libertarian argument for gay rights and agreed not to talk publicly about it. Nor did he. That was a typically neo-con position, as well as a libertarian one.

Scoop was so unphony it could be politically painful. He was a religious man. I pointed out to him once that it would be helpful to allude to that in his campaign speeches. No, he said, that was private. Ever since the 1976 advent of Jimmy Sanctimony, the praying president, that notion has gone by the boards. Scoop never took a dime for a speech. Honoraria went directly, and quietly, to a scholarship fund.

I spent about three weeks in Florida in the winter of 1972, which is not bad duty. I roomed with Gerry Hoeck in a duplex hotel suite provided in some roundabout way by our Florida public relations team. (Legally, I hope.) Our first statewide survey, taken by the respected pollster Oliver Quayle, showed Scoop running at zero. Gradually our polling numbers began to grow: to 2 percent to 5 percent to 10 percent and then to 15 percent, almost tied with the widely known Humphrey, who had finally decided to enter his name for the presidency a second time. Also running was John Lindsay, the liberal mayor of New York City, carrying his full kit of handsome liberal charisma with him and having switched his registration from Republican to Democrat. He advertised heavily. George McGovern was on the ballot but did not compete. Muskie, the former front-runner, also campaigned.

At an early fund-raiser for Scoop at the plush New York City brownstone home of tycoon Meshulam Riklis—with Renoirs on the walls—I was pulled aside by Abe Beame, then the comptroller of New York City and a future mayor. He grabbed me by the arm, squeezed it hard, and asked whether I would be in Florida with Scoop. I said that I would. He said, "Tell them the truth about Lindsay." Later, in Florida, small planes cruised along the Atlantic coast of Miami Beach displaying large streamers reading "Lindsay Means Tzuris" (*tzuris* is Yiddish for "trouble" with a capital Tz). Miami Beach had a heavy concentration of elderly Jewish voters hailing from New York City. To the best of my knowledge, the little planes with their L.M.T. message was not a Jacksonian operation.

Your author—Mr. Smoothie himself—shone like a naked lightbulb at the Riklis gathering. Bess Myerson, a former Miss America and formerly a resident of the same apartment complex in which I lived as a child, was in attendance. In a conversational circle of about ten people we chatted away. (Bess, an intelligent and talented woman, was very interested in politics. She would eventually run a losing campaign for senator of New York State under Pat Moynihan's tutelage.) Then I heard myself say, "Bess, you may not remember this, but in the old days you were my babysitter." That was, as Casey Stengel used to say, a "true fact," and part of my family's lore. But the silence was deafening, as this balding windbag put a date on the age of the still-beautiful beauty queen. Maybe that's why I never ran for any office higher than board of representatives in Stamford, Connecticut (I lost).

In Florida, I was asked to brief the press to show how Jackson was gaining support. I stressed Scoop's climb. But I was under strict orders from Sterling Munro not to give out the numbers for a candidate who had run as an independent in 1968 but was now running as a Democrat—Governor George Corley Wallace of Alabama. Some members of the press can add and they got on my case, particularly columnist Jules Witcover, who insisted it was sneaky and unfair to give out only part of a poll. Upon reflection that may well have been so, although I didn't think so then. I thought: Let Witcover and other media bigfeet take their own poll if they want all the numbers. (I love jousting with the press. When I left LBJ I told myself the only job in government I would ever accept was White House press secretary. No one has asked.)

I stopped by a Wallace rally in Miami in the ballroom of the hotel in which we were staying. His remarks that day were almost entirely about national defense. By 1972, a few years after the passage of the LBJ civil rights laws, Wallace had given up his racist exhortations ("segregation today, segregation tomorrow, segregation forever!"). As he left the hall Wallace recognized me. He asked, "You're Wattenberg, aren't you?"

I responded, "Yes, Governor, I am."

He said, "You're a good man. You ought to come to work for me."

I was petrified, lest someone overhear the exchange. "I'm working for Senator Jackson," I said.

"Well," said Wallace, "he's a good man."

I retreated with speed. Actually, I may have run away: Someone might think I was too close with the once-racist devil.

After Wallace's talk, columnist Robert Novak asked me a good question: "Other than race, what did you disagree with Wallace about? About 'pointy-headed bureaucrats'? About 'law 'n' order.' About big government?"

Actually, I have never been against government, big, small, or medium size. I recall as a young man in Stamford feeling proud to pay taxes. Only later did I come to understand the complex scandal of the IRS code. (While running for the presidency in 1976, candidate Carter called it "a disgrace to the human race," and I agree.) I had some major disagreements with what governments did at whatever level—national, state, and municipal. And that is still roughly my view. Many—most?—conservatives and most libertarians deplore government spending whenever they can. Such was not the case then or now with many neo-conservatives. Some bureaucrats are talented and selfless civil servants.

THESE WERE THE final election results for the 1972 Florida primary: Eugene McCarthy, 0.5 percent; Congresswoman Shirley

Chisholm, 4 percent; Senator George McGovern, 6 percent; Mayor John Lindsay, 6.5 percent; Other, 7 percent; Senator Edmund Muskie, 9 percent; Senator Henry Jackson, 14 percent; Senator Hubert Humphrey, 19 percent; and Governor George Wallace, 42 percent (!). At least we beat Ed Muskie, the putative Democratic front-runner. When the final 1972 results for all the primaries were tallied, Mc-Govern, Humphrey, and Wallace each got about one-third of the popular vote. With his camp's knowledge of the rules, however, Mc-Govern walked away with the lion's share of delegates.

Jackson unofficially dropped out of the 1972 race, but officially remained a candidate. One of the nominating speeches for him at the Democratic National Convention in Miami was delivered by the young governor of Georgia, Jimmy Carter.

The spin race went on into the general election. One day Mc-Govern's boy wonder, pollster Pat Caddell, stopped by a table at the Federal City Club where Dick Scammon and I were having lunch. He told us that McGovern had a real shot at carrying South Carolina. South Carolina? McGovern lost it to Nixon 71 to 28 percent. I often wonder: Do spinners know they're slinging bull? Or have they come to believe what they want to believe? I often wondered whether Soviet officials were subject to the same introspection. I often wonder that about speechwriters and authors, including me.

One neo-conservative lesson I learned clearly was that what applied to the Washington, D.C., political debate did not necessarily reflect what was going on in the country. In Washington, Scoop was sometimes called a conservative Democratic candidate. But Florida showed that Democratic Party primaries had at least three parts: liberals (like George McGovern and John Lindsay), moderates (like Scoop Jackson and Hubert Humphrey), and real conservatives (like George Wallace, with or without his racist background, and with some populism tossed in). This enumeration doesn't even count the handful of vocal radicals. It is a lesson that many Democrats never do seem to learn: There are lots of different kinds of Democrats voting in primaries, not just liberals.

For many years the American Enterprise Institute's Karlyn Bowman and I followed a generally ignored but vitally important survey run by The New York Times. The Times aggregated all the popular votes cast in all the state presidential primaries and presented the characteristics of those voting in each party. The results show clearly that the Democratic primary vote is not dominated by liberals, although that is axiomatic in practical politics. Moreover, the differential among attitudes of Democrats of different persuasions on most issues (e.g., crime, the military, religion, etc.) is relatively small. There is not even a large gap between Democrats and "all Americans." And yet every four years the same story comes up with a lede roughly like this: "The Democratic Presidential primaries, dominated by liberal activists, moved on today to . . ." And that is strange. If the Democrats could ever get their act together and be seen again as a mainstream party of the center left, they would be the natural governing party in America. Little guys still beat fat cats. Alas, it never seems to happen.

A president is deeply influenced by his staff and by the interest groups that work them over. I find the Democratic interest groups—super-feminists, super-environmentalists, and the like—less palatable than the Republican ones—fat-cat businessmen, cultural conservatives, and so on. I got to know a lot of fat cats through American Enterprise Institute. I have generally found them to be decent, public-spirited people. Like most everyone else in Washington and elsewhere, they will typically violate principle for practicality. A CEO of a steel company will be proprotectionist on steel and antiprotection on everything else.

I WILL NOW tell you whom this neo-con voted for in the past forty years. In 1968, for Humphrey, whom I had come to know and admire during my LBJ years. In 1972, for the first time I voted Republican, for Richard Nixon over George McGovern, because I believed that McGovern was espousing isolationism that could yield disaster. (I kept that vote to myself for years.) Yet McGovern had been a B-24 bomber pilot in World War II who flew thirty-five combat missions in Europe and was awarded the Distinguished Flying Cross. In 1976, I voted for Carter, who ran a primary race to the right of Scoop Jackson. In 1980, I voted for Reagan because Carter had proved to be ineffective and weak on the Cold War.

In both 1984 and 1988 I voted for Walter Mondale and Michael Dukakis over Ronald Reagan and George H. W. Bush, respectively, because I was active in the Coalition for a Democratic Majority, a factional Democratic group (see chapter 5). I did not want to be in a position of saying I was an activist Democrat and then not voting for one. But, if in 1984 or 1988, I thought my vote would have chosen the president, I would have voted for Reagan and Bush over Mondale and Dukakis because I thought the Democrats—as a party, not Mondale or Dukakis themselves—had already been infected with the soft-on-the–Cold War virus. I voted for Clinton in 1992 because he was saying all the things I had been preaching all those years about the social issues. In 1996, I voted for Dole because Clinton was not governing as he had campaigned; he staffed up with only a few moderate Democratic Leadership Council types but plenty of leftists, often apparently chosen by Mrs. Clinton. In 2000 and 2004 I voted for George W. Bush, even though Gore in 2000 ran as more of an internationalist than Bush. But I no longer trusted Democrats. In 2004, after what I saw as George W. Bush's heroic actions in Iraq, it wasn't even close. Like Harry Truman, I think Bush may well be rated as a near-great president after having finished his term in relatively low regard (although almost twice as high as that of the Congress).

The election in 2000 deserves special comment because it shows another difference between neo-cons and conservatives. In the course of writing my column I traveled with Senator John McCain for a couple of days as he campaigned in the New Hampshire primary on the famous Straight Talk Express bus (commonly called Bullshit One by the regulars of the traveling press corps). The bus rolled from town to town, with McCain shmoozing, pontificating, and joking with the scribes, almost always on the record, something quite unusual and much admired by the journalists. He treated me like a bigfoot. You don't usually go wrong in politics or life by praising people, especially when the praise is valid, or at least not preposterous.

I didn't believe in everything McCain said but I bought most of it and was particularly moved by his stock line that Americans had better start thinking "about things greater than themselves." He was a hawk; he was an idealist; he was an internationalist; he believed in an assertive global role for America; he was a military hero. Gov.

George W. Bush, meanwhile, was talking against the idea of nation building, which can sometimes be code for a mild isolationism. My column was very favorable to McCain. Many, probably most, of the neo-cons were entranced by McCain. The conservatives mostly stuck with Bush. McCain won the New Hampshire primary big, beating George W. Bush 48 to 30 percent.

Remembering how Jimmy Carter created an incredible and nearly unstoppable media wave with some early victories in 1976, I thought I was witnessing a replay. I bet $100 with conservative John Fund of *The Wall Street Journal* that McCain would be nominated. It was not a bad bet, but I should have demanded odds. I lost and paid up. My problem: I had neglected to fully factor in that independents couldn't vote in many of the upcoming Republican contests.

My CHOICE BETWEEN Muskie and Jackson in 1972 was simple: Go with the clear front-runner or go where my heart was. I went with my heart and never regretted it. It opened up a whole new political world for me. Scoop took a shine to me and often asked me to travel with him on campaign trips. It was said of Jackson that he was a poor speaker. I sometimes felt that he regarded giving speeches as a duty that had to be performed. (Given his stolid and responsible Norwegian heritage, he performed his chores.) But I recall speeches at which sweaty audiences shook the beams as Jackson delivered one applause line after another, clearly speaking from his heart. Charisma is in the eye of the beholder.

Both the Muskie and Jackson 1972 campaigns collapsed. One amazing aspect of Scoop's ideas was their staying power. After all, he was only one senator among one hundred. But on the issues he cared most about—a strong national defense in the cause of America's protection and the advancement of human rights and democracy—the national dialogue is still full of references to Jackson Democrats. I was asked to be one of the eulogists at Jackson's funeral in 1983. Senator Ted Kennedy was another, and it was there that George Will, yet another eulogist—no neo-con—declared himself to be a Jackson Republican. I don't know of anyone who called himself a Muskie Democrat.

In May of 2003 Donna Brazile, a tough-minded liberal and the former campaign manager of the 2000 Gore-Lieberman campaign, coauthored an op-ed in *The Wall Street Journal* with Timothy Bergreen entitled "What Would Scoop Do?" It blasted Democrats, saying they were "AWOL on national security" and that they ought to "adopt the policies of Scoop Jackson."

THE SECOND JACKSON presidential campaign, in 1976, did much better than the first. The early signs were good. *New York* magazine ran a cover article with a picture of Jackson and a cover line reading, "Dawn of an Old Era: The Inevitability of Scoop Jackson," written by Richard Reeves.

I wasn't asked to be on the paid Jackson staff. As it turned out, I could not have done it. I had committed to do a PBS series of documentaries with WGBH in Boston. But I was asked to do a number of tasks for the campaign and remained in close and regular touch with the candidate and many key staffers. There is a certain advantage in being unpaid yet close. It is very easy to speak up in disagreement. It is said that the best job in Washington is when the press says you are "known to be close to the president."

Jackson's principal opponent turned out to be Jimmy Carter, no longer governor of Georgia, no longer the man who thought so highly of Scoop that he nominated him at the 1972 convention. Carter and his staff spun a good one: Carter was so much the common man that he carried his own bag on and off the campaign plane, his way of saying—post-Nixon Watergate resignation—that if he was elected he would be no "imperial president," unlike the portrait painted of Nixon. I have been told that Carter's luggage shtick was a purposefully staged photo-op, part of the peanut farmer image he promoted. But Scoop was the real goods. I have a photograph of Jackson carrying his own bags off the plane. The standard gag on the campaign plane was that Scoop would carry your bag as well as his own if you didn't act quickly and grab it first.

And in public, Carter's people always called him Jimmy. In private, I have been told, he insisted they call him Governor Carter.

Scoop, however, was always Scoop. I once heard Sterling Munro berate him in front of others: "Goddamn it, Scoop, make up your mind!"

Carter executed a political masterstroke by campaigning heavily for the Iowa caucuses. The first contest of the political year, it had always been ignored in the media in the past. The caucus had no secret ballot, voters had to spend the better part of an evening to participate, turnout was low, and it was a typical, almost lily-white state that yielded only a handful of convention delegates. I suspect it is somewhat akin to voting in Communist Bulgaria. Carter was the choice of 28 percent of the Iowa caucus participants, less than the 37 percent who chose "uncommitted." Yet "uncommitted" is not a person; Carter reaped a massive publicity bonanza.

Don't ask me how the details of delegate selection process worked in Iowa—then or now. My job was to try to get voters to vote for candidates by helping them express ideas they typically believed in before I got their ear.

Carter had a great advantage in Iowa: no longer governor in Georgia, he could run full-time. He personally met many thousands of likely caucus participants, often sleeping over in their homes. It was truly retail politics, and he did it well. The next week, with the New Hampshire primary coming up soon, his picture was on the cover of *Time, Newsweek,* and *U.S. News & World Report.* Wallace won the Mississippi caucus five days later, but no one paid much attention.

Carter won the next contest on the schedule—the first real primary with a secret ballot and voting booths—in New Hampshire. Demographically it, too, is a sparsely populated, almost lily-white state with only a few convention delegates at stake. But it was the first real voting in the 1976 process and yielded another bonanza in publicity. As in 1972, Jackson stayed out of New Hampshire, again a wrongheaded decision in my judgment. Then came the big boys, in which Jackson did compete head to head with Carter: Massachusetts, Florida, New York, and Pennsylvania.

I happened to be in Boston at the time of the Massachusetts primary, working on my PBS advocacy specials. I had a drink at the

Parker House with Jody Powell, Carter's press secretary and advisor. He told me, "We're going to take votes from Jackson's well, but we can do a better job of it." They were acting like neo-cons. That seems to be about what happened.

DANIEL PATRICK MOYNIHAN had been appointed as the United States' permanent representative to the United Nations on June 30, 1975, by President Gerald Ford, a job that at that time not only carried the title ambassador but held the rank of a member of the president's cabinet. Pat served for less than a year, leaving in 1976, just one month before the Massachusetts primary. During his tumultuous tenure he gained great attention for his condemnation of the UN General Assembly resolution that "Zionism is racism" and for vigorously "standing up for America." What went on is described in his book *A Dangerous Place*, coauthored with Suzanne Weaver (now Garment).

When Moynihan left the UN I was asked by Jackson's people to secure Moynihan's endorsement, which he gave. The Jackson team subsequently did a poll in Massachusetts. One question asked respondents about endorsements and what kind of person would carry the most weight with them. At the top of the list was "a professor." Moynihan had been a professor at both Harvard and the Massachusetts Institute of Technology, and had received his doctorate from the Fletcher School of Diplomacy, also in Boston.

Accordingly, the Jackson team prepared a full-page advertisement featuring Moynihan's endorsement, to appear in *The Boston Globe*. I informed Arthur Klebanoff, an attorney and a Moynihan factotum, that such an ad would be running. A few days later Klebanoff called me and said Moynihan wanted the ad cancelled. I immediately called Sterling Munro and told him of the conversation with Klebanoff. Without missing a beat Sterling said to tell Klebanoff that Scoop knew Pat as a man of honor and could not believe that he would do that, and moreover the ad was already on press (which was not true). I called Klebanoff back, repeated the falsehood, and that was the last we heard of the matter. The rumor on the campaign was that Pat's wife Liz disapproved of either the endorsement, the ad, or both. I did not check that out but I do know that over the years Liz played a very important role in Pat's unique and successful political career.

With heavy union support (and Moynihan's endorsement) Jackson won the Massachusetts primary solidly. This time his slogan was "Jackson means jobs." He received 22 percent of the primary vote; Arizona Congressman Morris Udall got 18 percent, Wallace got 17 percent, and Carter got 14 percent. That night, at about 10 P.M., I took a cab down to the headquarters hotel for the Jackson campaign. We had finally won one! I literally pinched myself to make sure I wasn't making it up. The mood in the Jackson suite was euphoric. Scoop called me into the bathroom for a private word and said, "We're going to get the nomination."

Florida was again a very important primary. Carter beat Wallace 34 to 30 percent, with Jackson running at 24 percent, almost twice his 1972 total. But the big news, much deserved, was that a Southerner could beat Wallace. (Although by that time Wallace was campaigning in a wheelchair after an assassination attempt in Laurel, Maryland, late in the 1972 campaign.)

During the Florida campaign I was asked to do a fly-around with Moynihan in a small jet to do brief press conferences in six major media markets. One of our companions was Theodore H. White, author of the ground-breaking *The Making of the President* series of books. Another was R. W. "Johnny" Apple of *The New York Times*. On the jump seat was my son Danny, then seventeen, who had taken a few days off from school.[2]

Moynihan's principal opponent in the New York Democratic senatorial primary in the fall was the Far Left congresswoman Bella Abzug, who had been an active member of the Young Communist League and of whom it was said, "If she wasn't a Communist Party

---

2. When Moynihan died in 2003 Danny did an article for *The Weekly Standard* and reported on his experience with Moynihan when he ran for a U.S. Senate seat from New York after Scoop had dropped out of the race. During that summer of 1976 Danny worked with John Moynihan, Pat's teenage son. The two boys hustled street crowds for Moynihan's primary campaign. Moynihan, according to Danny, was "running bravely as a social moderate and foreign policy hawk for the nomination of an ultraliberal New York Democratic Party." Not a bad description of a neoconservative. Danny reported that Moynihan was "extraordinarily kind to me. . . . I was a very shy teenager and he was one of the few adults with whom I succeeded in actually conversing."

member, she was a dues chiseler." Moynihan beat her by a single percentage point. After the primary, Moyhihan called Danny at home during school hours and told his mother (my then-wife Marna) that he was calling to thank Danny and that the only other person he called prior to Danny was New York's Terence Cardinal Cooke. It was clear to me Moynihan's intention was to reach Marna, not Danny. Why her? As Danny later wrote: "Because he wanted to make her proud of me. Now that, I think, was the kindest thing anyone outside of family has done for me."

I go on about this because Moynihan was a central, sometimes puzzling, neo-conservative figure for many decades. He had a relatively liberal voting record but wrote in the neo-con mind-set in his books and articles. Some people found him hard to deal with. He is discussed and quoted in many places in this book. I liked and admired Moynihan and never had any personal problems with him. In early 1980 I asked him to consider running for president in a unique way while Ted Kennedy and Jimmy Carter were duking it out. My idea: Give ten major speeches in ten cities to show the difference among Democrats. He said something like "hmm," and that was the end of it.

I have heard the stories about how Moynihan drank too much. During our Florida travels we often dined and imbibed together. He did drink a lot, but I never saw him lose control. Later, he answered a question about his drinking in a press conference. He said: "For many decades when I come home at night I have a few drinks—with the same woman." Pat had a wonderful way with words. To combat the notion that Jackson was dull, he said Scoop had "the charisma of competence," probably the most beneficial remark I heard about Scoop that year.

Jackson next faced Carter directly in the April primary in New York. Again, I did a one day fly-around press conference tour with Moynihan. At each stop Moynihan graciously and at some length introduced me to the journalists. Jackson won 38 percent of the delegates; Udall got 26 percent; and Carter, 13 percent. "Uncommitted" received 24 percent. That made it two in a row following his Massachusetts win. Jackson should have been accorded media garlands for winning the second-largest delegation to the Democratic nominating convention. Instead, the media line was that Scoop won because his votes came from New York City and its suburbs, and that these areas had many atypical Jewish voters. Some of the uncommitted votes were from the Buffalo area, said to be holding out for Humphrey, who allegedly encouraged such voting among the party leaders through Buffalo party boss Joe Crangle. Scoop was not pleased. Humphrey was still deciding whether or not to run for the presidency in 1976. (He didn't, for health reasons.)

More important by far was that Scoop's campaign did almost no advertising or campaigning in upstate New York, where delegates were ripe for the picking. It was a major blunder. A win in a few upstate districts would have nullified the Jewish spin. Scoop felt betrayed by his staff. Coming down on the train I sat next to him. He said, "We have no campaign." He had come to the conclusion that campaign chief Bob Keefe was not cutting it. True? I have no idea. The ultimate blame, however, always goes to the boss: Saint Scoop himself.

There was one more Carter-Jackson showdown state: Pennsylvania. I did no work there, spending time putting on a fund-raiser at my home for Jackson's six-person Maryland delegation, of which I was one and Jeane Kirkpatrick was another. Jeane and I drove down to the Maryland capitol in Annapolis to file our papers as Jackson primary delegates. My form listed my ballot designation as "Ben Wattenberg." The clerk asked to see my identification. I showed him my driver's license. It read "Joseph Ben-Zion Wattenberg," my legal name. *Ben-Zion* was the pen name of my grandfather, a distinguished Hebrew writer, poet, and publisher. The clerk said "Sorry. You can't use nicknames on a Maryland ballot, and *Ben* is only part of *Ben-Zion*." I complained. Jeane raised a ruckus and said I wrote books as "Ben." The clerk would not be moved but said that if there were no hyphen in *Ben-Zion* then *Ben* would not be a nickname. I went to a Maryland lawyer, who made the change from Joseph Ben-Zion Wattenberg to Joseph Ben Zion Wattenberg. Like President George Herbert Walker Bush, I now have four names. I was on the ballot as a Jackson delegate as Ben Wattenberg. (How many male candidates do you know who lost their hyphen?) Our slate lost; by that time Scoop was out of the race. If there is a small neo-con moral to this tale it is that the whole incident reenforced the growing sense I had that governments at all levels could sometimes go wild with bureaucratic regulations and should be watched. On balance, I still believe that government is more of a solution than a problem.

The battle of the moderate Democrats went on to Pennsylvania in late April. Both Carter and Scoop were very short of cash. For bureaucratic reasons the Federal Election Commission was holding up all matching payments. Moreover, in Jackson's case, there was not enough time to raise money after his New York victory. But according to election law a candidate could spend his own money. Carter took out a very controversial loan of $1 million, backed by the deed to his peanut warehouse and arranged by his media director, Gerald Rafshoon. Scoop's money men said he should execute a similar strategy and advised him to take on similar debt. They said that come what may they would see to it that he got reimbursed. I am told Scoop said this: "I'm not a wealthy man; I'm not a young man. I have two young children. I can't risk their future. Besides, you couldn't raise money when I was a viable candidate; how could you raise it when I'm not?"

There was no loan. Carter won the Pennsylvania primary, 37 percent to Jackson's 25 percent. Did the money make the difference? Would Jackson have made up the twelve missing percentage points with more cash by perhaps getting six points of Carter's vote? I don't know. But Jackson was finished for 1976, finished as a national presidential candidate, and dropped out. I urged him to stay in, living off the land, to give him enough delegates via proportionality to perhaps put Carter over the top and bargain for the vice presidency. He refused (and described Carter with a profane word). But later when Carter interviewed four people in Plains, Georgia, for VP, Scoop was among them. The job went to a liberal, Fritz Mondale, who played a powerful role in the Carter presidency. We can only speculate on how different things might have been for Carter, America, and the world had Scoop been selected. I doubt that Carter would have suffered from the soft-on-the-Soviets charge.

There is some political justice. When the Jackson campaign folded, Scoop not only endorsed Pat Moynihan's candidacy but asked his financial backers to help Moynihan, which they did. Was the money worth the one percentage point by which Moynihan beat

Bella Abzug? I would surely think so. Moreover many New York Jackson supporters, inspired by Scoop, worked very hard for Moynihan.

When Scoop died suddenly in 1983 I was asked to do a column about him in *The Washington Post*. Then his staff asked if I would deliver a eulogy at the Washington Cathedral. I was so very honored to be asked. Herewith, a few excerpts:

> Scoop liked his own nickname and had an all-purpose nickname for those around him. "Leader," he would say, "what's the schedule?" Or, "Leader, how do we get the votes we need?" It was a game we all understood. Scoop's Troops knew who their leader was.
>
> After the shock of his death began to wear off, some of us started thinking that there ought to be a memorial for the leader, a monument, a building named after him, something. For me, the urgency behind such a quest for memorialization has diminished. Scoop already has his memorial.
>
> In the decades that followed World War II, great Americans devoted their lives to securing peace and learning how to make peace from strength, each in their own way: Truman, Acheson, Marshall, Russell, Vinson, Eisenhower, Dulles, Kennedy, Johnson, Humphrey, to only begin a very long list of patriots. But always, remarkably, from the end of World War II until last Thursday night, that's thirty-eight years, there was Henry Jackson: Jackson on the Joint Committee on Atomic Energy, Jackson on defense, Jackson on NATO, Jackson on the Middle East, Jackson on intelligence, Jackson's powerful hearings on statecraft, Jackson on strategic arms, Jackson on China, Jackson on trade with the Soviets, and most recently Jackson on Central America with what he called a Marshall Plan but [which] was, of course, a Jackson plan.
>
> Day in and day out, decade after decade, Scoop labored in the vineyard of freedom with presidents and vice presidents and prime ministers, with secretaries of state and defense,

with CIA directors and admirals and generals, each toiling with vigor during their season in the sun. But always, there was Scoop, not just a season in the sun, but a generation in the sun, two generations in the sun, the young man from Everett who came to participate in the contest for freedom. And human freedom, always a fragile flower, always threatened, survived and in many ways flourished on this planet during Scoop's time. Year in and year out, decade after decade, did any man contribute as much toward shaping the policies and the power that kept freedom alive in this perilous era?

So let us not worry too much about a memorial for Henry Martin Jackson. He has one. It's called the free world.

So our leader is gone. His tasks are now our tasks, and for our children's sake we can pray that there are those in this church and elsewhere who will pick up the leader's lance. In that spirit then, we say, "Goodbye, Scoop, you are still our leader."

CHAPTER FIVE

The Coalition for a Democratic Majority

ARCHIMEDES SAID, "GIVE me a lever and I can move the world." After the 1972 Jackson campaign I became interested in a certain kind of political leverage that could help spread the ideas of neo-conservatism. The vehicle for the leverage was the Coalition for a Democratic Majority (CDM). Over the years I have often been asked about CDM by doctoral candidates and by students working on honors papers. To use a British term, it was a "ginger group." The dictionary definition: "an organization inspiring others with demonstrated enthusiasm and activeness."

The prototypical and probably most famous such organization was the Fabian Society, founded in January 1884 in England. It was named after the Roman general Quintus Fabius Maximus, who advocated weakening the opposition through harassing operations rather than pitched battles. Alas, Fabians believed that capitalism had created an unjust and inefficient society. They agreed that the ultimate aim of the group should be to reconstruct "society in accordance with the highest moral possibilities." The Fabians were concerned with helping society make the move to a socialist society "as painless and effective as possible." The group was small but had enormous influence in England and all throughout the far-flung British Empire. Pat Moynihan believed it set back economic progress by decades, particularly in the third world (a notion that came into his full focus when he served as ambassador to India, during which time Prime Minister Indira Gandhi declared martial law and installed a form of socialism).

For somewhat more than a decade starting in 1972, the Coalition for a Democratic Majority was regarded as the political wing of the neo-conservative movement, even though it had many members who were not then, nor would they ever be neo-conservatives. CDM members regarded themselves, in Governor Howard Dean's 2004 phrase, as "the Democratic wing of the Democratic Party." Rank-and-file liberals at first regarded CDM as the conservative wing of the Democratic Party—and later as turncoats. The issue of which Democrats morphed into what, however, is an ongoing theme in this narrative.

It was a unique organization. One charter member was Jeane Kirkpatrick—before she was *the* Jeane Kirkpatrick—who characterized CDM as "a state of mind, not an organization." That was accurate. We had made a decision that our job was to try to change the climate of opinion and not be a membership group, which typically requires local chapters and a good deal of hand-holding of people who want an answer to the most difficult question in politics: What can I do to help? (Answer: Raise money.) I often thought of CDM as a sort of a political embodiment of *The Wizard of Oz*. There was a small group of cause-oriented, self-appointed political mischief-makers with a megaphone, standing behind a curtain, while the political world thought perhaps there were masses of people ready to march. (Not such an unusual practice in political life at any spot on the spectrum.) Representative Bella Abzug was particularly infuriated by CDM. "They don't have anything," she would bellow, "it's a fake." She would go on: "It's not a wing; it's a feather!" Oz-wise, she was correct. Indeed, Bella's people had an organization—in fact lots of organizations. But CDM's views pretty well coincided with the views of many—perhaps most—Democratic voters, and quite possibly a cross-section of all American voters.

In terms of *The Real Majority*, we saw CDM as an embodiment of a centrist organization. Centrist voters are notoriously hard to organize. Voters in the center of a political spectrum do not believe that the world will end if a species in the rain forest goes extinct or if a Miss is called Mrs. or Ms. But if they believed that Western civilization would go out of business if there weren't a tight lid kept on potential Soviet expansion, they would be very interested indeed. From that taproot, CDM became a surprisingly important organization.

Like so many things in my early professional political life, CDM came about through Dick Scammon. By mid-1972 it was quite apparent that through the McGovern candidacy the so-called New Politics, the New Left would capture the Democratic Party's presidential nomination and that its leftist views would yield a mighty defeat that would reverberate. It did. The final 1972 results were McGovern 37.5 percent, Nixon 60.7 percent. Scammon used to say that 60 percent was a true landslide. The 1972 election was the greatest landslide in all American political history.

One afternoon, in his office, Scammon said to me, "I've been thinking; we need a new ADA." After the end of World War II the Americans for Democratic Action (ADA) had been the strong voice of liberal anti-Communism. Scammon felt, with merit, that the ADA had bought into far too much of the countercultural, pro-Vietnamese, and neoisolationist ideas of the New Politics. He suggested that I call Dick Schifter, then the boss of liberal Montgomery County (Maryland) Democrats and work together to set up such a new organization. When I lived in suburban Maryland I would call Schifter on election days and ask him whom to vote for in local races because I respected his judgment. I still do, but as political allegiances and views shifted we went our separate ways.

And so, during the summer and fall of 1972 our organizing committee would meet furtively at the proletarian hideout of the Federal City Club, planning its strategy. The "secret" held, and it was good that it did. Had it surfaced, it would have been listed as another factor in McGovern's loss to Nixon in 1972. At one point Scoop Jackson and Hubert Humphrey were set to become chairmen of CDM. I met in Humphrey's office with Jackson, Humphrey, and Ken Gray, the administrative assistant on Humphrey's Senate staff. We talked for close to an hour and all went well, with Gray saying little. Just as we were about to seal the deal with a handshake, Gray said to Humphrey, "Senator, don't you think it would be wise to sleep on it." (I think Gray was afraid of a reaction against Humphrey from some liberals, although many CDM members were old-fashioned liberals and union people.) Humphrey immediately acquiesced to Gray's suggestion, leaving me thinking about the rap on Humphrey as being indecisive.

We left it on hold. I was dismayed. Later Humphrey agreed to become an *honorary* co-chairman along with Scoop. The distinction between chairman and honorary co-chairman turned out to be minimal. What counts is name association and the connotation that the name brings with it. Later on I became "chairman for life" of CDM, in which capacity I served for about a dozen years.

Shortly before Humphrey died in 1978 he called me just to chat. He opened with "Hi Ben, it's Hubert." We talked for a while—nothing to do with CDM. Puzzled, I called Norman Sherman. He said, "He was telling you he's dying." I thought that was an act of courage and honor.

CDM did two smart, important things right off the bat. First, we hired young Penn Kemble to be the executive director. Penn had been the head of Frontlash, the labor movement's answer to Governor George Wallace's attempt to capitalize on the white backlash that formed during the roiling sixties. Penn was an excellent executive and brought CDM credibility in the labor movement. Several presidents of the national independent unions—the bricklayers, the painters, the garment workers as well as Albert Shanker, a very special man and president of the American Federation of Teachers (AFT)—gave us some financial, moral, and ideological support. Shanker was a man of great intellect, and, arguably, had a neo-con mind-set. But the AFT is a *big* union. And the AFL-CIO, on whose executive committee he served, was a *big* confederation of unions with a vast array of positions on the issues of the day. As I understand it, Shanker struck an interesting deal with both organizations. He would say what he wanted and what he believed on national issues of the day. On local bargaining issues he would back his AFT chapters, and on national issues he would endorse the AFL-CIO positions. This was a doable deed when most neo-cons felt they had an identity of interest and beliefs with the unions. Once labor joined up with the Left cause groups, this would have been a more difficult situation. Shanker managed this honorable but strange balancing act for many years, fighting for his beliefs within both organizations. Al died in 1977 at age sixty-nine, another big loss to the broad spectrum of the neo-con orientation.

Later the executive director slot was filled with some people who proceeded to ever-greater achievements. These included Josh Muravchik, who went on to get a Ph.D. at Georgetown University and has become a leading foreign policy expert and author (he is now a scholar at the American Enterprise Institute), and Jay Winik, who has become an author with at least one bestseller to his credit, *April 1865.*

Our effort to fund CDM drew us to Al Barkan, the director of the AFL-CIO's Committee on Political Education (COPE). Barkan was probably the most outspoken man I have ever dealt with and quite charming in a blunt way. Penn and I would go up to his office seeking money and hear him rail and rant, often profanely, against the "weirdos, homos, and peaceniks" of the anti-union New Politics faction. Barkan believed that the "New Politics" cause groups had taken over his beloved liberal Democratic Party and insulted the entire American trade union movement. We got money. I will have a lot more to say about Penn as we go on. He died in late 2005 of brain cancer at age sixty-four. He was sometimes known as a behind-the-scenes man, but that was far from the truth. Over the years, he was my best friend in Washington, but what I will offer here I believe to be the straight goods.

The American Federation of Labor and Congress of Industrial Organizations, almost always referred to as the AFL-CIO, has changed dramatically in recent decades. Rather than fighting many of those leftist cause movements, it has become one of them, in an activist coalition supporting many positions that labor previously opposed. Some fairly big unions have broken away because of this tendency.

In early 1992 I had lunch at the Hay-Adams Hotel with Lane Kirkland, then the AFL-CIO president. In the course of our meal Kirkland—a man who had often shown distinct neo-conservative tendencies and with many close neo-con and conservative friends— told me that he supported Iowa Senator Tom Harkin for the Democratic nomination. "But Lane," I said, "Harkin supports quotas." Kirkland responded, "So do I." That shocked me, but it probably shouldn't have. The trade unions were becoming a smaller part of the American economy, with more minority members, and were turning left. Their leaders followed suit.

But on balance I applaud Kirkland, as would most all neo-cons. The AFL-CIO, under President Kirkland's hands-on direction (and with Tom Kahn as his active assistant) was the chief American supporter of Solidarity, the Polish labor union that defied Poland's Soviet puppet government (and became much more than a union). After one defeat by the Soviets, Solidarity did not give up and turned out to be the principal agent in ending Soviet domination of Poland. That triggered the astonishing anti-Soviet revolutions in the other European satellite nations, which in turn set the stage for the ultimate dissolution of the Soviet Union itself.

My parents were somewhat to the right of the generally leftist Jewish immigrant society; my father's older brother Elya, however, had been a Communist back in the old country. Along with his family, Elya emigrated to America. My father, Judah, went to Palestine after World War I, and then came to America so his family could help him cure a case of malaria he contracted in the still fairly primitive British Mandate. (My father was born in late December of 1899. He died in 1996, at age ninety-six.) In the early 1930s my father's older brother Elya became a leader at Amtorg, the Soviet-U.S. trading corporation. He was then invited to go to the Soviet Union, where he ended up heading the lumber trust—a very big job. But like so many others, particularly Jews, he got caught up in Stalin's murderous paranoia. When my father cabled that their father had died, he received a cable back saying only, "Don't write again." In the early 1950s he and his wife were put on trial and, according to eyewitnesses, shot and killed *in the courtroom*. So don't ever wonder what was wrong with Communism. When I was exposed to political anti-Communism at CDM, it fit like a glove.

By my lights, the labor movement in those days was a force for great good. Labor lent massive political muscle to the LBJ agenda: Medicare, environmental laws, higher social security payments for the elderly, and education reform. My eldest daughter, Ruth, who has worked at the American Federation of Teachers for almost three decades, has a bumper sticker on her car that reads "Unions: The Folks Who Gave You the Weekend." (Good writers don't scorn clever bumper stickers; they applaud.)

I salute the trade union movement for decades of promoting democratic views and values everywhere. After World War II their agents in Western Europe did a great deal to keep those nascent democracies from becoming communist. (Irving Brown was their key man. I interviewed him at a sidewalk café in Paris for one of my early television programs.) There were some political reasons for such activity—as Kirkland used to say, "What labor leader would want to negotiate with an employer who ran the government, ran the police, ran the army, ran the judiciary, and was the only employer?"

But their big players—Presidents George Meany, Lane Kirkland, and Tom Donahue—stand out because they did what they did for more than mere parochial reasons. They believed in the cause deep in their political hearts. Despite some nepotism and corruption, labor leaders in America are *elected*. As freedom fighters, they beat the business community cold. It was Lenin who said that capitalists, driven by the profit motive, would sell Communists the rope with which to hang capitalists.

CDM PUBLISHED BIG advertisements in *The Washington Post* and *The New York Times* under the big headline "Come Home, Democrats." (McGovern's plea in his acceptance speech in Miami Beach was "Come home, America," a reference to Vietnam.)

The organizing committee included Jeane Kirkpatrick, Bayard Rustin, Tom Foley, Max Kampelman (a former Humphrey bigwig later turned neo-con who became Reagan's arms control advisor),

Penn Kemble, Dick Schifter, and me. Some signers of the ad included Zbigniew Brzezinski, union leaders Albert Shanker and William DuChessi, author James T. Farrell, attorney Peter Rosenblatt, White House aide Harry C. McPherson Jr., and congressional committee chairmen Richard Bolling and James G. O'Hara. We should have gone after some movie stars.

We received hundreds of responses with membership checks and donations. Much of the mail had heartwarming messages of support. Therein was another message for neo-cons, an old one true in most every circumstance across the political spectrum, perhaps best expressed by the labor union slogan "In unity there is strength." In the case of neo-conservatism there were many active, public-spirited people who felt quite isolated politically, knowing that something was going very wrong in their Democratic Party. As individuals they felt politically homeless and weak. Some of them thought it best to remain silent. They knew they weren't Republicans. But they were deeply offended by the message of the McGovern anti-war Democrats and by the highly publicized counterculture. Some of them wondered if they were overreacting. But CDM, with its neo-conservative undercurrent, offered a way to stay in the game and remain true to long-held principles. To borrow from Reverend Jesse Jackson's later language, CDM was an organization that kept hope alive.

As time went on some CDMers came to feel that the neo-conservative persuasion was not for them, that it was too harsh on modern liberalism—or not conservative enough. Kemble, who later moved from executive director to chairman of the executive committee of CDM, was a unique case. He had been president of the Yipsels, the Young People's Socialist League. But Yipsel socialism, in fact and then in name, was social democracy (the group is now the Social Democrats USA). In Europe they call social democracy the welfare state. But *welfare* is a bad word in U.S. political usage, and so Social Democrats and some neo-cons often use "the safety-net state" instead. That may sound like big government, but show me the elected officeholder who is against clean air and water, the interstate highway system, language training for legal immigrants, Social Security, and Medicare. (I exempt Dr. Ron Paul.)

To the end, Penn Kemble still regarded himself as a Social Democrat. But as the union movement joined the Left coalition, he paid ever-greater attention to foreign policy. Penn had worked for Daniel P. Moynihan when Pat was first elected to the Senate in 1976. He was the *acting* director of the United States Information Agency in the latter years of the Clinton administration. Clinton and/or his special-interest staff apparently did not dare to make him *director* lest the lefties think that Clinton had let in one from the other team. I knew Penn understood the full-bodied nature of Moynihan's call for a global Liberty Party better than anyone. He was instrumental (together with Mort Halperin, a man of the Left) in starting what has come to be called the "democracy caucus" or the "community of democracies" within the UN. The columnist Jonathan Rauch, an astute observer who writes for the *National Journal*, noted in 2004: "Predictions are risky, but where you see an acorn, it is not crazy to foresee an oak. With a little light and water, the democracy caucus will inevitably grow. It may overshadow the UN regardless of which party is in charge in America."

I used to tease Penn about the Yipsel's secret plan to take over the world in a blizzard of letterheads. Indeed, before and after CDM, he was engaged with small organizations, often with inter-locking directorates, that in one way or another had the promotion and extension of liberty as a central goal. These included Freedom House, the Institute for Religion and Democracy, and the Foundation for Democratic Education, some of which received grants from *conservative* foundations because they were the smartest anti-Communists around.

Sidebar: This meant redirecting funds from old-guard conservative grantees. This drove Pat Buchanan and the paleo-cons to distraction, because the neos took his money! I think that lies at the heart of the odium paleo-cons like Buchanan have for the neos: We broke his rice bowl. As my American Enterprise Institute colleague Michael Novak likes to say, "When someone says 'It isn't the money, it's the principle of the thing,' it's the money!"

Penn had an additional advantage. He came from an old New England Protestant family; he was muscular, looked like a mini-Superman, and had attended the University of Colorado. In a crowd heavy with Jews, blacks, and union activists, he was perceived for a while as the vanguard of mainstream American Yankeeism, finally seeing the light of socialism. In fact, his father was a psychiatrist.

And Penn was right about those letterhead organizations that I playfully mocked. A few people of common belief and a just cause expressing themselves in a free society can indeed cause great change. Penn understood in the fiber of his being that the promotion and encouragement of democratic views and values was America's cause. He believed that even when it occasionally involved military force.

He did not support the Vietnam War but had no truck with the notion that the war was immoral or that Ho Chi Minh was a great national leader. Uncle Ho was a totalitarian Communist getting arms and supplies from the Soviet Union and Red China, murdering his own people who had the effrontery to disagree with his Communist notions.

Prior to CDM, Penn had participated in one of the Yipsels stunts in New York City to promote civil rights, staging a sit-down on New York's Triboro Bridge during rush hour. Did it further the cause of civil rights? Surely not. It sizzled the commuters. He didn't repeat that trick.

Penn was the man who was always there—to set up a conference and to see to it that papers and articles got published and attention was paid. He knew that neo-conservatism was a critical player in the great game of our time, although he rejected the label neo-con for himself. Now that he's passed on and can't defend himself, I appoint him a posthumous neo-con. That is a compliment.

At the time of Penn's death I spoke at a meeting in his honor and in the course of my research for that speech I googled him. For an allegedly behind-the-scenes operative, he did all right. There were 29,600 entries with his name in them.

CDM WAS IN business. But what would we do? We would have opinions. Many of the ideas in our first text-rich advertisement were, or would become, part of the neo-con fabric. It offered political guidance. Much of it is still operative three and a half decades later.

Midge Decter had drafted the body of the text; I added a somewhat more politically and organizationally oriented beginning. ("For too long now the voices of common-sense liberals have been barely audible in the blare of the New Politics.") Midge's text stressed *national defense* (no withdrawal from international responsibilities); *American greatness* (notwithstanding inequities at home, which we would work to oppose); *merit over proportionalism* (honest affirmative action over quotas); *domestic security* (we were not soft on crime); and *anti-elitism* (no cavalier attitude toward American voters).

Could Oz work in politics? We learned that the opinions and the megaphone of a group cause could become a potent instrument. A journalist's first call for an opinion on a story on so-called crisscross busing to achieve racial balance might go to the National Association for the Advancement of Colored People (NAACP), a group with many tens of thousands of members. After the McGovern victory, the Democratic National Committee itself became an all-purpose organization ready to promulgate its leftward line or refer a caller to an appropriate feminist, environmental, civil rights, or consumer group. Members of Congress could be called. For "balance," however, a rich vein of quotes might well come from CDM, where the pontificators didn't have to worry much about single-issue group voters and funders. A bright writer might then call me or Penn. And they did—regularly.

We would explain that we believed in affirmative action with goals. But when racial balance demanded timetables enforced by the government, that was code for quotas, a concept alien to the American ideal. We might note that there could be somewhat demeaning about the idea that black children could only learn if they were able to sit next to white children—always provided that legal segregation had been struck stone cold dead. The resultant story was that Democrats were split on this critical issue, which was correct. CDM—under my chairmanship—did its best to make the split into a chasm. A party faction in opposition is not looking for unity, but to draw bright, clear lines that try to explain what's wrong. The compromise, always necessary in a free political system, would come later and carry the marks of the battle of ideas. Why would journalists call Penn or me? Because CDM's name carried organizational and intellectual heft and they knew we spoke for more than ourselves.

One day I was invited to a Yipsel–Social Democratic meeting to debate Tom Kahn on socialism vs. capitalism. Tom—the Yipsel theorist—was smart, articulate, and learned, much admired by the audience, and with good reason. I was mostly flying by the seat of my pants, but the consensus was that I won. It's not a hard case to make. People work hard and are innovative when they get rewarded for their efforts. To be sure, not all rewards are monetary, but it helps. There is much more. Read the internationally famous *Spirit of Democratic Capitalism* by my American Enterprise Institute colleague Michael Novak.

For quite a long time I would meet most weeks for breakfast with Penn, CDM president Peter Rosenblatt, and Elliott Abrams. On other occasions, with a somewhat larger group, we would meet at Jeane Kirkpatrick's house to plot our next move. One thought frequently came up during these meetings. The mainstream Republicans had not worked hard to capture bedrock Democratic ideas—merit-based civil rights, immigration, and real feminism, for example. The New Politics and the New Left Democrats had mostly abandoned such ideas, handing over great substantive and electoral issues to their competitors.

Toward the end of CDM's life in the early 1990s, Penn set up a separate subcommittee dealing with defense issues that drew in some money from the defense industry and published a newsletter, *The Defense Democrat*. It went on to survive after CDM shut down. One issue attacked the first President Bush's proposed cuts in defense spending, noting that Defense Secretary Dick Cheney announced support for a $10 billion cut for fiscal year 1990. Kemble's publication wondered whether the Bushies had quietly put into place a plan to shift from guns to butter too soon. The Soviet Union was out of business, but America had disarmed between the two world wars with catastrophic results.

Among the members of CDM's Task Force on Foreign Policy

and Defense, which backed *The Defense Democrat*, were Democratic congressional military heavyweight Congressmen Les Aspin of Wisconsin (who later became secretary of defense), Norm Dicks of Washington, and Dante Fascell of Florida, as well as a former marine officer who served in combat in Vietnam, Virginia senator Charles S. Robb, Lyndon Johnson's son-in-law.

Over the years I would make calls to Scoop's funders for CDM and was rarely refused. His bedrock backers were mostly Jewish businessmen and lawyers who lived all around the country. Scoop once told me he was amazed that his Jewish contributors never asked for anything. I suspect that because of his heartfelt support of Israel they knew they didn't have to ask. I wish I had done more for CDM; I sometimes think that if I had, the organization might still be up and running, making good trouble. But fund-raising takes work and time. It was time that I lacked.

CDM would hold an annual fund-raising dinner; I have a picture on my wall that shows the center part of a dais with Pat Moynihan speaking, Scoop Jackson and Tom Foley listening, and me busily scribbling on some papers. It is inscribed by Moynihan "To Ben Wattenberg, who doesn't even listen to his own speeches." Funny, but *no one* put words in Pat's mouth.

CDM had lost its momentum, but history repeats itself. Just as CDM was triggered by McGovern's massive loss to Nixon, the idea for a new Democratic centrist factional group, to be called the Democratic Leadership Council (DLC), was quietly put forth by Rep. Gillis Long of Louisiana at the 1984 Democratic National Convention in San Francisco.

For many years a principal supporter of the DLC was Bernard Schwartz, who was also Clinton's biggest financial supporter. He is also the biggest supporter of *Think Tank*. He is a real mensch with major wealth, much of which he uses to support an array of causes that explore political ideas from center-left to center-right. I met him at a DLC meeting.[1]

After the DLC set up shop, Kemble, Rosenblatt, and I met with the

---

1. The Reverend Jesse Jackson later characterized the DLC as "Democrats of the Leisure Class."

two key DLC hands-on organizers, President Al From, who remains in that job today, and Will Marshall, who now heads the Progressive Policy Institute, the think tank not-so-informally linked to the DLC (with an IRS 501(c)(3) status, allowing it to receive tax-deductible contributions). Al From is a particularly tough political hombre: He calls the Democrats of the Far Left "the Taliban wing." The idea on the table concerned a possible merger of the two groups. The DLC people mentioned that they had already given some thought to the idea. In fact, they mentioned that the DLC's idea was based on CDM's experience. But the DLC leaders had come up somewhat negative on the idea of a merger. DLC *members* were all *elected officeholders*. Accordingly, the group had to be careful about what it said and how it said it. Even its Progressive Policy Institute twin had more constraints than CDM. The CDM trumpet could sound a mightier note.

The DLC was a bigger and more influential operation than CDM ever was. One of the early chairmen of the DLC was Governor Bill Clinton of Arkansas. When he was elected president, the expectation was that he would load up the White House with DLC people. Like CDM before it with President Carter, the DLC pretty well got stiffed. Hillary Clinton, then appropriately seen as a woman with clear leftist tendencies, played a major role in both policy formulation and hiring decisions.

All in all, I think the DLC does good and useful work. But pushing moderate ideas against the powerful, very liberal special interest groups that work over Democratic officeholders is very difficult (think Sisyphus). Like CDM, they have played the Oz game, to good effect. I would not call the DLCers even closet neo-conservatives, lest I impose the kiss of death. But I did once set up a lunch meeting at the American Enterprise Institute with Al From, Will Marshall, Bill Galston, all of the DLC, Irving Kristol, Penn Kemble, and myself. It was friendly, and I don't recall any major differences of opinion. Kristol, in his fey manner, told me once, "It's better to control two parties than one." That has not happened.

That was a similar stance to that of the staunch conservative Republican multimillionaire Henry Salvatori. In 1972 he gave campaign money to Scoop Jackson, a domestic liberal tough as nails on the Soviets. At a Scoop fund-raiser in California, Salvatori told me:

"If Nixon wins we'll be tough on the Soviets; if Scoop wins we'll be tough on the Soviets. I win both ways." (One minor matter: George McGovern got the nomination that year.)

In 1988, I was asked to do a one-hour PBS special entitled *The Democrats*. David Gergen did a matching show on Republicans. It is a stretch today to call me a Democrat, although that is how I am registered. Nor is Gergen a Republican. Both of the programs were updated, changed somewhat, and rebroadcast in 1992. The executive producer was Michael Pack, who later became the vice president for programming for the Corporation for Public Broadcasting and was then pushed out during one of public television's periodic bloodbaths. Pack is one of the very few television producers who ever made programs by neo-conservatives.

I was very proud of my effort. I tried to show the recent history of the Democratic Party and where the party had gone wrong. After the show appeared, the DLC asked me if I would like to show a tape of the program to its members at a meeting in Philadelphia; there was a slot available between the last of their afternoon break-out sessions and the festivities set for the dinner program. Attendance would be purely voluntary. It was the best audience I could think of. Though I anticipated low attendance, the room was packed with about two hundred people, most of them elected Democratic officeholders from every level of government all over the country.

Early on in the program we showed the famous clip from John F. Kennedy's inaugural address: "Let every nation know, whether it wishes us well or ill, that we shall pay any price, bear any burden, meet any hardship, support any friend, to assure the survival and the success of liberty."

The program marched through the Cuban missile crisis, Kennedy's doctrine of peace through strength, and the first major nuclear weapons agreement with the Soviets, the Test Ban Treaty. It quoted Democratic senator Gary Hart of Colorado saying that Kennedy "was a pragmatist. . . . He resisted that effort to pin him on the spectrum. I was attracted to him in part because the liberals in the party thought he was too conservative and the conservatives thought he was too liberal." It dealt with Johnson's push for civil rights, the Wallace backlash, the Chicago "police riot," and Chicago mayor Richard Daley saying "I have given instructions to shoot arsonists and to shoot looters."

Students for a Democratic Society leader Tom Hayden said the Vietnam issue was very concrete and personal. "In my own case, my father wouldn't talk to me for fifteen years." Hayden said that Humphrey stole the 1968 nomination. But McGovern said, "It was absolutely fair in terms of the ground rules we were operating on." McGovern was correct. And it showed McGovern at the Gridiron Dinner saying, "We opened up the doors of the Democratic Party and thirty million Democrats walked out." It had McGovern saying, "I was not a 'McGovernite,'" that is, that the press had treated him unfairly. (Sound familiar?) It tried to explain New York senator Robert F. Kennedy's messianic presidential campaign and his tragic assassination by a Palestinian who had recently read a pro-Israel remark Kennedy made.

The film picked up on Carter's 1976 victory and the challenge to him in 1980 by Ted Kennedy, who refused to hold Carter's hand in the air in the traditional convention podium photo. Carter literally chased him around the stage, seeking such a picture. It never came off and demeaned President Carter and the presidency.

The program moved forward to Lane Kirkland denouncing Gary Hart in 1984 for Hart's denunciation of labor as a special interest. It praised Jesse Jackson for broadening the election process through his candidacy in 1988 but noted his support of Fidel Castro and Yasir Arafat, and his refusal to oppose the anti-Semitic, antiwhite Louis Farrakhan. Included was an interview with Democratic candidate Michael Dukakis, who compared the Boston-Austin axis of Kennedy and Johnson with the new Boston-Austin ticket of Dukakis and Senator Lloyd Bentsen.

As the film rolled, I looked around the hall and saw the audience nodding in agreement, laughing when appropriate, grimacing at the right spots. I remember the highly influential Senator Sam Nunn of Georgia watching it intensely, clearly showing approval.

I closed the program saying, on camera:

"In the not-so-distant past, the Democratic Party was the great engine of progress in America. It was a party of international responsibility, of economic vigor, of solid social traditions. Times change. But values can and should endure. If Democrats can be credible about those ideas, they can be competitive this year and for years to come."

There was silence in the DLC audience for a moment, and then a standing ovation. Viewers shook my hand and clapped me on the back. But the Democrats have yet to recapture those values.

CHAPTER SIX

The Liberty Party

HOW I CAME TO UNDERSTAND IT

SCOOP JACKSON'S CAMPAIGN and the subsequent formation of the Coalition for a Democratic Majority opened my eyes to the issues that for me became very important in my neo-conservative career. Loosely those issues are called human rights, or democracy, but there is more to it than that. I cite here some further bolstering experiences. They should form a pastiche that I hope explains itself as the story unfolds.

Peasant Under Glass

In 1976 President Gerald Ford fired Secretary of Defense James Schlesinger because he was too tough on the Soviets in an era of détente. It was also said that he patronized Ford. Ideologically, Schlesinger was somewhere in and around the neo-conservative and conservative community, although he had been Carter's secretary of energy.

By that time the Sino-Soviet split had emerged. The Communist giants, the Soviet Union and China, had been feuding, actually killing each other in border clashes. The Chinese saw an opportunity.

They invited Schlesinger to visit China to poke a finger in the eye of the Soviets. This was at a time when there were no diplomatic relations between Red China and the United States. Schlesinger told the Chinese that what he could learn in Beijing (then called Peking in the West) he could learn from briefings in America. But if the Chinese would include visits to the Russian border in Sinkiang, to Inner Mongolia, and to Tibet, then such a trip would be most appealing.

The Schlesinger party included five staff advisors, including Richard Perle, then on Scoop's Senate staff; Edward Luttwak of the Johns Hopkins Center of Foreign Policy; "Bing" West, a professor at the United States Naval War College; and William Whitson of the Congressional Reference Service's foreign affairs section. The small press contingent included Robert Bartley, editor of the editorial page of *The Wall Street Journal*; Jerrold Schechter, diplomatic editor of *Time*; Lloyd Shearer of *Parade* magazine; syndicated columnist Joseph Kraft; and me, a freelancer at the time who was invited at the last minute when author Richard Whalen had to cancel. Because of the lack of diplomatic relations, there were no regular American correspondents stationed in China. Before the trip I talked with Howard Simons, the managing editor of *The Washington Post*. I told him I was on the Schlesinger team and if anything of interest should turn up I would like to file for the *Post*. He agreed.

China was a peasant country and still is, notwithstanding great but tumultuous progress. One day we were taken out to see high-tech Chinese defense tactics against putative Soviet invaders. One highlight was booby-trapped chicken coops that would kill hungry and predatory Soviet invaders. The next day we were driven about thirty miles from Beijing to see Chinese soldiers marching in parade and get briefed at the headquarters of the Third Division of the People's Liberation Army. No news there.

Suddenly, we heard the strains of "The Internationale," the Communist anthem, on the loudspeaker. We were told by Chinese officials that Chairman Mao had died.

In our automobile caravan on the way back to Beijing all the writers started taking notes. Black armbands suddenly sprouted everywhere along the narrow roads. One peasant pedaled his bike down a country lane with a slaughtered pig on the back of his bike and a black band on his arm. By the time we reached the outskirts of Beijing, Chinese flags were being displayed at half staff by storekeepers. When we got back to the hotel I started scribbling out a story. Good friend Jerry Schechter explained to me how to place an international phone call to Washington. As I hurried out I was so excited I opened the door of my armoire to get my foreign correspondent's trench coat and slammed the door against my forehead. Bravely, I ignored my war wound and called Washington. It was like a scene from *The Front Page*. The *Post*'s man on the other end said "rewrite" . . . and I dictated. I felt like Ernie Pyle. Later, I went to the American Hospital in Beijing for two stitches. (I have never applied for a Purple Heart.)

As I was writing, Joe Kraft came by to say that Ben Bradlee, editor in chief of the *Post*, had called from Washington to ask him to write the news story, not just a column about the situation. Bless Kraft: He told Bradlee that I had been given the assignment, and that I should write the story. For four consecutive days I filed. Three of the stories ran on page one, two in the upper-right corner: the page one "lede." I played it very straight. I noted, for example, that China watchers were saying that Mao had filled the past and present equivalent roles of "George Washington, Thomas Jefferson, Abraham Lincoln, Mark Twain, Franklin Delano Roosevelt, and Gerald Ford." Not by my lights. Those Americans were democrats. Mao was a totalitarian, murderous thug.

It took the Chinese almost a week to put together a suitable state funeral, to which our delegation was invited. Our out-of-Beijing trips were put on hold. We ate our meals together in a special room in our hotel, featuring a lazy Susan loaded with Chinese delicacies that were very tasty until identified: e.g., locusts and scorpions, with their little tails stuck in the air and a slightly bitter taste. The highlights of my day came when I received cables from the *Post* foreign editor, who sent me cute little messages saying my stories were running on "p. 1."

Our team was cooped up and we occasionally drove each other nuts. But we were allowed to wander around the city. It really was the proverbial blue ant society: everyone on the street, both men and women, wearing the same quilted blue jackets and blue pants. I wondered why God had made beautiful women in every country in the world but China. I was to learn otherwise.

Because of the delay due to the funeral and commitments made previously for the public television series in Boston, I had to peel off from the group and was not able to take the delayed side trips in China. When I got back I wrote an article for *Harper's* that ran in February 1977 entitled "Mao's Funeral," explaining the funeral protocol that took place in the Great Hall of the People.

In the first places on line to pay respects to Mao in his glass-topped catafalque were China's big pals, the liberty-lovers of the world: the crazy anti-Soviet Albanians, the imprisoned North Koreans, the murderous Vietnamese, and the gentle peasant genocidal reformers from blood-soaked Cambodia. The Schlesinger group went next; we were guests of the Chinese, not representing America officially and consequently put ahead of all other nations. As we passed the chairman's remains encased in a catafalque, Perle—who has a wicked sense of humor—murmured to me, "Peasant under glass." Schechter and Kraft, who knew something about the country, told me that Mao's widow (Jiang Qing) was not in the receiving line with other members of the Politiburo. That was important to know because it meant something in the ongoing power struggle within the Chinese government. In fact, she had been denounced to us only a few days earlier in our meetings as a member of the infamous Gang of Four (which also included Zhang Chunqiao, Yao Wenynan, and Wang Hongwen)—revisionist communists, according to our briefers. Others were trashed as "capitalist roaders." I thought perhaps Mrs. Mao misplaced the car keys too often. Back at the hotel, Perle said to me, "Dead fellows make strange bedfellows."

I put forth my personal impressions of the trip in the *Harper's* piece. I was troubled. China was a peasant totalitalian society. Yet the liberal line in America about China at the time was, *Well, of course, it's not something we'd want for ourselves, but it's a good solution for the Chinese*, a view that is still held by many liberals. I asked whether Stalinism had been a good solution for the Russians, whether Nazism had been a good solution for Germans, whether Tojo had been the solution for the Japanese, and whether General Pinochet was a Chilean solution for the Chileans (which was somewhat gratuitous, since the Chilean situation, while ugly, was different, not involving any border-crossing invasions). I noted that Freedom House had ranked China seventh in a descending scale of seven in the areas of political rights and civil rights.

I learned in China that the government—in effect, the Communist Party—decreed that sexuality was bad, that each city block had a political commissar/spy, that the government decided on a semiofficial age for marriage (in the late twenties), that reproduction (the most private and personal decision) was limited to one child per family and checked by block captains, who kept track of a woman's menstrual cycle—and that such information was publicly posted on factory bulletin boards. The one-child family edict may yet prove catastrophic—all those old people with few younger people to pay for their retirement benefits. Female infanticide only exacerbates the situation.

I learned that there could be no entertainment, only propaganda, and the state could, and would, issue decrees regarding what kind of clothing could be worn. I saw work gangs of stoop labor in the paddy fields ("revolutionary teams") working in the mud, the same way their ancestors had. I had been able to look into ground-level apartments and see a single tiny room packed with a three-generation family, with pallets stacked two and three deep along the walls.

I asked how one went about creating a global freedom coalition when American presidents (Nixon and Ford), an American secretary of state (Kissinger), and a multitude of American writers and intellectuals make public political love to one of the most repressive and murderous governments in history. An estimated twenty million Chinese were killed during Mao's tenure. The rationale: You can't make an omelet without breaking eggs. To paraphrase Churchill: some eggs . . . some omelet.

I wrote that a brush-fire war of ideology was growing in America. Pat Moynihan had called for a global Liberty Party. Aleksandr Solzhenitsyn was using forums provided by the AFL-CIO's George Meany. The former, somewhat improbable governor of California—a far-better-than-grade-B movie actor named Ronald Reagan—came within a thin whisker of winning the GOP nomination from President Gerald Ford. Reagan's biggest issue was morality in foreign

policy, which included a wrongheaded objection to the turnover of the
Panama Canal to the Panamanians. But it made a point. After Vietnam, America was back in business and Feisty was Uncle Sam's middle
name. Suddenly, politicians—following the public opinion polls—
were clamoring for higher defense spending. The Jackson-Vanik
Amendment, which denied important trade benefits to nations that denied their citizens from emigrating, had already been signed into law.
And in a campaign debate in 1976 Jimmy Carter, always a model of
consistency, said he endorsed the *Republican* foreign policy plank!

I more fully understood that most all Americans seem to lust for
meaning in their lives and that meaning for Americans in a political
context was often tied to the promotion and preservation of liberty. I
suggested that such a commitment to liberty—mildly messianic and
nonjingoistic—was more important than the size of the defense budget, the specific resolution of the Strategic Arms Limitation Talks, or
whether we should pursue parallelism with Mao's successor, Chairman Hua. Not for the first time, nor the last, I suggested that for
America idealism is the best realism. William F. Buckley, whom I did
not then know, wrote me a charming note praising the piece.

In 1993 I took another trip to China as part of a Chinese-American
business friendship group led by former congressman and World Bank
President Barber Conable (he had also been a visiting fellow at the
American Enterprise Institute). We went from one luxurious guest
house to another, talking with Chinese businessmen and officials, in a
very different, burgeoning, market-oriented China. My role was to
speak out *against* granting Most Favored Nation trading status to
China, enabling the group to say it had balance. The line I used regularly with our Chinese hosts was that it would be in China's best
interest to move toward political democracy. "Wood bends," I said,
"plastic breaks." Democracies adjust; totalitarian states like China are
fair game for revolution. I still believe that. As an investment I'd take
India over China without a second thought. (It was later pointed out
to me that there were many plastics that bent quite well.)

One of our last stops was Hainan Island, where we were taken to
see a fashion show featuring some of the most statuesque and beautiful women I have ever seen. They were not wearing quilted blue jackets. (Even a small dose of democratic capitalism can do wondrous

things.) For a few days we were joined by Robert MacNamara, secretary of defense during a good part of the Vietnam War. One day I sat next to him on the luxury bus and asked him whether he planned to write a book about Vietnam. He said: "Not until I hear what the experts have to say." Huh? He *was* the expert. But he did write such a book—*In Retrospect: The Tragedy and Lessons of Vietnam*, saying it was the wrong war at the wrong time at the wrong place—thirty years after he promoted it. If he had gone public with these sentiments in the 1970s, might not some lives have been saved?

Helsinki Accords

Notwithstanding the neo-conservatives' criticism of *détente*, they were almost surely wrong about the third basket of the Helsinki Accords agreed to by Gerald Ford, a much underrated president.

Henry Kissinger was at the helm at the State Department. No one describes what happened better than former Soviet dissident Natan Sharansky, whom I interviewed in 2005 on *Think Tank* shortly after the publication of his book, *The Case for Democracy: The Power of Freedom to Overcome Tyranny and Terror* (a book that President George W. Bush carried onto planes, jacket facing outward, clearly designed to push sales).

> BEN WATTENBERG: Many of the hawks, and neo-conservatives, I believe even you, were originally against the Helsinki Accords because it was said that, "Oh, it's just another Soviet promise they won't keep."
>
> NATAN SHARANSKY: In 1975, after years of negotiations, finally thirty-five countries—America, Canada, and all European counties, including the Communist bloc— came to the final Helsinki act agreement, of which there were three parts. First part: The free world accepted the occupation of Soviet Union of Eastern Europe, and the occupation of Baltic republics. They recognized the fact that those nations belong to Soviet Union.

BW: And President Ford was criticized for legitimizing those conquests.

NS: Exactly. The second part was about economic co-operation between East and West, but that also was in the interest of the Soviet Union. And there was the so-called third basket, which was about principles of the respect to human rights; to the right of people to emigrate, to the right of people to freedom of speech, the arrest of the people because of their con-victions, and so on. The fear was that, as in many other cases, the Soviet Union will give it only lip service. We were eleven dissidents who founded the Helsinki Group. We declared that we will start monitoring the fulfillment by the Soviet Union of this third basket. We knew that it meant that we were taking a big risk.

BW: You say in your book that the Soviet officials shrugged off this group as "students and housewives."

NS: Our group started out as a very small group of dissidents in Russia. But the minute we started pub-licly doing it, thousands of Soviet people sent us—or came to us—to tell us their case: that the Soviet Union was clearly violating their human rights. And we helped them to communicate. We sent information to the American Congress, to different human rights or-ganizations, and very quickly we were all arrested. But the issue of human rights, the issue of fulfillment with Soviet Union of this third basket, became a cen-tral issue in international relations.

BW: And you were in prison then for nine years.

NS: Yes. I was threatened that I would be executed. I was interrogated for eighteen months and tried. I wasn't executed because of big pressure from the free world. President Carter personally intervened and said that he checked all the archives of CIA and certified there is no such a spy as Sharansky. Then I was sentenced to thirteen years, and after nine years of imprisonment I was the first political prisoner who was released when Gorbachev came to power. Then there was one day when we forgot about all precautions. When we read in Soviet newspaper *Pravda* the article condemning Reagan for calling Soviet Union the Evil Empire. We knew that here is the day when a Western leader said the truth . . . and now there'll be no more illusions about the nature of Soviet Union. We thought then that the days of Soviet Union were numbered.

BW: You were communicating with your cellmates through the toilet; is that right?

NS: Yes. One of the most dangerous but most effective ways to speak from cell to cell was to talk through toilet. You pump water from your tubes, your neighbor from his tubes, then you put your head deep into the toilet and you speak like by phone. The moment the guard will see that you're in such a strange position you'll be sent to punishment cell.

BW: Is that solitary confinement?

NS: No, solitary confinement means simply that you are alone. But a punishment cell is very small room: two meters by two meters, very dark, very cold, they take away all warm clothes. It's dark and no furniture. Officially it's no more than 15 days. But under different pretenses they make it longer. Altogether I spent 405 days in punishment cells.

BW: Ultimately you were released and allowed to walk across a bridge. They told you to walk straight across, no funny business.

NS: They asked me to go straight and they said, "Agreed?" I said, "Well, for so many years I never agreed with you . . . and on that you want me to agree with you? Of course I don't agree." I went across the bridge zigzagging.

BW: Tell me about some of the other personalities during this great Cold War era that we lived in. Just your own quick view: Kissinger and Nixon.

NS: Well, Kissinger and Nixon believed in the policy of *détente*, which I believe meant appeasement of the Soviet Union; it was a policy that helped the Soviet Union to survive and to continue exploiting its own people and to be a threat to the West.

BW: What about President Carter?

NS: President Carter, even before he became a president, during the presidential campaign, made an issue of human rights. But later we were disappointed with the fact that his words about human rights were very tough but his policy on this issue was not tough.

BW: What about Mikhail Gorbachev?

NS: He was relatively young leader who wanted to *save* the Communist regime. But he was fresh enough to understand and to say publicly that we are losing in our competition with capitalism. The system is not working. In order for it to start working we have to make people a little bit more free.

BW: This was perestroika [restructuring] and glasnost [more open information].

NS: But as a Communist, Gorbachev couldn't understand that there is no such a thing as a little bit of freedom.

BW: It's said that a little bit of freedom is like being a little bit pregnant.

Sharansky also said that he believed that the three most important figures in the global democracy movement were the Soviet academician Andrei Sakharov, President Ronald Reagan, and Senator Scoop Jackson.

I interviewed Sharansky again in 2008 in Israel—when I was invited to be a panelist at the renowned Herzliyah Conference to speak on global demographics. Natan had climbed high in Israel's government, serving as a deputy prime minister at one point. He is as spunky as ever, still zagging when he is expected to zig.

I had no disagreement about the idea that Secretary of State Henry Kissinger was, as Sharansky said, "a great statesman." That was not the case that neo-cons had against Kissinger. He knew the whole world, he knew diplomatic history and how power politics traditionally worked. He was shrewd—and sometimes he lied. He was surely an American patriot. But he had one great failing: He didn't fully understand Americans. Recall when President Reagan was told that certain things could not be done he responded "But we're Americans."[1] He understood what Kissinger did not.

Surveys show that Americans are the most patriotic people in the world, even as they may be trashing their government for corruption, inefficiency, unfairness, and unpopular wars. But many Americans believe, perhaps subconsciously, that they were put on this earth for

---

1. My very wealthy friend Bernard Schwartz tells of a dinner he had with multibillionaire George Soros and Felix Rohatyn, who is also wealthy. The discussion turned to recession, deficits, the debt—standard stuff. Soros and Rohatyn were gloomy; it would all catch up with us. Schwartz said it would work its way out. He later explained to me: "They were born in Europe. I was born in America." Bernard has been a key funder of *Think Tank*.

a purpose. Their political ancestors, after all, were the modern ini-
tiators of mass democracy, and they don't usually have a problem if
we try to promote the idea to others, even though they can be very
impatient.

I think Kissinger (and President Carter, too) thought that after
the traumatic defeat in Vietnam, Americans would be unsure of
themselves for a long time to come. That was the root of *détente*:
At the least, they believed we were temporarily weak and perhaps the
tides of history were finally beginning to run against us—so let's cut
the best deal we can. And when Jeane Kirkpatrick returned to the
American Enterprise Institute after her heroic term as UN ambassador, she told a small group of her colleagues that she feared that history had turned and the bad guys were in ascendancy. But as Reagan
showed, that's not how Americans react to national misfortune.
Americans will still look any man or nation in the eye and tell them,
"America is number one."

Carter

When Jimmy Carter was elected president in 1976 most CDMers,
liberty purveyors all, were pleased—for a very short time. We had
been pitched by some of his leading foreign policy players, including
trade attorney Sandy Berger, who subsequently blatantly stole classified documents. We officially supported Carter, and we expected
that some of our players would have a role in the policy-making
community. I had served for three days and many nights, along with
Pat Moynihan, as a Jackson delegate to the Democratic drafting subcommittee, coming up with some of the language that ultimately appeared in the Carter platform. Stuart Eizenstat was chairman of the
Carter delegation. The chairman of the subcommittee was Michael
Dukakis, the young governor from Massachusetts.

There was a foreign affairs forum four days after Carter's election. I pointed out that one wing of the Democratic Party had been
zeroed out on appointments and I said:

> It is no secret that there are at least two distinct and main-
> stream points of view about foreign policy within the

Democratic Party. The wrong way to describe these points of view is hard and soft, hawk and dove, pro-détente and anti-détente—all catch-phrases that by no means capture the subtleties of the arguments. But two sides do exist and that is healthy.

But the foreign policy appointments of the Carter administration do not reflect that blend. The mix consists mostly of neutral technicians and those who represent only one side of the (so-called) hard-versus-soft argument. . . . I cannot think of a single State Department appointee whom I do not consider able or competent. My problem is not the appointees but the missing persons. Accordingly, like-minded Democrats have been huddling to determine a course of action. Our options are many. We can look to the Hill, or go public, or go private. All these thoughts are under active consideration.

I then closed, saying, roughly, "It is normal to give a new president a hundred days' grace period, but President Carter deserves only a hundred hours."

As recounted in Jay Winik's *On the Brink,* which occasionally went over the edge on those he regards as the good guys, he writes of me that I was a man "of boundless energy. . . . He never walked into a room, he swept into it, immediately capturing the attention of everyone in it. . . . [He was] a darling of the Washington press corps. . . . He rarely fought personally . . . but when he fought, and fought hard. . . ." Jay writes so well.

But as Moynihan later pointed out, all that CDM got in the appointed foreign policy realm was the glorious post of ambassador to Micronesia, which went to one of our key members, Peter Rosenblatt. Moynihan bellowed: "We didn't even get *Macro*nesia!" (Peter asked Scoop Jackson if he should take the position; Jackson said yes. Peter solved a difficult diplomatic problem that had been festering for years.)

I believe Pat's was a sound analysis. The appointment of a largely center-dovish foreign team played a major role in Carter's defeat in his bid for reelection four years later. The disaffection with Carter grew. The neo-cons were concentrating on the Cold War. We were interested in extending human liberty. But Carter gave a famous speech in which he denounced America's "inordinate fear of Communism." That outraged us. Carter later said the remark was taken out of context: the standard rollback.

In May 2006, at a meeting of *The American Prospect* magazine, I asked Brzezinski whether he had been involved in that language and if so, whether he still accepted it. He said he was and he did. His fear, he said, concerned the power wielded years before by the demagogic Senator Joseph McCarthy, who had claimed that the State Department was infested with Soviet agents. Fair enough. But ironically, that situation was verified in some large measure far beyond the belief of all but Commie-hunting conservatives. The instrument of such revelations was the release of the Venona papers, which cited chapter and verse on Soviet penetration.

The last straw was a meeting attended by about a dozen key CDM members, President Carter, and Vice President Mondale in the late 1970s, after the Soviet invasion of Afghanistan. Held at the White House, the meeting had been arranged by CDM member Max Kampelman, a Minnesotan, a former administrative assistant to Hubert Humphrey, and a good friend of Mondale's, also a Minnesotan.

Carter didn't even understand who we were. His briefing memo had said that we were interested in human rights. Carter went on about a difficult human rights situation in Ecuador. (Ecuador!) Perhaps we could help there. Perhaps we could. But we were interested in human rights not only for idealistic reasons but because it was an issue with which to hammer our superpower adversary, the Soviet Union. (The picture in this book shows the meeting in the cabinet room. As I divine and recall, the expressions on the faces of Jeane Kirkpatrick, Midge Decter, Max Kampelman, Norman Podhoretz, and me reflect not anger but incredulity.) After about half an hour Carter left the meeting and Mondale remained for about an hour. Unlike his boss, Mondale understood exactly who we were and what we were up to. Mortified, he gave us a full-bodied and quite hawkish briefing, just what we had hoped to hear from his boss. But he wasn't the boss. I had voted for Carter in 1976. He lost my 1980 vote at that meeting. I chatted with Mondale at a New Year's Eve party on December 31, 2005, and he vividly remembered the meeting's surreal quality.

Carter did appoint me to his Board of Ambassadorial Selection, a group of about twenty distinguished Americans who would see to it that cronies of the president were not given plum ambassadorial selections merely because they had contributed money to his campaign, as had been the custom—and still is. The first chairman was former governor Ruben Askew of Florida. The board's job was to come up with four qualified candidates. Then Carter and the secretary of state would make the final appointments. The board met with Carter at the White House before its first meeting. He explained how diverse his appointments to the board had been: men and women of both parties, blacks, whites, Hispanics, and so on. I asked whether the diversity would extend to ideology as well. He said it would.

At the meetings I did my share of putting in my names. One was Jeane Kirkpatrick, fluent in French and Spanish, an articulate scholar with strong foreign policy views, and a staunch supporter of Israel. I recommended her for ambassador to France, several Latin American countries, and Israel. Nothing came of it.

The board would take a break every hour or so. During one of them former Secretary of State Dean Rusk and I chatted. Rusk had served the full eight years in the Kennedy-Johnson administration. Bill Moyers's name came up. Rusk, an apparently bland man, trashed Moyers as unmercifully as I have ever heard one man in public life talk of another. I will not repeat what he said because I have no written notes. But if Moyers's forthcoming book on LBJ is critical of Rusk—which I imagine it will be—rest assured that the feeling was reciprocated. In all, we neo-cons thought Carter's foreign policy pronouncements were back-assward: criticizing your allies publicly and your adversaries privately.

The Radios

The neo-cons believed that the war of ideas was at least as important as the defense budget in winning the Cold War. I had another chance to play a role in this contest when Ronald Reagan was elected in 1980. I got a call one day from Richard Allen, Reagan's freshly appointed director of the National Security Council. He asked if I would like to serve on the board of directors of Radio Liberty and Radio Free Europe, as well as on the board of directors of the Board of International Broadcasting (BIB), which was responsible for oversight of the other two.[2]

By federal statute, both boards had executive staff offices in Washington. The operational broadcasting headquarters was in Munich (it is now in Prague). There were nine members of the boards confirmable by the Senate, of whom no more than five could be from any one party. This meant a board made up of five Republicans and four Democrats. I was asked to serve as a Democrat. So was Michael Novak who, although he had worked for the McGovern campaign in 1972, was a solid neo-con. We both accepted the offers. I discovered that even in this hothouse of freedom the split within the Democratic Party between the neo-cons and the liberals flourished.

I filled out the lengthy paperwork required for confirmation. The forms included a request for a list of all honoraria received in the past eighteen months. I listed them. Several months later I still had no word about my appointment. Then I got a call from a man at the Office of Personnel Management, which handled White House appointments. He said, "Mr. Wattenberg, do you realize that if you are appointed and confirmed to this job you will have give up your work lobbying for foreign governments?" *What?* "Your list of honoraria includes $100 from the Canadian Broadcasting Corporation, which is a government entity." It turns out I had done a brief skybox interview for the Canadian network during the 1980 Democratic convention; because it is government-owned, it pays those who appear. The matter was cleared up. Message: Skepticism of government bureaucracy is often well-founded, even when it is representing Ronald Reagan.

---

2. At the time, Radio Liberty broadcast to the various ethnic republics of the Soviet Union in their native languages. Radio Free Europe broadcast to the Soviet satellite nations. There was 24/7 service in Russian. Some of the smaller republics got as little as half an hour of programming per day.

When I finally went to the Senate for confirmation, only one senator, Republican Larry Pressler of South Dakota, appeared for my hearings. He started asking staff-prepared questions of this sort: Mr. Wattenberg, what do you think of the role of the BIB? Mr. Wattenberg, what do you think of how the BIB deals with thus-and-such? Then he turned to a staff aide and said, "What is the BIB, anyway?"

THE NEWLY APPOINTED chairman of the Board of International Broadcasting, Radio Free Europe, and Radio Liberty was Frank Shakespeare. He was as dynamic, loyal, conservative, and anti-Communist as any man I've ever met. No neo-con he, not even close. He accepted the position with the condition that he be given the authority to recommend the other nominees for the boards, which he did with bold strokes. It was regarded as the best board in Washington. Among its members were novelist James Michener (quite liberal and very anti-Communist); Ed Ney, chairman of Young & Rubicam, the largest advertising agency in the world (or close to it); and, most intriguing of all, Lane Kirkland, the president of the AFL-CIO, an institution that was no friend of Ronald Reagan's. We ended up with an almost all-hawk board. (A not uncommon practice on Washington boards: The members of the minority party, when chosen by the majority party, are often those who hold views close to those of the majority party.)

Frank asked me to go with him to meet Kirkland when he asked him to serve on the boards. The head of the AFL-CIO does not go out of his way to do favors for an anti-union Republican president. But Lane was as fierce an anti-Communist as Frank or Reagan. It was like pushing on an unlocked door. Kirkland said to us, "The only Reagan appointment I would accept is with the radios."

That the board was so high-powered played a role in its ability to get money from Congress—at least early in Reagan's term. The Democratic majority in Congress paid some extra attention when Lane Kirkland and James Michener stood behind our budget requests. Moreover, its principal competitor for government money within the bizarre federal budget accounting system was the Voice of America, with which it shared a line item, creating a zero-sum game. This was tricky because at the time the head of Voice of America was Charles Wick, a close personal friend of Reagan's.

Unlike the Voice of America, which broadcast principally American and global news, the radios served as surrogate broadcasters, offering listeners what they would learn if they did not live in circumstances where censors exercised tight control.

Despite sophisticated jamming by the Soviets, Radio Free Europe and Radio Liberty offered a full-bodied menu of programming featuring local news as well as some history, culture, and political opinions (which were labeled as such) and broadcast in about twenty languages. Some liberal, too-pure journalists from free countries maintained that the Radios were propagandistic. It's a pretty good rule of thumb that the free media all over the world tilts left, especially when they are on a public payroll. The BBC offers a great radio service with a clear left-wing slant. In America, NPR was almost as bad, but getting fairer. (RFE/RL were the exception that proves the rule.)

Brit and Aussie radio journalists were heavily represented on the Radios' payroll in Munich and were often in the lead in criticizing them publicly for being too hard-line. I didn't buy the criticism. Every hour of broadcasting on Radio Free Europe and Radio Liberty began with a ten-minute rundown of the news of the day, well prepared by Tom Bodeen, a top-drawer American broadcast journalist. The balance of the programming was idiosyncratic and of interest to the listeners, who were drenched in real propaganda and starved for credibility.

After a while Shakespeare appointed me vice chairman of Radio Free Europe, Radio Liberty, and the Board of International Broadcasting. Frank and I would go up to the Hill to testify to various congressional committees and subcommittees to explain what a splendid job the Radios were doing and why we deserved still more funding. We needed another programmer for Kyrgyzstan, for example, even though unbelievable German labor laws might draw out that process for a couple of years. Yet everyone associated with the Radios acknowledged that somewhere between one-third and half of the professional staff were "deadwood," sucking a teat for a lifetime. But the time and costs of trying to fire someone in Germany usually made it a fool's game to even attempt it. On the plus side, the Radios had quite sophisticated audience survey research. It was based on respondents from the USSR vacationing in satellite states. The polling was run by Gene Parta, a bright American.

Soviet citizens could not generally travel outside Iron Curtain countries but, as rewards for good work or as political patronage, they could visit, say, the beaches in Bulgaria. While there, an interviewer from the Radios might engage the Soviet visitor in a casual conversation about what he knew about the world and where he had learned it. Survey researchers also queried respondents in the Soviet satellites about what sort of government they would prefer if the Soviets were to leave them alone.

The Radios in Munich also had superb research facilities, which not only provided source material for programs, but were a repository of information for scholars and journalists everywhere. Where does source material come from in totalitarian societies? Free or unfree, there is information that must be published. For example, journals, magazines, and articles provided information about agriculture, oil, transportation, steel, as well as personnel changes. Much of the information was kept on handwritten index cards at Radio Liberty's headquarters in Munich. But when a new commissar was appointed, the Radios had his full biography, as well as that of the man he replaced—who may have died or been imprisoned. From such material came the grist for program items. Journalists who were publicly critical of the Radios relied heavily on our research.

When reports came in following the end of the Cold War, it turned out that what the Radios' research provided was just about right on the money. Those "votes" for what sort of political system would be preferred in free elections were uncanny in their accuracy. After the Cold War ended we heard reports from many Russian and Eastern European listeners that could only be described as ecstatic. Lech Walesa, the brusque chief of Poland's Solidarity union, said the Radios had been "the sun and the stars" to him during the Cold War years. Václav Havel, a much nicer man, was equally demonstrative. So was Andrei Sakharov. Later, Russian émigré cabdrivers in New York City would invariably light up when I told them that I had worked for Radio Svoboda. I used to say to Frank, "All those lies we told on the Hill were true!"

The political split at the Radios were embodied by two great Russians: Scientist-activist Andrei Sakharov and the angry man of letters, Aleksandr Solzhenitsyn. Sakharov was seen as the Western-style democrat who married a Jewish woman, Yelena Bonner, a well-known dissident in her own right. Solzhenitsyn, author of the path-breaking *Gulag Archipelago,* was often denounced as a right-winger with anti-Semitic and autocratic tendencies. His supporters saw him as a Russian nationalist hero who harked back to a brief moment of democracy in pre-Bolshevik Russia.

The Russian émigrés who put on the programs from the Radios' home base in Munich were bitterly split about both Solzhenitsyn and Sakharov. How much of Solzhenitsyn's material should go on the air of an American-funded radio station? What kind of material? Wittingly or unwittingly, might we be putting anti-Semitic or antidemocratic material on the air? Would Sakharov's view not be tough enough or devoid of patriotic feeling?

When the board met annually in Munich, radio staff members would call us at our hotel and meet with board members after work. They came telling horror stories about who was broadcasting what, and how so-and-so was really a Communist agent or an undercover fascist. The Soviet agents killed a Bulgarian broadcaster working for the Radios in London: They played for keeps and had no congressional critics badgering them.

A Senate subcommittee, chaired by liberal senator Claiborne Pell (sometimes called "Stillborn" by his foes) oversaw the board and the Radios. Pell's chief staff man was Peter Galbraith, who later served ably as ambassador to Croatia at a critical moment. The liberal congressional watchdogs were concerned about Shakespeare. At his confirmation hearings Pell shook his finger at Shakespeare and said, "I'm going to keep an eye on you." The watchdogs wondered: Was this new board—mostly made up of conservatives and neo-conservatives—too anti-Communist, too authoritarian, too hawkish, too soft on anti-Semitism? Against *détente?*

Me, insufficiently attuned to anti-Semitism? *Me,* antidemocratic? With Frank, I testified before Pell's subcommittee. I had been asked by Shakespeare to review some of the questionable transcripts of the various broadcasts by and about Solzhenitsyn. I saw nothing in them that was either anti-Semitic or antidemocratic and so testified. Aha! said the anti-Solzhenitsynites, the transcripts were no good, the buried messages of autocracy were to be found between the lines, and the anti-Semitic stuff came through in the "tonality" of the broadcaster's voice. The State Department periodically got into the act, nervous that the Radios would start making their own hawkish foreign policy, although our authorizing legislation had some restraining language.

When I testified, I told the subcommittee a story my mother had told me many times. During the Kishinev pogroms in Russia in the early twentieth century, her father, a Hebrew writer, poet, and publisher, journeyed from his home in Odessa to Kishinev to survey the damage. He returned to Odessa with a gruesome souvenir—a brick covered with the brains of a slaughtered Jew. This brick remained on my grandfather's desk until the end of his life, a reminder of the intensity of European anti-Semitism. In the end, the stations broadcast both Solzhenitsyn and Sakharov.

The Board of International Broadcasting had a meeting one day with the professional staff at which Walter Roberts, the director, suggested that because Solzhenitsyn and some other historical material we broadcast was getting us in trouble, we should just drop historical programming altogether. I happened to be watching James Michener. His face fell. Here was a man who had done as much as any person at the time to explain history, through intergenerational historical fiction read by tens of millions of people around the world, being told by a minor bureaucrat that history wasn't so important after all. The change was not made.

Dimitri Simes, who now runs the Nixon Center in Washington, D.C., had recently emigrated from Russia and aligned himself with the anti-Solzhenitsyn board members. He came to my office one day and told me I had better behave properly or he would see to it that I paid a price for it. I not very politely asked him to leave my office and told him he still had a lot to learn about how American democracy worked.

In the mid-eighties Shakespeare left his post at the Radios and hand-picked his successor, Malcolm "Steve" Forbes Jr. Steve not only worked at his new job diligently but had a softer touch than Frank. Moreover, on occasion he flew the board over to the annual

Munich meeting in his private 727. Rank has its privileges—so does wealth.

Steve is a very decent and knowledgeable man, albeit with a quirkiness about him. *Forbes* magazine was one of the most interesting publications in America. On those long flights Steve taught me some economics, most of which seemed to make sense. I am certainly for tax simplification, flat or otherwise.

I ultimately resigned from the Radios when, in the early 1990s, I was asked to serve on two separate commissions investigating the wisdom of setting up a Radio Free Asia for unfree nations in that corner of the world. The idea was to replicate the model of the radios, featuring local news in the native languages of the target nations: Cambodia, Burma, Laos, North Korea, and of course, mainland China. It was a controversial notion.

One of the invitations to participate came from the first President Bush. The second came from then–Speaker of the House Tom Foley, a good friend from the Scoop Jackson campaigns, who needed to fill a designated Democratic slot. (Like the Soviets before them, the Chinese still try to jam the broadcasts, but it's getting tougher: Chinese listeners use their cell phones to participate in call-in programs!)

Both commissions were chaired by John Hughes.[3] An important behind-the-scenes player was Senator Joseph Biden. Both Hughes and Biden vigorously supported Radio Free Asia. But the vote was close: just 5 to 4 in favor. Those opposed, including many China experts, felt it would be regarded as a hostile act by the Chinese (*détentists* once again)!

On the second commission it was pretty apparent that the votes of eight of the members would cause a 4-to-4 tie. The ninth vote was that of Mike Cuthbert, a young radio executive from Kansas appointed to a

---

3. I often wonder: How does America get such highly qualified persons to do what is essentially volunteer work? Consider: Hughes is a Welshman, was schooled in England, came to America in his midtwenties, and was naturalized a decade later. He is a Pulitzer Prize–winning journalist and former editor of *The Christian Science Monitor*, for which he wrote a nationally syndicated column and for a time served as its Africa and Far East correspondent. He was an assistant secretary of state and an assistant secretary general of the United Nations. He was director of the Voice of America. And he is as soft-spoken, fair, likable and decent a man as you will meet, who worked as diligently as if he were making a fortune from public service.

Republican slot on the commission by Kansas senator Bob Dole. All during the hearings Cuthbert was quiet. At the final meeting we held our breath. Cuthbert voted in favor. I have been told that the positive 5-to-4 vote, and the majority report that went with it, played an important role in gaining congressional approval. Those radios will play an ever-growing role in bringing democratic views and values to a part of the world that needs them. As this happens, it should help bring stability and prosperity to a dangerous place.

Recently there have been Radio Free Asia broadcasts to China twenty-four hours per day: twelve in Mandarin, eight in Tibetan (in three dialects—Uke, Kham, and Amdo), two in Uygur, and two in Cantonese, broadcast principally to Shanghai, much of which are in Wu, a Cantonese dialect. The Chinese try to jam the signal, working particularly hard to block the Tibetan and Uygur broadcasts. But that's harder to do than it once was. High-tech has expanded the web of communications, and as it does, the democratic revolution expands globally.

Waging Democracy

The war of ideas, under whatever name, was very much a part of the ongoing Cold War. In 1967 it was revealed that the United States government had not just been sitting back and letting the Soviets do all the ideology purveying. The Central Intelligence Agency was providing covert aid to a variety of nations and organizations.[4] Front-page newspaper stories and the evening news programs trumpeted the story.

What sort of aid? Principally money. To do what? To help democratically inclined political parties (Right and Left), to assist democratically oriented newspapers and magazines (Right and Left)— sometimes with communications equipment as trivial as mimeograph machines—to fund delegations (Right and Left) to go to international

---

4. Contrary to popular belief, the CIA was a mildly liberal sort of place. With some exceptions, it was staffed mostly by Ivy Leaguers, many of whom were moderate Democrats, but hawkish (not a bad description of a neo-con). The agency gets dumped on regularly. But spying can be dangerous work, and since its inception many CIA staffers have been killed.

meetings with intellectuals (of the Right and Left). Most all of the recipients of the CIA aid were unwitting, although a very few were "witting" (great word).

There was a media firestorm concerning covertness. Questions were asked in the councils of government: Why did the CIA have to do things secretly? Weren't we proud of who we were and what we stood for? And so slowly (as is characteristic of democratic bureaucracies) things began to happen overtly. But by and large what happened overtly was right in the neo-con game plan: up-front freedom fighting. Among the key players were Democratic congressmen Dante Fascell of Florida and Donald Fraser of Minnesota; activist George Agree; Senator William Brock of Tennessee, a former Republican National Committee chairman; and Charles Manatt, then serving as Democratic National Committee chairman.

I received a call from Brock to be the go-to guy to help organize what would eventually become the National Endowment for Democracy (NED). Up to my ears in books and projects at the time, I turned down Brock's request but did serve as one of two vice chairmen of the Democracy Program, the study that ultimately led to creation of the NED. (Tony Lake, later Clinton's national security advisor, was the other one.)

The first big meeting that I recall was one that I arranged at the main conference room at the American Enterprise Institute. The original idea was that congressional monies would go to the national Democratic and Republican parties, to business (through the U.S. Chamber of Commerce), and to labor (through the AFL-CIO). In each case separate institutes were established to insulate them from internal pressure from their parent organization.

I said that these were all worthy institutions but they were organizational "whales." I asked, what about the "minnows"? Why shouldn't the nascent NED have the ability to give grants directly to groups that were not affiliated with the big boys? After much discussion the idea of independent grants became part of the NED package. Today, grants to minnows, mostly private organizations, now amount to 44 percent of the total NED budget, or $45 million.

In 1982 President Reagan spoke at Westminster Palace and said he favored a plan whereby America would "foster the infrastructure of democracy—the system of a free press, unions, political parties, universities—which allows a people to choose their own way, to develop their own culture, to reconcile their own differences through peaceful measures."

In 1983 the National Endowment for Democracy was established. As president, the board chose Carl Gershman, previously the senior counselor to the U.S. representative to the United Nations serving under Jeane Kirkpatrick. Gershman still serves more than twenty years later. No surprise: he was a former chairman of the Yipsels, the omnipresent sort-of socialists and always prodemocracy activists. They have always been right up there with all the big players. Penn Kemble used to quote political scientist James Q. Wilson's remark that in our time "most great debates have begun as factional debates within the Socialist Party."

There was extended congressional wrangling over appropriations and mission. But waging democracy caught on. By late 2003 the Congress (the Senate, unanimously, the House, 391 to 1) commended NED "for its major contributions to the strengthening of democracy around the world on the occasion of the twentieth anniversary of its establishment." America is now into democracy-building in a big way. A number of other nations are doing similar work, including many European nations, Japan, and Taiwan. Ironically, the first was Germany, with a party-based *Stiftung*, probably as penance for its damnable record under Hitler's Nazism.

Funding for NED has grown to a core budget of about $60 million, plus special funding of about $20 million for special countries such as China and the Muslim nations, and about $60 million for Iraq. In addition, much money comes from the Agency for International Development and other federal agencies, including now the Millennium Challenge Corporation to aid Africa (with the money conditioned on a nation being free, which is a new development). At one point President George W. Bush proposed doubling the funding.

In fact, President George W. Bush has been a particular fan of the endowment. At its twentieth anniversary he paid tribute to its staff, directors, and global program: "By spending for and standing for freedom, you've lifted the hopes of people around the world and you've brought great credit to America."

NED is a small organization, but it has been at the center of much of the turbulent global explosion of democracy. And *explosion* is the right word. Freedom House (founded after World War II with the help of liberal high priestess Eleanor Roosevelt) is a tell-it-straight organization that assesses the status of democracy, civil liberties, and other indices of human freedom around the world. In 1975 it ranked forty nations, representing 25 *percent* of the world's population, as fully *free* nations. At that time, sixty-five nations, with 41 *percent* of the global population, were ranked *unfree*. (The balance were scored partly free.) Thirty years later, at the end of 2005, the numbers had just about reversed: eighty-nine nations, with 46 *percent* of the world's population, were free (almost a doubling), while forty-five nations, representing 24 *percent* of the population, were "unfree" (the lowest number in more than a decade), almost a halving. Moreover, the rate of countries moving from unfree to free or partly free was accelerating.

The great majority of unfree people live in mainland China, with its estimated population of 1.3 billion. That is one reason that observers who speculate about the future, like me, find China the greatest potential threat to global peace on the horizon.

Although the Muslim countries lag the rest of the world, from 2000 to 2005 there were major gains—and some backsliding. Some came in Muslim countries outside of the Middle East. Indonesia, for example, went from partly free to free. Few Middle Eastern nations are wholly free, but there have been important advances into the partly free ranks. Women's suffrage has been introduced in Kuwait; some uncensored media has surfaced in Saudi Arabia. Dubai has moved forward, albeit in its own way. Perhaps the clearest victory occurred when Libya moved away from its nuclear development program and gained full diplomatic recognition from the United States. Supporters of the second Iraq war—particularly many neo-cons—have linked the mild growth in Middle Eastern democracies to American involvement in Iraq. When people or nations feel they are not alone, they can behave in a bolder fashion. The unresolved mystery is what happens if free Middle Eastern nations *vote* to limit their own freedom. That complicated scenario actually happened in Algeria in 1991, leading to a brutal, ongoing civil war. Today Algeria is ranked unfree by Freedom House.

The satellite television station *Al Jazeera* has appropriately been seen to be anti-American and sympathetic to jihadist terrorist activity. But when *nine million* Iraqis voted, the pictures of *women* proudly waving their marked purple fingers (indicating participation at the ballot box), *Al Jazeera* aired it. These broadcasts engendered remarkable reactions in the generally repressive Middle East. People there thought: *If they can do it, why can't we?*

The other area that showed major progress in the 2005 assessment was among some former republics of the Soviet Union. In Ukraine, population 47 million, the Rose Revolution moved the nation quickly into a fully free ranking, although economic development has been sluggish. Other former Soviet republics or Soviet satellites also moved forward, including Kyrgyzstan, Georgia, Latvia, and Lithuania. As we have seen in many nations, the advent of greater liberty does not yield to automatic economic progress. On the other hand, with the exception of some oil-producing nations, there are no unfree rich countries.

Freedom House calls them straight: The Philippines was recently downgraded from free to partly free. In all, it tallied twenty-seven nations and one territory advancing and nine retrogressing in 2005. The notion that encouraging democracy—with all its complexities—is a pastime for intellectuals writing papers at think tanks is incorrect. I have been on the Freedom House board and over the years served with Mitch Daniels, former director of the Office of Management and Budget and more recently governor of Indiana *and* Donald Rumsfeld, notwithstanding his reputation as a strictly military man. They and others like them served because the extension of democracy yields the likelihood of greater peace in the world.

The NED does not *initiate* grants; it *responds* to requests from democratic groups abroad. Nevertheless, the NED's grants range far and wide. The Democratic and Republican parties helped Iraqis prepare for their election and made sure it included the participation by women. The Chamber of Commerce Institute supported fifteen grantees in Iraq; they encourage entrepreneurialism and train political parties in economic policy making. In Cambodia a NED grantee is playing a critical role in bringing the murderous Khmer Rouge leadership to justice. A NED grantee in Sudan is working on environmental issues that include mediating disputes over grazing rights among competing tribal leaders. In Egypt a NED grantee is training lawyers who will investigate the use of torture. Some projects do fail, often due to ongoing terrorism.

The key issue of democratic development these days concerns the Muslim world. It is said that these nations will never go democratic, and consequently they remain largely violent and hospitable to terrorists. Perhaps so, but the same was said of South Korea because it lacked a democratic heritage. Today it is a vibrant democracy and increasingly prosperous. El Salvador was the hardiest of the Central American tyrannies, sustained by twenty years of brutal civil war. Today it is essentially democratic. The attempt to foster democracy in the Muslim Middle East is vital. It may mean that there will be no repeat of 9/11.

All this yields some history that may have relevance to this tale of firsthand neo-conservatism. Certain names, certain organizations, and certain ideas stand out in ways that might not have been previously apparent. The Social Democrats USA were an offshoot of the U.S. Socialist Party, which saw its greatest days in the early part of the twentieth century. In 1908, Eugene Debs, the Socialist candidate for president, received 6 percent of the national vote. But socialism as a U.S. electoral force never went any further; there have been many millions of words written to explain why America and socialism never did mix. Every major European democracy has had an active, and powerful, Socialist Party, sometimes called the Social Democrats.

The Young People's Socialist League—the Yipsels—were the youth arm of the Socialist Party in America. But do not be fooled by the word *socialist*. These Yipsels were (then) principally pro-union; their hero was George Meany, then president of the AFL-CIO. Meany was in the tradition of 1890s labor leader Samuel Gompers who, when asked, "What does labor want?" answered "More." Not a society based on "from each according to his ability; to each according to his needs," the Marxist formula. The trade unions, with some exceptions, have been deeply involved in democracy promotion, They believe in democracy. They have been hassled from the Right, including by neo-cons, whose case is that unions restrain market forces. Their best counterargument is that a unionized company may pay higher wages, but unions provide a guaranteed force of workers (except for the occasional wildcat strike). For the record, whatever the role of unions was, it is less now. The percentage of American workers covered by unions has declined from 23.3 percent in 1983 to 12.5 percent in 2005.

Not so earlier. In the postwar years America dominated international manufacturing, creating good union jobs. As such work has migrated to poor, less-developed nations, that has changed. Today most unions are against free trade (some observers chalk it up to clear self-interest) and have taken much of the Democratic Party with them. This was clear in the congressional fight for CAFTA, the Central American Free Trade Agreement, which was barely passed into law in 2004.

In some ways the Yipsels have been victims of their own success. Many of their young and now graying bright young men of earlier decades hold, or have held, important government positions. Some have taken the neo-conservative track—others are liberals or conservatives. Perhaps what changed the Yipsels most was the nature of their opposition. Starting in the sixties, the Yipsels had new young people to contend with. On campuses around the country chapters of Students for a Democratic Society (SDS) organized and denounced the old Socialists. At its peak the SDS probably had one hundred thousand activists in its ranks. But it captured the attention of mainstream media during the Vietnam War.

The SDS manifesto was issued in 1962 as "The Port Huron Statement." The public figure associated with it and SDS was Tom Hayden (later married to Jane Fonda, herself a Far Left symbol). Of course, SDS trashed the Vietnam War. Even most of the Yipsels did that. SDS was not in itself pro-Communist, but it repudiated any activists who were anti-Communist. It favored participatory democracy, calling for direct New England–style town meetings and decision making by college students, not voters. SDS belittled elected legislatures, maintaining that representative democracy doesn't work. SDS activists became front-page news; they were pro-Maoist; their anti-Vietnam chant was "Hey, hey, ho, ho, LBJ has got to go! Hey, hey, ho ho, Ho Chi Minh is gonna win."

I interviewed Kemble (a former Yipsel president) shortly before his death. He drew some further distinctions between the SDS types with all the headlines and the Yipsel types who never achieved that notoriety. Kemble noted that the Yipsels insisted that democracy and elections are inherent to socialism. The Yipsels would not allow SDS-types who actively sought Communist victory to participate in their councils. The Social Democrats, Kemble maintained, could prevail in truly free and fair elections. In that sense, Kemble said the new democracy movement was defined by its adversaries. Democracy was the answer to the antidemocrats. It was yet another example of a response to the runaway liberalism that sparked neo-conservatism.

In one of his books, Senator Daniel Patrick Moynihan describes searching for an answer to deal with the Communist threat and "stumbling" into some of the Yipsel thinking. So powerful is the idea of the promotion of democracy that President George W. Bush has listed it as one central factor in the second Iraq war. The number of Yipsel players has been small but they were part of the alleged cabal that convinced the key players in the Bush administration that the Iraq mission was worth the risk. And the democracy movement grows, two steps forward and one step back, but clearly moving forward.

President George W. Bush's second inaugural address on January 20, 2005, was a remarkable document. Except for one paragraph that dealt with Bush's domestic plan for an "ownership society," the entire speech dealt with the issue of democracy-building. It is the kind of speech that would be almost impossible to deliver unless the speaker, even a practicing politician, endorsed it heart and soul. Bush had come to believe in what had previously been the hallmark of the neo-conservative case. If you have been asking yourself, "What on earth are we doing in Iraq?" I urge you to go online to the

White House Web site and read the speech in its entirety.[5] I excerpt it here at some length because he says it better than I could.

> There is only one force of history that can break the reign of hatred and resentment, and expose the pretensions of tyrants, and reward the hopes of the decent and tolerant, and that is the force of human freedom. The best hope for peace in our world is the expansion of freedom in all the world.
>
> So it is the policy of the United States to seek and support the growth of democratic movements and institutions in every nation and culture, with the ultimate goal of ending tyranny in our world.
>
> This is not primarily the task of arms. . . . Freedom, by its nature, must be chosen [by citizens of unfree states]. . . . The great objective of ending tyranny is the concentrated work of generations. The difficulty of the task is no excuse for avoiding it. America's influence is not unlimited, but fortunately for the oppressed, America's influence is considerable. . . .
>
> My most solemn duty is to protect this nation and its people against further attacks and emerging threats. Some have unwisely chosen to test America's resolve, and have found it firm. . . .
>
> America will not pretend that jailed dissidents prefer their chains, or that women welcome humiliation and servitude, or that any human being aspires to live at the mercy of bullies.
>
> We will encourage reform in other governments by making clear that success in our relations will require the decent treatment of their own people. . . . [*Author's note:*

5. Bush's second inaugural address can be found at: www.whitehouse.gov/news/releases/2005/01/20050120-1.html.

overstated.] In the long run, there is no justice without freedom, and there can be no human rights without human liberty.

Some, I know, have questioned the global appeal of liberty—though this time in history, four decades defined by the swiftest advance of freedom ever seen, is an odd time for doubt. . . . Today, America speaks anew to the peoples of the world:

All who live in tyranny and hopelessness can know [that] the United States will not ignore your oppression, or excuse your oppressors . . . Democratic reformers facing repression, prison, or exile can know: America sees you for who you are: the future leaders of your free country. . . .

I ask our youngest citizens to believe the evidence of your eyes. You have seen duty and allegiance in the determined faces of our soldiers. You have seen that life is fragile, and evil is real, and courage triumphs. America has need of idealism and courage, because we have essential work at home—the unfinished work of American freedom. In a world moving toward liberty, we are determined to show the meaning and promise of liberty. . . .

From the viewpoint of centuries, the questions that come to us are narrowed and few. Did our generation advance the cause of freedom? . . .

We go forward with complete confidence in the eventual triumph of freedom. Not because history runs on the wheels of inevitability; it is human choices that move events. Not because we consider ourselves a chosen nation; God moves and chooses as He wills. We have confidence because freedom is the permanent hope of mankind, the hunger in dark places, the longing of the soul. . . . When our Founders declared a new order of the ages; . . . when citizens marched in peaceful outrage under the banner "Freedom Now"—they were acting on an ancient hope that is meant to be fulfilled.

> When the Declaration of Independence was first read in
> public and the Liberty Bell was sounded in celebration, a
> witness said, "It rang as if it meant something." In our
> time it means something still. We are ready for the great-
> est achievements in the history of freedom. . . .

With all the hoopla that has surrounded President Bush's handling of the war, I don't see that his vision has changed. Whatever
the label Bush and his team claim as their own, this speech represents
the essence of what neo-conservatism stands for. There is something
grand about the American presidency in my view. The men who
occupy the office—regardless of past policies of prejudices—move far
above the hurly-burly of partisanship and are single-mindedly dedicated to the best interests of America as they see them. They are not
perfect—this nobility is more apparent in a second term than in a
first term.

The USSR

I made two trips to the Soviet Union at the invitation of what was
then called the United States Information Agency.[6] My first trip was
in 1975. The Soviets were interested in me because of my Scoop
Jackson connection. The public affairs officer in Finland had business in Leningrad (now St. Petersburg). I asked if we could drive in
from Finland. He agreed. The Finnish countryside was lush and
green. Then we crossed the border checkpoint and had our papers
checked. Suddenly the landscape turned brown and dreary. It was
as if the political border seen on a map was real as we passed into
the poverty of Communism.

------

6. I made many of these trips. I found it was just about the best way to travel for a fidgety fellow like me, who gets antsy sitting on a beach during a vacation. The State Department Public Affairs Office would arrange for me to talk about America to elite groups. It set up small meetings
with journalists, provided transportation, and handled the bothersome details of foreign travel.
There was even a small fee. I typically had some unusual requests of my sponsors: I asked to see the
host country's leading demographer and to be driven through the worst slums. Ask me about
Howrah across the river from Calcutta, or the Tondo in Manila. The downside was that the United
States Information Agency often asked for long trips. One, in 1969, included four weeks in six
cities in India, from which I still have not quite recovered. Talk about culture shock.

Arriving in Moscow, I spoke at the Institute of the USA and Canada Studies, whose director, Georgy Arbatov, can probably best be described as a politician-scholar-propagandist-operator. He is part Jewish with a Nazi background(!). He was widely covered by the Western media. After the Cold War, he talked about how he really tried to reform the system from within. That's what they all say.

I was astonished at the knowledge displayed at the institute. One question concerned the presidential race of 1976 and I listed, or tried to list, the top four candidates. I named three, but had a momentary lapse and couldn't come up with the fourth. A voice from the back of the room piped up and said, "Bahntzen"—Democratic Senator Lloyd Bentsen of Texas.

Meanwhile, in Moscow, the stores were almost empty of goods, and there were lines of Russians waiting to enter to get whatever was available. The bureaucracy was bizarre. It took three separate receipts to get a box of paper clips.

One day I was told that I was to meet with a General Milshtein. The topic concerned the intricacies of the Strategic Arms Limitation Talks, about which I knew little except that I supported Scoop's positions. Milshtein did almost all the talking, thinking that he was sending a message to Jackson. I made believe I understood what he was talking about when the translator repeated his remarks about nuclear weapons, multiple independently targeted reentry vehicles (MIRVs), and throw weights. Luckily, the American embassy sent a political officer with me; he took notes. I asked him to make sure that Jackson received a copy of Milshtein's remarks.

I asked the embassy to set up some meetings with dissidents, many Jewish, some not. A political officer named Mel Levitsky knew them all and arranged meetings that were deeply frowned upon by the Soviets. Levitsky just stared them down and went about his work. The U.S. diplomatic personnel in the Soviet Union were a gutsy group. Over the years, I found Americans diplomats in the field to be hard-nosed. The problem was back home, typically in the State Department and the White House, where supreme caution was too often worshiped. Most neo-cons share in such a critical view of super-cautiousness.

I went to some dingy apartments crowded with dissident Jews. They told of their plight as refuseniks, people who had applied to emigrate and were refused the right to leave, even though they had visas to Israel. Seen up close, the power of a police state is even more awesome than when viewed geopolitically. Scoop was right: If you can't leave a place you are in prison.

I met with one the most prominent dissidents, Vladimir Slepak. We chatted, and I asked him if he could arrange for me to meet Andrei Sakharov, the "father of the Soviet H-bomb," who had become the most prominent of the Soviet dissidents. Slepak called me back and said the meeting was set up for a couple of days later, on a Saturday night, at Sakharov's apartment in Moscow. When we arrived we were told that there had been a misunderstanding. Sakharov and his wife Yelena Bonner, also a leading dissident, were at Sakharov's dacha in the suburbs of Moscow. Slepak phoned out to the dacha and Sakharov said to come on out. Slepak hailed a cab and gave the driver the address.

The driver said the address was in a restricted area. Slepak argued with him, and told him that I was an important official. Grudgingly the driver proceeded, for about forty-five minutes. We arrived at a guardhouse protecting the area. It turned out to be where the big-shot commissars and officials had homes. Former Foreign Minister Vyacheslav Molotov was one.

The guards had automatic weapons, which made me nervous. They gave Slepak a hard time, but he managed to talk his way in. Sakharov was an "academician of the Soviet Union," and despite his outspoken views was not a man to be trifled with in the post-Stalin USSR. (In Stalin's time he probably would have been shot or sent to the gulag.) Europeans think much more highly of academics than Americans. After the Left came to dominate much of the American academy, I tended to side with the American view.

We got to Sakharov's home rather late in the evening. It was a pleasant, old three-story house—nothing grand by American criteria, but a mansion in the USSR, where whole families often lived in a single room with shared kitchen and toilet facilities. We rang the bell. Once. Twice. Three times. No answer.

Slepak, who had astonishing courage, began pitching pebbles at the lit windows. In a moment someone let us in. Sakharov spoke no English, so the conversation had to be translated for my benefit.

He had heard about my Jackson connection and said one thing I remember: "Jackson knows how get things done." *That* I reported back to Scoop personally.

Soon, the conversation lapsed into Russian, and after a while I went back to Moscow, by train, in the company of a young mathematician recently released from prison, where he had been treated with psychotropic drugs. The theory was that a dissident must be crazy to oppose the regime.

The next time I was in Moscow was in the early 1980s, traveling with Diane Abelman, the woman who would become my second wife. Again we got the red-carpet treatment. In Moscow we stayed at the Spasso House, the elegant American embassy. We were assigned a "guide" by the embassy, whom everyone knew was a KGB agent. Diane and I walked around. Once again the stores were mostly empty. We met with dissidents. Diane (no neo-con) was outraged at what she saw and heard.

One evening we went to the Soviet equivalent of a nightclub accompanied by a Russian-Armenian pollster and Alan Coombs, a political officer from the American embassy. We were seated in a big booth designed for six people. After a while I asked Diane to dance and gave Coombs my camera to take a picture of us. The flash went off. A moment later we returned to the booth, with Coombs taking an inside seat. A burly, high-ranking Soviet military man with lots of stripes on his sleeve — maybe a general — came to the booth and began berating Coombs. He said it was against the law to take photos of Soviet military men, and he believed he was in the background of the shot. (Or maybe he was dancing with a woman who wasn't his wife.) He vaulted across the table and grabbed the camera from Coombs. Coombs jumped back and wrested the camera back from the big striped one.

I had a third contact with the Soviets that might shed some light on the nature of our Cold War adversary. I was invited by the Chautauqua Institution to a U.S.-Soviet conference in Jurmala, a resort town in Latvia not far from Riga. After considerable research from transnational polls and with much help from the staff of the American Enterprise Institute's *Public Opinion* magazine, I gave a talk on how the Soviets were regarded in the rest of the world. It was straight stuff:

no spin. The data was remarkable. Around the world people thought that the Soviets were the greatest threat to peace, that they had a terrible record on human rights, that they prohibited freedom of expression, that they were potentially expansionist, and so on.

One of the Soviet speakers was a high-ranking Soviet diplomatic official, who said two things that were truly incredible. First, that the wall in Berlin was built to keep the Americans *out*, not to keep the East Germans *in*. Second, that America deserved condemnation as antihumanitarian for using atomic weapons in Hiroshima and Nagasaki to end World War II.

I responded that his statement about the wall was odd. East Berliners were being shot for trying to cross into West Berlin and away from Soviet domination. Most visitors to East Berlin came from West Berlin to visit family.

The argument against the use of atomic weapons to defeat the Japanese is usually made by dovish Americans who think that the war could have been won without their use in early August 1945. I think it was a wise use of power. Most neo-cons believe it saved many millions of lives, both American and Japanese. So does Pat Moynihan, a gunnery officer on a ship slated to take part in the invasion of Japan. But what about the Soviets? Evil and murderous things happen during wars, on all sides. The Soviets had taken tremendous human losses but had also committed mass atrocities. For a while they had been allied with the Nazis. They had killed tens of millions of their own subjects. For a high-ranking Soviet to plead humanitarianism in the Hiroshima and Nagasaki atomic bombings was not what I had expected. I reminded my Soviet partner the bombings had also saved the lives of Soviet troops because the Soviets had joined the allied forces in the Pacific against Japan shortly before the war's end.

I wondered: Over the years of the Cold War, there were very smart, quite knowledgeable Soviet officials. Were they purposefully lying to us and the world? Or had they come to believe what they were promulgating? That happens often in life.

When the Jurmala event ended, I traveled on to Moscow for a few days. Senator Charles Robb, a man I greatly admired, was in our party. One night he and I went to visit a group of Russian Jewish immigrants. The pitiful surroundings were as they had been years

earlier. I asked, in all innocence, expecting the usual negative answer, whether freedom of expression had expanded in the USSR.
Almost in chorus, the dissidents answered, "Da."

The era of glasnost had begun. Mikhail Gorbachev had become
general secretary. The Cold War was beginning to end in a way that
led to the disappearance of the Soviet Union.

CHAPTER SEVEN

Ideas Have Consequences

THINK TANKS

R ECALL THAT PAT Moynihan, a professional Democrat with neo-conservative inclinations, said that the Republicans had become the party of ideas in the early 1980s and that we Democrats were left as "the stupid party." I ascribe Moynihan's sentiment principally to the growth and expansion of neo-conservative and conservative think tanks, which started seriously in the mid-1970s.

In 1978, I was asked to join the American Enterprise Institute for Public Policy Research—AEI. Over the years it has played a major role in the development and promotion of neo-conservative, conservative, and centrist ideas, some moderate ones, and even a few left-of-center ones.

Earlier, the Brookings Institution had been the big fellow on the block, with roots going back to 1916. AEI has a history going back to 1943, starting as a very small business-oriented group, the American Enterprise Association, funded by a few businessmen afraid that the United States would continue World War II price controls after the end of the war. I think Irving Kristol and economist Richard McCormack had recommended me to Bill Baroody Sr., AEI's president.

People sometimes ask, "What does a person who works at a think tank do—sit around and think? That must be a good job." It has indeed been a good job for me. Before AEI, the longest I'd worked at one job was a couple of years in the Air Force. In 2006 I concluded twenty-eight years as a senior fellow in residence at AEI, and continue my affiliation today off-site. I'm also affiliated with the Hudson Institute, another major think tank. For someone with a hop-skip-and-jump freelance mentality like mine, the years at AEI have been just what the doctor ordered. I don't want this chapter to be an AEI puff piece, but it is a very important place.

The AEI official motto at the time I joined was, "The competition of ideas is fundamental to a free society." It was a time, as non-liberals saw it, when the conservative or the neo-conservative message was drowned out by what seemed to be a wall-to-wall liberal media full-court press. Baroody believed that if the conservatives, or neo-cons, or nonliberals, could get even *half* of the barrel of media ink or *half* the video face time they would be ahead of where they were.

Sometimes, when a book title is so good, you may not have to read it. The buzz phrase among the scholars at AEI at the times was *ideas have consequences*, which was also the title of a seminal, gloomy, dense, conservative and philosophical book by Richard M. Weaver published in 1948. I never read it, and I'm not sure many other have. But it was the title, succinct and straight to the point, that drew our attention. It was a truism, but there it was: a call to try to influence things by thinking them through.

When I arrived, one project AEI was sponsoring was called Rational Debates. They would get, say, liberals Ralph Nader and Ted Kennedy and two others—perhaps from AEI, perhaps not—with opposing views. AEI would typically tape and edit a one-hour television program derived from the session, thereby presenting both sides of an issue. The program was then "bicycled," as television coinage had it in those presatellite days, from station to station—for free use. A traveler could end up at 1:00 A.M. in a Pittsburgh motel and see—in his bedroom—a program showing why competition of ideas was fundamental to a free society. (Ted Kennedy and AEI were both instrumental in the deregulation of the airline industry.) A weekly radio program, *National Policy Forum,* was aired by an estimated eight hundred stations. In different formats, vastly expanded, AEI still does the same sorts of promotion.

Baroody was a very intelligent man. But I believe his central contribution to the world of scholarship was elementary: *publicize.* He didn't want the product sitting on musty bookshelves read by a few hundred academics. He wanted his players to be in the action. Over the years that notion did a great deal to bring both conservatism and neo-conservatism to the forefront. And today it is standard operating procedure in the growing world of think tanks of whatever persuasion, and even in the academy.

One day shortly after I began working for AEI, I was walking down Seventeenth Street with Baroody. Suddenly, displayed on a public garbage can, was—me! There it was: a full-can ad promoting WGBH's new program *In Search of the Real America,* based on my first non-Scammon, non-collaborative book. It aired in a rather unique format—a half-hour documentary series with an up-front point of view: mine. Baroody was dumbstruck. His scholars, fellows, and academicians at AEI were not featured in advertisements, certainly not in the late 1970s—certainly not on garbage cans!

That notion of—promote! promote! promote!—plays out in a number of ways, both tactical and psychological. Over the years I have counseled younger colleagues that if they believe in what they've written, there is a coincident duty: Promote it. That may mean doing fifty "phoners" to talk shows around the country, repeating yourself endlessly. It may get you called a publicity hound. But if you want your ideas to have consequences, that's what you have to do. Given the disparity in audience size between books and radio and television, writing a book may only be a ticket to get on the shows.

On a book tour it is not hard to notice that there are some big dopes who serve as radio and television hosts; you can often tell when you see that your book has not been cracked, the pages laying flat and virginal. The host works from canned questions provided by the publisher. But there are also many times when you see earmarks and underlines throughout the book, yielding incisive questioning from hosts—most of whom were and are right-of-center, a circumstance that goes back long before Rush Limbaugh and Fox News came on the scene. They had high ratings. In fact, that is *why* they did so well; they understood which way the wind was blowing.

In 1991 I wrote *The First Universal Nation*, which dealt in some large measure with immigration. I was then, and now, very much in favor of a reasonable amount of legal immigration (probably somewhat higher than our current levels). I even have mixed emotions about illegal immigrants (to be explored later).

As I did the phoners, a pattern emerged. About half the callers said I was wonderful, had good insights, and that immigration was what made America great. The other half thought I was a big jerk and said so. One caller told of a Bangladeshi family that lived in the apartment above him and tossed their spicy garbage out the window. Didn't I know that immigrants weren't assimilating? (They are, by the way, assimilating as rapidly as ever, probably even more so.) If I had a better sense of some of the personal anguish involved I think I could have dealt with the topic more wisely. If I could figure out how to do it, I'd make it a publishing axiom: Do the phoners first, then write the book.

Bill Baroody Sr. was a second-generation Lebanese Melchite with seven children. He was known as a real operator in Republican circles. He was high on the totem pole with the 1964 Goldwater campaign and had been an economist with the U.S. Chamber of Commerce. When he became president of AEI in 1954, the place started jumping. He had the two key skills necessary in running a think tank: understanding ideas and the ability to raise money. That allowed him to begin a substantial expansion of AEI by the mid-1970s. There is a general pitch for all think tanks with a point of view. When the opposition party is in power, fund-raisers say, "We have to keep them honest and keep surfacing our good ideas." When your own party is in power, the line is, "We have so much influence." These are good lines, although at AEI and some of the better think tanks, the scholars and fellows are not at all shy about publicly criticizing pols who are generally associated with their own view. It's tactically sound, too; no one takes you for granted.

In the early 1970s the American Enterprise Institute had only a handful of resident scholars—people who worked full time on the premises. The two of greatest eminence were economists of the Austrian School, Gottfried Haberler (who signed on in 1972) and Willy Fellner (who joined up in 1973). They were regarded as world-class economists. (I learned that economists are sometimes ranked like yachts.) When they signed on as resident scholars, AEI moved from being seen as an intellectual broker and a specialty publisher to something akin to a school—that is, a university with top-grade faculty but no students. As it turned out, over the years many of the research assistants of the resident fellows—working one-on-one with top-grade scholars—were themselves receiving a world-class education.[1]

One way Baroody Sr. raised the money for AEI was different: He hired Democrats. Within a few years' time in the late 1970s Jeane Kirkpatrick, Michael Novak, election scholar Austin Ranney, and I were asked to join. Norm Ornstein came aboard shortly thereafter. Bringing Democrats on board showed potential funders that the ideas in play at AEI, albeit regarded as somewhat right of center, were somewhat ecumenical—not a bad chit to have in a fund-raising kit. Personally, I was delighted at the prospect of having a place to hang my hat. I remember seeing the Coke machine at AEI, with *free* drinks, and thinking *these are some capitalists!* The idea of regular paychecks, office space, health insurance, and later, a research assistant of my very own, was also most appealing. I would guess that in 2008 dollars, the total package, with overhead, ran about $200,000 when adjusted for inflation.

I met Baroody in his office, along with his deputy and son, Bill Baroody Jr. Senior said to me, "OK, come on board. Let's give it a shot for six months and see how it works." Then he asked, "Would you like to do something here beside write?" He turned to his son and said, "Why don't we start Ben right out as a senior fellow"—the highest rank in a sometimes bewildering array of the regulars (Gerald Ford and Arthur Burns and perhaps a few other eminent individuals were called "distinguished fellows").

I was forty-five at the time and didn't feel like a senior anything. After a couple of days I got back to Baroody Sr. and said I would like to start two AEI magazines: one on public opinion and one on demography. (I heard that when Irving Kristol was asked about the idea for a magazine on public opinion he said: "Why bother? All you

---

1. Much of this material on AEI history comes from an unpublished work put together painstakingly by my AEI colleague Karlyn H. Bowman.

have to do is call Marty Lipset.") Baroody thought the *public opinion* idea might fly most easily. Within a few months we were rolling with a bimonthly magazine of that title. My first managing editor for *Public Opinion* was David Gergen, then a moderate Republican. He is a conscientious man, a good friend, and did a very good job. (There are Republicans who don't like Gergen at all, regarding him as a traitor and turncoat.) Over the years we have fried fish together many times. Karlyn Bowman was an associate editor and is still with AEI. Bill Schambra, who later went on to be a key official at the Bradley Foundation and to serve in government, rounded out the staff. They, too, were top-drawer. (Later, under private aegis, a magazine called *American Demographics* came on the scene.)

Public Opinion had some ongoing themes. Looking at the polling data from all over America along with our expert advisors Seymour Martin Lipset and Everett Carll Ladd, we came to the notion that the American value system represented "continuity, not change." It was not a brand-new idea: ink always flows toward what may seem to be sharp opinion shifts, but values tend to remain constant. Take a simple question like *Is America the greatest country in the world?* A chart of many decades' responses would consistently show about 90 percent of them affirmative; you could balance a full glass of water on the line and not lose a drop. Every transnational survey places America at the top in terms of proudest and most patriotic nation on earth.

Public Opinion published the first important work by social scientists describing an overwhelming leftward bias among print and television journalists working for top newspapers and television networks. Entitled "Media and Business Elites," it was written by professors Stanley Rothman and Robert Lichter; it set off a firestorm. Its general conclusions are now widely accepted. (A fuller explaination is offered in chapter 11, "Media Matters Most.")

We talked and wrote a lot about a new "realignment," or "dealignment," of the political parties, noting that the last great such political shift came about during the Depression, when the Democratic Party of President Franklin D. Roosevelt established political dominance. We talked and kidded a lot about the question *"Is this the end of an era?"* The answer seems to have turned out somewhat in the affirmative—hence all the talk about "America moving to the right." At the least Republicans have regained an equal footing—and perhaps done a little better than that. We did mostly general interest articles, usually, but not always, with a right-of-center tilt. The magazine helped grow the neo-con orientation.

Much later on, there was a reorganization, and *Public Opinion* was folded into AEI's new flagship publication, *The American Enterprise*, with Karlyn editing a special section on survey research. She has become the go-to source for scores of journalists, and writes a regular column for the congressional newspaper *Roll Call*. She is a dear friend and my only good source of AEI gossip. The editor of *The American Enterprise* was Karl Zinsmeister, a remarkable man, an all-American oarsman at Yale, my first research assistant, and as this is written, the domestic policy czar for the Bush #43 White House. Simply called *The American* today, the magazine became an even finer product under the direction of James Glassman, one in which I am proud to continue having an occasional article published. In 2008, Jim left to also join the Bush administration and was replaced by the immensely talented Nick Schulz, who had worked on *Think Tank* projects for many years.

I have hired a clunker or two, but have mostly been very fortunate in the other young people who have worked as my research assistants over the years. Some subsequently shifted over to *Think Tank* to learn television production skills. Many have gone on to fine careers in politics, writing, law, and business.[2]

MUCH HAS BEEN going on at AEI in recent years. Below are a few highlights that elucidate how neo-conservate thinking has grown.

---

2. An item by Jonah Goldberg in *National Review Online* in May 2006, when Karl Zinsmeister was appointed to the White House staff, read this way: "Great news for my friend Karl, who has replaced Claude Allen. Karl is a brilliant guy and the White House made a good choice here. Though this is perhaps bad news for my old and dear friend Tevi Troy, who was up for the job and who also would have been an outstanding pick. Tevi was Claude Allen's #2 at the White House and I have no idea whether he will stick around or not. But there's a nice conspiracy theory in the offing here. Karl Zinsmeister was Ben Wattenberg's first researcher at the American Enterprise Institute many years ago. He was replaced by Tevi. In turn, I replaced Tevi. So far, I've received no job offers from the White House (nor do I expect any are in the offing). But clearly, working for Ben is—statistically speaking—a better springboard to the highest levels of power in America than, say, attending Harvard."

Included are some portraits of my colleagues, some in greater depth than others, in order to provide a portrait of the people who make up what many have called the most influential think tank in the world.

One important development was the initiation of the American Enterprise Institute–Brookings Joint Center, in whose formation Christopher DeMuth played a big role. (Baroody Sr. used to tell potential corporate donors, "Brookings looks for governmental solutions; AEI looks for private solutions." DeMuth does, too.) Ideology aside, there are parts of government that just don't work from whatever perspective. The joint center examined these issues and made recommendations. Such ideas carried great weight with Congress and the executive branch, offering "cover" for pols of most every persuasion.

For a six-year term ending in mid-2006, I served as a member of the Domestic Advisory Council of a reorganized Smith-Richardson Foundation, often referred to on the left as conservative or very conservative. In fact, it is a pretty hard-headed group dedicated to funding social science research based on its merits. It is true that it always has some conservatives or neo-cons on its council, to screen out some tilted, liberal claptrap. But it was a principal supporter of the joint AEI-Brookings venture as well as my *Think Tank* program (antedating my service on its council). It has had moderate liberals on the council, like economist Isabelle Sawhill. Some of the family members are moderately liberal as well.

The liberal foundations have been by far the biggest givers to good causes. The MacArthur, Ford, and Rockefeller Foundations, and more recently the Bill and Melinda Gates Foundation, all have huge endowments. They have spent much of their money on do-good programs, often doing good, but sometimes counterproductively. Think health clinics for the poor, AIDS programs, education projects—but also racial quotas, far-out global warming themes, and super-feminism. Often to the dismay of their original founders, they had been "turned" by their left-leaning staffs.

The resignation letter of Henry Ford II from the Ford Foundation is a classic:

In effect, the foundation is a creature of capitalism, a
statement that, I'm sure, would be shocking to many
professional staff people in the field of philanthropy. It is
hard to discern recognition of this fact in anything the
foundation does. It is even more difficult to find an understanding of this in many of the institutions, particularly the universities, that are the beneficiaries of the
foundation's grant programs.

The non-liberal foundations, mostly on the small side, invested their
dollars in promoting ideas that had consequences. A handful took
the lead: Smith-Richardson, Bradley, Searle, Scaife, Carthage, and a
few others, often helping both neo-cons as well as conservatives.
Some have helped me over years, some not. (Of the major foundations, only the nonliberal Lilly Endowment was top-top tier, although
many of its grants were for local Indiana projects.)

Follow the money: The paleo-cons suffered most, driving poor
Pat Buchanan to great anger. His money had been swiped! Soon, the
liberals figured out that ideas had a bigger bang for the buck than
bricks-and-mortar projects. Now there is a good deal of money do-
nated to all sides for both purposes.

In 1991 AEI made a quantum jump, with the construction of the
Wohlstetter Center, a state-of-the-art conference facility named for
major AEI contributor Charles Wohlstetter, brother of nuclear
strategist Albert Wohlstetter. It takes up most of the entire top floor,
has a variety of configurations, and can hold about three hundred
people.

I convened and moderated the first major session at the center for
an all-day conference entitled *The New Global Popular Culture: Is It
American? Is It Good for America? Is It Good for the World?* Among the
participants were Jack Valenti, the president of the Motion Picture Association of America; AEI historian Walter Berns; neo-con film critic
Michael Medved; U.S. Court of Appeals Judge Robert Bork; liberal
intellectual Todd Gitlin; neo-con survey research expert Everett Ladd;
Irving Kristol; Francis Fukuyama; Charles Krauthammer; ground-
breaking publisher Erwin Glikes; former editor of *Reader's Digest*

Kenneth Tomlinson; historian Daniel Boorstin; scholar/bureaucrat William Bennett; AEI's Karlyn Bowman; Michael Schneider of the United States Information Agency; entertainment writer Pico Iyer; and film critic and author James Bowman (Karlyn's husband and author of the recent book *Honor*).

The keynote luncheon address was given by film director Sydney Pollack, who won two Academy Awards for *Out of Africa*. He said: "The theme of all American movies is the same—the hero shapes destiny." I don't know Pollack's politics, and I wouldn't want to poison him should they be Hollywood Left. But that idea of the hero shaping destiny is at the heart of neo-conservative thinking. Neo-cons tend to believe that action can yield results. There's not much nihilism in the neo-conservative playbook.

IN MY EARLY days at AEI in the late 1970s I remember standing in a corridor chatting with Nino Scalia, Bob Bork, and Larry Silberman, later a federal judge in a key Washington, D.C., federal court. It's not a bad way to learn about what's going on in the legal world.

SOME AEI PEOPLE have been personally involved at the highest level of electoral politics. In a 1992 presidential run, Dick Cheney, then a fellow at AEI, "explored" a presidential run (on his own time). Alan Keyes was at AEI for a while, and he ran for president several times. AEI Senior Fellow Newt Gingrich has long been in the mix as a possibility. Jeane Kirkpatrick was seriously mentioned but declined to move forward. Fred Thompson was at AEI before he left to run for the presidency.

Vice President Dick Cheney has been both a fellow and a trustee at AEI. His wife, Lynne, worked there before and during his vice presidential years. Since becoming vice president he has taken much grief about his tenure as chief executive of the oil exploration firm Halliburton and its subsidiary, Dresser Industries. But there is a critical part of the story that is rarely mentioned. At a trustee luncheon one day I asked Cheney about what Halliburton actually does. Among other things, it has been the leading firm in pioneering the new technologies of oil extraction in relatively ecologically safe ways. Some fields are now yielding up to 50 percent more fossil fuels from old wells.

Over the years some AEI scholars have received the very highest presidential honors, the Presidential Medal of Freedom among them. A short list of AEI honorees includes Irving Kristol, Jeane Kirkpatrick, James Q. Wilson, Dick Cheney, and Walter Berns. Quite a number of AEI folks have run for the presidency, or at least been mentioned by the Great Mentioners in Washington as attractive potential candidates for the highest office in the land.

SOMETIMES AEI HIRES out-of-office Democrats. One was Paul London, President Clinton's deputy undersecretary of commerce for economics and statistics. He was at AEI for three years shortly after Clinton left office, working on his book *The Competition Solution: The Bipartisan Secret Behind American Prosperity*, published by the AEI Press. Paul's theme is that we have lost sight of what caused recent American prosperity. Mainstream economists have had a wide variety of ideas concerning what moves the American economy one way or the other, including the notion that anything under a 6 percent unemployment rate would ignite inflation, that prosperity was not essentially linked to partisan policies, and that stock market behavior was critical—or new technology, or deficit spending, or government surpluses, or tax cuts, or Federal Reserve policy, or monetary policy, or government spending. Paul doesn't dismiss these concerns, but concentrates on something he feels has been more important.

London maintains that special interests sought (undeserved) anti-competitive help from the government—and *mostly did not get it*. It is his view that recent unemployment rates below 5 percent[3] were caused in large part by competition that kept prices low and in effect gave consumers a bonus every time they went through the checkout counter even if it was to buy a 747 or oil-drilling equipment. These low rates occurred during both the Clinton and Bush #43 administrations.

---

3. For sound technical reasons, unemployment rates below 5 percent are considered to be "full employment." About a decade earlier the figure was 6 percent.

Paul is teased by some of his Democratic friends as pro-Wal-Mart. I'm pro-Wal-Mart, too. He asked: Why has the idea of competition—as old as apple pie—received relatively little attention? Paul dug in and showed a sequence of case histories of deregulation leading to greater competition that have emerged in recent decades. These included the airline industry, retailing, financial services, foreign trade, telecommunications, "junk bonds," steel, import policies, and much more. Too often politicians promised voters and companies protection from both foreign and domestic competition. But London shows that there was little competition and on balance, most Americans gained from the new competition. (For those who don't there must be buffers: retraining, buyouts, and more.)

When I first arrived at AEI Jude Wanniski was in residence, writing his influential book on supply-side economics, *The Way the World Works*. It proved to be a very important work. There was only one problem. We would periodically have some meetings of about fifteen scholars around our big conference table. Jude could not stop talking about his book—on and on and on—until it would drive his colleagues crazy. Now, being excited about your book in progress is usually a very good sign. (I have been hopping on this one.) But Jude went over the top. He recently went to his final reward, so it makes it easier to tell you he was not one of my favorite colleagues.

Another highly influential book that came out of AEI's warrens was Michael Novak's *Spirit of Democratic Capitalism*, which was well received in America and became somewhat of a bible in nations seeking to break the yoke of authoritarianism, specifically in Latin America and Eastern Europe. At the height of the arguments about poverty and female-headed families, Michael examined the data and provided a four-word solution for staying out of poverty: "Get married; stay married." Michael has been my department head: he is the official chief for AEI's Social and Political Science Department. His office was close to mine. But I don't think I have ever met with him to talk about his bureaucratic duties, although our colleague Karlyn Bowman says there was one such meeting some years ago at which Michael told his troops that he wouldn't bother them. I am told that most scholars at other think tanks actually report to their superiors. AEI's trick, going back to Baroody Sr., was to hire the best people then leave them alone (and let them go if they didn't cut it).

Michael arrived as a full-time resident scholar in April 1978 but had been an AEI adjunct scholar a year earlier while teaching at the University of Syracuse, where he had already begun work on the democratic capitalism book. At Syracuse he held a university chair in religious studies, which allowed him to deal with students in several departments. He holds two masters degrees from Harvard. After elementary school in his hometown of Johnstown, Pennsylvania (forty miles east of Pittsburgh), he attended the Catholic seminaries at Notre Dame (in South Bend, Indiana) and Gregorian (in Rome). Later, he was a program officer at Rockefeller University, where even in the 1950s they were trying to figure out how to connect with mainstream America. His parents were Slovak immigrants who arrived in America and settled in Johnstown shortly before the famous Johnstown Flood that killed 10 percent of the town's population. There were five children in the Novak family. Here, the story takes a different turn from the typical poor-son-of-immigrants tale. Novak's father had quit school in the sixth grade to help the family. But Pop Novak became a salesman for Metropolitan Life Insurance. He recalls bringing checks to bereaved widows and feeling proud helping people make do in times of trouble. He told his children that one day they would live with the swells "on the top of the hill" in Johnstown. And they did. A tip-off to Pop's values was the first major family purchase: a set of the Harvard classics. So Michael did not grow up poor or ill-informed. For some of his childhood he lived very well in a family that valued learning in a serious way.

By 1976 Novak was working on Scoop Jackson's campaign. In 1980, President Jimmy Carter, seeking help in Archie Bunkerland, sought out Novak's counsel on ethnic issues. Novak refused. By then he was voting for Reagan and regarded himself as a "neo-liberal" — not a neo-conservative. He is now a neo-con. His interests are eclectic, to say the least: At one point he helped Senator Dan Quayle on the Strategic Arms Limitation Treaty, not a topic to be dealt with in a cursory way. Novak has catholic interests as well as Catholic ones. His 1960 novel, *The Tiber Was Silver*, is the story of a young man preparing for the priesthood in the 1950s. It contained valuable insights into the pre–Vatican II church and was reissued by Doubleday in 2005.

I have two problems with Novak's ideas and work. He believes that abortion is immoral and regards himself as pro-life. But like President George W. Bush, he does not believe that American law should *punish* or *imprison* those who provide abortions, which I believe is the pure pro-life position. He and I argue about it. By my lights his position is essentially pro-choice; he doesn't like abortion but doesn't effectively punish it. I am mildly pro-choice. During the first Scoop Jackson campaign, I came up with a mock bumper sticker: "It's murder and I'm for it."

Over the years that I have been at AEI there have been many books and articles of significance that have appeared, some which I have agreed with, some not. Charles Murray's *Losing Ground* was a seminal book that attempted to show that LBJ's programs hurt poor people. I had two problems with that, which we discussed at a symposium at the LBJ Library in Austin. First was that the worst parts of LBJ's monumental programs were effectuated not by laws but by regulatory agencies, massively built up congressional staffs, the leftward movement of courts, some Far Left members of Congress and—of all people—Richard Nixon, who not only (wisely) accepted most LBJ programs, but played quota games with them. LBJ's civil rights laws specifically did not endorse quotas. Further, even with all the mistakes that were made, the lot of poor and lower-middle-class people in America has improved substantially. Moreover, the intent of most of the laws made eminent sense. Who wants to live in a country with no environmental protection? And while welfare was an enormous problem in America for many years, increasing it was not Johnson's intent. Again and again he said he sought "a hand up, not a handout." Murray was right about how counterproductively welfare was doled out, but the law was eventually changed in 1996 by a Republican Congress pushing President Clinton, who had pledged "to end welfare as we know it."

Charles's big book was the huge bestseller *The Bell Curve*, written in collaboration with Richard Herrnstein of Harvard, who died shortly before its publication. The book was highly controversial and a huge commercial success. One key chapter did the job, maintaining, as Charles told me on a *Think Tank* show, that "if you take the mean on most tests of cognitive ability that have been given, including up to recent times, there's about a fifteen-point difference between blacks and whites." (Murray maintains that about 60 percent of this is heritable, and about 40 percent environmental.) Did this mean that blacks were less intelligent than whites? Not really, according to Murray; there was a great overlap between the two, meaning any given person of color could be as intelligent as a white person.

The statement of differential intelligence was highly combustible. It seemed to me that I never could get a clear answer from Charles to the question, "If I saw two men walking down the street, one black, one white, of similar dress and bearing, should I assume the white one is more intelligent?" We later did two *Think Tank* programs featuring Charles, and others, offering a variety of views on the book. The furor passed. The country has not publicly acted as if there is such a difference. Moreover, I wonder if the numbers may have changed somewhat. Much of the research studied by Murray and Herrnstein dated back to when almost all blacks were descendants of American slaves.

More recently, there has been a substantial emigration of sub-Saharan and Caribbean blacks to the United States, many from middle- to upper-middle-class background, often with college or university training—some using it, some driving cabs seventy hours a week. Many of them harbor ill feelings toward traditional African Americans, whom they say are always looking for a government handout as if it were owed them. There may be some truth to that, especially as expressed by some black leadership groups. But there are many blacks in America, men and women, who are also working those seventy-hour weeks to support a family. These days they are making out much better than before and for young blacks, test scores have been climbing steadily.

And just what is intelligence? Assume that there are disproportionately fewer black mathematicians and physicists. But consider some of the more stereotypical occupations. For many years many professional football coaches assumed that blacks did not have the smarts to play quarterback. Then along came Steve McNair, Daunte

Culpepper, Donovan McNabb, Kordell Stewart, Michael Vick, and the 2006 number three draft pick, Texan Vince Young. The future of the Washington Redskins may lie in the hands of Jason Campbell. It is a job that requires split-second timing, strategic thinking, strenuous training, and enormous courage. The same is true of the black players in the National Basketball Association who dominate the league. Watch the Wizard's Gilbert Arenas one day and tell me he is not smart. Or Kobe Bryant. Or twenty-three-year-old LeBron James. The phenomenon holds water for the sharply increasing number of Latinos playing major league baseball.

Or consider a couple of more prosaic occupations: bank tellers and airline ticket counter clerks. These are high-tech jobs that require brains and stamina. A technophobe like me couldn't do them. (This may run in our family. My dad—a brilliant man—once couldn't figure out how to open a Dixie cup of ice cream: Pull the little tab.)

In any event, no one would deny that there is a black-white problem in America. Clearly there is still a good deal of racist sentiment. Perhaps there is a partial solution in sight: the sharp increase in black-white intermarriage in recent decades, albeit from a low base, about 2 percent, to about 10 percent and climbing. The vast majority of Americans will no longer tell pollsters about their race-oriented feelings. ("Who, me? I don't have objections to a black family moving in next door.") That any other response is no longer an acceptable public sentiment, even to an anonymous pollster, is in itself a sign of progress. But there is a central problem that has not gone away. Blacks still have a rate of violent crime about five times that of whites. It poisons progress. In all, the situation is improving but remains a problem.

I HAD PROBLEMS with two of Judge Robert Bork's bestsellers, *Slouching Towards Gomorrah* and *The Tempting of America*. Both are gloomy books, and there has surely been some cause for concern about our coarsening popular culture. Bork is a very nice man, without a bone of condescension in his body. I think he was shabbily treated when he was "borked" by the Senate and denied a seat on the

Supreme Court. Given his own background, when I hear Senator Edward Kennedy's moralistic preachings, there are times I want to gag.

The profane language used cavalierly by many women is a case in point. I grew up at a time when cursing was common among boys: f-word this, f-word that. I have not worked hard to cure it, except when my research assistants have been religiously inclined, in which case I try to remember to apologize. The case can easily be made that what's good for the gander is good for the goose. But I still find it mildly offensive when some *nouveau* feminist women come into my office and seem to purposefully use four-letter words.

Still, I do not believe that what has happened in the realm of popular culture is nearly as bad as Bork describes. The Beatles—as an obvious example from a musical simpleton like me—were clearly wonderful musicians. In an earlier era, bobby socks–wearing swooners flocked to hear World War II draft dodger Frank Sinatra. He and they were regarded as a threat to the culture. But he turned out to be both a wonderful singer and a fine actor—with criminal thugs for friends. I still listen to him via CD in my car.

Some younger AEI research assistants were contemptuous of Bork's work on popular culture. They maintained that he only read a few rap and rock lyrics but didn't really know the music.

Bork still does some legal consultation and has recently moved from AEI over to the neo-conservative Hudson Institute, a solid place. And he still writes with despair about the horrible influence of popular culture. I debated him on the issue before quite a large crowd. I think I won. A man as smart as Bob Bork must also think I won.

Sarath Rajapatirana is another colleague I had an opportunity to learn more about in the course of writing this book. He is an economist hailing originally from the larger-than-you'd-think island nation of Sri Lanka, which has a population of over twenty million. Since 1998 he has been a visiting scholar at AEI; he was the first scholar to come over from the World Bank, although others have come since. Sarath's principal field of study is trade from developing countries, an increasingly important subject. Rajapatirana's books include *The Trade Policies of Developing Countries* and *Boom,*

Crisis, and Adjustment. One of Rajapatirana's routes to AEI was through his association with economist Allan Meltzer, author of the magisterial two-volume *History of the Federal Reserve.* Meltzer combines his work at the Carnegie Mellon Institute in Pittsburgh with his role as a regular, one-day-per-week visiting scholar at AEI. One conclusion Meltzer came to in his second volume was that former Fed chairman Arthur Burns (subsequently an AEI distinguished fellow) made policy decisions prior to the 1972 election that gave every indication of being purposefully in the political favor of President Richard Nixon, who had appointed him chairman. (The material came from the Nixon tapes.) Meltzer called it as he saw it about a colleague. Such is the AEI code, although any lack of cordiality in public communication, as in a conference, is grounds for a big fat black mark.

DeMuth asked Sarath to become a "member of the AEI Family." Sarath thinks things out. He told me that he came to AEI because he believes in liberty over equality, that a moral compass and social responsibility are legitimate fields of study for an economist, and that his economics come out on the free market side. In February 2006, Sarath became a naturalized American citizen.

Jeane Kirkpatrick was at AEI in 1979 when she wrote her famous article "Dictators and Double Standards" for *Commentary.* Its theme was clear and powerful: "Rightist authoritarian regimes can be transformed peacefully into democracies, but totalitarian Marxist ones cannot. In the final analysis these enemies of freedom can only be deterred from greater aggression by the military capacities of the United States."

It was a highly influential article and drove the Left nuts. I agreed with it. So did Ronald Reagan; he read it and asked her to be his ambassador to the United Nations, where she made America's case with great vigor, along with a team of neo-cons each with ambassadorial rank (many of whom were AEI affiliated and whom she selected). Her theme made much sense to me and still does as far as it went: Military deterrence was critical. But in the end the Soviet Union and its Eastern European satellites changed peacefully because its ideology was desperately flawed and it lost the battle of ideas.

Here is a lift from President Reagan's address to the AEI annual dinner in 1988:

> The American Enterprise Institute stands at the center of a revolution in ideas of which I, too, have been a part. AEI's remarkably distinguished body of work is testimony to the triumph of the think tank. For today the most important American scholarship comes out of our think tanks—and none has been more influential than the American Enterprise Institute.

At a later AEI dinner President George W. Bush made a similar point and put a number to it: He said that twenty AEI scholars had joined his administration!

FOR MANY EVEN-NUMBERED years I moderated and participated in AEI's monthly Election Watch series, held principally for journalists, Washington corporate representatives, and foreign embassy officers. The three AEI regulars were Norm Ornstein; Karlyn Bowman, who knew the polling material inside and out; and Bill Schneider, a Harvard-trained political scientist and coauthor (with Seymour Martin Lipset) of a seminal work, *The Confidence Gap*. Schneider later became a well-known regular political commentator for CNN. Many in the audience would ask questions and then communicate back to their employers: "I talked to Bill Schneider today about the political situation, and he said . . ." The panel had no noticeable political tilt. Ornstein and Schneider had Democratic proclivities, but the mix gave the sessions credibility. A few years ago, as I began work on this book, a very smart and young AEI political scientist, John Fortier, replaced me as a regular on the panel. I once met Egyptian President Hosni Mubarak at a session hosted by the American Jewish Committee. Schneider was in front of me in the receiving line. Mubarak boomed out, "I know you, I see you on CNN."

I do have one problem with Schneider's CNN work. He will often say, "Candidate Jones has achieved a wall-to-wall win; he cap-

tured a greater number of votes than expected, including Southerners, skilled workers, Westerners, Jews, blacks . . ." and on and on.
What typically happened was that Jones appealed to all Americans,
and the demographic dominoes fell in tandem.

WHEN SO MANY universities became radicalized think tanks of the
right-of-center and the right filled a yawning gap, and Washington
was their epicenter. In my jaded eyes AEI is the hotbed of neo-
conservatism.

I am a Washington booster; it's home base for so many neo-
cons—as well as the Wizards, Redskins, and the Nationals. I have no
data to back this up, but I would make a big bet that the combined
academic resources of AEI would be superior to that of any great
American university. If you added in the resources of other think
tanks and of the National Institutes of Health, the Census Bureau,
the National Academy of Sciences, the Office of Management and
Budget, to begin a long list, the intellectual firepower could probably
surpass the academic totality of five to ten of the best universities in
America, or the world.

AEI keeps up with the times. When the second Iraq war erupted,
our foreign policy staff was expanded, something President Chris
DeMuth apparently had in mind to do in any event. Most—all?—of
the new appointees supported the Iraq II war. It was said that AEI's
briefings on the situation played a vital role in President Bush's decision to proceed. In many quarters we caught hell for that. We shall
see; I think it will turn out all right. There were arguments about
Iraq's new constitution. But Americans still argue about our own
founding document. We fought our civil war about it. We have
terrorists—like the Weathermen and Timothy McVeigh.

As this is written, the situation in Iraq is looking much better.
America tried. We don't use force very often. When we do I believe
it has almost always been for a good purpose. (Invading the Philippines in 1898 was stupid.) The world is not going to do very well if
America opts out. Iraq II made sense even if we "lose." Vietnam was
a losing battle in a war that we ultimately won.

What is the staying power of neo-con players? By early 2006

some were bailing out on Iraq, in part because the mere word "neo-conservative" was used as a rallying cry by opponents. Not very gutsy. Some of the bailers were from AEI.

The American Enterprise Institute has come a long way. The place teetered on the brink of bankruptcy in the mid-1980s and had virtually no endowment. In 2006, AEI had revenues of $28.4 million. That supported the work of about 160 people, 50 of whom are scholars and fellows. AEI has more than 70 adjunct scholars around the country. In 2007 AEI had more than 110 interns in three sessions. In the first 9 months of 2007, AEI held 130 conferences and other events, 22 of which were covered by C-SPAN.

Such a change is enormously important. But it is not the numbers that tell the tale. By dealing seriously with ideas, AEI and other non-Left think tanks have helped give Americans a true competition of ideas when some of the influential Left went over the edge. That is what participants in a democratic society deserve, and they got it. The views put forth at AEI as well as those at other right-of-center think tanks, many of them of a neo-conservative persuasion, make sense. Furthermore, most Americans agree with those non-Left ideas. We are no longer the underdogs. Ideas do have consequences.

CHAPTER EIGHT

Measuring
Neo-Conservatism

IMMIGRATION, ASSIMILATION, AND
DEMOGRAPHICS

I BECAME INTERESTED in social demographics in the early
1960s when I read Theodore H. White's *The Making of the President, 1960*. It is a wonderful narrative of the presidential race between Senator John F. Kennedy and Vice President Richard M.
Nixon. It had a powerful impact on subsequent journalism. For me it
yielded some of the building blocks of what would become my neo-
conservative orientation.

Suddenly, in chapter 8, White breaks away from his political
yarn and makes the point that only once every twenty years does a
presidential election coincide with the taking of the U.S. decennial
census. And 1960 was such a year. On that observation White hangs a
long chapter, mixing social and economic data from the 1960 Census
with anecdotes based on shoe-leather reporting. He writes of blacks
from the rural South thrown out of farm work by new farming equipment and arriving in Chicago on the Illinois Central late at night with
their paper suitcases, eyes blinking at the harsh lights. He sets forth a
portrait of the population boom in America's suburbs and of forlorn
parents watching as their children leave the small towns and farms
of the American midcontinent, victims of the mechanization of

agriculture. (That rural-to-urban migration is still happening in America and around the world.) He emphasizes the shift of home heating from coal to oil and natural gas and speculates about the changes this could bring to American and global politics and economics. For me, something clicked. White's book tuned me in to the treasure of social demographic data that is produced by both government and private sources. I have fondled some of that data for more than forty years.

At that time I was in my late twenties and was editor and half-owner of a small book publishing imprint called Boldface Books. My partner was David Boehm, owner of Sterling Books, a grade B publishing firm. Dave was very savvy in the ways of publishing and more than a little quirky. He was wholly financing our little venture. The morning after I read Teddy White's chapter I ran his office and said, "Dave, I have a great idea. Let's get a poet or a novelist to write *a whole book* on America based on social and economic data." He responded with unaccustomed vigor: "Ben, that's the worst publishing idea I ever heard."

DIVERSION WITH A neo-con point to it: The little book publishing firm ultimately collapsed, not because it was doing poorly, but because it was doing well. Boehm hadn't realized we would start making money from the get-go, but when we did, he didn't much like the idea that I would have something of value without having invested anything. Our big book was *A Boy's Life of John F. Kennedy*, and it took off as if catapulted from a carrier, based on orders placed at the 1961 convention of the American Booksellers Association in Washington, D.C. Alas, the orders were generated only by a piece of posterboard bearing the title of the book and a designer's rendition of a jacket cover picturing JFK as a youngster, wearing an old-fashioned football helmet. Orders are only orders. There were no books. The book had been Boehm's idea. I recruited an author, Bruce Lee of *Newsweek*. I put him on a tight deadline so we could quickly turn the orders into books delivered to booksellers to get cash into the firm. Lee's manuscript was based mostly on clippings and had very few original interviews, which was probably to be expected with such a tight deadline. But I had huge problems with Lee's writing. I worked days, nights, and weekends to edit it, and actually wrote whole parts of it myself.

When it got to the bookstores, more or less on time, it sold very well. Why? JFK was handsome and articulate, and the First Lady, Jackie Kennedy, was beautiful. Their children, Caroline and little John-John, were photogenic darlings. But why was Kennedy elected over Nixon? (He won by a very thin margin: 49.7 to 49.5 percent.) His 1961 inaugural address gives a clue. It was probably as hawkish as anything ever uttered by an American president. It has been quoted ever since, most times favorably, but sometimes not, and sometimes by JFK admirers saying "that's not really what he meant." Some key lines:

> The world is very different now. . . . And yet the same revolutionary beliefs for which our forebears fought are still at issue around the globe—the belief that the rights of man come not from the generosity of the state but from the hand of God. . . .

> Let the word go forth from this time and place, to friend and foe alike, that the torch has been passed to a new generation of American—born in this century, tempered by war, disciplined by a hard and bitter peace, proud of our ancient heritage—and unwilling to witness or permit the slow undoing of those human rights to which this nation has always been committed, and to which we are committed today at home and around the world.

> *Let every nation know, whether it wish us well or ill, that we shall pay any price, bear any burden, meet any hardship, support any friend, oppose any foe, to assure the survival of liberty.* [Emphasis added.]

> All this will not be finished in the first hundred days. Nor will it be finished in the first thousand days, nor in the life of this administration, nor even perhaps in our lifetime on this planet. *But let us begin.*

Thus, an open-ended commitment to liberty: at *any* price, no matter the burden or hardship. Moreover, Kennedy had campaigned on the notion of a "missile gap" between the United States and the Soviet Union—with America on the short end, at the height of the Cold War. (The gap turned out to be nonexistent.) JFK was an anti-Communist hawk with some neo-con tendencies. Like many neo-cons today, he was not against the federal government taxing and spending. By some definitions JFK couldn't be a real neo-con because he wasn't formerly a liberal. His father, multimillionaire financier Joseph P. Kennedy, who played a large role in the development of JFK's political views, was an isolationist and a conservative. But as supply-siders never let us forget, JFK proposed tax cuts to "get America moving again." He was a practical politician. He had no problem in campaigning for votes in the sinfully segregationist solid South (solid for Democrats, that is).

Kennedy's hawkishness was not idiosyncratic. Senator Frank Church delivered the keynote address to the 1960 Democratic Convention that nominated JFK. Church was known as a stem-winding orator. What follows is quite remarkable, given Church's later dovish conversion.

> A Red Empire now engulfs all of Eastern Europe and vast China—[it] encloses a third of the world's people within its spreading reach. Its method of expansion has always been conquest, either from within or from without; in no Communist land have people ever freely voted the system in, and in no such land have the people ever been given the chance to vote it out.
>
> I have listened to Nikita Khruschev, behind the closed doors of the Senate Foreign Relations Committee. I have heard his certain prediction that Communism would win history's verdict. He has said that, although we may be free men, our grandchildren will be Communists.
>
> These are the grave stakes deeply involved in the coming national election. The mission of the Democratic Party is to reawaken America to the mighty task before her: the

> maintenance of peace, the preservation of freedom. The
> fate of the world all ultimately depend upon American
> principle, American prestige, and American power.
>
> I will never forget the words of an old Polish lady, spoken to
> me last year in Warsaw. She looked back with the wisdom
> and perspective forged in nearly a century of life. "Senator,"
> she said to me, "America is truly the hope of the world!"

Church later changed his views. He condemned the war in Vietnam. He exposed the "family jewels" of the CIA. He voted squishy soft on defense. I wonder what the old lady from Warsaw thought about that.

American voters generally approved Kennedy's language and thinking. They knew the costs of World War II and the Korean War (1950–1953), but they sensed a rationale in it. After all, Ralph Waldo Emerson had said, "Our whole history appears like a last effort of divine providence on behalf of the human race."

So: The quest for global liberty, and the strength to back it up, now ascribed principally to neo-cons and too often denigrated, had long been a central part of the American creed and that of the Democratic Party. The idea that neo-conservatism broke new ground is wrong. It is the Democratic Party that changed. Liberal Democrats today too often sound as if they are not willing to pay *any* price or bear *any* burden. That is one big reason they have been losing more elections than they should have, and why Jimmy Carter's 50.1 percent in 1976, more than three decades ago, was their last popular majority in a presidential election.

In the mid-1980s Speaker Tom Foley was invited to address at the Ditchley Park conference in England. He came to my house to sound out some ideas. We sat on my deck in the Forest Hills section of D.C. for several hours. Foley pointed out to me a high irony: Democratic members of Congress end up voting for large defense budgets but are always perceived as being afraid of doing so because they oppose one or two high-profile weapons systems. Why do they do that? Not necessarily on the intrinsic merit of the weapons, but to keep their credentials with peacenik special interests.

Ditchley is about as prestigious as these BOGSATTs (bunch of guys sitting around a table talking) get. Foley is a splendid man whom I had come to know during the two Scoop Jackson campaigns. We had a few drinks, exchanged views, and told tall tales. As the leading Democrat in Congress, his thinking had evolved since we were on the front lines of Scoop's Troops. The Democrats had moved to the left and so, too, had Foley. He had no choice, but as so often happens with so many of us, he came to believe what he had to believe, and his views were surely augmented by authentically changing convictions.

He wanted to know my opinions of the matters of the day: defense, domestic spending, race, neo-conservatism, and so on. Our views had diverged on a number of issues. Foley and Senate Majority Leader George Mitchell, the Maine Democrat, had paid a visit to President-Elect Clinton in Little Rock. As the story goes, they told him what the Democratic majorities in both houses of Congress would and would not accept from the new president. This allegedly had the effect of moving Clinton leftward, a move he later said he regretted, as he discussed with me at length (see chapter 9.)

Foley told me an interesting story. He received a call from Gordon Culp in Seattle. Culp is a solid citizen and had worked with us on the Jackson campaigns. He told Foley: "What's going on is crazy; they've passed a bill that instructs Americans how best to perform sadomasochistic acts! It's in use in San Francisco!" Foley said that was impossible, but that he would check. He did and it was true. The little program had been tucked away in one of those huge complicated pieces of legislation. He was dumbstruck. I was dumbstruck. But it was not really so surprising given the leftward cultural lurch of the Democrats. Hence the need for the commonsense views of the neo-cons.

I thought John F. Kennedy was great. So do many people with whom I disagree. They point to his softer side (e.g., a proposed nuclear test ban treaty with the Soviets). But what actually does, "Ask not what your country can do for you, but what you can do for your country" mean? Is that downplaying the safety net? I think not. Instead, it's a call for resolve in the American people to help their country pursue the nation's intrinsic mission of expanding liberty.

The positions later taken by his younger brothers did not pursue that star with similar vigor.

In any event, my short career as a book publisher begat my love of data. I lost my job because of Boehm's peculiarities. That job had been supporting my first wife and three young children. I learned that bill collectors are not nice people. Leaping from the frying pan, I decided to turn to freelancing and write a book based on 1960 Census data. I was told by my first editor, Sam Vaughan of Doubleday, that I was an unknown and I should get a better-known collaborator. Richard M. Scammon, the director of the U.S. Census Bureau, was neither a poet nor a novelist. Neither, for sure, was I. But the book materialized under the title *This U.S.A.* and led to my White House job with LBJ. His first major speech to Congress after JFK's assassination was in November 1963. He took Kennedy's line of "Let us begin," and turned it into "Let us continue."

THIS U.S.A. WAS published in 1965, when many young leftist academics were pouring out their theories and theses in great volume, using ever-more sophisticated data. They had regression analyses to prove just what they wanted to prove: that America was a bad place and would get worse unless the New Left or the New Politics or the Far Left or even the violent left acted and prevailed. Such views were gaining traction in the ever-more radical academy. Scammon and I didn't see things their way.

We looked at the numbers and reported on what we believed the data showed about America, absent manipulation. Ever since the publication of that first data book I have been called an optimist. We wrote that in America the optimists have been the realists. The social demographic data showed that America was making progress in most ways that are measurable. Social measurements can usually only track growth of the material aspects of life. Trying to measure human *happiness* is a different matter and is not simply the reciprocal of better living conditions. And as some research reports, rich people commit suicide at greater rates than poor ones.

When Scammon and I finished that first book, I remember thinking to myself: Wouldn't it be wonderful if I could write one

every ten years through the turn of the twenty-first century, adding
other dimensions of measurement as I went along. It sort of worked
out that way. In the 1970s I wrote *The Real America*. In the 1980s the
title was *The Good News Is the Bad News Is Wrong*. At that time,
I also authored *The Birth Dearth*, a book on global vital statistics.
In the 1990s I wrote *Values Matter Most*. Each book added additional lenses: about public opinion data, foreign policy, birth and
fertility rates, global demographics, elections, economics, and more,
notwithstanding my lack of the academic credentials that normally
go with such topics. There were other books as well. Alexander
Trowbridge, formerly LBJ's secretary of commerce and then head of
the National Association of Manufacturers, asked me to write a book
about trade. I recruited Richard Whalen to work with me. The National Association of Manufacturers put up some advance money
and hoped our book would advance a straight free-trade stance. It
didn't. The book was ultimately published as *The Wealth Weapon*,
and offered a *faux* dialogue among various views. The hero turns out
to be the fellow who wants to use trade to advance liberty, as in the
Jackson Amendment. The book was published by Transaction Press,
run by Irving Louis Horowitz. He is an angry man who screams a lot.
I hung up on him once.

Although I read a great deal, I learn best from talking things
out. Washington, D.C., has a remarkable base of talkers willing to
share: It is the talk-and-data capital of the universe. It is not hard to
book panelists for *Think Tank*. Social and economic measurement
has a long and distinguished history in America. The call for a decennial census is in the U.S. Constitution. After all, how could
seats in the House of Representatives be apportioned without such
data?

In 2000 I coauthored *The First Measured Century*, a book of
fairly simple charts with explanations covering the whole twentieth
century (written in collaboration with academics Theodore Caplow
and Louis Hicks); it is slated for update and republication by the AEI
Press.

In 2004 my book *Fewer: How the New Demography of Depopulation Will Shape Our Future* followed the spoor of *The Birth
Dearth*, showing how the slide in fertility rates continued to plunge,

and speculated on the potentially staggering meaning of that development. I believe that book has enormous significance for everyone in the world, yet it did not attract great attention, nor did it originally sell well. Later, sales grew as it became a standard work in the great demographic debate of our time.

I think *Fewer* may be the most important book I have written. I am going to give you the theme, some new numbers, and new projections as well. I believe that the situation is unprecedented, and no damned good for the whole world, even though it boosts American influence and power. I think that the medium- to long-range demographic situation is the most serious one mankind faces. That would include Iraq, terror, HIV/AIDS, avian flu, third-world poverty, crime, and more. (I am not particularly afraid of global warming.)

Let me set the context for my popularized data books. I sensed that America had a corps of data-twisting professional "pessimoans" (recall "lying for justice"). Their gloomy claims should be examined; insofar as these distracting factoids are being used to push for misguided actions. Prominently liberal, sometimes conservative, the gloom team has not given up. It seems to me that the data is being more distorted and politicized than ever before. The fight for reality, at least as I see it, is at the core of the neo-con persuasion.

Here are some of the things we hear: *that* Americans are the world's greatest greenhouse gas emitters and the chief culprits of global warming; *that* we live by borrowing from other, poorer, nations; *that* Social Security and Medicare are going broke; *that* the balance of trade deficit is killing us; *that* America is the gravest threat to the world; *that* we have no sympathy for people on welfare; *that* the American dream has been shattered; *that* our democracy is crooked; *that* American businessmen are thieves, living the good life while unemployment is high; *that* permissiveness has eroded our values to the point that homosexuality and abortion are glorified; *that* dangerous drugs are peddled in our schools; *that* computers provide pornography that corrupts children; *that* marriage is giving way to "hooking up"; *that* we aren't really making more money than we used to; *that* the rich get richer and the poor get poorer; *that* tax cuts go the rich and not to the middle class; *that* poor people don't get medical care; *that* neither blacks nor Latinos are making progress; *that* crime remains rampant; *that* fat cats run Congress; *that* the American education system is a scandal; *that* we kill prisoners inhumanely; *that* we can't even handle a flood; and *that* fundamentalist Christians call the shots, trying to force their Jewish, Muslim, Hindu, Confucian, agnostic, and atheistic neighbors' children to worship the baby Jesus.

In short, if you believe most of the items on that list, then the neo-cons must be wrong: America doesn't work.

LET US DEAL with the demographic situation first. Some neo-cons see parts of the problem as I do, but many are unaware of the full ramifications of the data, as are most people. I promise to keep the demographic complexities as simple as I can, but I assure you that the basic points are worth your consideration. The root of the problem concerns what has been called the population explosion, and for six decades it has been applied to so very many of our modern problems, sometimes correctly, usually not.

Much of the explosion idea rests on the flawed pillars constructed by Reverend Thomas Malthus (1766–1834), the English political economist who was concerned about what he saw to be the decline of living conditions in nineteenth-century England. Malthus laid the blame of the perceived decline on three notions: too many babies being born, the inability of resources to keep up with this rising population, and the irresponsibility of the lower classes. The whole idea was often summarized as "population outruns food supply," an idea that Malthus later conceded was foolish. That has not slowed down armies of latter-day Malthusians, who are rarely neo-cons.

Malthus recommended that the family size of the lower classes be regulated so that poor families could not produce more children than they could support. This was echoed two centuries later by China's coercive and nefarious one-child-per-family regulation instituted by Mao Zedong.

OF THE MAJOR modern nations in the world, only America is on a path to continuing demographic growth. How can it be that most of the other modern nations will have subreplacement total fertility rates, leading to population decline, and yet America will grow from three hundred million people today to four hundred million by 2050 and five hundred million in 2100?

The root of the answer is this: America takes in as many legal immigrants as the rest of the world combined. Perhaps I am so pro-immigration because my parents came to America in that brief window of time between the end of World War I and the harsh, restrictive immigration laws of 1921 and 1924. And neo-cons are more likely than most other Americans to favor legal immigration. But despite the recent furor about illegal immigration, Americans have a soft spot for people from elsewhere. Everyone in America is a descendant of people who came from somewhere else. George Washington, the "father of our country," was a descendent of English immigrants. Albert Einstein, whom *Time* magazine named man of the century, was a German Jew fleeing Hitler. The father of Andre Agassi, one of the best tennis players in history, was an émigré to America from Iran. African Americans are not exactly immigrants, having arrived in stinking slave holds, but some generations later two of their descendants—General Colin Powell, via Caribbean ancestry, and Secretary of State Condoleezza Rice—were at various times ranked number one in public opinion polls for president of the United States. And so it goes. It is interesting to speculate on how much the American high-tech industries would have grown without émigrés from India, China, Japan, and Taiwan.

It used to be said that Americans come from everywhere. That wasn't quite right. For example, there were laws, like the Asian Exclusion Act, that specifically put tight quotas on certain groups of people. To be sure, most every other group of arrivals was hated (although not quite so specifically in law): Italians, Jews, Slavs, and the Irish come immediately to mind. There were organizations like the Ku Klux Klan, to handle such peoples. Contrary to popular belief, the state with the most Klan members was not a Southern one, but Indiana, where at times the Klan ran much of the state government. The Klan was not only antiblack and anti-Jewish, but anti-Catholic as well.

The anti-immigration laws of the early 1920s had the effect of greatly increasing the immigration of northwestern European immigration and sharply diminishing the "dangerous" newcomers from southern and eastern Europe.

That was then, now is now. I wrote a book in 1991 entitled *The First Universal Nation: Leading Indicators and Ideas about the Surge of America in the 1990s*. Such a surge occurred. If there was one piece of legislative action that led to that boost it was the ongoing efforts of the Immigration Reform Act of 1965, passed as part of President Lyndon Johnson's Great Society.

The demographic experts I interviewed at the Census Bureau in the early 1960s for *This U.S.A.* seemed to know everything. Over the decades they have been gracious and prompt in their dealings with me. I only received one bum steer, through no fault of theirs. I was told that it was a great time to write the kind of book I was talking about because the era of immigration in America was over. But from 1981 to 2002 a total of 19 million legal immigrants arrived in the United States. For the record, during congressional hearings Attorney General Robert Kennedy predicted that 5,000 Chinese immigrants per year would come to America; from 1981 to 2002 the total was 813,000.

Mountains of studies have sought to show that immigration is either good or bad for the United States. One of the biggest questions raised about immigration concerns assimilation. It is said that in the old days immigrants were purposefully assimilated: in schools, by businesses, by settlement houses, and other similar institutions that taught American civic lessons, the English language, and patriotism. But in this day of runaway multiculturalism (so it is said) we are afraid to purposefully push assimilation lest we be called cultural chauvinists. But the immigrants *are* assimiliating, and the ability to assimilate them more quickly may be our greatest competitive advantage in the twenty-first century. National television plays a big role. Polling regularly shows that immigrants are even more patriotic than other Americans.

The Department of Defense has numbers on everything, except sometimes on which side is going to win a war. In proportional terms, Mexican Americans have been awarded the Congressional Medal of Honor more than any other ethnic group. The medal is the nation's highest military badge and requires "courage above and beyond the call of duty."

The linguistic history of the phrase *the brain drain* is fascinating. In the old days it referred mostly to highly educated young people seeking to further their learning in America. That was seen as a problem principally for the country *sending* students here. The students' elementary and secondary schooling was paid for by their home country, as was their transportation. For America, it was the ultimate gift. Great scientists and engineers came to America, producing new goods and services, some of which would be sold back to the brain-drained nations.

But in reality there were also low-skilled immigrants coming to America, some illegally. There was an open border with Mexico. By American standards many of the illegals worked for low wages, typically in jobs that Americans were unwilling to do. Consider the "stoop labor" in our agricultural industries, often done by people working below the minimum wage. Still, that wage was higher than what they could have earned back home. Gardeners and construction workers working at low wages are picked up by contractors at designated spots and also provided goods and services that subsidize other Americans. In effect, every bite of food that Americans consume has been subsidized.

As their education and aspirations climbed, few black women would do domestic work. Latinas picked up the slack, enabling many American women to enter the labor force, advancing feminism. My housekeeper, for example, is from El Salvador. She came here illegally, stuffed in the trunk of a car filled with fifteen other people. Now she has a green card. We have a deal. I correct her accent. She teaches me Spanish (*Buenas tardes, señora*). Her teen-aged son Rudy gets excellent grades, weighs 210 pounds, plays fullback at a high school noted for high educational and athletic achievement, and loves computers. I frequently lecture him about a sound mind in a sound body, and he pretends to listen. Ignore the dueling studies about the efficacy of immigration. No study can factor in what Rudy will do for America.

The general neo-con support for immigration is not generally matched in the other parts of the conservative constellation. Many conservatives have been anti-immigration, or very nervous about it. Paleo-conservatives like Pat Buchanan have written radically anti-Mexican tracts. One of his books was high on the bestseller lists and has a theme that goes back many decades. Its title says it all: *The Death of the West: How Dying Populations and Immigrant Invasions Imperil Our Country and Civilization.* In brief, it substitutes Mexicans for the vicious feelings once felt for Italians, Jews, and Irish. Anti-immigration sentiment is not a new story; Benjamin Franklin wrote nasty screeds about Germans coming to America. Ironically, the new Americans are mostly Catholic, family-oriented, and patriotic — just what Pat admires. What is Buchanan's problem?

Before the 1965 law, about 80 *percent* of the immigration to the United States was of *European* origin. Since 1965, about 80 *percent* has been *non-European*, or to put it more bluntly, as some conservatives see it, nonwhite. The new immigrants have come mostly from Mexico, China, Taiwan, the Philippines, South Korea, and India, although there have been plenty of English, Poles, Russians, Russian Jews, Irish, and Germans.

The big demographic story after the 2000 Census was that by 2050 half of America would be nonwhite. This frightened many Americans. It should not have, either numerically nor substantively. In the old days census enumerators looked at a respondent and decided whether he or she was white, black, Asian, or Hispanic, terms that today no one seems able to define satisfactorily.

When America becomes "majority minority" it's going to be hard to notice it. The rates of marriage between groups are astonishing. More than half of Jews marry non-Jews (many Jews regard this unhappily). Japanese-Americans marry WASPS. Italo-Americans marry Irish-Americans. (Kerry Kennedy — of the vast Irish-American political clan — married Italian-American Andrew Cuomo, son of New York's Governor Mario Cuomo. Years ago that would have been a scandal in two communities. Today, such a story is a yawner.) Bobby Jamil, from *India*, is the new governor of Louisiana, a mostly Catholic state. Perhaps the most remarkable story of exogamy (the uptown sociological term for intermarriage) concerns African Americans. As noted, these days nearly one in ten blacks marries a nonblack; a few decades ago the rate was just one-fifth of that. And one hears that African-American women complain bitterly that they can't find potential black marriage partners because most black exogamy occurs among black men and because the rate of black men in prison is so high. The law of unintended consequences: Will the children of such unions be judged black under the ugly "one-drop" rule? I hope not. Tiger Woods calls himself Amerasian because he has black, Thai, and American Indian ancestry.[1] Americans should decide what, if anything, they should be called. American Jew works for me.

The general rule of exogamy is that the smaller the pool of immigrants, the larger the rate of exogamy. Iranian-American parents may hope that the child they send away to college will come home with an Iranian-American mate. But there aren't that many young Iranians in college. I'm for immigration. When I take a cab in Washington or New York, most of the drivers are immigrants, with foreign accents. I usually ask the driver how long he has been in America, what he thinks about it, and then wait to see how long it takes until I hear the words *opportunity* and *hard work*, as in, "You have to work very hard here, but there is plenty of opportunity." It's usually in the first full paragraph. (The second paragraph is about the damn traffic.) It can often take a seventy-hour week for a cabdriver to make ends meet.

Moreover, immigrants are the best explainers of America we have, at a time when we need all the help we can get. Those cabdrivers take advantage of cheap global transportation, cell phones, and e-mail. Immigrants have established a global information network that beats the best that public diplomacy can offer. They speak to the world and say that pluralist democracy works pretty well at a time when anti-Americanism is running high.

Immigrants play an important and positive role in international economics. Many recently arrived American immigrants send money back home—the formal term is "remittances." Most international economists believe it is the best form of foreign aid. It goes directly to poor people who need it, with no skimming by third-world plutocrats who are too often corrupt. It is said the "skim" in Asia is 10 percent and 90 percent in Africa.

Immigration is as an enormous asset in the geopolitical realm as well. A larger population tends to yield greater geopolitical influence. If you are interested in promoting and extending democratic values,

---

1. Joke: Q: How do you describe one black man being chased by 100 angry white men? A: The PGA tour.

as most neo-conservatives are, geopolitical power sometimes comes from a strong military. American population will grow from three hundred million to five hundred million between 2000 and 2100. It takes no mathematical genius to see that a defense budget split among four or five hundred million people is easier to pay for than one split among three hundred million people, especially if every other major nation is not only shrinking but shrinking more quickly than the tricky UN projections indicate. Look at the nations of the European Union theme park. They will not have the manpower to field a serious young volunteer force. Belgium makes do with portly forty-year-old draftees.

Not everything about immigration is just plain good. Sometimes it has caused more than a little torn fur at the Department of State. The central question: Should America have a foreign policy based on American interests or on the interests of Americans? A great country, *the* great country, needs a professional diplomatic corps that sees a grand national interest. But a country whose founding document begins "We, the people . . ." must respect the interests of its citizens, all of whom are immigrants (and many of whom vote). And so, while Turkey is geopolitically more important to America than Greece, we have tended to tilt toward Greece because there are more Greek Americans than Turkish Americans. There are more Muslims than Jews in the world, but America tilts toward Jews and Israel because there are more Jews than Muslims in America, because Jews vote at high rates and are particularly active politically, sometimes quite hard-nosed about it, and because Israel is a democracy. When the British fought Argentina in 1982 over the flyspeck Falkland Islands, America sided with our British ancestors and allies, not our Argentinean hemispheric neighbors. The U.S. action broke with the tradition of the Monroe Doctrine. (UN Ambassador Jeane Kirkpatrick wanted to help Argentina.)

So, just how does the case for gloom I introduced at the beginning of this chapter stack up to the data? Regarding global warming, fewer people should create fewer greenhouse gases. I reviewed environmentalist Bill McKibben's book *Maybe One* for *The Wall Street Journal* in 1998. His logic flowed this way: He wanted a second child but had a vasectomy instead, to prevent global warming. He wants other people

to behave similarly. My bottom-line question was this: Is Bill Mc-
Kibben an extremist? I was on the edge until I finished his book with a
sense that something was missing. Something was. Right there, in the
index, between Notre Dame and nutrition was—nothing. No mention of nuclear power. Why not? Nuclear power produces energy
without emitting greenhouse gases. Why not open that conversation?

Many environmentalists like McKibben have difficulty endorsing nuclear power. Jane Fonda told them not to. The green Clinton-
Gore administration bragged about selling nuclear power plants to
China, but we couldn't build new ones here. I find it hard to take
global warming very seriously until environmentalists talk very seriously about nuclear power. McKibben doesn't, preferring vasectomy. He's an extremist.

I am not an expert on global warming, but I can certify that the
debate has become highly politicized. A 2006 comprehensive study
run by Duke University climatologists showed that the likely increase
of global warming comes in at the low end of the much-publicized
probabilities. There may be some change afoot: Patrick Moore, the
former director of Greenpeace, now publicly endorses nuclear power.

Are Americans living on borrowed money? Given the demographic and power circumstances, where else would foreign investors
put their money in order to guarantee a safe payout to pensioners?

Are Social Security and Medicare going broke? We shall see, but
the average age of a legal immigrant to America is twenty-nine, which
means about forty years of Social Security insurance payments to the
federal government before any monies are withdrawn. Moreover, as
the gross domestic product grows from $12.5 trillion in 2007 to $25
trillion in 2025 there will be lots of taxable income to pay for entitle-
ments, quite possibly without a tax increase. Changing the formulas
for Social Security or Medicare is no longer "the Third Rail of American Politics." They were changed in 1982 and can be again.

Are we mortgaging our children's future? Sure, but that process
resembles life; parents care for their children, when parents age their
children care for them. Entitlement programs like Social Security
and Medicare tend to partially institutionalize the traditional human condition. What are we agonizing about? That Americans are
living longer healthier lives?

Is the negative balance of trade eroding our economic strength? Given the current situation, the nations that hold our dollars will keep holding them because they are the safest form of liquid wealth in a world where America is the only large, stable, and free country that is growing while the rest are shrinking. We give them paper. They hold the paper and send us goods. Not a bad deal.

Is American democracy crooked? Has there been thievery among American businessmen? Sure there is some, but on any international scale it is comparatively small. New transparency laws, even the dreaded Sarbanes-Oxley Act, yield a safety net for investors. Ultimately, such additional transparency makes American markets more attractive. Nor is there any evidence that the American Congress— despite some recent high-profile cases of serious corruption by lobbyists—is worse than that of other free political systems, and it is probably much better. The French are far more corrupt. Most American federal elected legislators of whatever ideological persuasion are honest and patriotic.

On the so-called hot-button social issues, many neo-cons would tend to agree that homosexuality and abortion are too often glorified in the media but would not favor making either illegal. Do neo-cons think that permissiveness has eroded the American our way of life, that dangerous drugs are peddled at most every school in America, that computers provide pornography that corrupts children, and that marriage is under threat? Yes, but they have no good solutions. America has its problems.

Are neo-cons concerned about high violent crime rates? Yes, and they have been for fifty years. But violent crime rates have come down substantially in America and gone up in many places that used to point to American violence as a symptom of American decay. Think French suburbs.

Is American unemployment very high when calculated against most other modern nations? No. It is substantially lower.

Do neo-cons think that tax cuts go the rich and not to the middle class? They may not like the current tax structure, but they tend to understand that if tax rates are to be cut, and such cuts offer incentives to economic growth, then the cuts must come from the people who pay most of the taxes—the well-to-do. As bank robber Willie

Sutton said, go where the money is. Moreover, every federal tax cut for the well-to-do has been matched by taking many less fortunate Americans off the IRS rolls or providing them with a bonus through the Earned Income Tax Credt.

Are Americans really making less money than they used to? Are the rich getting richer as the poor get poorer? Again, many neo-cons could think of ways that income could be distributed more fairly, but the economic evidence is overwhelming: Americans are doing much better than they did in days past. Gordon Green, the former chief of the Census Bureau's Income Division, is a visiting fellow at AEI working with Doug Besharov. Green recently showed the bureau, to its satisfaction, that the core poverty rate was not about 12 percent but about 8 percent. The Census Bureau will be making that change. He believes that, counting the noncash benefits like food stamps, the true rate is about 4 percent.

The income numbers do remain complex, but I think the best way to measure the well-being of Americans over time is by looking at what they have: nearly double the number of automobiles per household since 1960; more than double the average size of a new home over the same period; air-conditioning in 85 percent of those homes. And better educations: in 1960 8 percent of Americans held bachelor's degrees. Today the number is approaching 30 percent, and 1 in 3 of those college graduates go on to attain advanced degrees.

Do some middle- and lower-middle-class Americans live without medical insurance? Of course, but the very poor receive Medicaid, while poor and lower-middle-class children receive "Kiddie-care." The elderly receive Medicare, which now includes a prescription drug benefit. Veterans can turn to their local Veterans Administration facility. Problems remain, but there is not yet a consensus about how to cope with a difficult situation. People living in countries with universal coverage like their systems, but those with money often fly here for private care: They resent waiting five years until hip replacement surgery can be scheduled. But the lower-middle class is left out—they don't have the money to travel.

Do most American politicians keep spending more and more taxpayer money? Yes. Some neo-cons don't like it; most all conservatives don't like it. Since President Reagan came into office, federal spending has climbed substantially, yet because of continued economic growth, today's deficits are relatively low by historical standards. We need to spend. The biggest "pork-barrel" projects—the roads, bridges, airports, and harbors—are all things America needs.

Surveys show that most Americans believe in the death penalty for heinous crimes. But there is a very lengthy review process. Surveys in some European Union nations show sizable populations endorsing capital punishment, notwithstanding the EU's demand that candidate states for membership must outlaw the practice before joining. And the surveys I'm referring to were conducted *before* Theo van Gogh was carved up by a Muslim terrorist in early 2006.

What about education? America has some of the greatest schools in the world—both public and private. Yet there are schools in poor areas that are dreadful. Once again, there is little agreement regarding what to do about it and with whose money. (Scoop had the right idea. See chapter 4.) Are children learning more and better? Test scores are rising, but the full picture is dicey.

Some liberals maintain that neither blacks nor Latinos have made economic progress in recent decades. There are legitimate ways to argue this, but the overwhelming evidence is that substantial progress has occurred. And so it goes. It is said that in America we can't even handle a flood and we didn't during Hurricane Katrina. The U.S. Army Corps of Engineers is usually a top-flight organization, but the perfect storm . . . was a perfect storm. It is said that American fundamentalists and Evangelical Christians call the shots— but the religious Right claims that all it gets is rhetoric from politicians they helped get elected.

The game is called politics and it thrives on declarations that the other side creates all the bad news. I would maintain that the evidence shows clearly that America is the most successful nation in the world. The American dream is alive and well.

WELFARE WAS A mess. From its inception, the program known as welfare, Aid to Families with Dependent Children, was a federal "entitlement." That is a budget term of art which means that recipients get their welfare payments automatically, by formula, with no need for the legislation to go through the crazy-quilt congressional authorization and appropriations procedures. In 1996, President Clinton signed legislation eliminating welfare as an entitlement. Although he had campaigned in 1992 to "end welfare as we know it," it was the 1994 Gingrich Republicans that put teeth into a law that the Clinton White House sought to finesse. It was Clinton's re-election year, however, and because most Americans believed that welfare was counterproductive, he signed. Some softening amendments followed.

Senator Moynihan, a welfare expert, said it would result in little children not having enough to eat. Secretary of Health and Human Services Donna Shalala denounced her own president's act. Hillary Clinton's mentor, Marian Wright Edelman of the liberal Children's Defense Fund, declared it a scandal. The number of welfare recipients dropped. And huge amounts of long-rumored fraud was proved true: Many recipients stopped drawing welfare because the new law stipulated that recipients had to pick up their checks in person.

The new welfare law did provide former recipients with jobs, job training, day care, and food stamps as needed. And the former recipients took advantage of the new provisions, in some large measure because the new law said no American could draw welfare benefits for more than five years in the course of a lifetime. People with serious disabilities were exempt. People in real need received more. Welfare cheats got less. That is how it should be. In the end more money was spent in total than before the entitlement abandonment. Observers said the reforms might work during economic boom times but catastrophe lurked around the corner if the economy ever headed down. In 2000 the economy tanked, but the number of people on welfare stayed low. In all, in 1995 there were 13.4 million recipients; in 2000 it was 5.8 million. And in 2005 the estimate was 4.5 million, in a growing population.

As neo-conservatism developed it was clear that an optimistic view of America was one of its hallmarks. The data showed that

America was making clear headway, despite remaining problems. By emulation, other nations might do better. Only America could lead.

I LIKED TO think I was on to something new: "data journalism." I was trying to build a case fact by fact telling the story straight and debunking what needed debunking while trying to keep a narrative flowing. Fine. But who was purveying what needed debunking? The most publicized of the crisis-mongers were liberal interest groups and the radical Left, although many moralistic conservatives and GOP businessmen had their own grim tales about how terrible America had become.

For me, it became more than just data journalism; it was counteradvocacy, and it fit right into the neo-conservative view. Like most of the American public, we neo-cons understood that although there was always plenty of room for improvement, America was doing well and stood for something very important and good in the world.

1967. President Johnson, flanked by Special Assistants Douglass Cater and Harry McPherson Jr. and (with hair!) the author. *(Author's collection)*

The publication of *The Real Majority* in 1970 caused a political sensation, pro and con. Almost forty years later, the book is still regularly hailed as a classic. At right: myself (with mustache) and my psephological mentor, Dick Scammon. Center: *Meet the Press* moderator Lawrence Spivak. The panelists are David Broder, Kevin Phillips, Bob Novak, and Paul Duke. *(Courtesy of NBC News)*

The kick-off advertisement for the Coalition for a Democratic Majority. It drew a heavy and enthusiastic response and told Democrats, bewildered in the wake of the 1972 campaign, that they weren't alone. *(Author's collection)*

Come Home, Democrats.

Notwithstanding his note, Pat Moynihan's words were his own, always. At left are Senator Scoop Jackson and Representative Tom Foley, later Speaker of the House. Contributing to the start of the CDM in the mid-1970s is one of my proudest accomplishments. *(Author's collection)*

Scoop Jackson remains my number-one hero. He was one senator out of a hundred, and today's American foreign-policy strategies can still be evaluated in "pro-" or "anti-Jackson" terms. (*Author's collection*)

Scoop really did carry his own bags . . . and if you weren't careful, yours as well! Jimmy Carter only *claimed* to do it. The senator here with his wife, Helen, myself, and aide Don Donahue in the early 1970s. (*Author's collection*)

The famous—or infamous—meeting between the CDM and President Carter in 1979. He thought we were concerned about human rights in Ecuador! I am at the president's left. Proceeding clockwise around the table: Midge Decter, Jeane Kirkpatrick, National Security Advisor Zbigniew Brzezinski (a CDM founding member), Max Kampleman, Norman Podhoretz, Elliott Abrams, Dan Flanagan, Vice President Walter Mondale, (obscured), Austin Ranney, (obscured), Maria Thomas, S. Harrison "Sonny" Dogole, (obscured), and Admiral Elmo Zumwalt. *(Official White House photograph)*

Taping a PBS special in the early 1980s in a replica of Johnson's Oval Office at the LBJ Library in Austin, Texas. As I see it, the job criteria for being president includes wisdom, ideology, vision, and an inspirational character. Legislative experience and "knowledge" come in a distant second. *(Author's collection)*

The Board of Directors of Radio Free Europe and the Board of International Broadcasting in the early eighties. From the left (rear): President Gene Pell, Ken Tomlinson, Michael Novak, Lane Kirkland, Clair Burgener, Ed Ney; (front): Arch Madsen, Chairman Malcolm "Steve" Forbes, the author (vice chair), and James Michener. The Board was known as "the best in Washington." *(Author's collection)*

To Ben Wattenberg - With Every Good Wish & Best Regards
Ronald Reagan

Interviewing President Reagan in the early 1980s. His remarks about the relationship between liberalism and fascism made big news. *(Official White House photograph)*

VALUES MATTER MOST, a one-hour television documentary will premiere Monday, November 13, at 10 p.m. (ET) on PBS (check local listings). Host Ben Wattenberg (pictured) argues that the number one political issue among American voters is values. According to Wattenberg, values issues are the reason why Republicans won in 1994; why Democrats must change in order to hold on to the White House and regain strength in Congress; and why an independent presidential candidate may yet surprise us all in 1996.

VALUES
MATTER MOST
With Ben Wattenberg

VALUES MATTER MOST is a production of BJW Inc. in association with New River Media and is presented on PBS by Thirteen/WNET. (Photo: Sigrid Estrada)

The promo picture for the PBS special based on my book *Values Matter Most.* (Author's collection)

President Clinton and the author in 1995 just before the announcement "subsuming the Radios" into the United States Information
Agency. Vice President Gore and columnist Fred Barnes were also in
attendance. The schmooze went on for about a half hour while the
press cooled its heels. (*Official White House photograph*)

Vice President
Cheney has
an undeserved
sinister reputation.
I find him humor-
ous, bright, cordial,
and open. (*Courtesy
of the Office of the
Vice President*)

CHAPTER NINE

Values Matter Most

A POLITICAL FIRESTORM erupted in 2004 when an exit poll showing that moral values were the most important issue in the election failed to report that the issue was actually only cited by 22 percent of the respondents. In second place was the economy, at 20 percent, well within the margin of error. Terrorism was the choice of 19 percent of the responding voters, and Iraq scored 15 percent. More important, this was the first time the phrasing moral values had been used by the consortium of newspapers and television networks that sponsored the poll. There was no time line, and no way to know whether moral values were waxing or waning as an issue. Soon, the commentariat zeroed in on the strange aspects of the poll. With merit, liberals said it meant next to nothing.

Almost entirely unnoticed in the postelection polling brouhaha (as AEI's Karlyn Bowman pointed out to me) was that there was another national exit poll, taken by *The Los Angeles Times*. It *had* asked a values question for three consecutive presidential elections, and *had* asked the question with near-identical phrasing. The results were clear:

Q. Which issues, if any, were important to you in deciding how you would vote for president today? (Up to two
replies accepted.)

2004
> 1. Moral/ethical values: 40 percent
> 2. Jobs/the economy: 33 percent

2000
> 1. Moral/ethical values: 35 percent
> 2. Jobs/the economy: 26 percent

1996
> 1. Moral and ethical values: 40 percent
> 2. Jobs/the economy: 35 percent

The issue of values in many of its forms has been at the root of
much neo-conservative activity. It is not a new issue by any means,
nor is it going away.

Exit polls are not of much value these days. After the 2000 election fiasco in Florida I was called by Tom Johnson, then the CEO
of the news division of CNN. He asked me to serve on a three-
person commission to investigate the matter. My colleagues were
Joan Konner, a professor and dean emerita of the Columbia University Graduate School of Journalism and the former executive
producer of *Bill Moyers Journal*; and James Risser, a two-time Pulitzer
Prize–winning journalist and a professor emeritus of communication
at Stanford University. The first sentence of the preamble to our report
was this:

> On Election Day 2000, television news organizations
> staged a collective drag race on the crowded highway of
> democracy, recklessly endangering the electoral process,
> the political life of the country, and their own credibility,
> all for reasons that may be conceptually flawed and com-
> mercially questionable.

Joan wrote it; I loved it.

Among the problems: 1) There are higher rates of absentee ballots cast, and those voters cannot be surveyed as they leave a polling place; 2) More voters than in earlier years brush off pollsters as they exit their polling places; 3) Fewer voters will answer a pollster calling on the telephone, probably due to the rise in maddening telemarketing calls; and 4) Both television and newspapers rush to judgment before sufficient data is available. Still, there is a role for exit polling if it is examined carefully and if there is more than one source used. The polls can give us hints about the *reasons* voters cast their ballot as they did. Simple election returns just give numbers.

President Bill Clinton understood the values issues well. In 1992 he had campaigned with great effect by calling for "personal responsibility," and, my favorite, "no more something for nothing." In late 1995 my book *Values Matter Most* was published. Before publication I had the publisher send bound page proofs to a number of important people, trying to create a buzz. I succeeded beyond belief. One of the people I sent the book to was President Clinton. (I had heard him speechifying at an event at the Greenbrier in White Sulphur Springs, West Virginia, a few weeks earlier and mentioned it to him as he masterfully worked the entire room filled mostly with CEOs.)

Weeks later I was in a hotel room in San Diego taking a nap in the late afternoon following a luncheon speech I had delivered. The phone rang. It was the White House operator, who had tracked me down through my office. "The White House calling," she said. I knew that game; I asked her *who* at the White House was calling. "It's the president, Mr. Wattenberg." In a moment, President Clinton came on the line. And we talked—for almost an hour! I took notes.

This was shortly after the Republicans had taken control of both houses of Congress for the first time in forty years. Newt Gingrich had become Speaker and was promoting the Contract With America, assailing Clinton at every turn, often on issues of values, sometimes validly, sometimes wildly. Gingrich's Republicans had gained fifty-two seats in the House, more than even Gingrich had expected. The GOP stayed in the majority through 2006. In 1994 the GOP also gained eight seats in the Senate.[1] All this occurred despite an economy that had recovered solidly from a shallow recession: The gross domestic product growth in 1994 was a robust 4 percent.

President Clinton said he had been reading and skimming my new book, and was very complimentary. He said it was the "most honest criticism of the administration," that it "hit on substance and helped him gain perspective," and that it was "honest [and] open, not mean-spirited . . . the kind of book any president would appreciate." (I cannot resist repeating those phrases.) He also noted that there were some things in the book with which he disagreed. He told me that he had been thinking about the current political landscape and had come up with a phrase to describe it—"values matter most." (I choose to believe that.) And so he was more than taken aback when a book of that title ended up on his desk.

Clinton analyzed his problem: He told me that in 1993 and 1994 he was too interested in the "legislative scorecard rather than in philosophy." He said he was "so anxious to fix the economy" that he had "changed philosophically and missed the boat"; that he had "lost the language" that had originally shaped him in the eyes of voters as a New Democrat who had paid great attention to issues of values. He said that he had behaved "like a prime minister, not a president." He believed that he had created a "cardboard cutout of himself." He added that he had "let Democrats down" by not talking out more forcefully about values.

I said that I was not pleased with his weak welfare reform bill proposal and he responded, "I wasn't pleased with it either." We agreed that his education bill ("Goals 2000") started the legislative process as an excellent piece of work, but didn't end up that way.

Clinton vowed to publicly recapture his New Democrat image and ideology. In late 1994 the draft *National Standards for United States History: Exploring the American Experience* was issued. Much controversy ensued. The standards stressed what was left out of earlier histories. Fair enough. But once again, the cause groups went too far. For example, there were six mentions of antislavery heroine Har-

---

1. The day after the election Senator Richard Shelby of Alabama changed parties, from Democrat to Republican, bringing the total GOP gain in the Senate to nine.

riet Tubman (a black woman, and hence a "two-fer" in modern hiring parlance), but no mention of the Confederate hero General Robert E. Lee—not even unfavorable ones. I interviewed Professor Gary Nash, the codirector of the project that had produced the book, for my column. He said that the document was against "triumphalism," and that too many nations had suffered from telling their stories as "us, the good guys, versus them, the bad guys." The sainted Albert Shanker, arguably neo-conservative in many ways, and president of the American Federation of Teachers, issued a statement. It was not entirely negative, but noted that "the section on the Cold War doesn't even mention Soviet aggression in Eastern Europe." (He called for substantial revisions.) I have not seen survey results on the word or the concept of *triumphalism*. But I would bet Professor Nash his salary that over 90 percent of American parents would like their children taught that America has triumphed in a parlous world. Clinton said that he agreed with me on that but was not aware of the argument.

The president had not said that his comments were off the record, nor on background, nor deep background. I was a known scribbler with a weekly column. Naturally I decided to write a column about the long conversation with the president. I checked with my old friend and media maven Dave Gergen (who had by then left Clinton's staff), and he agreed that I would not violate any journalistic convention by publishing. I called Clinton's press secretary Mike McCurry and told him about my long talk with Clinton and that a column was on its way. McCurry said I certainly had every right to write it. I wrote it and faxed an advance copy to a list of all the White House correspondents actually stationed in the White House rabbit warrens. (I then lost the list, a valuable commodity for a self-promoter with a cause.)

The column generated a controversy and dominated the regular White House press briefing for not one, but two, news cycles. (McCurry told the press corps that President Clinton said the story and quotes were accurate, except for one item. I checked my notes; I was right, he was wrong. In any event it concerned a matter that Clinton had covered in another, unchallenged, statement.) It was news: the president shmoozing and baring his soul to a columnist, for almost an hour, admitting important errors, many of them on the values issues.

The story appeared on page one above the fold of *The New York Times* and was featured in most every other newspaper. I quickly appeared on just about every public affairs television and radio show in Washington, from PBS's high-end discussion program to the scream-fest known as *The McLaughlin Group*. Regular group member uber-columnist Bob Novak said to me, "No president ever called *me*."

I was profiled in the style section of *The Washington Post*, which was quite favorable in places but quite smarmy in others. Media columnist Howard Kurtz seemed to think it was not nice to promote your own work, and that I had a sinecure at the American Enterprise Institute. Kurtz works hard. So do I. His work is not very original. I think mine is. (Authors of thesis books like *Values Matter Most* tend to believe that they do the most important work on the planet.)

So I had my minutes of media celebrity. It was fun. There was one downside: When the book was reviewed, almost entirely favorably, a good piece of the review space was typically devoted to the infamous phone call, not the substance of the book, which was values and how a neo-con sees that issue.

I talked to McCurry after the furor, and he said that when White House aide George Stephanopoulos told Clinton the uproar would get him into trouble, Clinton said, no, it would help him. This was about the time Clinton was thinking of "triangulation," the theory that he could do mildly conservative things—particularly on values issues (like school uniforms, which were mocked)—and still retain liberal support. Presidents are almost invariably shrewder than their aides. (School uniforms are a good idea if parents and teachers agree to them.)

MY VOTE FOR Clinton in 1992 was largely based on values. Here was a Democrat—a New Democrat—who preached "no more something for nothing" and always drummed home the point that people's well-being was mostly dependent not on government activity but on personal responsibility. Clinton had pledged to "end welfare as we know it," very tough words for a Democrat to utter. He was four-square for values—governmental and personal; just my kind of stuff.

In *Values Matter Most* I defined the often amorphous term *values* from *Webster's New World Dictionary*: "The social principles, goals or standards held by an individual, class, society, etc. That which is desirable or worthy of esteem for its own sake; a thing or quality having intrinsic worth."

In *The Real Majority*, coauthored with Dick Scammon, we had written that values (i.e., the social issue) had become *coequal* with the economy as the most important voting issue in American politics. In *Values Matter Most* (written alone) I maintained that values had become the *most* important voting issue.

I divided values into social issues and cultural issues. The social issues concerned things that governments did wrong and could correct, and that most voters agreed were wrong. The case histories in the book that I discussed with President Clinton concerned parts of his legislative package: crime, welfare, education, and affirmative action, which I maintained was often really quotas. I made every effort to be objective, and I believe I was.

In 1993 I traveled to Kansas City, Missouri, to get some material for a PBS special based on the book. Focus groups—one for women, one for men—were set up for us by a local self-help group, certainly not of a conservative mind-set. Most but not all of the interviewees were African American. They loved their children deeply. Most of the panel was in school or getting ready to begin work. In the interview with the women, I apologetically began asking a neo-con question:

> ME: Some people say that teenage girls are having out-of-wedlock babies in order to get welfare. [The rest of the question was supposed to be cowardly and contradictory, roughly this: *Now I don't really believe that, but isn't it likely that the package of welfare benefits does reduce the restraints against such births and therefore make them more likely?* I didn't get to finish the question. The women jumped in vehemently.]

> WOMAN #1: Right, there are women out there just having children to get it.

WOMAN #2: That's what they'd rather do, is sit at home and do nothing.

WOMAN #3: Young girls out there will brag that "I have four kids, so I get this and this amount of money, and this amount in food stamps."

I was shaken. When it came to interview the men, one of them said that while in prison he had been listening to Rush Limbaugh and he thought that Limbaugh made a great deal of sense.

The cultural issues in *Values Matter Most*, sometimes disparaged these days as wedge issues, are much harder to pin down. But something had happened. Some conservative concocted a poll that gained great currency because it seemed so relevant to what was going on. It was called the "Top Problems in Public Schools, Identified by Teachers." In 1940 those top issues were allegedly talking out of turn, chewing gum, making noise, running in the halls, cutting in line, dress code infractions, and littering.

And in 1990 the top problems were allegedly drug abuse, alcohol abuse, pregnancy, suicide, rape, robbery, and assault.

Quite a difference. The poll turned out to be phony, but was still credible to many because so much had changed in America.

The book also listed some other cultural issues that had come to the fore, among them (alphabetically): abortion, amnesty, bra-burning, busing, capital punishment, draft dodging, drugs, flag burning, gays in the military, Gennifer Flowers, gun control, homosexuality, movies and television, *Murphy Brown*, patriotism, the Pledge of Allegiance, political correctness, pornography, prayer in school, Troopergate, and Willie Horton.

Some of these cultural issues are long gone, but many are still with us, like abortion, homosexuality, and what can be seen on television and on movie screens. And there has been at least one big new one: gay marriage. Thirteen states in the election year of 2004 held referenda on gay marriage, "a union between a man and a woman," or a variant of that phraseology. The pro-gay side of the issue lost in all thirteen states, some by massive majorities.

The hot-button issues of gay marriage and homosexuality are interesting ones. They again point up the difference between neo-cons and the rest of the conservative constellation. So-called paleo-cons (like Pat Buchanan, for one) and many plain conservatives would regard homosexuality as a sin. The neo-con position is usually quite different. Neo-cons would tend to say, Let people alone. Talk about homosexuality if you wish. Do not stigmatize it. But do not glorify it.

I have mentioned the (arguable) idea that the true pro-life position means punishment for OBGYNs and hospital personnel who help in the abortion process. That position is emphatically rejected by the American public. In any event, contrary to popular belief, abortion is not a big voting issue in America. Karlyn Bowman, the American Enterprise Institute's polling expert, says that abortion usually ranks in about tenth place on a scale of most important issues.

I am pro-choice — barely. I was influenced in the early 1960s, when I interviewed a Hungarian OBGYN over a meal of elk in a restaurant looking out over the Danube. (Hungary was among the first nations to legalize abortion. I was researching a book tentatively titled *This World* that never came out due to my recruitment by the White House.) The doctor had delivered thousands of babies, and performed thousands of abortions. I asked him if terminating a pregnancy troubled him. He said, "I have learned over the years that there is nothing you can do to prevent a woman from having a baby if she wants one, even if she is putting her life at risk. And there is nothing you can do to prevent a woman from aborting a fetus if that's what she has decided to do." Many years later I saw a sonogram of my youngest daughter. It did nothing but fortify my position. I am pro-choice, but no one will convince me that life is not present in the womb. Over the years pro-life groups have asked me to speak because of my view that the world is not overpopulated and that legalization is not needed as a crude form of birth control. I have refused such invitations.

In his very interesting 1998 book *One Nation After All*, sociologist Alan Wolfe sets out an interesting thesis, as well as one of the longest subtitles: *What Middle-Class Americans Really Think About God, Country, Family, Racism, Welfare, Immigration, Homosexuality, Work, the Right, the Left, and Each Other*. Wolfe, along with some fellow researchers, conducted two hundred interviews in eight suburban localities.[2]

Wolfe (a liberal, a former sixties radical, vigorously anti–George W. Bush, and no neo-con) held lengthy conversations with the respondents. Rather than ask the simple yes-or-no, make-a-choice questions featured in public opinion polls, the researchers asked for free-form, conversational answers. His conclusion was that Americans are a quite tolerant people on most cultural issues, seeking a "sensible center" and content to live and let live (sound familiar?). His exception was homosexuality—a topic about which he found vigorous opposition. But since the 1998 publication of the book, Wolfe has done further research and found that attitudes toward homosexuality are softening. Wolfe's findings, as I read them, are not far from where most neo-cons stand on these issues.

Given that values (broadly seen) are the most important issues in our political life, and that surveys show Democrats routinely far behind Republicans on the issue, why are Democrats still potent vote-getters, albeit less so than before?

When all is said and done, Democrats are still regarded the party of the little guy, and Republicans are still seen as the party of the fat cats. There are still more self-perceived little guys than fat cats. That plutocratic image has been a heavy albatross for the GOP at least since the times of the Great Depression, when the idea of the lower-middle-class forgotten people was used by President Franklin D. Roosevelt to powerful effect. President George W. Bush's "just folks" public image seemed to help the GOP early on, but the fat-cat image is still there, regularly reinforced by scandals or alleged scandals (think Enron, Global Crossing, Jack Abramoff, etc.). If they could get straight on the values issue, the Democrats would be the natural majority in America. But I don't see that happening any time soon.

Why do voters care so deeply about values? "Wedge issues" are commonly regarded pejoratively, but cultural values are not just

---

2. Atlanta (DeKalb and Cobb counties), Boston (Brookline and Medford), San Diego (Eastlake and Rancho Bernardo), and Tulsa (Broken Arrow and Sandy Springs).

wedge issues. They give a sense of how a candidate sees the world; a voter appropriately wants to feel comfortable with the worldview of his or her representative. After all, no one can tell what the issues will be during the time an elected official holds office. Who could have thought that gay marriage would be an issue? Or 9/11?

Values Matter Most was published in 1995 with the subtitle *How Republicans or Democrats or a Third Party Can Win and Renew the American Way of Life.* It was dedicated in part to the memory of Erwin Glikes, a path-breaking neo-con editor and publisher who had died suddenly in 1994. I still remember Erwin walking up and down the halls of the American Enterprise Institute, plucking potential authors like ripe grapes. Many of the books he acquired in that way became important ones that helped shape the climate of opinion.

As an appendix, the book carried a column of mine entitled "Why I'm For Clinton." It was a nervous column to be sure. Its central theme was that President George H. W. Bush would not attack knee-jerk liberalism, and that Clinton, as a "different Democrat," *might*. (He didn't.) There was also an epilogue that showed how skittish and even inconsistent I was about it all: "I confess I was a Democrat more concerned about Democrats winning than Democrats losing."

The gist of the book was that, in the words of a chapter title, "It's not new, it's normal." The Franklin Roosevelt years of the Great Depression (the 1930s) had focused journalism on the psephology of economics. The idea, still widely held, is that if the economy is doing well (say 4 percent gross domestic product growth with 2 percent inflation), then the party in power likely has a lock on electoral victory, particularly in presidential election years when the political lines are drawn with greater clarity. The problem was history. I cited Michael Barone's book *Our Country*, which listed four great *noneconomic* issues of the years just prior to the Depression: racial segregation, immigration, Prohibition, and American participation in World War I.

But there was much more. President William McKinley not only beat candidate William Jennings Bryant in 1896 on the economic issue of the cross of gold (so-called bimetalism), but the campaign also served as a platform for Bryant's rural fundamentalist voters from which to stage a last stand against the growing number of secular and metropolitan voters who flew McKinley's flag. Before that, in 1824, Andrew Jackson's big issue concerned a charter for a U.S. national bank, but also drew on regional and cultural attitudes—this time the rugged frontiersmen versus the Eastern establishment. Women's suffrage was a battle that went on from the early days of the republic until they were given the right to vote in national elections in 1920.

And to all of that add the periodic issues of foreign policy: the Revolutionary War itself, the Civil War, the Spanish-American War, and more recently World War II ("Don't change horses in midstream"); "Who lost China?" (1948); Cold War spending (1948 to 1992); "Korea, Communism, Corruption" (1952); Hungary and Suez (1956); the missile gap (1960); Vietnam (1968 and 1972); and President Reagan's campaigns against President Carter's maladroit handling of American diplomatic hostages in Iran (1980), always mixed in with his panoply of values: family, work, neighborhood, peace, freedom, as well as an optimistic vision that Americans can do most anything if they set their minds to it. (American researchers recently created a new bladder from stem cells.)

The so-called wedge issues properly play an important role in American life and politics. My son Danny, now the arts and entertainment editor of *The Washington Times,* has made an interesting point over the years that I cited in *Values Matter Most.* In the good old days, he maintains, Hollywood turned out movies that portrayed American heroes: Abraham Lincoln, Thomas Edison, and Alexander Graham Bell, to name a few. Some were clunkers, others not. More recently (when *Values Matter Most* came out), the antiheroes our children were treated to were—for example—the thug labor leader Jimmy Hoffa, gangster Bugsy Siegel, and Jim Morrison, the rock star who died from a drug overdose. But where are the new movies, in suitable tones of gray, about Bill Clinton, Colin Powell, Ronald Reagan, Condoleezza Rice, Henry Kissinger, Curt Flood, Arnold Schwarzenegger, and Oprah Winfrey? Americans do not want their history or biography sugar-coated. (*Ray,* a recent movie about the blind pianist Ray Charles, was on the right track.)

Regarding family values: When my youngest daughter was *really* young, there was a handwritten sign on the wall of her room that read "On my honor, I will try to serve God and my country, to help people at all times and obey the Brownie law." Recent number of all girl and boy scouts: 9,548,963! (I used to tell her stories at night about a made-up character, "Peter Politics." Another set of made-up yarns concerned "Proud Puffed-up Peter," modeled on Peter Jennings. Sometimes some of my kids have complained, with some merit: "Dad, all we do is talk about politics." But they did learn some things most youngsters don't know, just as I had at my parents' dinner table.)

Even with plunging polls about American foreign policy keyed to the Iraq war, we should not forget that the world holds *Americans* and *America* in high regard. Around the world long lines form at American consulates as foreigners seek to emigrate to the United States. Many foreigners admire our system of relatively free markets. They admire our ability to bring new people into our way of life and our ability to freely and publicly express ourselves. They know that despite its problems, the American experiment has been a successful one. U.S. Ambassador to the United Nations Adlai Stevenson once told that body: "Americans can gag on a gnat, but we swallow tigers whole."

Republicans, trashed by the mainstream media, have sometimes been nervous about how they discuss values. Democrats attacked what Pat Buchanan said at the 1992 GOP convention in Houston. The Bush I campaign team chose not to promote a more moderate version of the values debate, fearful that they might lose the backing of the likes of Buchanan and Pat Robertson. There had been thirty-nine Republican primaries that year; Buchanan contested thirty-six of them. He lost all of them—in Mississippi by a *margin* of 56 percentage points.

Buchanan's moment of glory had come in the always high-profile first-in-the-nation primary in New Hampshire. It is not customary for a sitting president seeking a second term to be challenged by a member of his own party. But Buchanan saw a golden opportunity to promote his agenda and campaigned vigorously. He *lost* to Bush #41 53 to 37 percent in what would normally be considered a

Bush landslide. But the national media, always looking for a combat story in New Hampshire, gave the story—and Pat Buchanan—the full monty.

For reasons never fully explained—possibly a threat not to back the Bush-Quayle ticket—Buchanan was scheduled for an opening night prime-time appearance at the Republican National Convention in Houston, sandwiched between Condoleezza Rice and former President Reagan. Buchanan's speech ran long, and reporters could see Reagan backstage pacing nervously, watching his prime-time minutes tick away. Rice's speech wasn't even aired by the networks. Buchanan's remarks had been OK'ed in advance by Rich Bond, chairman of the Republican National Committee, perhaps because Buchanan did not bring up some of his most inflammatory issues: immigration, protectionism, and isolationism. He gave pornography only a glancing blow. But the gut paragraph was tough enough:

> This election is about much more than who gets what. It is about who we are. It is about what we believe, it is about what we stand for as Americans. There is a *religious war* going on in our country for the soul of America. It is a *cultural war*, as critical to the kind of nation we will one day be—as was the Cold War itself. And in that struggle for the soul of America, Clinton and Clinton are on the other side, and George Bush is on our side. And so, we have to come—and stand beside him.

Now, Buchanan was making a real point when he talked of the divisive fight between cultural and religious values in America. The battles between the secular and the religious, between abstinence and condoms, over gays in the military, homosexuality, and a variety of religious issues including prayer in the schools and the trashing of St. Patrick's Cathedral—are serious. I think that what has driven Buchanan over the edge is that in some quarters it has become all right to be publicly anti-Catholic.

But religious *war* and cultural *war* seem European: the Holocaust, pogroms, the Crusades, Nazism—these seem great overstatements of whatever America was going through, which was plenty. Buchanan is one of the best pundits in America. He had been in the soup before on this sort of language. He could have stayed within the lines. He has a crystalline mind; he speaks in brief sentences. But he deserved whatever calumny he received. The astonishing part of the whole event was the wholesale transference of Buchanan's views to the Republican Party.

After all, the Houston convention was a big tent. Bill Bennett said, "When we talk about traditional family values we are not using code words. We are not seeking a political wedge issue. And we are not seeking to demean or belittle others. Rather we are seeking to honor and affirm the 'better angels of our nature,' and of our children's nature."

Jack Kemp related policy to values: "The Democratic Party has dictated the policies governing our cities: higher taxes; redistribution of wealth; a welfare system that penalizes people for working, discourages marriage, punishes the family, and literally prohibits saving. It's not the values of the poor that are flawed; it's the values of the welfare system that are bankrupt."

Pat Robertson pushed too hard in one spot: "When Bill and Hillary Clinton talk about family values, they are not talking about either family or values. They are talking about a radical plan to destroy the traditional family and transfer its functions to the federal government."

Marilyn Quayle, the sitting vice president's wife, got a slot. She was a mother of three, an attorney, and a promulgator of family values. Recalling her college days, one passage drew great media attention: "But remember, not everyone joined the counterculture. Not everyone demonstrated, took drugs, joined the sexual revolution, or dodged the draft."

The battlefield was clearly arranged. Clinton made his points about being a New Democrat with all that implied. But neither did he duck a fight or some complexity. He said that gays ought to serve in the military. He said he would reduce deficits, not cut taxes, which turned out to mean big defense cuts and increased domestic spending. He came out against handguns. He said he was in favor of legal abortion. He got tough once on race—citing the inflammatory language of rapper Sister Souljah who thought killing whites was not a bad idea. He came out for a convoluted position that can only be described as pro-quotas. He was vulnerable to the charge of draft dodging and massive sexual dalliance. He told audiences that if he were elected Americans would get two for the price of one. The second was his wife, Hillary Rodham Clinton, whose very liberal record was clear. (But her 2008 run for the presidency periodically took on a centrist flavor, often running as if she were following directions laid out in *The Real Majority* almost forty years earlier.)

And what was the response to the 1992 values debate? By mid-September sources at the White House were telling reporters that the campaign would back off the issue that was their most powerful. Where was the counterattack? Where was the substantive discussion about welfare, quotas, crime, and discipline in the classroom? Where was the discussion of handgun control? Where was the talk about the role of the religious Right? What about military budgets? What about feminism, abortion, draft dodging, and sexual behavior? The role of Jesse Jackson in the Democratic party? Ross Perot? About the corrosive role of female-headed households? About policies that were "soft on crime" and "police brutality"? Where was the story about the mostly solid views of the convention delegates at this allegedly right-wing zany convention? Most delegates were conservatives, moderates, and neo-cons. Where was the sort of symbol-laden values campaign that George H. W. Bush had put forth in 1988?

The press played a big role in Bush's loss. Collectively, the media had come to view values as something unclean and not worthy of a politics that should concentrate on issues. The issue of values itself had been trivialized and mocked by a series of mini-events, like actress Candace Bergen's portrayal of Murphy Brown bearing an out-of-wedlock child in the eponymous national sitcom. The convention and the subsequent campaign were so disorganized that the press didn't even understand what was going on and allowed one speech by Pat Buchanan to define it.

The gentlemanly Bush #41 and his campaign team had apparently come to believe that young, hip Americans wouldn't buy that social stuff any longer. The economy had been souring and was just turning the corner. When Bush #41 announced that the recession was ending he was laughed at by the press. The recession ended. Bush was suffering from Graves disease, which slowed him down and apparently made the campaign seem less important.

All this allowed candidate Bill Clinton to run principally on the theme of "It's the economy, stupid," created by his campaign manager, James Carville, and displayed in the war room in Little Rock. Clinton, too, ran on an old-fashioned economic campaign—not challenged on values, he could easily do so. The final results were Clinton 43.01 percent, Bush 37.45 percent, and Perot 18.91 percent. That 5.5 percent margin by Clinton over Bush was solid, but not sensational. In theory, a switch of 2.8 percentage points would have given Bush a popular vote majority. But English psephologist David Butler calculated that because of Clinton's huge "wasted vote" (about 1.5 million in California and about 1 million in New York State) the actual additional margin Bush would have needed was about 1.9 additional percentage points for a popular vote majority.

If Bush had run a campaign with a greater stress on values, who would have won? I don't know. But the campaign robbed American voters of that legitimate debate, and he deserved to lose.

SOME LIBERAL ECONOMIC analysts make the case that income, too, is a values issues. It is true that in the last few decades the *share* of total personal income earned by the very rich has gone up faster than that of the poor and middle class, although for many decades prior to that the shares had remained constant. However, those at the lower ranges of the income distribution have *gained* real income even as the disparity between *shares* of total income between rich and poor grew. Further, the shares of income have recently leveled off, albeit at a greater disparity than previously, according to economist Marvin Kosters of the American Enterprise Institute. Moreover, a *doubling* of income in a family earning $50,000 per year means a bigger boost in its standard of living than a tripling of income in a family earning 2 million per year.

In an article published in 2005 in the *EPI Journal* which is put out by the Economic Policy Institute, a left-of-center think tank that takes a decidedly pro-union stance, Lawrence Mishel called this disparity itself a values issue. Mishel, a frequent guest panelist at American Enterprise Institute conferences, writes that "the social class you belong to really matters—it determines your health, how long you live, your exposure to crime, your success in school and the likely success of your children." He maintains that these, too, should be seen as values issues.

It is a devilish problem, with built-in contradictions. Neo-cons are certainly not looking for a country of the very rich and the very poor. They generally approve of a safety net. But they are also free marketeers. And if the board of directors of a big private company believes a dynamic CEO can lead to billions of extra dollars of additional earnings, shouldn't the compensation committee of that company be entitled to bid for the services of that potential CEO on the open market? In fact, isn't it the *duty* of the CEO to try to raise shareholder value, especially now that more than half of Americans own shares of companies through financial instruments such as pension plans, mutual funds, and 401(K)s? On the other hand, huge bonuses and options have gone to executives whose companies have not done well, and most people, including me, find this distasteful.

I favor the partial privatization of Social Security. I think people will end up with much larger pensions if they are free to reasonably invest their own money. The ultimate plan should have a government guarantee that stipulates that those entering the privatized plan would get reasonable payments (perhaps 75 percent to 85 percent of others') should their investments collapse. As an added bonus, more investors could ameliorate the us vs. them tone of the political argument, which would be good for all of us.

George W. Bush's tax cuts were described as tax cuts for the rich. Indeed, they were. But *proportionately* the middle class received greater cuts. I generally approved of Bush's tax cuts, but not the elimination of the inheritance tax, or death tax, as conservatives like to call it. The untaxable portion of an estate should be raised, perhaps up to $5 million, and then price adjusted. Then estates of the wealthy can pay a modest tax at a modest rate. Most important, the *beneficiaries* should pay an appropriate tax. A poor beneficiary should pay less in taxes than a rich one. The elimination of the estate tax is wrong, however, principally because it can ultimately yield a near-perpetual aristocratic class of families. America does not need a few more potential wastrels living as economic royalists.

In recent years the percentage of working Americans who pay *no income taxes at all* has gone up dramatically. Through the Earned Income Tax Credit, lower-income Americans receive a form of negative income tax—money from the Internal Revenue Service based on income they did not earn that year. (Neo-cons mocked the notion when George McGovern proposed something similar in 1972. Time marches on.)

I do not have a solution to all this. At root, the economic arguments revolve around the idea of income redistribution made into law by democratically elected governments. And the issue of income redistribution will always be a major one in democratic countries. I don't have a problem with that at reasonable levels. Some Libertarians mindlessly say taxation is theft. Really? What protected them from a Soviet-dominated world?

The "Safety Net State" makes sense to me. Keep the market system alive. Let innovation flourish in such a system. Punish the financial crooks. But see to it that the non-rich have the wherewithal to live decent lives in the richest country on earth, sometimes through big government programs, as long as they are carefully scrutinized to determine that they do more good than harm.

All within a system that honors the idea that values matter most.

CHAPTER TEN

Think Tank

THE TELEVISION PROGRAM

TELEVISION IS WRITTEN on the wind. As proud as I was of the half-hour documentary programs we produced, there was a problem: regularity. I was interested in promoting a set of ideas — neo-conservative ones — that I believed were not getting sufficient attention.

Herb Schmertz's garbage-can ads notwithstanding, within a few weeks after a series of our half-hour documentaries aired, its message was gone. While it aired, people recognized me on the street. I liked that. A few weeks after we went dark, the reaction was, "Aren't you, uh. . . . I know you, you're, uh. . . ." And then — nothing.

And so late in 1993 I started drawing up some plans along with Andrew Walworth, who was just starting New River Media, his television production company, and who would become executive producer of *Think Tank with Ben Wattenberg*. Our arrangement is still operative as this is written more than fourteen years later. He and I have always been roughly in tune ideologically (although the subject of many of our programs are nonpolitical: Duke Ellington, alternative medicine, professional sports, George Gershwin, gambling, infertility, whether animals think, Alzheimer's disease, and baseball statistics).[1]

In late 1993 Andy and I paid a visit to Jennifer Lawson, the director of programming at PBS headquarters. I told her I wanted to do a program every week and that I believed I could raise the necessary funding. Jennifer had lots of questions. One was whether the new program would have a sufficient number of women as panelists. I said we would try, but we were going to put on the best, most knowledgeable, and most articulate panelists we could find, regardless of gender. After a few days she called me and said PBS would *not* air the program. In the bizarre political marketplace of public television she was generally considered to be left wing. I was convinced that her decision was mostly an ideological one; she would not willingly commit neoconservatism on her PBS schedule. Jennifer is now head of WHUT, the Howard University public television station in Washington, which airs *Think Tank*. And when I go to the supermarket the people who come up to me are disproportionately black, many of them foreign born, who often watch the program on WHUT. They tell me they love the program and watch it because it teaches them about America. Thank you, Jennifer. She and I are now on warm and cordial terms.

The system of public broadcasting in America is not only bizarre, but weird, strange, crazy-quilt, bureaucratic, and somewhat left wing. It has one saving grace: It airs a great deal of good television, probably the best in America. It also airs junk, particularly during those wonderful "beg-a-thons" during pledge weeks, whose numbers expanded and then expanded some more. There is a certain quality of sanctimony in public television. In commercial television everyone understands that the object of the enterprise is to earn money. Much the same is true in the world of public television, except that the players have convinced themselves, the Congress, and the public that the ongoing activity is solely in the public interest.

There are more than three hundred public television stations in America. They get their funds not only from incessant dunning of local contributors, but from the Corporation for Public Broadcasting,

---

1. A full list of the programs and guests can be found at www.pbs.org/thinktank.

funded by Congress, from "underwriters" (i.e., advertisers), and from selling DVDs, tapes—and more. Those stations then buy much, but not all, of their programming from PBS, which is thought of as a network, but is in reality mostly a program distribution service.

One of the biggest and best purveyors of public television programming is the American Program Bureau in Boston, then run by Gene Nichols. When Jennifer turned me down, Andy suggested I call Gene. I did, and asked him if he would be interested in the new program. Gene knew who I was and said he was indeed interested. In a matter of a few minutes we had a deal. In fact, Nichols said the American Program Bureau was having its annual convention in Dallas in a few weeks, and he invited me to make a pitch to the stations. I did, and got an excellent reaction. Many public stations signed on. The people there were not noticeably of the Left. And so, in the spring of 1994, I began *Think Tank with Ben Wattenberg*. Later, it was aired by PBS. David Gerson, the executive vice president at the American Enterprise Institute (AEI), wished me well on the venture, smiled, and predicted that we would run out of material within six weeks.

Ironically, the big, liberally tilted networks do not buy public affairs programs from private producers. Sitcoms are purchased from outsiders, but not programming about things that matter more. Such content is produced solely by the news divisions of the big networks, inordinately by reporters on the Left as indicated in chapter 11. But in fact—and notwithstanding all the often-true conservative talk of public broadcasting being a haven of liberal thinking—it was public broadcasting that was, in its way, the last bastion of free enterprise in the most important part of the video world, the part where new ideas are surfaced. Go figure. That's why *Think Tank* was able to get started.

The plan for *Think Tank* was unique in a number of ways. Unlike *The McLaughlin Group*, it was to be entirely civil in tone—no food fights. Unlike most of the other public-affairs shows, its guests would not include politicians, spinners, or journalists (with an exemption for journalists who had written serious books). (In all our years of broadcasting we had only one active politician on the program: Senator Daniel Patrick Moynihan, the eclectic neo-con scholar who appeared on three separate occasions.) We would deal with only one topic per program. Our panelists were typically authors, think tank scholars, and experts from the academy.

We had two other criteria, in possible contradiction. Those programs that were to deal mostly with issues of public policy were to be discussed *within the forty-yard lines*, where I believe the essence of public policy wisdom resides. That was a very neo-conservative way of looking at things, and quite different from much of what was on public television dealing with public affairs. The neo-conservative journal *The Public Interest* also looked at public policy with an open mind. This was very far from the CNN *Crossfire* model, which was a hot show for many years. It was looking for panelists who were on opposing *ten*-yard lines, which often yielded either extremists as panelists, or panelists who would overstate their case.[2]

The other idea I insisted on was that I speak my mind on *Think Tank* unless the topic was one I was wholly unfamiliar with. My first task, obviously, was to be the traffic cop, to see that all the panelists had their say and that there was coherence in the flow of the program. But I would not only ask the questions; I would express my opinions. There were several reasons for this. I had written books and a newspaper column for many years; most viewers would know where I was coming from. I couldn't get away with being neutral even if I tried. Second, I felt there was no real sense for me to do the program if couldn't make my points. Although I was officially the moderator of *Think Tank*, I often called myself the "immoderator," sometimes on the air.

There was yet another reason for my opinion-mongering: I have a big mouth and am hard to silence. Luckily, from the beginning the program had good, tough, young editors. They were not at all afraid to tell me when I was talking too much, either through an earpiece on the set, or in the postproduction editing process. In theory, the

---

2. In the early 1980s I was asked to fill in for Bob Novak for about a month as one of the provocateurs on CNN's *Crossfire*. I would hear producer Sol Levine directing me through my earpiece: "Go get him," "Hit him in the balls. . . ." The standard end was: "From the Right, I'm Bob Novak" and "From the Left, I'm Tom Braden." I invented my own close. I would say "From Tom Braden's right, I'm Ben Wattenberg." Most everyone was on Tom's right. It was a modest neo-conservative act. We neo-cons are not necessarily people of the Right. When I didn't think I had a position that was tough enough for them, I would tell the *Crossfire* producers to get someone else to argue with Braden.

final calls were mine, although I have learned to trust their judgment. I usually don't see the very final version of the program until it airs on one of two stations in Washington, WHUT, or the flagship Washington station, WETA. Recently, the national carriage of *Think Tank* increased dramatically through the advent of the *PBS World* cable network. We now have four plays each week in Washington—points we make sure aren't lost on potential funders seeking influence where the laws are made. Voice of America airs the program globally, and our Internet presence at *thinktanktv.com* makes the program available worldwide and holds an impressive archive of transcripts and video from our four-hundred-plus episodes.

PAST *THINK TANK* episodes offer a pretty good picture of what neo-conservatism—and its adversaries—were thinking about from the mid-1990s onward. I have now asked some occasional cohosts to ensure continuity. The first two have been former Secretary of Defense Bill Cohen; and Michael Gerson, an author and former chief speechwriter for President George W. Bush. We expect they will be joined by Francis Collins, who directed the Human Genome Project at the National Institutes of Health, and Newt Gingrich. A selection of notable *Think Tank* material is offered here, in several formats.

Our first program (in April 1994) was entitled "Does Punishment Pay?" We had four panelists: Judge Robert Bork; Professor Philip Heymann, former director of Harvard's Center for Criminal Justice and former deputy attorney general in the Clinton administration; John DiIulio of Princeton University, and a fellow at the Brookings Institution; and law professor Lani Guinier of the University of Pennsylvania.[3]

---

3. Guinier is a tall and handsome woman who had recently been in a media firestorm about her idea of passing new legislation mandating that election districts be determined by race, and she was of natural interest to viewers. But I learned something else that was perhaps more important from a television point of view: She wore a fire engine–red dress. The video screen told the tale: Four guys in dark suits competing with a red dress. Not fair! Over the years we tried to book as many women as possible, for substantive and for television reasons, not for proportionality. We were only partially successful. My conclusion is that there are fewer women than men involved at the top rungs of public affairs. In early 2005 there was a mini–media firestorm about the revelation that men far outnumbered women on the op-ed pages—even at liberal papers like *The Los Angeles Times*, *The Washington Post*, and *The New York Times*.

Bork and DiIulio are of the conservative or neo-conservative persuasion; Heymann and Guinier, on the liberal side. Although both sides said they were for *both* punishment *and* prevention, it was clear that the conservative/neo-con side was stressing punishment while the liberals were stressing prevention. The program aired after William Barr, the first President Bush's attorney general, had issued a report entitled *The Case for More Incarceration*. According to Barr, the best way to stop crime is to put criminals in prison. I had described the position this way: "a thug in jail can't shoot your sister."

It was a very important situation. In many polls, crime had been ranked as the Most Important Issue. The violent crime rate had gone up nearly fivefold in the previous forty years. Violent criminals served only about one-third of their sentences, and while on parole one in three committed new crimes. A Brookings Institution study showed that a typical criminal committed thirteen crimes before being apprehended for the first time.

In subsequent years incarceration did indeed go up. There were 330,000 prisoners under federal and state jurisdiction in 1980—and 1.4 million in 2000! This has exacerbated another situation: so many children without fathers in the house. There are no full solutions to issues of public policy. Recall that the neo-con mantra concerns "the law of unintended consequences." But violent crime rates dropped dramatically. Americans feel safer today than before incarceration increased. Most neo-cons believe that the liberal Democratic view on crime had turned too soft.

A few weeks later, on May 28, we were on the air with "Adam Smith: Twenty-First-Century Man." The panelists were Robert Lawrence, Jagdish Bhagwati, James Fallows, and Thea Lea.

Lawrence was an author and professor of economics at Harvard University, Bhagwati was a professor of economics at Columbia University, Fallows was a long-time analyst of East Asian economic strategies, and Lea was an international trade economist at the Economic Policy Institute, a think tank with close ties to unions. I introduced the program noting that Smith's famous *The Wealth of Nations* (actually *An Inquiry into the Nature and Causes of the Wealth of Nations*) was published in 1776 and that it remains one of the great cornerstones of modern economic thinking, and not just among those on the right of the spectrum. It represents a notion of how the world works—an intelligent design in the non-creationist sense. Smith's core idea is that individuals are better than governments at determining their own economic interest, and this self-interest in turn positively contributes to economic well-being in general. Smith argues that free trade between countries benefits consumers. He illustrates his point using the modest example of a household: It is the maxim of every prudent master of a family never to attempt to make at home what it will cost him more to buy. Why make your own clothes when you can pick them up at a department store more cheaply? Why should the United States make all its steel at home if it can buy steel less expensively from South Korea?

The four panelists had some disagreements about where Smith had taken us. Some had problems with the North American Free Trade Agreement (NAFTA), some about the huge new trade treaty, the General Agreement on Tariffs and Trade (GATT). But they agreed that Adam Smith was the man whose doctrines (including "the invisible hand") now set most of the economic markers in the world. I felt it was a good day's work to help get that idea in play to the intelligent viewers of America's public television stations.

In late 1995, long before it became Governor George W. Bush's campaign motto in 2000, we did a program called "Can Conservatives Be Compassionate?" We paired former Governor Mario Cuomo, famously liberal and author of *Reason to Believe,* with the then-conservative Arianna Huffington, author of *The Fourth Instinct: The Call of the Soul.* Arianna said "conservatives like myself" believe in faith-based solutions to social problems. (A few years later Arianna's faith called her well to the left.)

I was sufficiently impressed with our first interview with Lani Guinier that I invited her back in 1995 to do a one-on-one interview with her, entitled "Affirmative Action and Reaction." One-on-one interviews were fairly rare in the early days of *Think Tank.* (Today many of our programs are in that format. Not only are they less expensive to produce, but viewers often enjoy a program with fewer interruptions. We started out doing forty-eight original shows each year. Now, with stations preempting more often with beg-a-thons, but mostly because we have a superb library of old, evergreen programs, we do about thirty-five original programs each year. No one has written us to say, oh no, not that two-parter about Irving Berlin during Christmas again.)

I thought that although we had dealt with the issue of race before, Lani could shed further light on the matter. It was an important moment in the ongoing struggle between affirmative action and quotas. President Clinton's quest for "diversity" in his administration turned out to be a sad joke. The word quickly went out that certain executive branch jobs were earmarked for "skirts." But white females were complaining that they were losing out to black or Latino women ("twofers") and claiming diversity box score credit for both. James Adams of *The Sunday Times* (of London) wrote that the chief of one Clinton transition team didn't get a job because his team was found to have no OGs (openly gay men) on it. Clinton also sought to get around the strictures of "race-norming."

Into this atmosphere Clinton nominated Guinier to be head of the Civil Rights Division of the Justice Department. That can be a very influential position. A media firestorm ensued. In her recent law journal writings, she had endorsed very wide concepts of proportionalism. These included quotas for local legislatures, the right of minorities to veto many important laws, that the minorities must be "authentic" (i.e., not middle-class blacks [like herself?]), and that minorities in legislatures be entitled to enact a proportionate share of legislation *alone*, for example, establishing set-asides. I read it and some of her other material quite carefully. It was neo-conservatism upside down.

Such ideas would need a constitutional amendment to become law. But there was little public support for such a course. A Gallup/*Newsweek* poll taken at the time showed that by 77 to 20 percent, Americans rejected the idea of racial preferences. Polls also showed that *blacks also rejected the notion, albeit by a lesser majority.*

The Wall Street Journal used a special name for Lani Guinier: "the Quota Queen." It stuck to her like Crazy Glue. After much uproar President Clinton inelegantly pulled her nomination. Later, I did a playful column adding some variations to the *Journal*'s alliteratives: the Princess of Proportionalism, the Duchess of Diversity, the Vicar of Victimization, and the Czarina of Czeparatism. I don't

think she had seen the column at the time of our interview—
although I later sent it to her.

Her new book was *The Tyranny of the Majority: Fundamental
Fairness in Representative Democracy.* In person she was much more
moderate—but less interesting. I asked her about the current state of
play in the race preference struggle. She said, "We are not con-
fronting our prejudice . . . we are talking past each other." The conversation moved to the possibility of violence. She said, "There is a
rage . . . and that rage is at the boiling point." Middle-class African
Americans, she said, feel that they are "being punished twice, first
for being black and second for being angry." She said African
Americans were experiencing "microaggression," quite different
from the old segregation. She told the story of "a judge I clerked for,
who was at a conference wearing a suit and tie in Williamsburg, Virginia, and was asked by a white gentleman to park his car for him,
gave him the keys, and said, 'Could you please take care of this?'"

We talked about white cabdrivers passing up black customers. I
then asked my favorite question in the preference debate. "What
happens when a *black* cabdriver passes by a potential *black* fare because he, too, knows the crime statistics and knows that violence by
blacks is five times disproportionate [to the white rate]. . . . How do
you deal with that? The black cabdriver is certainly not a racist."

She responded: "It's not that the white cabdriver is a racist. I
think we are subconsciously harboring assumptions that affect a
group of people in a way that [denies] them the same opportunity to
compete." She chose not to address the question about a black cabdriver, and implied that blacks did not commit crimes substantially
higher than white rates. I did not push the matter. I did note in passing that Judge Robert Bork had said that while he opposed quota-
style preference, he believed that if they were to be retained they
should only apply to blacks because of their particularly tragic history due to slavery, but that he opposed them for women. That makes
some sense to me.

Guiner said women ought to be included as a preferential category and called for mentoring programs for women in law schools.
Adding women, with their great numbers, was a political gold mine
for the quota-meisters. Neo-cons would later hail the war in Iraq as a

huge advance for women, which it was. Liberal women were not impressed. I guess Lani did not appreciate my alliterative descriptions of her. She turned down invitations to appear on further programs.

WE DEALT WITH the difference between equity feminism and gender feminism in two *Think Tank* shows. Equity feminists want fair treatment and no discrimination against women; gender feminists believe that women are trapped in patriarchal hegemony and in thrall to men and a male culture. Or so believed Camille Paglia and the AEI's own Christina Hoff Sommers, the two feisty equity feminists on a *Think Tank* program entitled "Has Feminism Gone Too Far?" Then as now, gender feminists were in full throat and full of factoids that never seemed to prove out. Said Sommers:

> A few years ago feminist activists announced that on Super Bowl Sunday battery against women increases by 40 percent. NBC was moved to use a public service announcement to encourage men "to remain calm during the game." *The New York Times* began to refer to it as "the day of dread." But Ken Ringle at *The Washington Post* did something very unusual in this turbulent sea of media credulity. He checked the facts—and within a few hours discovered that it was a hoax! I interviewed a young woman at the University of Pennsylvania who came into the Women's Center. She said, "Oh, I've just suffered a mini-rape," and I said, "What happened?" She said, "A boy walked by me and said, 'Nice legs.'"

Think Tank interviewed James Q. Wilson several times. He is a true hero in the neo-con pantheon because he was an academic who had clearly changed things. His ideas had consequences. In 1982, Wilson published "Broken Windows" in *The Atlantic* in collaboration with George Kelling. In our interview he explained:

> We proposed an idea based on a common observation: If there's an abandoned building with one window broken,

within a very short period of time, all the windows will be
broken. We had to avoid having the first broken window.
This meant that the police take very seriously small signs
of disorder, such as graffiti on walls.

Wilson had been researching the idea for sixteen years! A tough-on-
crime idea, it was adopted in many places. Many observers believe it
played a significant role in reducing violent crime. In New York
City, the new Mayor Rudolph Giuliani based his police strategy on
"Broken Windows" combined with detailed statistical analysis. The
rate of violent criminality plummeted.

Wilson also explained a strategy that went further. He came out
for extending family shelters to boarding schools for teenagers living
in at-risk neighborhoods and in single-mother families. He caught
hell when the media characterized his idea as orphanages. But he
stuck to his guns. Neo-cons knew that crime had to be confronted in
many ways, or it would corrode America.

It was fine to have Lani Guinier as a sole guest on *Think Tank*.
The combat helped make the program interesting. I got my licks in,
but it was giving perfectly fine PBS airtime to an ideological adversary. There has been much talk about whether there is media bias
found on television or in the newspapers. But the argument is usually misrepresented. The way to get a point across is not by misstat-
ing facts or slanting the words or pictures. It is often a question of
agenda and who is offered a spot on the air.

We talked again with James Q. Wilson in 1998, then of the University of Southern California, previously of Harvard, and later of
Pepperdine University. He is one of the smartest, calmest, and most
learned men I have ever met.

The title of the second program was "James Q. Wilson on
Crime, Welfare, the Family, and America." His two most recent
books were *On Character* and *The Moral Sense*—not what you
would normally associate with a political scientist who had investi-
gated the mean streets of Chicago and New York. Wilson went to the
roots of the tension between freedom and discipline to the attempt
to reconcile order and liberty and about the rise of modernity and individualism. We acknowledged that the relatively new mixture of

capitalism, democracy, freedom, science, and technology was an
intoxicating brew. Wilson spelled out a global dividing line:

> On one side are the children of the Enlightenment, those
> who believe in reason, individualism, and personal free-
> dom. On the other side of the dividing line is the world
> of Islam and Confucianism, the world that believes that
> man's reason cannot grasp his own state, that tradition, au-
> thority, and religion embedded in the state ought to govern
> the state. And they're betting that we're wrong, and they're
> pointing to crime, drug abuse, and family dissolution as
> evidence that we're wrong and they're right.

The discussion aired a half a dozen years before 9/11. (Wilson, from
California, is the son of an auto mechanic.)

And so it went: rat-a-tat. We reran the Paglia-Sommers show a
number of times. Around our male chauvinist production shop
(which included women) the show became known as "The Babes."
Sommers even attacked the holiest of feminist numbers: that women
earned only 59 cents for every dollar made by men. Research had been
done by the Independent Women's Forum (and published as a booklet
by AEI foolishly entitled *Women's Figures*) showing that when cor-
rected for age, length of time in the workplace, and whether women
had children—the number was 90 cents. And the number was about
equal if a woman had no children. But the feminist mantra changed
from "equal pay for equal work" to "equal pay for comparable work"—
a system by which earnings would be decided by government boards,
not the market. It would be a system not far from socialism. That
would help working women. Under such criteria a waitress might
make as much or more than a long-distance trucker. Ironically, the
original case establishing comparable worth was decided by Judge Jack
Tanner, a supporter of Scoop Jackson's. He was later overruled.

WE HAD PROMISED a rebuttal on Sommers and Paglia, and some
months later we delivered the superfeminist Catharine MacKinnon,
law professor at the University of Michigan who had previously

THINK TANK: THE TELEVISION PROGRAM

taught at Yale, Harvard, Stanford, and the University of Chicago. She confused me. Most everything was either rape or pornography. That women were the majority of the electorate and could in theory make the laws under which they suffered had no bearing on her views. I asked her what she thought of Marilyn Quayle's speech at the 1992 Republican Convention in Houston. Mrs. Quayle had said this:

> I sometimes think that the liberals are always so angry because they believed the grandiose promises of the liberation movement. They're disappointed because most women do not wish to be liberated from their essential natures as women. Most of us love being mothers or wives, which gives our lives a richness that few men or women get from professional accomplishments alone.

MacKinnon answered:

> I'm not a liberal. She may be right. There is the impression that the women's movement was about deciding what freedom for women constitutes is wholly and exclusively engaging in what had been male roles. Women being mothers is something that the women's movement has sought to allow without the punishment that comes with being women. It includes being in committed relationships with men but still having a full human life that includes being able to work in fulfilling ways.

I asked her if in its early years the women's movement did not scorn the idea of women staying home, being a homemaker, and bringing up children. She said: "I think some people gave off that attitude. But I think that came across because it was the role that women were forced into. Therefore it made it impossible to conceive of it as a choice. If the role that was equally available to men as to women, then it wouldn't be forced on you based on gender." (I didn't quite understand that last remark. I still don't.)

MacKinnon said that those women who are working do not have a free choice, that they have to work, and that "they are being discriminated against." I said most men had to work also, otherwise no one would eat in their families, and asked if that implied inequality or subordination. She said, "We could discuss capitalism. . . ." I said I'd like to do that sometime.

I returned to her remark about not being a liberal.

Me: "You said you're not a liberal."

Her: "That's true."

Me: "What are you?"

Her: "A feminist."

Me: "Are most feminists liberals?"

Her: "Probably not, but increasingly so."

Me: "I'm getting confused. What do you have against liberalism?"

Her: "Ah."

Me: "Ah."

Her: "It has male supremacy built into it, and that's true on the Right in certain other ways. Liberalism has a large tradition with much to recommend it. I have a lot against it."

It went on. I asked: "Was there male supremacy in the 1980s in England when Mrs. Thatcher was prime minister?"

MacKinnon: "Yes."

I asked: "About 53 to 54 percent of the American electorate is female. Don't they get it that they are being subordinated, discriminated against, made unequal. Why don't they vote the right way?"

MacKinnon: "Voting doesn't determine social power. You can vote any way you want and still get raped." She said rape is not taken seriously in this society.

I said, "Rape is against the law. Rape is a vulgar, terrible, murderous crime. Who says that rape is okay? Don't people who are husbands and fathers and brothers of those raped take rape seriously?"

MacKinnon: "Not only don't they, but the incest figures suggest that they participate in it to a considerable degree."

Me: "How much incest is there in America?"

MacKinnon: "There's a tremendous amount." (She may be right.)

We came back to the issue of gender feminism versus equity feminism. She said: "It's a phony distinction." She went on to say that Americans are also discriminated against on the basis of race, class, and rank (as in a CEO of a company—which is changing these days). She said women had nothing to do with setting up such a society and that ". . . nobody asked us." It went on for a while in this manner; the program ended; we shook hands.

In an unexpected way, the wars in Afghanistan and Iraq expanded my own view of feminism. I consider myself a feminist. The women in my immediate family were well-educated professionals. My sister went to NYU, raised three children, and became an actress and playwright. (For nine years she was in the ensemble cast of the sitcom *Wings*, in which she played the role of Fay, the ditzy stewardess. She was the best one in the cast. The program is on the air in reruns and she is still recognized on the street. Her one-act play about Eugenia Ginsburg, the heroic anti-Stalinist dissident in the 1930s, appeared off-Broadway. She was in the cast of *United 93* and wrote a well-publicized journal of her experiences regarding the filming of that remarkable movie.)

My mother had a graduate degree in nutrition from Columbia, which she attended after World War I. She had come to New York with the intent of going back to what was then called Palestine to supervise nutrition on a kibbutz. But, as she liked to recount, she met my father, got married, had a baby (my sister), the Depression struck, had another baby (me), and then World War II almost destroyed the planet for nearly six years. At that point she had two teenage American kids who were not interested in going back to what was later to be called Israel. She was a fine mother and a woman of great culture—also quite outspoken.

I thought I knew the general situation of women in the Arab world. But the graphic televised revelations and depictions of half of humanity treated as third-class people knocked me for a loop. I thought of the MacKinnon interview. Once again, the American activist Left had taken a good idea—feminism—and let remaining problems distort enormous progress.

Environmentalism is another good-cause movement idea run amok. In 2005, we did a program on lobbying with AEI Visiting Fellow James D. Johnson, former vice president for industry-government relations at General Motors, and author of *Driving America*. He quotes climatologist Stephen Schneider of the National Center for

Atmospheric Research, who in 1989 wrote this about scientists with a point of view:

> We must include all the doubts, caveats, ifs, and buts. . . .
> [But to get action] we have to get some broad-based sup-
> port to capture the public's imagination. That entails get-
> ting loads of media coverage. *So we have to offer up scary
> scenarios, make simplified, dramatic statements. Each of
> us has to decide what the right balance is between being ef-
> fective and being honest.* [Emphasis added]

Schneider added: "I hope that means doing both" (which doesn't soften the statement, although it sounds as if it does).

Again, lying for justice. We all know it goes on. I had not seen the quote before. I find Dr. Schneider's statement irresponsible and barely acceptable for a public relations practioner and certainly not for a scientist.

Most of the cause movements have raised legitimate issues: feminism, environmentalism, peace, racism, consumer rights, and business responsibility, just to begin. But there has been a catastrophic tactical misjudgment. Suppose the environmentalists had just publicized the quiet but accurate time-series data from the Environmental Protection Agency that show dramatic improvement in environmental quality. It was, after all, a cabinet-level department they were largely responsible for creating. Instead too many of them, or the most publicized of them, go about saying the sky is falling, or the earth will fry, or nuclear power will blow us up. And so, many fair observers think they are greeno nuts.

Such exaggeration allowed the neo-cons, with credibility gained from their prior backgrounds, to call their bluff, publish the counter studies, and take the political offensive. The conservatives did the same thing but their material was often discounted on the basis of their earlier, stop-the-world ideas.

No one believed more in the power of ideas—sometimes to a fault—than Norman Podhoretz. He did a one-on-one *Think Tank* program in April 1999 entitled "Intellectuals at War." It dealt mostly with his book *Ex-Friends*, which recounted his falling out with New

York intellectuals Allen Ginsberg, Lionel and Diana Trilling, Lillian Hellman, Hannah Arendt, and Norman Mailer. It gives some idea of splits between Left and Right, conservative and neo-conservatives and even between New York and Washington.

I asked Podhoretz about "the neo-conservative heresy." He said of the combat in small-circulation policy magazines circa late 1960s:

> When we came along our arguments against the Left were much more effective than the arguments that had been made by traditional conservatives like Bill Buckley and the people around the *National Review,* who really didn't know the enemy as well as we did. We knew where the vulnerabilities of the Left were. And we won those arguments partly because the old Right was out of shape, but partly because we were right. That explains why we had the effect that we had. We were tiny in numbers but like those movies in which six cavalrymen are attacked by one thousand Indians and they would run from one rock to another to try to fool the Indians into thinking that there were more of them than there were.

He took credit for a lot, I thought. I asked him where the vigorous American anti-Communism, championed by neo-cons, had come from: "The view about the Soviet Union being a major threat was enunciated by Harry Truman and Dwight Eisenhower and John Kennedy, and my hero Scoop Jackson, and a lot of other people."

NP: These are people operating in the political realm who implemented policy. But before they did so there were many years of debate and analysis of the phenomenon. Finally, and I say finally,[4] they came to recognize it as the kind of threat it actually was. And it had to do with defining what the true reality

---

4. Finally? Podhoretz had been an anti–Vietnam War radical. He later wrote a book entitled *Why We Were in Vietnam.* Scoop Jackson, Richard Nixon, Lyndon Johnson, and many of their supporters had lash-marks for defending that position long before Podhoretz came to it.

of what the Soviet Union was. As you know, there were many apologists for the Soviet system, including important politicians like Franklin Delano Roosevelt's vice president, Henry Wallace, whom we narrowly escaped having as president.

BW: But Harry Truman was not educated and shaped by intellectuals in New York.

NP: I think there's a kind of trickle-down effect in the culture as there is in the economy. Ideas are the moving forces of history. I'm the opposite of a Marxist. I don't think it's "the economy, stupid," that drives history, I think it's ideas in the heads of men.

BW: What about the idea that this process doesn't go on as trickle-down but as bubble-up? People understood the evils of totalitarianism. There is a huge ethnic population in the United States who, by the grapevine of their people in Eastern Europe and in the Soviet Union, knew damned well what was happening. Didn't Susan Sontag write, when she finally partially turned the corner, that "you would have learned more about the Soviet Union from the *Reader's Digest,* which had a circulation of twenty million people, than from all the combined intellectuals"?

NP: Yes. But what she failed to say was that where the *Reader's Digest* learned it was from Max Eastman, who had been an ex-Communist intellectual and translator of Trotsky. The answer to your question is yes and no. I'm a great believer in the common sense of the American people, and I'm a great believer in Bill Buckley's classical dictum that "I'd rather be ruled by the first two thousand names in the Boston phone book than by the combined faculties of Harvard and MIT." I will, however, say that voters on their own don't have a glorious record in this context.

BW: More glorious than the intellectuals. We agree on that. These arguments that you describe in your book were particularly intense in New York. We had these arguments in Washington all the time, but most people remained fairly cordial and fairly friendly because they had to do business on a lot of other things—for example, agriculture policy.

NP: You've just given the answer: They had to do business on a lot of things. It's also part of the art of politics to obfuscate differences in order to make it possible to cooperate, and even somebody like Joe McCarthy, it is said, would run into someone he had been harassing or ruining at a committee hearing, throw his arm around him and say, "It's nothing personal. Let's go have a drink." Well, I mean, I would have decked the guy. [And faced charges of assault?] Intellectuals don't play the game that way. They feel it their duty to sharpen and clarify differences in order to understand what the logic of a particular view leads to.

BW: But, does that mean getting bitter and personal about it? Because some of that comes through in your book.

NP: I'm always asked that question. If you take ideas with the kind of seriousness that the people I write about did and that I did, they were matters almost of life and death, held with a religious intensity. It becomes extremely difficult to maintain civil or cordial relations . . .

BW: Doesn't that lead, then, to a certain parochialism—you hang out with your guys, they hang out

> with their guys—instead of getting the blend that
> many of us would think is the source of wisdom?
>
> NP: I would call it sectarianism, except that you have
> an obligation to keep at least reading what the other
> guys are saying, and to make yourself aware of what
> the opposing arguments are.

We are lucky that policy is made in Washington, not in New York. In some ways Washington is the most representative and typical city in America. The 535 members of Congress are elected from 435 congressional districts and 50 states. There are something like 7,000 trade associations, most with national constituencies and most with their own lobbyists. Just about every important corporation has an office in Washington, with its own lobbyists. There are embassies from most every nation on earth. There are tens of thousands of journalists. If there is a point of view that is not pushed in Washington, please tell me what it is.

But do the competing players become "ex-friends"? Usually not. Washington is said to be more polarized these days than in a long time. But still, the players—the special interests, the lobbyists, the think tankers, the members of Congress, the president and the executive branch personnel—do work together, not as ex-friends, but usually as competitive colleagues in a rough-and-tumble realm. Washington has another advantage over the broken ranks of New York City. I know this from creating programs for *Think Tank*. Booking a program in D.C. is a movable feast, surely the best locale in the world to sign up panelists from every spot on the ideological spectrum. A steady diet of New York–based guests would be overwhelmingly liberal, no matter how tenacious the effort to achieve balance. A discussion program from Dallas would have the same problem from the Right.

MY UNDERSTANDING IS that going back to the 1945 conference in San Francisco when the United Nations was formed, many conservatives were dubious about it. But the neo-cons, or those who would become neo-cons, were more idealistic and had high hopes. Those whose hopes were high became bitter when those hopes were dashed. A flavor of the neo-con view about the United Nations was offered in September of 2004, when we ran a *Think Tank* program entitled "Does the UN Work?" Our panelists were Tim Wirth, the former senator from Colorado, former State Department undersecretary for global affairs, and president of the United Nations Foundation,[5] and Joshua Muravchik, a resident fellow at AEI, author of *Exporting Democracy: Fulfilling America's Destiny* (1991) and *The Imperative of American Leadership: A Challenge to Neo-Isolationism* (1996).

I began by asking Muravchik the question before the House: "Does the UN Work?"

He replied:

> The UN was conceived of as an institution that would be the bulwark of world peace and it never grew into that role. In this post–Cold War era, the main structure of peace is the United States itself. The UN can't keep the peace and succeeds sometimes at tying down the U.S.

Wirth countered:

> The idea of the UN is still valid. Nations ought to get together and make sure that no single country is able to impose its will on others. The UN is now working very hard

---

5. Wirth, a dedicated environmentalist and population alarmist, achieved notoriety for an item on his State Department desk: A bowl of condoms, free to any visitor. It's not your father's State Department. Wirth now works for the United Nations Foundation, which was established with a $1 billion pledge from CNN founder Ted Turner, since reduced. Turner was originally a fierce conservative; in fact, that was one reason his earlier attempted buyout of CBS was condemned and turned down. Then he met and married Jane Fonda—a fierce radiclib—and resurfaced as a far-out liberal. Cause and effect? Who knows what goes on in a marriage? Muravchik, another former president of the Yipsels in New York, later became executive director of the Coalition for a Democratic Majority. He is also the author of *Heaven on Earth: The Rise and Fall of Socialism*, a strikingly interesting and highly readable book, later presented as a three-hour PBS *Think Tank* special by our television team.

with the people who care about the UN, which is almost everybody, to modernize itself to the threats of the modern world.

I asked Wirth about the concern that the U.S. dominates the world as the "sole super-power." He said:

> The UN is a political institution like the Congress. People have their own agendas. Put yourself in the position of understanding that some of these members are looking at the big United States and saying, well, maybe there's some way we can gain an advantage . . . but if we want something to happen at the UN, it generally happens, and if we don't want it to happen, it generally doesn't happen.

I responded, "In the General Assembly, 44 percent of all votes have been one-sided, anti-Israel resolutions, so that's not the U.S. having control over those kinds of votes."

Wirth likened the General Assembly to a debating society. "What the General Assembly says is like a congressional resolution. It's like a 'national salute to Eisenhower.' What's important is what happens in the Security Council."

Muravchik demurred:

> The reality is that in the now nearly sixty years of the UN's existence, there have only been two occasions on which the UN Security Council has responded to put the aggressor back in its place: Korea in 1950 and Kuwait in 1990 and 1991. Both times it was a U.S. response under a slight UN fig leaf.

THINK TANK WAS into the argument on "intelligent design" before that was a controversial phrase in play. Our guest was Robert Wright, a former writer at the New Republic, who takes a deep interest in the hot fields of sociobiology and evolutionary psychology, which have become topics of deep interest in the never-ending argument about Darwinism.

Wright had written two books in the field, *The Moral Animal* and *Non-Zero: The Logic of Human Destiny*. He then became a professor at the University of Pennsylvania, whose dean described him to me as an "academic superstar." We talked about his new book, *Non-Zero*. Wright presents a fascinating argument. One exchange has stuck with me:

> WATTENBERG: You say that this long train of human history has a genetic bonus on cooperation and liberty which leads us from families to chiefdoms to tribes, and so on, toward greater democracy, right?
>
> WRIGHT: Well, it's certainly toward greater and more advanced social complexity. I do think that right now technological trends favor the spread of democracy, and the diffusion of power, the decentralization of both economic and political power. And I think there are precedents for that in the past, during kind of thresholds in information technology. I'm optimistic about the future in that regard.

I don't know whether Wright considers himself a neo-conservative or not. But the sentiment expressed lets neo-cons believe that even in fields like evolutionary psychology and sociobiology, at least some smart people know what we are talking about.

ONE NAME THAT keeps cropping up in this tale of neo-conservatism is that of Daniel Patrick Moynihan. His three appearances on *Think Tank* were repeated several times. One, in 1997, was a straight interview on the occasion of his seventieth birthday and the publication of a Festschrift[6] by those who admired

---

6. A volume of learned articles or essays by colleagues and admirers serving as a tribute or memorial, especially to a scholar.

his work. He was the only active politician to ever appear on the program and we did not talk partisan politics. Moynihan died in 2003. In 2005 we aired a long interview, which we had originally taped in connection with a PBS documentary special we produced entitled *The First Measured Century* but had been able to air only a few bites of in the actual program. The third, from 1996, was a joint interview with his former Harvard colleague Seymour Martin Lipset, another seminal neo-conservative. The topic was Lipset's new book, *American Exceptionalism*, a notion that connects clearly to the neo-conservative orientation. Some excerpts:

> BW: Tell us about your new book, *Miles to Go: A Personal History of Social Policy.*
>
> DPM: I was asked if I would put together a series of essays that have a certain continuum in that they speak to matters that I've been going on about for fifty years and in which almost nothing seems to get better. But Americans are learning how to manage the business cycle. In the late thirties there was only one real question around. It was understood that free-enterprise market capitalism had failed. Indeed, if you look at the data the alternation of boom-and-bust and boom-and-crash and boom-and-bust had seemed to be amplified from the late 1890s onward.
>
> BW: I saw the chart in the book [*The First Measured Century*]. Those were incredible swings.
>
> DPM: That's over. In a half century we've had only four quarters of negative economic growth. Nothing like it in the history of the species. It would have been thought impossible.
>
> BW: Negative in a very minor way, 1 to 2 percent negative, and we have so-called "growth recessions,"

where the gross domestic product remains positive by 1 to 2 percent.

DPM: If the Bureau of Economic Analysis and the Commerce Department didn't tell you, you wouldn't know it.

BW: But not everything came up roses. What about welfare reform, or as you sometimes refer to it, as welfare repeal? What happened?

DPM: One of our largest social changes ever in this sort of modern era was the erosion of traditional family structures by which children were reared with two parents. But which way does the causal arrow point? Did the program create the social condition, or did the social condition take over and change the program? The assumption grew that the program caused the problem, and so we abolished it.

BW: We abolished that specific entitlement. We did not abolish federal aid to poor people. We turned over large sums of money to the states to do that.

DPM: That's right. But with this condition that no one can receive benefits for more than five years. And the average recipient receives them for thirteen. I fear we're going to find millions of children unsupported and possibly even abandoned. I don't predict it; I don't have any joy in talking about it. But it's the biggest gamble we have ever taken with social policy. [As of 2008, Moynihan's fears have not been realized.]

BW: Let's go into some labels for a moment. It is said of you that as an intellectual and a thinker you are a

neo-conservative, but as a senator you are liberal. Is
that so?[7]

DPM: There's a history. In the 1960s, the time when
you were in the Johnson White House, a certain kind
of liberalism seemed ebulliently triumphant. For years
there had been no real opposition, or none that anybody had noticed. Then in the middle of the 1960s,
the journal *The Public Interest* [began pointing out
some problems].

BW: You were one of the coeditors.

DPM: I was on the board of publication and I wrote
the first article in the first issue. We began to come
up with some social science findings that were very
troubling. One of the great examples is *The Coleman
Report*. The 1964 Civil Rights Act provided a little section that there would be a study of the quality of educational opportunity around the country, but
mainly the South. So sociologist Jim Coleman conducted the largest social science project in history,
asking what makes a difference between actual
achievements of the child? And I'll never forget a
spring morning there was a little reception at the
Harvard Faculty Club and Seymour Martin Lipset
walks in and says, "You know what Coleman is find-
ing, don't you?" And I said, "No." And Lipset said,
"All family." Family explained most of those differences. The reach of social institutions seemed much
more limited than we knew. This was not good news.
It was rejected [by liberals]. Then a great radicalism
came on with the Vietnam War, and at one point the

---

7. Moynihan's votes in the Senate from 1979–1980 to 1995–1996, as calculated by the
American Civil Liberties Union, averaged 78 percent liberal—not very liberal—one year as high
as 95 percent liberal, and then the next at 53 percent.

old traditional socialists in a journal called *Dissent* were under attack as being not left enough. In a celebrated article it was decreed that people like Moynihan and so forth were not liberals, we were neo-conservatives. But Irving Kristol said, if you say so I'm going to be so.

BW: He's proud of it. [Me too.]

DPM: But we hadn't changed. It was the debate that changed. I think it was decreed that I was no longer a neo-conservative about the time I came to the Senate. It was on a pretty crucial issue regarding the Soviet Union.[8] By the mid-1970s, I had come to the conclusion that the Soviet Union was going to break up and soon. I said it, wrote it, nobody paid it much heed. That was a point that was not worth arguing about, because I wasn't going to change the minds of my friends who continued to see a very serious Soviet menace.

BW: But they did have all those nuclear weapons, pointing at Chevy Chase.

DPM: So we might all go up in flames. Watch out. And they start pointing them at each other and it wouldn't make much difference. My early ideas were shaped by Nathan Glazer. In 1963 I was in the Kennedy administration. We published our book, *Beyond the Melting Pot,* which was a study of the ethnic groups of New York City. And there had been this idea that, you know, we'd all come over here, we were all different, we go into a melting pot.

---

8. Pat was a brilliant political hybrid. By my lights, there was plenty of neo-con left in him right to the end.

BW: Israel Zangwill. The play was *The Melting Pot*. I recently reread it.

DPM: It was set in Staten Island. There's the Jewish girl who is a violinist, and the Russian boy who's a singer, and his father is a general who carried out a pogrom, and they all fled. In Russia there should be no chance of them coming together, but love conquers all on Staten Island. We are building the New American Man. That was our creed and our hope. What Glazer and I looked at was a city [New York] in which that hadn't happened at all. We saw it as the test of the Marxist hypothesis: that industrialization will wipe out these preindustrial remnants, and social class will determine everything. The red flag is our flag because of all the blood of all men is red. And there will be no Estonian and Lithuanian and Ukrainian and Dane, and such. We checked it out it and it wasn't there. So if you have the idea that Marxism is fundamentally wrong about the power of ethnicity and you see a multiethnic empire sprawling from the Baltic to the Pacific, and you say, this isn't going to last either. You can't prove it, but you can predict it.

BW: Many years have gone by since the publication of *Beyond The Melting Pot*. The rates of exogamy—intermarriage—in America are now Zangwillian. More than half of Asian Americans out-marrying and about a third of Latinos out-marrying. Jews are above 50 percent exogamous. You have now for the first time a serious out-marriage among blacks. So at precisely the time when some people are talking gleefully or portentously about Balkanization and separatism it seems to me that the people who count, who are making these demographic decisions, Joe and Jane in the privacy of their bedroom, are going toward a melting pot.

DPM: It seems to me both things are so. We noted the exogamy, but more and more this society identifies people by race, religion, national origin.

BW: The government does.

DPM: The government does. OK, we can make a distinction.

BW: Right. I don't know that the society does. The government is race crazy.

DPM: Government is race crazy.

BW: You're in government; it must be your fault.

DPM: Well, yes. Whoever's to blame ought to be found out. Every appointment is a question of race, religion, gender. It is just the very opposite of the American creed, which is we're all equal. We're all classified. For the moment ethnicity is much more assertive here than it was.

BW: If you were a historian of the future looking back at the past fifty years, say, post–World War II to now, how would you weave all the strands together?

DPM: The United States became the most powerful nation in the world and the first nation ever nearly so powerful. We did it because in the main our values were right and our system worked. In the end the great challenge of totalitarianism, which had arisen by the end of the twentieth century, was over. American values, which were not American necessarily in origin but which we embodied as a major nation, had triumphed. And we were left with a lot of aftermath, but if you look around at our adversaries wouldn't you say how fortunate the century had been for us? And the only question that historians will really ask is, Did that make them overconfident?

BW: Tell us now about *The Report on the Negro Family.* How does that come about?

DPM: When the Kennedy people came in, . . . [u]nemployment was the big issue domestically. The attention was focused on places like Appalachia, and we were beginning to be very much aware of the problems of black Americans, especially in cities. In 1946 we did produce an unemployment rate. We didn't publish it. We weren't sure enough. But black unemployment was well below white unemployment, because blacks were on farms, and on a farm you may have scarcely enough to live on, but you are employed. When the black movement North came, black unemployment became a problem. I was able to show a striking correlation between the rise and fall of unemployment, the rise and fall of things like "married woman/husband absent," and the number of new welfare cases. . . . Then suddenly, the unemployment rate for minorities was going *down*, and the [welfare] dependency rate was going *up*. The lines crossed.

BW: When graphed this is what James Q. Wilson calls "Moynihan's Scissors"?

DPM: It meant that we had something bigger and more complex than we knew, and we still have.

BW: *The Report on the Negro Family: The Case for National Action* soon became known as *The Moynihan Report,* and still is. Can you describe the reaction?

DPM: Let me put it in context. In the summer of 1965 we had some wonderful things in Washington as regards race by that time. In 1964 the great Civil Rights Act was passed. In 1965 the great Voting Rights Act was passed. Then without any notice or warning or heads-up the rioting broke out in Watts, in Los Angeles. It was fierce. The reporters in the White House—a group you know well, Ben—were saying to Bill Moyers, the press secretary, saying, Bill, what's going on? What happened?

And he said, "Oh, we know all about these things. Let me just show you." And he handed out this report, saying, "Pat Moynihan did this for the president last June; we're on to these things."

Next morning Bob Novak and Rowland Evans, in their wonderful column, their headline was "The Moynihan Report." And it linked up the behavior at Watts with this other matter [family decomposition and welfare dependency]. People got very upset. It was rejected. The president had called for a conference "To Fulfill These Rights," to make it not just equality of opportunity, but equality of results. The opening line by the White House director of the conference said, "I'm here to assure you that there's no such person as Daniel Patrick Moynihan."

There is no argument about what Johnson said about the racial turmoil, but there is an argument about what he meant. The speech was delivered at Howard University in June 1965. The operative lines are:

You do not take a person who, for years, has been hobbled by chains and liberate him, bring him up to the starting line of a race and then say, "You are free to compete with all the others" and still justly believe that

you have been completely fair. Thus it is not enough
just to open the gates of opportunity. All our citizens
must have the ability to walk through those gates. This
is the next and more profound stage of the battle for
civil rights. We seek not just freedom but opportunity.
We seek not just legal equity but human ability, not just
equality as a right and a theory but equality as a fact and
as a result.

Those who have pushed for racial quotas or, euphemistically, "affirmative action with goals and timetables" or "race-norming" maintain
that LBJ in effect endorsed race-based quotas. But Johnson said that
we "*seek* equality of results." He did not say, "We should legislate. . . ."
He said he wanted equality of "opportunity," that is, a meritocracy with
a nudge from affirmative action but without the timetables that yield
quotas. That argument, about the intent of civil rights laws, has gone
on for more than forty years, and continues. I find it hard to believe
that LBJ would want quotas to be a part of the permanent condition in
America. He may not have written the speech, but as a former legislator he knew the importance of every word.

BW: Let's just pursue this track for a moment. Some
years later, as you pointed out, this high illegitimacy
rate—

DPM: Ratio.

BW: Right. Excuse me. The high illegitimacy ratio that
you saw . . . in the early 1960s climbs enormously
within the black community, but also climbs in the
white community, to a point where it is higher than
the original Negro crisis that you pointed out. A few
years go by and it's not just out-of-wedlock birth, it's
an increase in crime, it's an increase in welfare. There's
a lot of things going on. There's drug usage. And you
write an essay called, "Defining Deviancy Down." Is
there linkage?

DPM: I found myself thinking about all of the previous thirty years. Information would come up which was at first shocking to people and then they had to deal with it in ways that made it less so. One of the founders of sociology, a Frenchman named Émile Durkheim, wrote a book about the turn of the twentieth century in which he said that crime was normal. He said that you have to have a certain amount of deviant behavior such that you can establish what is correct behavior. It occurred to me that what we had been doing in the last thirty years was that as we got too much deviant behavior we began to define it down. So you say, "Well, there weren't *that* many murders in *that* many schools last month." Let me give you an example: I was reading *The New York Times*. There on page B-14 was a story about seven people having been found shot dead in a Bronx apartment building. That was a notable event because the mother, before she was shot, managed to shove her infant child under a bed. And I thought of that wonderful example of gangland violence, the St. Valentine's Day massacre in Chicago (1929), when Al Capone's men rubbed out seven of Bugs Moran's men. It became the subject of national legend. And so the idea clicked. We could no longer deal with the amount of murder going on in Manhattan and the Bronx, so we had to say only special murders get attention. And you can take this pattern of avoidance and of defining deviancy down all across the society.

BW: What would some of the other examples be?

DPM: Out-of-wedlock births. Drug use of very serious kinds. Very poor performance in school. School violence. And the Democratic Party—my party—moved into this denial mode.

BW: Frank Fukuyama's new book is called *The Great Disruption*. This great disruption on the social side happened, but starting in the late 1980s or the early 1990s we rebounded—not far enough, but crime is down, welfare is down. You and I could argue about out-of-wedlock births. But there are many positive social indicators now. So how do you put that all together?

DPM: I think we may be stabilizing at a much higher level than we'd known before, and we're beginning to congratulate ourselves on circumstances that would have been thought horrendous two generations past.

BACK IN 1996 we taped Moynihan and Seymour Martin Lipset together on the occasion of the publication of Lipset's book, *American Exceptionalism*.

SML: The phrase *American exceptionalism* was actually coined as far as anybody knows by Alexis de Tocqueville in his great book *Democracy [in America]*, which is in many ways still the most informed book about America. Tocqueville says America is exceptional as compared to other countries, by which he meant it was an outlier, it was different. The thing that interested him most at the time was that it was the only democratic country in the world. And he, coming from France, where the French Revolution had seemingly failed, came to America to try to understand: Why did democracy work?

BW: America's different. Is that to be interpreted that America is better?

SML: Better and worse. There are some things which, if you look at statistics of behavioral patterns, we are at the good end of the scale. But there are some in which we're at the bottom end of the scale. One of them is violent crime. Another is voting. We have close to the lowest proportion of the population voting. We have more people involved in organizational activities and community activities. We're still the wealthiest major country in the world. We're the greatest job producer by far. We're the most religious country in terms of church attendance and belief by far.

BW: Pat Moynihan, how exceptional are we?

DPM: Well, two things I might say, if you don't mind a New Yorker speaking for a moment. Tocqueville actually came here, as Marty knows, as a part of a three-person commission of the French government to look into our prison reforms.

BW: He was on a junket.

DPM: He was on a junket, and he had to get out of France. He was heading for Auburn, New York, where we had produced the reformatory, a pretty grim place.

BW: Finger Lakes, close to Hobart College.

DPM: That's right sir. Exactly. Your own. But we were innovating, trying to improve people, as against just punishing them. But there is something else since Tocqueville. We are exceptional in that there is not a major [democratic] country in which we do not have stationed American military personnel and American bases. The one exception is France. We had our armed forces all over the world in a peaceful participation, in a confrontation with the Soviet Union. It began with the German and Japanese empires. That surely is exceptional.

BW: Has that ever happened before in history?

DPM: No.

SML: I don't think so. It ties in with another aspect of exceptionalism. We're an ideological country. Americanism is an ideology in the same sense that communism or socialism or fascism are ideologies. [Historian Richard] Hofstadter once said it's been our fortune or misfortune as a nation to be an ideology.

BW: Fortune or *mis*fortune?

SML: Being an ideology leads you to want to change the world. And this is something Americans have wanted to do. They've wanted to be involved. In many ways up to 1917, up to the Russian Revolution, we were the center of the world revolution, the democratic revolution. Democratic revolutionaries came here from all over the world, when they were defeated, when they needed R & R or when they needed money. Sun Yat-sen did. Kossuth did. Garibaldi did. This was the place that they wanted to be. We didn't want to dominate them. But this notion that we should be concerned, that we want the rest of the world to be democratic, to be decent, is an old American orientation which other countries don't have.

(Moynihan had wonderful stories he delighted in telling. Like this one: After World War II ended, a European came here to find out about how America worked. While touring a factory floor, he met a man on the assembly line who thought he could help him. "Tell me about your boss," the European said.

"Well, he's likely to stop by my work station and just chat during the day."

"Really?" asked the European.

"Yes, really. And later he might suggest that we go out for dinner."

"Your boss might invite you out to dinner? That's amazing!"

The American went on: "And after that he might suggest that we go to his place for a nightcap. And he might well invite me to stay over."

The European was astonished: "Has this ever really happened to you?"

The American responded: "No, but it happened to my sister.")

> BW: Marty, you gave a list of the sort of classic American characteristics: individualism, meritocracy, optimism. Is there a grand theme that could put all these things together?

> SML: I suppose you could say it's individualism, democracy, or egalitarianism. You know, Tocqueville stressed the fact that America at the time was the most egalitarian country in the world. By that he didn't mean equal in income or equal in power, he meant equal in opportunity, and in terms of social relationships. Americans didn't bow down to others and didn't want people to bow down. Americans don't like to have servants and don't want to be servants, unlike the situation in the hierarchical, post-feudal countries of Europe.

> DPM: I absolutely agree with that. I think you would also say that in this individualism, some get plenty and some get none, and is leaving us at the end of this century, in which we are the wealthiest nation in the world, with the largest number of genuinely poor, isolated people. [The author disagrees.] We have a degree of societal breakdown which we never would have expected. A third of our children now are born to single parents.

BW: There's a whole history of words that have described that. It went from *bastard* to *illegitimate* to *out-of-wedlock* to *non-married*.

DPM: *Non-marital*.

BW: *Non-marital*, excuse me.

DPM: In the fifty largest cities in the country, the average is 48 percent. Now, no society has ever in history had to deal with this. We are exceptional in this, too.

SML: This is a Western phenomenon. In the province of Quebec, now one out of every two children is born out of wedlock. And in Britain, it's now up to a third.

BW: Pat, you once sounded the trumpet to set up a Liberty Party in the world. Is it fair to say that what characterizes America in most of these unique aspects is that it is more free than anywhere else in the world?

DPM: We are more given to asserting the individual right to do as you will and more busybody and nosy about the way people behave.

BW: And you pointed out in the book, Marty, we are also the most litigious people. We are willing to go to court and get lawyers for anything.

SML: The Bill of Rights was the only one of its kind until recently. And you know, it said Congress may *not* do, the government may *not* do this and that, because one of the characteristics of the founding fathers was they were suspicious of the state. . . . Well, setting up the Bill of Rights meant you can sue for your rights against the government. But it also led to people being concerned with their rights against each other. This in turn produced all this litigiousness.

DPM: Most of the sort of social issues we've dealt with, unemployment, old age, and so forth, we had European models. They got there first, with pensions in Germany and unemployment insurance in Britain. We followed on. Now we're facing a new set of situations of which there's no European counterpart. The Europeans are getting the problems that began here. We're going to have to work them out on our own, and I don't think we will do so successfully if we just take as a model something the Europeans might do. We're going to have to work this out in terms of our values.

BW: The conservatives would argue that this increase, for example, in out-of-wedlock birth, was caused not by too much liberty, but by too much government; that you set up a welfare net that is so high that it led to dependency, which encouraged welfare recipients to have out-of-wedlock children. We complain in this country about government being too large and too intrusive. How does it compare to other nations?

SML: We have the smallest government in percentage terms. I don't like a deficit any more than anybody else, but our deficit is under 2 percent of the GDP, the lowest by far of any developed country. We have the lowest tax rate. Americans complain, I do too, about their taxes, but taxes in every other major developed country are much higher. [Japan excepted.] They pay much more taxes; there's a bigger government. The Depression, which hit the United States harder than any other country except possibly Germany, resulted in a major change, which turned out to be an increase in the role of the government. Hofstadter said we had a social democratic tinge in American life for the first time. World War II increased it. But then since the war, we've gone through a period of returning to the American classic tradition, which is this liberal—European definition—tradition of being opposed to the state, of wanting small government.

BW: To the old-fashioned liberalism, which we would today call what, libertarianism, I guess?

SML: Now we call it libertarian.

DPM: Same Latin root.

BW: Meaning?

DPM: Freedom.

SML: Freedom.

BW: Back to freedom again.

CHAPTER ELEVEN

Media Matters Most

IN A DEMOCRACY, not only the political players seek change. In a nation with a free press—and America's press is certainly very free and getting freer—the media also reflects changing reality. A printing press, paper, and a fleet of circulation trucks cost much more than setting up a blog for $200. When life is unsettled and if people feel they are not getting the information that reflects change, the public often condemns the media. Mainstream members of the press, typically liberals, tend to pooh-pooh charges against the media.

At the end of the 1960s, neo-cons and conservatives tended to believe that most elite newspapers, newsmagazines, and television outlets were tilted left of center. Defenders of the media, typically of a liberal persuasion, claimed that all that the media was doing was telling the objective truth as it was known at the moment, creating "instant history." As conditions changed, the right-of-center forces responded, not only to proposed political change, but with new media. That proved to be critical to the nature and role of neo-conservatism. The players in the ongoing fray *agree* on several thoughts:

The media has—or appears to have—*great power and influence*. But there is even an argument about that. For instance, during both of Ronald Reagan's runs for president, the drumbeat criticisms of Reagan by two prominent *New York Times* columnists—the quite liberal Tom Wicker and the very liberal Anthony Lewis—seem to have helped, not hurt, Reagan. Still, many in Washington arrive at ridiculously early morning meetings to review the important newspapers, what was said on television, and what appeared on the 'Net. They do this not just to be informed but in order to rebut the journalism and even sometimes to change policy. Such scrutiny sometimes helps, but often not.

But even as people complain about the press, they tend to believe what they see in print. Gutenberg created a magical machine. But even among sophisticated observers, what people see on television probably has greater credibility. People say, "I saw it with my own eyes." Those morning meetings also cover the mean and funny gags that appeared on the previous night's late talk shows.

The power of the media: I visited Israel for the first time in 1969 shortly after I left the LBJ White House. It was a time when fedayeen attacks had sharply increased, with the perpetrators coming principally from Egypt. There was a great deal of newspaper and television coverage about the attacks, with the gory details shown on television. A still-valid axiom of television news is "if it bleeds, it leads." I was frightened. I would like to say I was frightened because I had three small children to support. I was, but I was also frightened for myself. I screwed up such courage as I had to make the trip. I arrived at Lod Airport (later renamed Ben-Gurion Airport) and took a cab to the Hilton on the Mediterranean Sea. I was very cautious, looking every which way for fedayeen ready to pounce. I bravely decided to take a short evening stroll along the boardwalk. It was totally peaceful. Lovers strolled—arms interlinked. After a while I felt safe. *What on earth had I been worrying about?*

I was working on a story as well as meeting family. Through the offices of the public relations professionals of the Israeli government, an interview had been arranged for me with David Ben-Gurion, the mythic first prime minister of Israel, who had by then retired. What was scheduled for a one-hour interview turned into three hours. (It turned out Ben-Gurion knew some of my family, which had emigrated to Palestine in the first years of the twentieth century, when

Palestine Liberation Organization could easily have been used to describe Zionist Jews, not Palestinian Arabs.)

After a while Ben-Gurion and I struck some common conversational ground: Israel's future in relationship to its demography. At that time Israel had a population of about 2.2 million. About 15 percent of the population was not Jewish, leaving about 1.9 million Jews. I asked Ben-Gurion how could Israel manage its safety in a neighborhood of tens of millions of hostile Arab neighbors publicly announcing their goal was to drive the Israelis "into the sea." The watchwords of Arab policy were, "We don't have to win every war, or some wars, just the last one."

Ben-Gurion was a small man, but he had a voice like a bell. "America," he said. "American Jews," he said, "are going to come to Israel in the millions."

"Mr. Prime Minister," I said, "with all due respect, I was born in America, I've lived there all my life, and in a pro-Zionist household. I write about demographics. There will be a few Americans emigrating, but only a few, certainly not enough to significantly change the population of Israel."

"Look at this!" he boomed, triumphantly handing me a copy of the famous *Time* magazine whose cover blared "Black versus Jew," with a picture of three blacks on one side staring at three white people (assumed to be Jews) on the other. He, too, had been paying attention to the media and believed what he read and saw. "See," Ben-Gurion went on, *"the pogroms are starting in America."* We were both gulled by sensationalism of the press.

I said there was indeed tension between blacks and Jews in America, but great numbers of Jews would not leave because of it. "Don't rely on many American Jews emigrating," I said. "Money? Yes, many Jews will be generous in giving money to a variety of Jewish causes. Visiting Israel? Yes, some American Jews will visit Israel; there is an emotional attachment and Israel is a great tourist attraction in its own right, for Jews and gentiles alike. Influencing Congress and the president? Yes, Jewish activists are among the most effective lobbying group in Washington.

"Some American Jews will send their children to a kibbutz for a summer," I continued. (My daughters Ruth and Sarah went. My son

Danny spent half a year at Tel Aviv University. My youngest daughter Rachel visited Israel as a child and saw my daughter Ruth and David Kusnet married in a small, beautiful ceremony in Jerusalem at a wide spot on the side of the road to Mount Scopus.) But at the end of the day, I said to Ben-Gurion, most American Jews were and would remain both Jewish and patriotic Americans.

I talked about how fertility rates of secular American Jews were diminishing sharply. At the same time, Israeli Jews had, and have, the highest fertility in the developed world. (This, I believe, comes from the addition of a third "insurance baby" among secular Israelis, who are afraid that one of their children will be lost in one of the periodic wars or terrorist attacks. So Arab hostility increases Israeli population, and power.) Ben-Gurion only had the country wrong: Since 1970, about a million Jews have come to Israel from the Soviet Union.

Israel may be considered a neo-conservative nation by American standards. By the nature of their circumstance, Israelis believe in strong national defense. They have dumped the old model of kibbutz-based socialism for high-tech entrepreneurialism. Next to the U.S. itself, Israel—population just six million—now has the most listed companies on NASDAQ. Israelis believe strongly in immigration. And, like a majority of Americans, they are pro-Israeli.

CELEBRITY IS ANOTHER aspect of the modern media acknowledged by all. Back in 1972, Scoop Jackson stayed in the race even though he had stopped campaigning. His delegates were in Miami in force, and they threw a party at the headquarters motel alongside the swimming pool. Eric Sevareid, the distinguished journalist and author, was at the time the main commentator for the CBS Evening News. At the party, standing poolside, Sevareid asked me some questions about the campaign. Of course, I was happy to provide both facts and opinions. The crowd at the party was not composed of local yokels gaping at a rock star. They were for the most part political professionals with at least some sophistication.

Gradually, a few individuals at first, and then more, came up and asked Sevareid for his autograph "for my grandchild" or "for the missus, who unfortunately couldn't make it here." Sevareid obliged, and after a while it was simply impossible to conduct a conversation. He motioned to me to come with him to one of the small balconies of the first-floor motel suites, up a half a dozen steps from the pool. That didn't buy us more than a couple of minutes. At first a few individuals came up to Sevareid, then a steady march. Up the stairs they came, this time clearly interrupting a private conversation. Sheepishly, Sevareid threw up his hands and said we'd pick it up later, time and place unspecified. He couldn't do his job.

I went back down poolside. Unrecognized, Senator Tom Eagleton came over to chat. He said, in effect: "Ben, there's some talk that McGovern is going to pick me as his vice presidential running mate. What do you think? Should I do it."

I said, "Sure, what do you have to lose?"

Eagleton later did indeed get the bid from McGovern, accepted it, and lost plenty. The press did its customary digging, and it was revealed that Tom Eagleton had been hospitalized three times for nervous exhaustion and twice received electric shock therapy. He was dropped from the ticket, replaced by R. Sargent Shriver, who had never held elective office, but only after many other big name elected Democrats turned McGovern down cold. The press had a field day with the issue.

Which leads to a *third* commonly accepted, and correct, view of the modern media. They may tilt toward the left, but they are piranha first and foremost: *If it bleeds, hit it.* The intense coverage given to the Eagleton affair harmed McGovern greatly, even though evidence is clear that the elite media favored his candidacy. More recently, the sexual relationship between Monica Lewinsky and a generally liberal President Clinton received vast coverage domestically and internationally. (By the way, the issue did not concern sexual activity but *perjury* before a grand jury, by a lawyer, a former law professor, and the employer of the chief law enforcement officer in the land, the Attorney-General.)

A *fourth* notion is that bad news is big news and good news is no news. We all know that it is *not* news when all the planes land safely; it *is* news when one of them crashes. But when mindlessly applied to America, and to Western civilization, such media guidelines are at the root of much of the neo-con complaint about contemporary journalism. An early liberal hero of mine, Adlai Stevenson, ran against Dwight Eisenhower in 1952 and 1956. He was also the publisher of an Illinois newspaper, *The Bloomington Pantagraph*. He understood the game. A newspaper's job, he said, is to "separate the wheat from the chaff and print the chaff."

A June 2005 survey conducted by the Pew Research Center for People and the Press asked the relevant question: "In general, do you think news organizations pay too much attention to good news, too much attention to bad news, or do they mostly report the kinds of stories they should be covering?" The results: good news, 3 *percent*; bad news, 67 *percent*; about right, 23 *percent*. Sounds fine, but even the great American public can be more than a little hypocritical at times. The public loves watching bad news, which is a main reason the media run so much of it.

A *fifth* idea concerns journalists from countries with a *free* press trying to cover the reality of what is going on in an *unfree* country. Official government censors edit out any unfavorable descriptions of life in an autocratic or dictatorial regime. "Minders" follow television crews wherever they go, granting or denying permission to tape. They accompany journalists when they attempt to conduct interviews to make sure that no interviewee says anything contrary to the official government line. (We get the straight goods only *after* the journalists leave the country.)

In Israel foreign journalists are not only free to cover what they choose but are often foolishly provided with police radios so that they can quickly get to the scene of violence and send the fresh and gory tape of Israeli-Palestinian violence home via satellite. Often the terrorists or activists wait for the journalists, a technique at least as old as Gandhi's protests in South Africa. By contrast, journalists in adjacent and autocratic Syria can not provide any realistic portrait of what is going on there.

I can think of one exception. The Soviets invaded Afghanistan in 1979—just the sort of thing the neo-cons had thought they might do. CBS anchorman Dan Rather got through the sealed border and reported about the situation on the ground with one of the *mujahideen* groups fighting the Soviets. This took courage. But Rather did not receive much credit. On camera for his standups he was dressed as a "mooj" guerilla, replete with turban. For this he gained the sobriquet Gunga Dan. Moreover, he quite clearly suggested that the Soviets would prevail in Afghanistan. Anchorman Rather was wrong. In 1989 the Soviets were forced to withdraw after taking heavy casualties. It was the only time a putative Soviet satellite successfully broke away from the grip of the USSR. The word was out: That dog won't hunt. There are those (like me) who believe that Afghanistan led to the overthrow of Soviet rule by the Eastern European satellites and ultimately to the dissolution of the Soviet Union and the end of the Cold War. (Times change: A dozen years later 9/11 was directed from Afghanistan.)

(There were nonmilitary repercussions to the Afghanistan invasion. In 1979 President Jimmy Carter determined that the U.S. Olympic team should boycott the 1980 Moscow Olympics. Sixty other teams joined in the American boycott, leaving only eighty-one participant nations. Reagan, the Commie-basher, opposed the boycott! In 1984 it was the Soviets' turn to boycott, citing the safety of their athletes in the anti-Communist environment of Los Angeles. But 140 nations showed up, including mainland China—for the first time in thirty-two years!)

CONSIDER NOW SOME items about which neo-cons and conservatives are in *disagreement* with prevailing wisdom concerning modern journalistic practices.

There has been a great deal of talk in recent years about *media bias.* The Right says the media is biased toward the Left. A few on the Left say the media is biased toward the Right—for example in the book *What Liberal Media?: The Truth About Bias and the News,* by slash-and-burn radiclib Eric Alterman, who is smart but sometimes mindless and nasty. Bill Moyers reports that "mega-media companies are driving journalism down the hierarchy of corporate values, silencing critics while shutting off communities from essential information," and let us further know on his PBS program NOW *with Bill Moyers* was subject to "relentless public attacks from the de facto Ministry of Propaganda in the right-wing media." The Ministry, I assume, is part of the government of President Bush #43. But just who is censoring what? If there is censorship, where is the Federal Communications Commission? Will Moyers name names? How come Moyers can broadcast on public air waves through all that censorship?

Neo-cons (and conservatives, too) generally believe the Right is right on the issue of bias. For example, the war in Afghanistan following 9/11 was only two weeks old before some in the press corps found (often unnamed) sources who maintained that Afghanistan would be a "quagmire," just like the earlier "immoral" war in Vietnam. Two weeks later American troops were in Kabul. Soon, elections deemed to be free and fair were held and women as well as men voted—a stunning event in the Arab world. A constitution was passed and a president elected. There is still plenty of domestic unrest in Afghanistan as this is written, but that is a statement that can made about a great many countries today.

The disparity between media reportage of what is going on in Iraq and the firsthand testimony of grunts on the ground has been astonishing. The GIs have seen great progress on all fronts in Iraq—political as well as military—that most of the journalists seem to ignore. One ongoing story concerned the adoption of a democratic constitution in Iraq. Those journalists who make a career of blasting America said that there were powerful disagreements in Iraq about what the new constitution might really mean. Ironically, at about the same time, in America, Judges John Roberts and Samuel Alito were going through Senate confirmation hearings regarding their appointments to the U.S. Supreme Court. Those hearings, and the heated rhetoric concerning Roberts and Alito, concerned the true meaning of the U.S. Constitution, almost 225 years older than the new one in Iraq.

Intellectual conservatives tend toward the "original intent" of the U.S. Constitution as written in 1789, often expressed by Justices Antonin Scalia (a former AEI scholar) and Justice Clarence Thomas (AEI's featured speaker at one of its annual black-tie dinners). Neo-cons generally don't like judge-made law either, but they are more prepared to accept the notion that times have changed a great deal since 1789 and that the supermajorities needed to amend the Constitution are hard to come by. Accordingly, most neo-cons are prepared to fight each judicial fight as it comes along, sometimes agreeing with Scalia and Thomas on outcomes, sometimes not. (Times change: There were no cars, computers, cell phones, or respirators when the Constitution was written. Slavery was legal.)

I HAVE A bag full of credentials that allows me to speak to issues of journalism. I have seen the game played up close and have standing to pontificate. The story of my life in media-land provides some neo-conservative aspects of what *was* going on and why, compared to what *is* going on and why.

I have worked in most every editorial capacity. I started as a delivery boy for *The Bronx Home News*, a local edition of the *New York Post* second only to the short-lived *PM* in its liberal leanings. At the time New York City had more than ten dailies in English, in addition to many foreign language dailies and weeklies. The *New York Post* was my favorite as a boy. Then as now the paper had the ability to keep readers reading—no small matter.

I find reading today's *New York Post* occasionally outrageous but usually quite enjoyable reading. The *Post*'s liveliness may have something to do with the nature of a tabloid, as opposed to the "serious" broadsheet papers. If today's *Post*, owned by Rupert Murdoch and operated at a loss, is regarded by some as a conservative rag, the old *Post* would be counted as a liberal rag. Today's *Post* is actually more a neo-con paper than a conservative one (but neo-cons don't like the idea of Murdoch doing business with the Chinese when they censor his television programming). In any event, the expansion of Murdoch's media empire on the American scene was a key element in the rise of neo-conservative media.

Murdoch can be quite eclectic. In 2006, he announced he would hold a fund-raiser for New York senator Hillary Clinton. Speculation mounted that he might even endorse her for the presidency in 2008. Senator Clinton, it should be noted, supported the war in Iraq and frequently allied herself with the positions of the Democratic Leadership Council, probably the only organization in the Democratic firmament that could be (with a stretch) deemed kindly to neo-con views and values. Clinton changed her view on Iraq when her presidential race foundered.

Murdoch has a history of political variegation. His English tabloid *The Sun* quite unexpectedly endorsed Tony Blair, the prime ministerial candidate of the Labor Party. Blair flew the banner of New Labor and become known as the example of the Third Way in politics, both movements regarded as somewhat sympathetic to neo-conservatism. It was Murdoch who backed both the neo-con *Weekly Standard,* also operated at a loss, and the "fair and balanced" Fox News Channel, which most neo-cons and conservatives think *is* fair and balanced. Fox News surely has a preponderance of right-of-center media personalities, but also moderate-right centrists such as Mort Kondracke, down-the-middle Ceci Connolly of *The Washington Post,* and Mara Liasson of National Public Radio, a thoughtful commentator whose day job is at a public radio network that has often been cited as an example of taxpayer money used to further advance a liberal agenda. Further, there are some up-front liberals on Fox News: Juan Williams and Alan Colmes of the Hannity & Colmes program, although conservative Sean Hannity is the star performer. The bombastic Bill O'Reilly is a conservative, but eclectic.

Perhaps most important, the success of Fox News forced other cable news channels to put on conservative or neo-con personalities. For example MSNBC, last in the cable news ratings and generally regarded as mildly liberal, gave a slot to paleo-con Pat Buchanan. Starved for nonliberal news, the public made Fox number one in the cable news ratings, far ahead of competitors CNN and MSNBC. Old leaders like the CNN softball pitcher Larry King have fallen precipitously in the ratings. When King was a radio talk show host, he was clearly swinging from the left side of the plate. In his dotage he now bitterly resents the rise of the neo-cons, which I have experienced firsthand. In Beverly Hills I had breakfast with him and a group of five of his acolytes. He went after me for being (eek!) a neo-con, in coarse language. I gave as good as I got. Of course, the yes-men were too afraid of their King to say a word.

IN EARLY 1976, I got phone call from a producer at WGBH in Boston asking if I would like to do a PBS series of programs based loosely on my recently published book *The Real America.* WGBH was known, and still is, as one of the very best public television stations and, in the quite liberal world of public television, one of the most liberal. I went up to Boston to talk to the two men who would become the key players in the new show, Austin Hoyt and Gerry Lange, probably the only two conservatives on the entire WGBH staff. We talked about the book and the potential program. I took a brief television audition, which I passed.

Austin then asked the question that is central to every public television discussion I have been in: "Where are you going to get the money?" (Later he mused, "Where are we going to get the money?") Ultimately, the series got on the air, and there was a neo-con twist to that as well. The major funder—secured by WGBH fund-raisers— was Mobil, one of America's biggest oil companies. (PBS has on occasion been called the Petroleum Broadcasting Service.) Thus began my career in advocacy television, which I still practice.

The person behind Mobil's funding of my program was Herb Schmertz, a quite remarkable man working in a quite remarkable role. At one point Schmertz had worked in Washington for Senator Edward Kennedy, but he had gone commercial. At Mobil, he was responsible for opening the lower-right corner of *The New York Times* op-ed page for high-minded public affairs advertising, a slot that still exists. His ads typically featured the Mobil-sponsored *Masterpiece Theater*, which aired on Sunday nights on PBS. But occasionally the advertisements dealt with ideological and political issues, such as why Adam Smith was a great man, and what was the wise position on natural gas. The high-culture public service advertisements, Schmertz once explained, served to lend credibility to what was an ideological agenda. Most of the ideology made sense to me.[1] Funding my program, with its clear neo-conservative viewpoint,

---

1. After the show ended, Schmertz hired me as part of a small, freelance floating idea group. Its job was to come up with ideas for op-ed ads. Former LBJ aide Horace Busby was another member of the group, as was Milt Gwirtzman, a former key aide to President John Kennedy, Senator Robert Kennedy, and Senator Ted Kennedy. I was paid $100 per week, which helped pay the freight for a struggling freelancer. I learned that politics and friendship can be thicker than ideology. In 1980 Senator Ted Kennedy ran against Jimmy Carter for the presidency in the Democratic primaries. Schmertz took a leave of absence from plutocratic Mobil to work for his old boss, Kennedy, a faux populist adversary of oil companies.

was a way of cashing in on Mobil's paid-for goodwill in print and on television. Neither Schmertz nor Mobil had any say in program content. But having read my book, and aware of the viewpoint of the producers, he could pretty well guess what he would get.

The series, when it finally began airing in 1977, was called *In Search of the Real America: A Challenge to the Chorus of Failure and Guilt.* The best single piece of TV advice I ever received was from the director of the program, Bruce Shah, who told me, "Never forget, the lens is your friend."

Along with Austin and Gerry, producer Elizabeth Dean played an important and very constructive role in the programs. We decided to do half-hour documentaries, a fine format but rarely seen any longer because local programmers say it disrupts their schedules. (Why?) The local stations are fiefdoms unto themselves and only follow the PBS "must carry" programming feed for a very few hours each week, if that. This makes it very difficult to get national advertising, or as the PBS folks call it, underwriting.

Let me brag: *In Search of the Real America* was a very good program, with high production values, viewpoints that were quite novel for either public or commercial television, and enough of a budget to travel anywhere. I learned to memorize stand-ups without a teleprompter and that I had a certain natural speaking rhythm that some viewers found appealing. Most important, I was enthusiastic, and it showed.

Then bias belted me. As is required for new programs, we sent rough cuts of a few of our programs to PBS headquarters. Word came back that the shows were indeed good, but because there was a point of view expressed, they would have to carry an opposing viewpoint as well. To our knowledge this had never been required of any PBS program before, and there had been plenty of programs with a point of view, stated or unstated.

When this ruling came down from on high, the key PBS executives were Lawrence Grossman, its president, and Suzanne Weil, the director of programming. Grossman later became president of NBC News. We had no choice on the matter; either we did what they wanted or they wouldn't feed the program. So we decided to do a five-minute debate between me and a known opponent of my views at the end of each program. Thus, on "There's No Business Like Big Business," my debating partner was the famous Harvard economist John Kenneth Galbraith. The central point of the program was that if big American corporations didn't compete effectively, they suffer, and many would go out of business.

The producers had the wonderful idea of a visual of a graveyard on a foggy night, with headstones made from papier-mâché and a smoke machine providing the fog. I walked through the mock cemetery in a raincoat and read off the names of corporate tombstones, which included Central Leather (the seventeenth largest company in 1917), International Mercantile Marine (the eleventh largest in 1917), as well as failures like Baldwin Locomotive Works American Woolen, Packard, Motor Car International Match, Pierce Petroleum, Curtiss-Wright, United Verde Mining, and Consolidation Coal.[2] When we showed the Central Leather tombstone, a sound effect mooed; behind International Mercantile Marine's, a steamship horn bellowed (I love shtick).

Galbraith argued that big business was just about invulnerable and challenged me to name even one that had gone bankrupt. I did: the five-and-dime chain W. T. Grant. It was a factoid that I had quite fortuitously noticed in the business section of one of the major newspapers just a few days before our shoot. Since then, many corporations, big and small, have folded. Many new ones formed in an economic process called "creative destruction" described by economist Joseph Schumpeter.

Our program "The Bomb That Fizzled" was about the decline in birth rates. My opposition was Judith Kunofsky, president of Zero Population Growth. The show "Pig of the World," about alleged resource depletion, featured LBJ's secretary of the interior Stewart Udall as my opponent. Among the other guest adversaries were Julian Bond, Anthony Lewis, Morton Halperin, and Ramsey Clark.

The best debater I faced was Milton Friedman. We did only one program that lasted a full hour, "The State of the Unions," and

---

2. The program was based on an article by James Michaels, editor of *Forbes*. For many years, people would come up to me in airports, recalling that one scene and complimenting me on the program.

it required two opponents to accommodate my split personality about the topic. William Winpisinger, president of the International Association of Machinists, argued from the Far Left of the union movement, and Friedman argued the anti-union position. Friedman was not only good but had an unnerving technique. While he was talking, I tried to keep quiet. When I was talking he chuckled, not audible on camera, but plenty audibly to me. I thought my fly was open.

We did the program at WGBH for two seasons: six the first year and seven the next, with rebroadcasts of the first year's programs, for a total of 13. Then the burden of commuting to Boston while doing a column and writing a new book grew too heavy, and I stopped.

A nonpolitical sidelight: The staff was excellent, but at times the pressure was enormous. Good television prose is written to fit the pictures and, accordingly, has to be drafted by the producers. Some arguments went nuclear. There were things that the staff drafted for scripts—which they maintained were based on the book—that I simply would not say on air because I didn't think they properly reflected my views. They often argued that the passage in question was needed for continuity, or for technical video reasons. I owe a great deal to the television producers I have worked with over the years. But it seems to me they sometimes say it *can't* be done, when in fact they don't *want* it done. Fortunately, in advocacy television, the on-air personality has a *de facto* veto over what goes on the air: If you won't say it, it goes unsaid. But peace came. Public affairs television producers typically have to sell a face and a distinctive personality; otherwise, it will be difficult to be able to build an audience. When the WGBH press release stationery arrived, my name and picture was prominently featured. And that kind of warfare no longer exists at *Think Tank*: I own the program. Still, nothing is perfect. The staff often tries to boss me around. I win about half the time.

Austin Hoyt has had a distinguished career at WGBH, producing many specials that have achieved wide acclaim. But he is still very proud of the series we did together, feeling that the idea of weekly half-hour neo-con advocacy programs was path-breaking television. In the halls of liberal WGBH are posters of the shows of which the station is most proud. Our show is not among them, to Austin's dismay. But some critics, even of a liberal persuasion, understood what advocacy television was. John Leonard reviewed the series in *The New York Times* and wrote:

> Wattenberg mounts his thesis as though it were a motor scooter and his mustache were the handle bars. Vroom. . . . He is the kind of guy you argue with all night, after the women have gone to bed in disgust. You are never going to agree but it beats playing cards and he won't steal the silver. Whether or not his America is "real," he is.

I skipped a year and then did a similar program of advocacy half-hour documentaries for WETA-TV in Washington. Mobil was no longer sponsoring. Among others, new funders included Dow Chemical, Conoco, and LTV (which was in Chapter 11 bankruptcy status at the time).[3] The five-minute debate was no longer required, although we often put in opposing views on our own. PBS apparently accepted our idea that balance could be achieved in the course of a season of *all* PBS programs, rather than in the course of *each* PBS program. The first year of the WETA program was called *Ben Wattenberg's 1980*; the second, *Ben Wattenberg at Large*. Again, the personality factor was crucial; this time the stationery and press releases carried a stylized portrait of me.

George Vicas, a commercial network producer with a fine eye for television and a great ear for music, was our executive producer. Penn Kemble, the pro-union Social Democrat, almost a neo-con, carried the title editor, an unusual one in the arcane realm of television credits. He was officially number two, after Vicas, but Penn understood in his bones what I was trying to do. Often I was doing what he had suggested

One program was entitled "Power Shift: Soviet Arms Buildup," filmed on the pitching deck of the USS *Forrestal*, on assignment in

---

3. A miracle moment: One day at AEI, Keith McKennon, the public affairs director for Dow Chemical, popped into my office and said, "If you ever want to do more public television, let me know." Dow CEO Paul Orefice was then on AEI's board. A few weeks later WETA president Ward Chamberlin and I were at Dow headquarters in Midland, Michigan. We met with Paul and Keith and got, as I recall it, a $500,000 grant. Asking people for money is not a pleasant task. After a while it became sort of a game to me.

the Mediterranean. The point was in the title. After the war in Vietnam the American military had cut back on many weapons systems, although there was an argument that the *quality* of our military was better than that of the Soviets'. Neo-cons maintained that the USSR was not only sharply increasing its military, but that it was developing a "blue water navy" including, for the first time, aircraft carriers. These ships would be able to project power all over the world. That was something that previously only the United States could do. It meant that nations around the world might change their mind about who would dominate the future. That could play itself out in ways that might give the Soviets what they wanted—in the oil fields of the Persian Gulf, in the Western European democracies, in India, and elsewhere. The neo-con term of art at the time was *Finlandization*. Finland was not a Soviet satellite. But it shared a long, common border with the Soviets. The Finns dared not make anti-Soviet noise, lest they find Soviet troops in their kitchens.

Working aboard the *Forrestal*, I got a glimpse of the capabilities of American naval and air power, with planes landing night and day, in good weather and bad, executing what pilots called a controlled crash. It was an experience I will never forget. Many of the pilots complained on camera that the Soviets had better technology. A Soviet "tattle-tale" ship disguised as a fishing trawler tailed the carrier, sending information back to Moscow. Below deck was a hatchway guarded by a marine with a drawn pistol, securing what one was led to believe were nuclear weapons. The crew of about five thousand men was inspiring. I (almost) wish I had served in combat.

Our four-day stay on the carrier ended with us being catapulted off the deck in a tiny COD plane (carrier on-board delivery). It felt like being shot from a cannon. We landed at the Sigonella U.S. Air Force Base in Sicily. From Sigonella we flew in a P-3 patrol plane over the Mediterranean, frequently below 300 feet, keeping track of Soviet ships. The P-3 was full of sophisticated observation devices. After a few hours, the radar observer called us over and showed us the submerged shape of a Soviet nuclear submarine. In retrospect, some of it seems silly. Would two nuclear powers have destroyed each other, along with most of the planet? No. But, could

America—refusing to act from strength—have allowed the Soviets to turn much of the world into a Greater Finland? Yes.

We did one program called "Specter Haunting Communism: The Polish Workers." In 1980 the roughly ten thousand workers at the Lenin Shipyard at Gdansk staged a sit-down strike that spread to other cities. The strike was called by the "independent, self-governing" union Solidarity. The movement spread throughout the country. In a Communist nation, the state, not unions, is supposed to represent workers. But in Poland, the Communist government gave in to Solidarity. Other freedoms followed unionization. The Soviets did not march in as they had in other instances. If the liberty could stick, it could result in a free Poland, a result devoutly desired by neo-cons, as well as by Poles and most everyone in the world who was thinking clearly.

It was critical that we get at least one small on-camera sound bite from Lech Walesa, the leader of Solidarity. We asked for an interview—and got no answer. Kemble and I sent word that we were close friends of Lane Kirkland, then secretary-treasurer of the AFL-CIO. That was true, and Kirkland had probably done more than any non-Pole to help Solidarity. Word came back that Walesa had said, "Everyone says he is a friend of Lane Kirkland." At his best, Walesa is a gruff man. But we ultimately got a short interview.

Television production on the road can get tense. I even had an argument with Kemble. I insisted that we film a shot of the train station from which Polish Jews were sent to the Nazi death camp at Auchshwitz, sometimes with the help of anti-Semitic Poles. As a Jew, I would not do a program that did not acknowledge the Holocaust. Vicas and Kemble understood but said that their job was to produce a program about the Solidarity uprising. I exercised my inherent veto power. The brief scene was filmed, and with a short voice-over, stayed in. It was a beautiful program, made all the more so by Vicas's use of the haunting choir music we taped in a Polish church. That *was* part of the story: the church was supporting Solidarity. Karol Józef Wojtyla, a Polish cardinal and staunch anti-Communist, had become Pope John Paul II in September 1978. His anti-Communism put him in the neo-con pantheon.

The Soviets rolled back into Poland eighteen months later. But in

1989 the Poles peacefully revolted again. This time the other satellites followed suit and the Soviets did not respond. Neo-cons rejoiced; the Evil Empire had collapsed. Soon, the Soviet Union dismembered itself. The Cold War was over; neo-cons were ecstatic. The (sort of) free country called Russia remained sometimes a friend of America's, sometimes an adversary, but no longer a dangerous threat, even with its rusting nuclear arsenal. The neo-cons had always argued that it was the *intent* of nuclear powers that was the problem. Russia today has no designs on bombing America. Neo-cons used to argue that Saturday night specials or steak knives in the wrong hands could and did kill more Americans than nukes. (The weapon that has killed the most people is believed to be the machete!)

One of my favorite moments came when we did a program entitled "Sri Lanka: Second Thoughts in the Third World." The country had been run into the ground by Socialist regulations discouraging entrepreneurialism and free trade. Citizens were subject to harsh repression, in at least one case believed to be murderous. In the late 1970s, under a Socialist prime minister, Mrs. Sirimavo Bandaranaike, free elections had been stalled for two years. Political observers feared another dictatorial Cuba just off the coast of India.

But in 1977, Sri Lankans finally got to the polls and elected J. R. Jayewardene, who promised free politics and free markets. Soon observers were talking about Sri Lanka turning into Thatcher South. In the Colombo hotel where we stayed, the gift shop sold little souvenir banners that read "The Democratic Socialist Republic of Sri Lanka." I interviewed Lalith Athulathmudali, the Sri Lankan minister of trade. I waved the little flag at him. In a golden television moment he told us, "To my mind today the path we have taken, which is broadly speaking a Socialist goal, but in practical terms means whatever can be employed to improve the lot of the poor, and if that includes private enterprise, that's good enough socialism for me." Off camera he said it more succinctly: *"Socialism is whatever works."*

I interviewed President Jayewardene and he told us about the prior regime.

> We have a public securities act, which when in force
> takes away all democratic freedoms. Meetings can be

suppressed, political parties can be made illegal. It becomes a complete dictatorship with no recourse through the courts or any other authorities. We said we would do away with that, and we did away with that.

Later he said: "I often use the words 'let the robber barons come.'"

These principles of President Jayewardene were market oriented and favoring human rights. They were highly regarded by neo-cons, conservatives, and most liberals. Later, the president asked our team to meet with him privately. And then we were invited to view a great holiday parade with him. I stood at his side on the reviewing stand, for three long hot hours, with George and Penn just behind us. (I never want to see elephants again, or their droppings.) I think President J. was showing off a bit to the public that Sri Lanka mattered to foreigners and foreign journalists. I think that we were white also made us good showpieces.

Toward the end of Jayewardene's term, tensions between the Sinhalese majority and Tamil separatists erupted into war. Over the course of two decades, tens of thousands died in ethnic conflict: paradise lost. In 2002 the government and the Liberation Tigers of Tamil Eelam reached a cease fire. In 2002 the Colombo stock exchange reported the highest growth rate in Asia, and Sri Lanka had the highest per capita income in south Asia.

President Jayewardene was later tendered a state dinner at the White House. At the request of the Sri Lankans I was invited. I sat at a table whose ranking celebrity was the *wife* of the secretary of state, Mrs. George Schultz. My then-wife Diane was seated at a table with President Jayewardene, Nancy Reagan, Tony Randall, an astronaut—and Frank Sinatra. According to gossip-monger Kitty Kelly's trashy book *Nancy Reagan: The Unauthorized Biography*, Diane told her that Nancy pretty well ignored the Sri Lankan president, talking almost exclusively to Frankie, and feeding the rumor mill.

ANOTHER PROGRAM WAS "France Goes Nuclear." A recent index shows that nuclear power accounted for more than 80 percent of French electric power, a larger percentage than any other country's.

The original goal was 100 percent, but knee-jerking Greens have put a stop to that. The French do many things back-assward, but this isn't one of them. They have their own way of disposing of nuclear waste, through vitrification (the encasement of the waste in canisters of solid glass); the canisters are then sunk into deep wells in the countryside.

Even though the French do it best, most all neo-cons and conservatives believe that nuclear power is one of the big answers to the twin problems of *global warming* and the *energy shortage*. It is clean power, emitting no greenhouse gases. It is not dependent on volatile Middle Eastern sources. The amount of power it can deliver is virtually unlimited. The safety record has been outstanding (people die in coal mine accidents, on oil rigs, etc., but there have been no deaths attributed directly to the generation of American nuclear power). Some liberals endorse the logic of nuclear power. But any liberals holding public office do so dangerously. *Nuclear power* has too often been used as an environmental veto phrase.

America has committed a self-inflicted wound regarding nuclear power. In March 1979 the Three Mile Island nuclear power station near Harrisburg, Pennsylvania, suffered a partial core meltdown. It took five tense days—massively headlined and televised—until government authorities were able to provide an evaluation of what happened. No injuries due to radiation were found. A number of independent studies have shown that the average increased dose of radiation to the approximately two million people in the area was about 1 millirem. The radiation from a full set of chest X-rays is about 6 millirems. The natural radioactive background dose for the Harrisburg area is about 100 to 125 millirems.

Just a few days before the accident at Three Mile Island occurred, the movie *The China Syndrome* appeared, featuring Jane Fonda as a news anchor at a California TV station doing a series on nuclear energy. In the movie, a nuclear accident almost happens while Fonda is at the plant. Fonda, a fine actress, had achieved both national fame and notoriety for her anti–Vietnam War activity, which included active support of the North Vietnamese. Her picture posing with an antiaircraft gun aimed at American planes had raised blood pressure across America. After Three Mile Island she used her

fame to lobby intensely against nuclear power. Newspapers and television breathlessly covered the antinuclear case she made. Her "balance" was provided by the vigorous seventy-one-year old Edward
Teller, the "father of the American hydrogen bomb" and an advocate
of nuclear power. But he soon suffered a heart attack, which he later
blamed on Fonda: "You might say that I was the only one whose
health was affected by that reactor near Harrisburg. No, that would
be wrong. It was not the reactor. It was Jane Fonda. Reactors are not
dangerous." Nuclear power has yet to reach its full potential in the
United States.

IN 1980 I was asked to do a nationally syndicated column. I turned
it down once because of television commitments, but in early 1981 I
accepted. The media world was not what it is today. Out of an army
of columnists in major dailies, there were only a few well-known
conservative stars: William F. Buckley, James J. Kilpatrick, and Bill
Safire, a conservative-libertarian hybrid. But there weren't many
columnists offering a straight neo-con view, and none with a social
demographic subspecialty. It worked out surprisingly well in some respects, due to some technical machinations that are worth exploring.
In another way, there were problems.

The instrument of my casting change was David Hendin, a
brash and bright young man who ran the United Media Syndicate
(an affiliate of Scripps Howard). Payments for the column ranged
from as little $5 per week per paper to as much as $50, typically dependent on the circulation of the purchasing newspaper. The syndicate kept half the receipts, which is general practice. In a unique
arrangement, after a few years of syndication Dave set it up so that
my column would also be included in the National Education Alliance (also owned by Scripps Howard) which is a newspaper service, not a newspaper syndicate. A service sells a whole package of
editorial goods to newspapers, including crossword puzzles and advice to the lovelorn in much the same manner that the New York
Times News Service offers a full package of goods to newspapers.
The National Education Alliance had about six hundred clients, all
dailies, most in smaller cities. Some of the smaller papers are jewels

for an opinion-monger like me: Athens, Georgia, ran the column and is the home of the University of Georgia. About 180 National Education Alliance papers ran the piece regularly, and I ended up with my column in more than two hundred dailies with about six to eight million potential readers. Ranked by size of circulation, I was among the top ten columnists in the country.

Op-ed editors, it was explained to me, must think first of weekly "holes" to fill, rather than substance, although the column had better be solid and distinctive: There are usually others around that are. A writer will never get rich doing a column. But it gives someone with opinions a platform from which to vent. It yields speaking invitations, which are often an easy payoff for very hard work.

How naive was I about the column business? Quite. I did realize that the two key outlets for a nationally syndicated column are Washington, D.C., and New York City. Those places are homes to megaphone papers with influential readers, and a global bounce, because they house embassies (Washington) and UN missions (New York). Given a choice, I'd rather have my columns run in those cities than all the others put together.

At a party at columnist Bob Novak's house on the eve of Ronald Reagan's first inaugural, I saw Meg Greenfield, the *Washington Post*'s op-ed editor, whom I had come to know and admire over the years. She had worked on the hard-line *Reporter* magazine, edited and published by Max Ascoli, a liberal who turned tougher in his later years, supporting the war in Vietnam. Meg worked in the magazine's Washington bureau, as had Douglass Cater, who was later a special assistant to LBJ and to whom, for a while, I reported. (It's a small town.) Meg was willing to stand by her columnists, which she did vigorously for me on occasion. On many issues she was a neocon. She, George Will, and Charles Krauthammer had a regular weekend lunch with an invited guest.

I told Meg I would be doing a column and asked if she would be interested in running it. Her answer was a straightforward "yes." Having established that the *Post* would buy it, I neglected to ask the questions any pro would have asked: *Would she run it?* and *How often?* I remember when the first column—about rising adult life expectancy—appeared, Diane and I went downtown to the *Post* offices, which also house the massive presses. I bought a copy at about 11:30 P.M., when the "bulldog" edition appears. Sure enough, there was the column, in the center of the op-ed page, boxed, uncut, and above the fold. I was thrilled.

After a while it became apparent that Meg did not intend to run each column I wrote. She normally had more columns than space, and then in 1982 when the rival *Washington Star* folded, the *Post* picked up some of its best columnists, like Mary McGrory and Bill Buckley. What was most agitating to me was that there seemed to be no rhyme or reason to her choices. Some of my best pieces, sometimes with real news as well as opinion, did not appear.

A woman of great culture, Anne Crutcher, was the op-ed editor of the new right-of-center daily *The Washington Times*, and had asked me several times to switch papers. I went to see Meg and said, "This has got to stop." I told her that unless we could establish some minimum number of columns to be published by the *Post*, I would go over to the *Times* (which had only one-tenth the circulation).

"You don't belong in *The Washington Times*," she said. We agreed that she would run a minimum of one out of three columns. Six weeks went by, and no column of mine appeared.

I called Anne and told her to sign me up. After Anne's untimely death she was succeeded by Mary Lou Forbes, an ex-*Washington Star* reporter who had won a Pulitzer Prize for her reporting on the struggle for civil rights. Although the *Times* was a good and lively paper, and in some ways quite innovative, my move there may have been a mistake. From the start the *Times* suffered from its ownership by the Reverend Sun Myung Moon and was known as the "Moonie" paper. The paper lost money each year, and its circulation was about one hundred thousand, compared with about eight hundred thousand at the *Post*. On the other hand, it was predicted that the *Times* wouldn't last long, but more than a quarter century later it is still going. Its circulation is climbing, while the *Post* has lost ground. The online edition of the *Times* does particularly well. It is an interesting and award-winning paper. Some of the young journalists working there were afraid that the conservative experience would in effect blackball them from jobs in the mainstream media. But many of them have gone on to do fine, well-paid work—Tony Snow for one. (I was later invited to pontificate at a Krauthammer-Will-Greenfield lunch. Meg told her colleagues she couldn't make it. Hmm. . . .)

The *New York Post* bought the column, but there, too, I had to fight to get it in the paper regularly. It was impossible to get a slot at *The New York Times*. It uses only its own columnists. Moreover, it only had one nonliberal voice appearing regularly on the op-ed page: Bill Safire. Now it has two. (And Bill Kristol writes monthly.) Withal, it was a great experience and I filed a weekly column for twenty years. And I've thought of a good line for my journalistic tombstone: Wrong Post, Wrong Times.

How journalism really works: I stopped by a neighborhood liquor store. The African-American clerk was reading *The Washington Times*. I asked him why. He said, "They give the neighborhood bowling league line scores."

AFTER I HAD done the column for a while I was asked to be a commentator on the CBS program *Spectrum*, which featured six pundits from various ideological spots in the political realm. (I think I was counted as a middle-of-the-road commentator in their array, but perhaps as a conservative.) At a reunion of my elementary public school in The Bronx, Mrs. O. K. Berger (who was my teacher in both third and sixth grades) came up to me and said: "Ben, it's really strange, but there's a person with your exact name on the radio. I listen to him all the time. I go to sleep with him on." I said to Mrs. Berger, "Does this sound familiar? 'For Spectrum, *I'm Ben Wattenberg.*'" (*Spectrum* was cancelled when CBS, in its wisdom, decided its listeners weren't really that interested in politics and public affairs. It decided to concentrate on lifestyle programming, a decision driven by focus groups.) If nothing else, *Spectrum* proved to me that pundits can get to sleep with their teachers. *Spectrum* was not hard work; typically, I just cut my weekly column by about 60 percent and that gave me the slightly more than the two and a half minutes I needed for a *Spectrum* piece.

For one year I wrote a data-oriented monthly piece for *U.S. News & World Report* on social demographics. I was recruited by Editor in

Chief Roger Rosenblatt—and paid a good fee. Alas, that ended when publisher Mortimer Zuckerman decided that editorial budgets at the magazine had to be substantially cut, a common practice of his (and others). The pieces reflected my neo-con public optimism. Zuckerman is sort of a neo-con (i.e., a common-sense liberal).

I have always found writing easy. But thinking is hard. A column that I take seriously forces me to wrestle an idea to the ground. Cutting it down by 60 percent, as I had to for *Spectrum*, forced me to narrow the beam further. Cutting anything written usually helps. There is an added advantage: Perhaps a year later someone at a Q & A after a speaking engagement would ask a question, the answer to which I had refined, years earlier, to a few good one-liners. When pulled from the hard drive of my mind and put forth as if I had just doped it out, you could see the audience murmur, "He's so smart. . . ."

The downside of this kind of a column was how much time it took. In the old days there were columnists who wrote five per week, but they mostly just summarized the day's news. I wrote weekly. It took me parts of a day or two to figure out what I wanted to write about, parts of another day or two to make some phone calls and perhaps get some quotes or dig out some data, and parts of one or both days of the weekend to sharpen the lines. Once I got everything straight I could often tap it out in about an hour. I was a very busy man. For about two years my son Danny would write every other column under a joint byline. Parental pride aside, his pieces were very good and quite different from mine.

A word here about the general media culture of the time. In 1981, Smith College political science professor Stanley Rothman and Robert Lichter, a Columbia University sociologist, published "Media and Business Elites," what I believe was the first systematic study of American journalists' attitudes. It appeared in *Public Opinion*, the AEI magazine I founded and edited. The study was written while Lichter was a visiting fellow at AEI. Some journalists believed that was a clue that the results of the study might have been preordained. But many other studies have subsequently shown the same sort of results. Rothman and Lichter administered the Thematic Apperception Test to 240 journalists from top-drawer media, both print and video, including *The New York Times, The Washington Post, The Wall Street Journal, Newsweek, Time, U.S. News & World Report,* and the news departments of ABC, CBS, and NBC, as well as the newspeople at PBS (PBS has no central news department). Of the ten, nine and a half were regarded as liberal: *The Wall Street Journal* had conservative editorial pages and mildly mainstream liberal news sections. Expanded and with a third author, sociologist Linda Lichter, the article later appeared in book form as *The Media Elite: America's New Power Brokers.*

What Rothman and Lichter found stirred up a hornet's nest. For example, in 1972 when Senator McGovern received only *37.5 percent* of the actual two-party vote, the elite journalists surveyed reported that *81 percent* of the elite journalists had voted for McGovern. In 1976 the journalists reported to the surveyors that *81 percent* had voted for President Jimmy Carter; the actual popular vote was *50.1 percent.* More than half—*54 percent*—of the elite journalists reported that they regarded themselves as left of center while just *19 percent* said they were on the right side of the spectrum; surveys of all Americans showed the ratio of conservative to liberal voters to be in the range of 3 to 2 or 2 to 1. The surveyed journalists solidly—*80 percent*—endorsed racial preferences, not what the polls were showing about all Americans. By a top-heavy majority—*90 percent*—the piece showed that the journalists were in favor of abortion rights, while the rate among all Americans was about half that, depending on how the question was asked. The journalists were overwhelmingly against the use of nuclear energy and strongly in favor of busing.

The demographics of the elite media reporters were also interesting: disproportionately upper-middle-class white male college graduates whose parents were likely to be college graduates, perhaps professionals. Almost seven in ten—*68 percent*—came from northeastern or north-central cities and demonstrated little sympathy for rural or small-town America. Only a few attended church or synagogue with any regularity. In itself, the inherent bias in the media should not be such a big problem. After all, other groups in American life tilt in other directions. Few would argue against the proposition that most big businessmen tend toward conservatism and the Republican party. But there are other problems. Journalists say, well, yes, there is a liberal tilt but a good reporter gives the facts, well-arrayed, interestingly, unbiased—no matter what his or her personal views may be. I don't buy that for a moment, even though I believe that most journalists believe it when they say it. As with think tanks, the issue is one of agenda. What does a person think is important and newsworthy?

A classic case concerns the *Washington Post's* failure to cover a major pro-life march on the Mall. This was not a conscious pro-choice decision. It came about because it didn't really register with the *Post's* assignment editor, and the pro-life people apparently didn't know whom to call, and when. It *was* covered by *The Washington Times*. Some years ago, *Time* magazine announced that it would no longer cover the environment as news: The situation was simply too dreadful to treat fairly. A strange view for the daddy of all news magazines. Ultimately, *Time* recanted and more recently has re-recanted. And there have been countless examples of stories reading, "Joe Blow, of the conservative American Enterprise Institute, said . . ." and very few reading "Joe Blow, of the liberal Brookings Institution, said. . . ."

Conservative media outlets do the same sort of thing. *The Washington Times* is a conservative newspaper, but not because its prose is tilted. Its reporters do not write, "Joe Blow, a well-known liberal slimeball, said today. . . ." Its editors choose events that cover its view of reality, just as the liberal editors do. Quite naturally, in the course of their daily duties, the editors would assign coverage of a pro-life march on the Mall. They would cover both sides of the global warming debate, and despite what you have read, it is not settled science in any seriously predictable way, even if the mainstream press has now become addicted to that phrase. (Has Al Gore ever heard of Noah's ark? Or that the Dutch built dikes? Or that the ice mass in the Antarctic is thickening?) A recent and comprehensive study run by Duke University say the chances are good that we will only get a slow and small climb in temperatures. The chance of a potentially serious bump were rated about 5 percent. Even that has been part of the rhythm of life on this planet. The snows on Mount Kilimanjaro started melting around 1800, long before serious industrialization. The liberal press also complains that the case against liberal bias is shooting the messenger. But do you know any messengers who sort through fifty messages and pick out which seven to deliver?

I must offer here a word of sympathy for the oft-battered members of the press. I, too, have experienced the thrill of the chase. In 1981, my ex-AEI colleague Dave Gergen was on Ronald Reagan's White House communications staff. I got a one-on-one interview with President Reagan for my weekly documentary program *Ben Wattenberg at Large*. I ran through many of his views and policies: his optimism, his conservatism, the federal budget, the role of the federal government in relation to the states, Cuba, El Salvador, the Soviet Union, the safety net, and more.

But not long into the interview I asked him about his support of President Franklin D. Roosevelt during the Depression years. Here are some excerpts of what he said, and the reaction I had:

> REAGAN: I have known [FDR's] sons for years. I know their own conversations about what he believed. I think [FDR] always thought that the things that were being done were in the nature of medicine for a sick patient. But people attracted to government and to government positions in those years, in many instances, did not view the medicine as temporary. If you remember, I was assailed during the campaign for saying that many of the New Dealers actually espoused what today has become an epithet—fascism—in that they spoke of how Mussolini had made the trains run on time. . . .

> ME (in my head): *Bing!*

> REAGAN: They saw in what he said he was doing—a planned economy. Harold Ickes [FDR's secretary of the interior] *said that what we are striving for was a kind of modified form of communism.*

> Me (in my head): *Bing! Bing!*

> REAGAN: I don't really believe that was really in Roosevelt's mind. I think that, had he lived, and with the

> war over, we would have seen him using government
> the other way.

What was I binging about? It was not about Reagan's views of the New Deal or Harold Ickes. It was about a news story for our program. I knew that Mussolini and Communism would be newsworthy. If I hadn't been wired for television I think I might have jumped out of my chair and given Reagan a big wet kiss.

Sure enough *The Washington Post* ran:

Reagan Still Sure Some in New Deal Espoused Fascism

> President Reagan remains convinced that many New Deal advisors to President Franklin D. Roosevelt espoused fascism and spoke admiringly of Mussolini's Italian Fascist regime. . . .

> It is an idea Reagan first voiced in 1976 and has repeated several times, most recently in an interview with Ben Wattenberg to be broadcast on the Public Broadcasting Service Friday night.

Publicity for a television program in the competing print media is very hard to get. There are *so* many television programs. . . .

SOMETHING NEW HAS happened. The media is giving the nonliberal side a growing, if still minority, share of the story. Why?

Irving Kristol often told businessmen that only intellectuals can argue with other intellectuals. I sense the same thing is so in the media world. They are listening now, and giving the right-of-center side a fairer shake, because they grudgingly accept the media-savvy, intellectually studious neo-cons in a way they would never have accepted criticism from rigid, old-fashioned conservatives. In fact, having been toilet-trained by the neo-cons, they now even listen to hear what conservatives have to say. In this respect, to use an old union phrase, it is the conservatives who are the "free riders." And the big new development in the media world is the advent of antiliberal programming run nationwide. As parts of liberalism went half crazy, repeating as gospel the political correctitudes of their liberal interest groups, a new media came about.

Consider book publishing. It is centered in New York City and traditionally liberal. But Erwin Glikes saw things differently. A Belgian-born Jew who had fled Hitler with his parents, he was on the faculty of Columbia University and witnessed student violence firsthand. He was repelled by what he saw. Irving Kristol, then a vice president at Basic Books, invited him into the world of publishing. Later, working with a number of different publishers, he specialized in providing a haven for conservative and neo-con authors ranging from George Will and Robert Bork to Francis Fukuyama, Dinesh D'Souza, David Horowitz—and me. Some of his titles were bestsellers. Alas, Glikes died suddenly in 1994 at age fifty-six. I wrote a column about him.

A number of other publishers had been in the neo-con or conservative field, or joined up as they saw sales grow among a reading public that had been turned off by left-wing authors. These included straight conservative houses like Regnery and Encounter, separate imprints of mainline houses like Random House's Crown Forum and Penguin's Sentinel, and just plain mainline publishers, like the fine people at Thomas Dunne Books of St. Martin's Press who published this book. I went out of my way to secure a mainline house for this volume. It's the other side that needs educating.

From 2000 to 2004, eighteen of the thirty bestselling political books were categorized as conservative according to *South Park Conservatives: The Revolt Against Liberal Media Bias* by Brian C. Anderson.[4] In fact, some were conservative and some were neo-conservative. That leaves twelve that weren't. Some of the conservative books, like former CBS correspondent Bernard Goldberg's *Bias*, were rather silly. I don't know Goldberg's political taxonomy, but his point that network television was tilted to the left, was based mostly on a few anecdotes. Plenty of liberals still got published. Al Franken's *Rush Limbaugh Is a Big Fat Idiot* was about as simplistic as *Bias*. There were much better books on both sides. In all, not a bad situation: choice for readers.

---

4. Other parts of this section are drawn from this book.

Limbaugh's name brings us to conservative talk radio. In some large measure it came about due to the repeal of the Federal Communications Commission's fairness doctrine, which required radio stations had to "provide a reasonable opportunity for the presentation of contrasting viewpoints."

The war was on. In 1987 Rush Limbaugh was a local conservative radio talk show host in Sacramento, California. The next year he moved to New York. His program was put out in national syndication via satellite. The audience for Limbaugh's daily three hours of eclectic, sometimes outrageous conservative humor grew very rapidly. People listened alone or in eateries with a "Rush room." By 1994 Limbaugh was given a large part of the credit for voting in a Republican Congress which then elected Newt Gingrich Speaker.

Conservative and neo-conservative talk radio pulled the biggest ratings. Among the stars were "Dr. Laura" Schlesinger, a neo-con whose tough family talk resonated with people fed up with social permissiveness; Sean Hannity, cross-promoting with his Fox News television program; G. Gordon Liddy, former Watergate jailbird and a straight conservative; Michael Medved and Dennis Prager, erudite neo-con modern Orthodox Jews; William Bennett, who is somewhere on the conservative spectrum; Larry Elder, an African-American non-liberal; as well as Laura Ingraham, Tony Snow, Pat Buchanan, and others. Once a week I would cohost Pat's program—and argue. Polls show that talk radio listeners are more likely to be politically informed than Americans as a whole, and are by no means solidly right-wing. The figures: 53 percent of the listeners declared themselves independents; 25 percent, Republicans; and 12 percent, Democrats.

Liberals fought back. Among the competitors were Mario Cuomo, the former governor of New York; Texas liberal populist Jim Hightower; the liberal and verbose Harvard lawyer Alan Dershowitz; former Democratic campaign operative and California attorney Susan Estrich; and Al Franken. There were many others. As a rule their ratings were poor. In a classic remark, revealing a classic liberal mindset, Cuomo told (bleeding-heart liberal) TV host Phil Donahue, that conservatives "write their messages with crayons. . . . We use fine-point quill pens." Talk about liberal sanctimony. I don't think many neo-cons would publicly say, "liberals are uneducated jerks."

There were other indicators that both sides would be heard. One day, in a crowd watching Pope John Paul II arrive at St. Mathews Church in Washington, I was standing next to Brian Lamb, a man I had never met. We started chatting, and he told me that he was going to organize a new cable channel that would televise Congress in its own words. I nodded profoundly, but didn't understand much of what he was saying. Then in 1979 C-SPAN went on the air. The first speech broadcast was one by then-Congressman Albert Gore. The original C-SPAN interview "studio" was an apartment in Arlington, Virginia. It was like going into a crack house or a brothel (I imagine). I have been a guest, interviewed on C-SPAN several times. Lamb has turned out to be a premier American television interviewer, letting the subject speak with almost no interruption (not my style).

C-SPAN started a second channel in 1986. *Booknotes* went live in 1989. Radio broadcasts began in 1997, airing all the available recorded tapes of President Johnson. C-SPAN has a vast online footprint. Its staple remains broadcasting the House, Senate, congressional hearings, press conferences, conventions, and think tank panels. In 1996 it broadcast the entirety of the Million Man March organized by liberal African Americans.

Lamb was once a Nixon campaign aide and Department of Defense public relations man. But C-SPAN's offerings are *totally* neutral. Most every important liberal voice has been heard. In a masterstroke, Congressman Newt Gingrich pushed his Republican members to speak up on "special orders" at the end of the day when the House chamber was typically nearly empty. C-SPAN cameras were permitted to show the congressional orators, not the vacant chamber. The publicity given to a second point of view, unfiltered, was instrumental in the GOP capture of the House in 1994. From the perspective of this book, it gave neo-conservatives a platform that did not exist before, no small matter. (In 2005, newly installed Chief Justice John Roberts said that Supreme Court hearings might be televised.)

MAINSTREAM NETWORK JOURNALISTS were outraged when the three big over-the-air networks began cutting expenses, particularly by shutting down foreign bureaus. Not me. They were feeding broadcasts with the same left-of-center point of view that was aired on their American parent companies.

Part of overplaying bad news involves the vast media attention that is given to sleaze and/or scandals. See if you can remember such world-shattering stories such as: "debategate" (columnist George Will helping to prepare President Ronald Reagan for a debate with President Jimmy Carter); Ed Meese's cuff links; Richard Allen's cuff links; "Lancegate" (about Carter's director of the Office of Management and Budget); Dr. Peter Bourne and Quaaludes; Koreagate; Billygate (about influence-peddling by Carter's brother); Nancy Reagan's new china for the White House; Abscam; or James Watt, Reagan's secretary of the interior, when asked about diversity, saying, "We have every kind of mix you can have. I have a black, I have a woman, two Jews and a cripple"—and getting fired for stating a fact. See if you can remember Congressman Wilbur Mills, chairman of the House Ways and Means Committee, and his frolic with stripteaser Fanne Fox; Congressman Gary Condit and the missing Chandra Levy; Congressman Wayne Hays and his sexual relationship with Elizabeth Ray, a member of his secretarial staff, who became famous for saying, "I can't type. I can't file. I can't even answer the phone." Or Paula Parkinson, Rita Jenrette, Janet Cooke, Jayson Blair, or the kid stuck in the well that sent CNN's ratings skyward.

It never stops. Republican and Democratic members of Congress have been found to be on the take. Recently, we have seen Tom DeLay indicted (but not convicted as this is written), and former Senate Majority Leader Bill Frist's alleged financial shenanigans. And brilliant *New York Times* reporter Judy Miller serving prison time for not revealing sources about a leak to a grand jury (this also involved columnist Robert Novak). Miller never even published the story.

The main problem with the media has not been getting the story wrong, but getting the wrong story. The advent of so many more and variegated outlets had created an opportunity to explain issues via video based on a persuasion, a tendency, a sensibility, an orientation, a mind-set—called neo-conservative. It was good news for neo-cons, but with a kicker. The sleaze/scandal stories—which will never go away—chewed up space and time when there were more important things going on in the world.

CONSIDER NEXT ALL the related aspects of the revolution in high-tech communication technology: the Internet, search engines, webzines, e-mail, blogs, and more. Although the liberals have often used it to stunning success, on balance it seems to have helped conservatives and neo-conservatives much more. Like talk radio, the newest forms of communication were a greater gift to those Americans who felt their views were not accommodated by the left-of-center mainstream media. Consider what Michael Barone of *U.S. News & World Report* wrote in late February of 2005:

> So what hath the blogosphere wrought? The left blogosphere has moved the Democrats off to the left, and the right blogosphere has undermined the credibility of the Republicans' adversaries in Old Media. Both changes help Bush and the Republicans.

It was an ideal time for Barone to take a look. The growth of the blogosphere had been almost unbelievable. In March 2003, before there was much of a presidential campaign for Howard Dean or John Kerry, there were approximately zero blogs. By November 2004, just before the presidential election were held in our own peculiar manner, the number of blogs was over *six million*, doubling in size about every five months to almost *ten million* by July 2005. (The data comes from Technocrati, a search engine for blogs.)

The blogs come in a wide variety of forms, from personal diaries and compendiums of hyperlinks to a variety of articles and viewer responses, often funny, sometimes profane, dealing with every conceivable topic—including plenty of porn—and in all of a somewhat more conservative bent than a liberal one. They are inexpensive to set up. And, in many ways, the blogosphere is the ultimate in free speech: They can be posted to any time, anywhere, by anybody.

The two main criticisms are that the material is often not edited and often posted by "some guy in pajamas." But if you believe, as I do, that the mainstream media had been tilted to the left, the lack of editing is a bonus. As for the guy in his jammies, there are some pretty smart folks who over the years have written at home, when their mind is fresh, before dressing or shaving (including me).

The first classic case of the political power and speed of the blogosphere was witnessed in the presidential campaign of 2004. Joe Trippi, the campaign manager of candidate and former governor of Vermont Howard Dean used the 'Net to identify Dean supporters and raise money from them. Primarily through the Web site of MoveOn, the Dean campaign put together an e-mail list of about six hundred thousand names and raised far more money than anyone had expected. But the voters in the Iowa caucuses did not rally around Dean. The ultimate Democratic candidate, John Kerry, won that critical and idiotic contest and later gained access to Dean's list.

The members of the Dean list were united in two principal ways: opposition to the war in Iraq, and a quite visceral hatred of George W. Bush. As an example of that hatred, Barone reported on Democratic consultant Markos Moulitsas, who runs the popular and very liberal site www.dailykos.com, which received funding from the Dean campaign—a fact Moulitsas acknowledged. After four American contractors were killed in Iraq, Moulitsas wrote: "I feel nothing over the death of the mercenaries. They are there to wage war for profit. Screw them." Dean himself has said, "I hate Republicans and everything they stand for."

Dailykos.com gets four hundred thousand hits per day and is believed to be the largest of the political blogs. Republicans have big problems with liberal Democrats and express it pungently, and some did just that during two full terms of the Clinton presidency, but the sad sentiment of hate has been coming mostly in recent years from liberals and, by my lights, with less reason.

BECAUSE OF THE blogosphere, in recent years Democrats have often raised more money than Republicans, the first time that has happened in modern times, although Republicans got their money in smaller amounts from more contributors.

But the Bush campaign used e-mail to compile a list of 7.5 million names, and a massive troop of 1.4 million political volunteers. On election day of 2004 Democratic turnout was up substantially. Kerry received more votes than any other Democratic candidate for president ever had. But the turnout for Bush was even higher. The final two-party vote was Bush 51 percent, Kerry 48 percent, a modest victory, but unlike the results in 2000 Bush got a majority of the popular vote.

In early July 2003 the Pew Research Center for People and the Press polled Americans on this question: "I'm going to read you some pairs of opposite phrases. After I read each pair, tell me which *one* phrase you feel better describes news organizations generally. If you think *neither* phrase applies, please say so." The results:

> Liberal 51%
> Conservative 26%
> Neither applies 14%
> Don't know/refused 9%

Other surveys, by other reputable survey research firms, taken at later dates, show similar results. With all the potency of the new media— Fox and Rush and Rupert and blogs—Americans still think their news organizations are tilted to the left. And they still don't like it.

CHAPTER TWELVE

Conclusion

NEO-CONSERVATISM'S ONGOING ROLE

HERE, I am permitted to repeat myself occasionally.

I find it marvelous that in our era, in our country, it certainly seems as if most every cause and every ideology has won some important victories. Freedom and wealth are two great catalysts.

There is much said these days about the intense partisanship and bitterness in the Congress and in America, which has obstructed action on important matters. No news there. But real legislative progress has not been halted. Neo-conservatism has been a key agent in this largely successful process. The whole process can in large measure be described in Tocqueville's term *American exceptionalism*—a central tenet of neo-conservatism. For many reasons I expect that America will become even more exceptional as the years go forward.

The liberals won some monumental victories, but not alone. Neo-cons helped. Look at three.

The end of segregation was probably the most important. No serious political players today are segregationists, although it would be naive to say there is no antiblack sentiment left in America. As shown earlier, the progress of African Americans has been substantial, the enormous problems remaining notwithstanding. One example not mentioned earlier: In *1970* there were *1,469 elected* black office-holders in federal and state legislatures, in city and county offices, in elected law enforcement positions, and in elected educational roles. In *2001* the comparable number was *9,061*, according to the Joint Center for Political and Economic Studies in Washington. (When people hold office, they wield power.) The number of women in elected office has also soared.

We tend to forget that desegregation is a relatively new situation. As a young boy of about ten (during World War II) I remember visiting Washington, D.C., with my parents. We lived in The Bronx in an all-Jewish neighborhood—it was neither a ghetto nor segregated. Of course, everyone was against what was happening to the Negroes in the South. It was surely a valid point, and Communists, domestic and globally, never failed to bring it up. But to me it was just words: Bad words describing a bad situation. When as a boy, I visited America's capital city with my parents and saw with my own eyes bathrooms marked "white" and "colored," I was amazed.

There properly remains a serious argument about just how desegregation should play out forty years after becoming the law of the land. Most neo-cons believe merit is the proper American way. But neo-cons have easily accepted affirmative action. You take better care of someone in your family who is having problems. But affirmative action with goals *and timetables* or "race norming" adds up to quotas. Most neo-cons say that is not the American way and has had the effect of embittering some whites. Perhaps it was necessary for a while. But neo-cons ask: For how long? Is forty years since the advent of big civil rights laws long enough to wipe out what is called by some "the legacy of slavery"?

(In passing, let it be noted that counting slaves as only three-fifths of a person, was a compromise to the *free* states to give *them* more seats in the House of Representatives, not a deal to help *slave* states, which got other great help in the totality of the Constitution. Like it or not, there wouldn't have been a Constitution without the recognition of slavery.)

The problem is not simple racism. It's hardly permissible to note that recent black immigrants from the Caribbean and sub-Saharan

Africa do better than American blacks. Nor can it be publicly mentioned that many new black immigrants often scorn American blacks, typically in private, sometimes publicly. They say American blacks expect the government to do everything for them. That is mostly untrue, but the sound of some black leaders makes the charge more credible.

Still, we have come a very long way. The immediate political thanks go to a variety of players. There was the public activism in the 1950s led by young people labeled the "New Negro." They were the ones risking physical harm, up to and including an occasional lynching.[1] Jews were among the most active civil rights activists. There were the media; it seemed as if every weekly issue of *Life* carried a photo essay of brave young blacks sitting-in at segregated lunch counters. There was the courage and eloquence of Reverend Martin Luther King, which reached its apogee at the 1963 March on Washington. Although rarely acknowledged, the major organizers of the march were civil rights leader Bayard Rustin, Tom Kahn of the Social Democrats, and Rachelle Horowitz of the Yipsels and later an important executive with the American Federation of Teachers. Rustin and Kahn in particular held many neo-con beliefs, at a time when the labor movement in America also held many such views. Proto-neo-cons and neo-cons today hate discrimination.

Things have changed. One can still find some anti-Semitic attitudes. Surveys show that African Americans are more likely than the population as a whole to harbor such views. The noise coming from

---

1. That is another unmentionable. *The Historical Statistics of the United States—Colonial Times to 1970* had a data series entitled "Persons Lynched, by Race 1882 to 1970." Remarkably, almost identical numbers of whites (1,169) to Negroes (1,170) were recorded as lynched over that time frame with the basic data coming from *The 1952 Negro Yearbook*, which incorporated a definition of lynching established in 1940 by a conference held at the Tuskegee Institute which used these criteria: 1) legal evidence of a killing, 2) illegality, 3) the killers were part of a group, and 4) they acted under the pretext of service to justice race or tradition. The idea was to quantify and expose a despicable practice (now extinct). Of course, demography somewhat discounts the data of savage mob justice. Over the years America has had a population 10 to 20 percent black. But lynch law for the most part occurred in the South and many of the Southern states had disproportionately large black populations. Lynching was disproportionately black, but present among whites as well, at a rate of about a dozen per year.

the radical Left, particularly in academic settings, may be called pro–Third World, anti-Israel, or pro-Arab, but to me it often comes across as anti-Jewish. And the war in Iraq is said to have been started by Jewish neo-cons, sometimes coupled with the old charge of dual loyalties, that is, that the real cause of the war was to help Israel. (I have dual *pride*. I am proud to an American and proud to be a Jew.) Some universities have unannounced quotas against Jewish applicants and Asian Americans because they score disproportionately *high* on college entrance exams. But today the very idea of anti-Semitism is generally scorned.

President Johnson played a powerful role. President Kennedy, recall, won the 1960 election with a good deal of electoral support from Democrats of the segregated "solid South." Once elected, he was accused of being dilatory in moving civil rights legislation and of not issuing certain pro-minority executive orders that required only a stroke of the pen to effectuate. He was coming around to a more activist stance when he was killed.

LBJ not only understood the morality of desegregation but he also knew the South. He knew the harm dealt to the region he loved when—as he put it—a Southern legislator in trouble would get elected by screaming, "Nigger, nigger, nigger!" Using the classic "Johnson treatment," LBJ brought together non-Southern Democrats and many Republicans to pass the three major civil rights laws of the 1960s. The opposition, deeply entrenched, were Southern Democrats.[2] Even after the laws changed, there was massive resistance to civil rights in the South. The rest of the country was better, but left a great deal to be desired. A variety of fights continue—it seems to be an American dilemma that will never fully go away. The most likely partial solution, for blacks, Latinos, and some other minorities, is the startling increase in intermarriage.

Still, the South has gone mainstream. Earnings in the South used be about 50 percent that of the rest of the country. Today it's in the 90 to 100 percent range, and with a cheaper cost of living. It wasn't only the breakdown of segregation. The mass availability of

---

2. Voters usually have long memories. Why so few blacks in America, even elderly ones who remember, vote Republican amazes me.

air-conditioning played a major role in the development of the South, where many more residences are now air-conditioned.

REAL FEMINISM PROVIDED real help for millions of women who deserved help. There were clearly inequities in law and in practice. Today most everyone says the law of the land should include equal rights for women as stipulated in the civil rights laws.

But nouveau feminism had its downside. The argument against the Equal Rights Amendment was not against equal rights, but that the rights were already inscribed in law. Luckily, we never were forced to call it *herstory* instead of *history* as a few feminists demanded. I am of two minds about the "Ms." business. It's true, it's no one's business whether the correspondent or respondent is married or not. But a lot of people seeking companionship or a mate would like to know. Gloria Steinman's phrase, "A woman needs a man like a fish needs a bicycle" is quite witty and monumentally stupid. Not being able to date someone from the office ends up hurting women more than men, and there are some desperate women out there. It may well be that homosexuality or bisexuality or gay marriage is part of that "penumbra" in the Constitution. But listen one day to the plaints of women who can't find a boyfriend.

Today, some women say that despite all that liberation, they prefer the job of raising children at home, at least for a while. A free society provides options with trade-offs; a woman may accurately say that her income is a necessity in the maintenance of her family. But it may not be if she chooses to live way out in the exurbs or in small towns like Cazenovia, New York. It's a choice. Most everywhere in the world young married people find it expensive to raise a child. It's not if you lower your sights a bit. An education at a good state university can be as good, or better, than one from Harvard, Yale, Cal Tech, or MIT. Moreover, I believe that bearing or adopting children and raising them is the most important thing people do in their lives, far exceeding even writing influential books.

Legal abortion (which I favor) came about on a 5 to 4 Supreme Court vote based on a penumbratic doctrine. It was bad law. It would not be much of an issue if it were voted on state-by-state. But

the results make sense. It is a decision yielding options for all—
except fetuses.

Rarely mentioned in the great abortion debate is that at the time
of the *Roe v. Wade* decision, several big states already had legal
abortion. And if *Roe* were overturned by the Court, the status of legal
abortion would revert to earlier state law and many other states
would surely adopt pro-choice status. Probably every pregnant poor
woman in a pro-life state would be within a one-day bus ride of a
pro-choice state. Perhaps wealthy foundations and individuals who
pour money into the pro-choice campaign could then give mini-
grants for a bus ticket to any poor abortion-seeking young woman.
As I have written, I am (barely) in favor of legal abortion, in part because there are so many couples seeking to adopt and so few children available to adopt. (My daughter Ruth will not take no for an
answer and knows all the bureaucratic wiles. But it took her years to
adopt two of my fine grandchildren. Ironically, they are from Romania and Ukraine, not far from where my parents lived before coming
to America via Palestine.)

EVERYONE IS NOW an *environmentalist*, or claims to be. LBJ
signed major environmental laws. The Environmental Protection
Agency was established on Nixon's watch. Nixon was more than a
little nuts, but often mildly progressive. (That's what "history says,"
although the historians keep revising the real meaning of most everything.) In any event, a new environmental awareness was surely
important, endorsed by neo-conservatives, even as many of them
said some of the reforms went way too far, were too expensive, and
in some cases were counterproductive. Those fights continue.

I used to think environmentalism was the default crisis; it would
pop up when nothing else was brewing. I was wrong. It is now big
time. A generation of young people think global warming will fry us
all. Insofar as that may be true, demographics may help save us. If
humans cause global warming, rest assured, there will be fewer humans left than we expected. Nuclear power would help, but antinuclear power has become another one of those maniacal liberal

causes. When the desalinization of ocean water through nuclear power becomes feasible, the world will change for the better.

That all these liberal victories were continuations of earlier trends does not diminish their importance. Life is a process, not an event. So is politics. Much the same can be said for law. Most neo-cons believe that when intent is clear and relevant there is good reason for "textualism" or "original intent." But the framers didn't know about birth control pills, or blogs, or cars, or TV, or reverse discrimination.

One other mindless word that drives me up the wall is "pristine." One of the symbolic issues of our time concerns whether America should open the Arctic National Wildlife Refuge (ANWR) for oil drilling. Most neo-cons approve it. Most environmentalists oppose it. Why? The operative word is *pristine*, as in "ANWR is *pristine*, therefore we shouldn't drill there." But where *should* we drill? Manhattan? Back Bay? Vermont? Yes, people do use hydrocarbons, even in those environmental havens.

CONSERVATIVES AND NEO-CONSERVATIVES have had plenty of big wins. *Inexorable* was another word that used to drive me to distraction. It is not a democratic word. A responsive democracy allows for change. It used to be said, here and in Europe, that the growth of the welfare state (European terminology), or big government, or the safety net state (American terminology) was inexorable. The idea was that each program had a constituency and the various rewarded constituencies would vote for those who gave them the goodies. Luckily, that's not the way it works.

Labor union members are putatively solidly Democratic, but about 40 percent vote Republican. Lots of union members are pro-gun, like me. I haven't touched a weapon since I qualified for a carbine and a .45 when in the service, but weapons can cut crime. Similarly, it is said that Evangelicals and fundamentalists vote Republican. But about 30 to 40 percent vote Democratic. The vast majority of Americans are not single-issue voters. Change via locked-in political allegiance is not inexorable.

In America the percentage of gross domestic product going for the military is on the low side. We really did what we said we'd do after the Vietnam War: "reorder our priorities." The percentage of GDP spent for defense has declined. In less than forty years it has gone from 10 to 7 to 5 to about 3.5 percent. (For my money, the key priority is in the preamble to the Constitution: "to provide for the common defense.")

The idea and ideal of socialism has pretty well collapsed or is collapsing, although even that should not be considered inexorable. Even China, still a politically authoritarian dictatorship, putatively runs a market economy, which has raised incomes in a nation where hundreds of millions of peasants remain pitifully poor. Market economics, once called capitalism, is the order of the day, as much as leftist intellectuals don't like it. Jean-François Revel (a good neocon) said it best: "They always compare socialism to what it could be, and compare capitalism to what it is."

THE EVIDENCE IS in. Nobel Prize laureate Paul Samuelson (whose much revised Econ 101 textbook earned him many millions of dollars) taught generations of American college students that socialist economies grow faster than capitalist economies. They don't. Not even close. The best way to get poor countries richer is through markets, individual liberty, innovation, hard work, and trade, with—most importantly—a culture that supports the others.

The right-of-center troops showed that values matter most. The plague of violent crime has receded. No one really endorsed it, but when some liberal Democrats (many now called neo-conservatives) said that *law and order* was not just a conservative buzz phrase but the root of civil society, it was important. Voters deserved to know that they were not alone in what they had observed and feared. Their elected leaders were thus more ready to respond, and did. The Europeans ("Old Europe" that is, like the French intellectuals) mocked America for its fixation on crime and racial riots. But Paris was torched in late 2005, mostly by young Muslims and some Francophone sub-Saharans. Prime Minister Jacques Chirac did not compare it to riots in Los Angeles, Cleveland, and scores of other American cities, but most everyone else did.

Those same Europeans scorned high American incarceration periods—a thug in prison cannot mug your sister—but then moved in the same direction when crime rates rose in their own countries. The European Union charter forbade any member state from having the death penalty on their books and once again Americans were called barbarians. But polls have showed that populations in Europe are changing their minds, especially since murderous jihadists have begun wreaking havoc.

Americans brag about our democratic ways. But every state has two U.S. senators, whether it be sparse Wyoming or populous California. That is not exactly "one man, one vote." We condemn disenfranchisement, but if you live in a "red state" like Texas, or a "blue state" like New York, your presidential vote doesn't really count. Only in a "swing state" does an American vote for president really matter. Under such circumstances, it takes real chutzpah to criticize the new Iraqi constitution. Let it breathe for a while. Argument is part of liberty.

Americans have been lucky as well as good. For the most part, our immigrants dispersed as they came here. It would be pretty hard for the English Americans to fight the German Americans; they wouldn't know where to have the war. It would be pretty hard for Irish Americans to fight the Jews except by neighborhoods, and there aren't many all-Irish or all-Jewish neighborhoods left (except among the ultra-Orthodox). The Jews were once largely situated in the greater New York City area but now are mostly not. And with all that we still managed to have one civil war—the bloodiest ever at that time and close to genocidal.

The opening up of the media is a neo-con triumph. The Internet, the satellites, the blogs, talk radio, Fox News, and whatever else allows everyone who wants to express an opinion has been monumentally important. That's what liberals believe in theory. But it is neo-cons and conservatives who crow about it these days because it gives them a better forum than they had. Of course it was never total, but there was a major bias in the mainstream media. It wasn't fair and balanced.

Next to the civil rights acts, the anti-quota Immigration Act of 1965 may well have been the most important legislation in the last half century. I don't know who gets the credit for immigration, and recently most everyone is complaining about it. Asian immigrants and their children form the so-called "model minority" and are now taking college slots from smart Jews and wealthy Episcopalians. Competition is good, not bad. That is even recognized by Jewish neos whose kids can't get into Harvard because of Asians with stratospheric test scores.

And America is going to keep growing because of immigration. Population yields power and influence. Polls show that immigrants are among the most patriotic Americans.

Who won that "culture war"? The liberals may still glorify homosexuality, but they know it costs them at the polls. Most all political observers say the country is moving to the right, and perception is a large part of politics. Actually, the crosscurrents have been many. Those conservatives who became neo-conservatives moved the right *leftward, toward* but perhaps not *to* the center. Some of the center left was dragged further left, apparently without much of a fight.

Some of the counterculture precepts made sense; some were a disaster. I don't have a problem with beards. I recently decided to grow one; I hate shaving. I then found I hated my beard worse than I hate shaving. Some rock music has become classic. But the loss of single-sex colleges robbed some young people of an option. The coarsening of the language, particularly among females, doesn't seem like progress. Hard drugs fried some brains. I am not against premarital sex, but some of the promiscuity has been physically and psychologically unhealthy. On the issue of crime in the streets, both neo-cons and conservatives won. It was a disaster. It is less of one now.

Neo-cons cleaned up big on foreign policy. There has never been a single country as influential as the United States, although it will likely continue to generate jealousy, and continued immigration to the United States by the jealous. All over the world people tap their toes to American music, read American books and newspapers, and learn (American) English. And foreigners sometimes eat our lunch, but I don't care whether a scientist who cures a form of cancer comes from America, Switzerland, China, or India. We will buy the drug if it works. Some bad actors on the global scene worry that if they ever crossed America it might lead neo-cons to go on the warpath with the greatest war-making machine in history. The idea that America is militaristic is mostly bunk. At any given moment there are usually about fifty wars going on. America may be involved in none or one. But the threat that we may act can make others behave better.

Since the second Iraq war, the popularity of America has diminished. That's too bad. But how come there are still those lines around the block at every American consulate in the world with people seeking to immigrate to America? How come foreigners continue to invest in America and hoard the paper called dollars?

That political and economic liberty has grown around the world at an accelerating rate may well be our greatest legacy—and the heart of neo-conservatism, although many Americans have believed in it all along.

Looking ahead, the European welfare state seems on the road to slow collapse. These economies are reforming, most of them foot dragging all the way. But they will likely face a tough economic time unless there is a massive (unlikely) reflation of fertility rates. Some European nations are quickly taking in many more immigrants. But they hate it. The Europeans don't do assimilation well.

Well, Americans do, sometimes with painful personal costs, but the second and succeeding generations of immigrants will shape the nation, as ever. Israel Zangwill was right.

Between a fertility rate that is almost at replacement value (about two children per woman) and healthy immigration in the decades to come America will be the only major nation in the world that is growing, and that includes China and ultimately India. It sounds amazing, even to me, but there will likely be about a half billion Americans by 2100 if present trends continue, which they often do.

Military strategist Eliot Cohen of the Center for Strategic and International Studies put a nice formulation in play. He counts four global catastrophes: World Wars I and II, the Cold War against the expansionist Soviets, and the current war against Islamic terrorists. If another global threat is coming, I would guess the perpetrators will be China some decades from now. And so, the anti-China—India— should become our greatest ally. (As with Argentina, it is often said that China will become a great modern power—but it never seems to materialize.) I'd work hard to put and keep the United Kingdom, Ireland, Egypt, Australia, Nigeria, Israel, New Zealand, Brazil, Mexico, and Canada in *our* club. Winston Churchill was on to something when he suggested an English-speaking union. Neo-cons love Churchill.

Some very good things have happened as the world has modernized. That no nuclear weapon has been detonated in anger for sixty years is almost unbelievable. America, of course, played a role in this, but all good things in the world aren't American or neo-conservative.

AMERICA WILL DO all right. America will remain number one. There is a story by Stephen Vincent Benét entitled *The Devil and Daniel Webster*. The ghost of the famous Senator Webster comes out of the night and says, "Neighbor, how stands the Union?" And the voice comes back and says, "The Union stands as she stood—rock-bottomed, copper-sheathed—one and indivisible."

Henry Luce said that "the twentieth century will be the American century." So will the twenty-first century. Neo-conservatism helped mightily in both cases.

But remember the first rule of history: Expect the unexpected.

Within those strictures, neo-conservatism—probably under a different label—will be the wave of the future. Scoop Jackson had it right: Common sense, for a change.

Bibliography

DeMuth, Christopher, and William Kristol, eds. *The Neoconservative Imagination: Essays in Honor of Irving Kristol.* Washington, D.C.: AEI Press, 1995.

Fosdick, Dorothy, ed. *Henry M. Jackson and World Affairs: Selected Speeches, 1953–1983.* Seattle: University of Washington Press, 1990.

Gerson, Mark. *The Neoconservative Vision: From the Cold War to the Culture Wars.* Lanham, MD: Madison Books, 1996.

Gingrich, Newt. *To Renew America.* New York: HarperCollins, 1995.

Goldberg, Jonah. *Liberal Fascism: The Secret History of the American Left, from Mussolini to the Politics of Meaning.* New York: Doubleday, 2007.

Heilbrunn, Jacob. *They Knew They Were Right: The Rise of the Neocons.* New York: Doubleday, 2008.

"An Interview with James Q. Wilson." *Think Tank with Ben Wattenberg.* 27 January 1995. (Television Transcript.) www.pbs.org/thinktank/show_144.html.

"Is America Exceptional?" *Think Tank with Ben Wattenberg.* 10 October 1996. (Television Transcript.) www.pbs.org/thinktank/transcript406.html.

"Is Public Television too Liberal?" *Hardball with Chris Matthews.* 10 June 2005. (Television Transcript.) MSNBC Online. www.msnbc.msn.com/id/8205914/.

"Is Social Science the God that Failed?" *Think Tank with Ben Wattenberg.* 1 January 1998. (Television Transcript.) www.pbs.org/thinktank/transcript601.html.

Jackson, Henry M. *Fact, Fiction, and National Security.* New York: Macfadden-Bartell, 1964.

Kirkpatrick, Jeane J. *Dictatorships and Double Standards: Rationalism and Reason in Politics*. New York: Simon and Schuster, 1982.

———. *Dismantling the Parties: Reflections on Party Reform and Party Decomposition*. Washington, D.C.: American Enterprise Institute, 1978.

Kristol, Irving. *Neoconservatism: The Autobiography of an Idea*. New York: Free Press, 1995.

———. *Reflections of a Neoconservative: Looking Back, Looking Ahead*. New York: Basic Books, 1983.

Ladd, Everett Carll, and Seymour Martin Lipset. *Academics, Politics, and the 1972 Election*. Washington, D.C.: American Enterprise Institute, 1973.

Lipset, Seymour Martin. *American Exceptionalism: A Double-Edged Sword*. New York: Norton, 1996.

———. *The First New Nation: The United States in Historical and Comparative Perspective*. New York: Basic Books, 1963.

———. *Neoconservatism: Myth and Reality*. Berlin: John F. Kennedy Institut für Nordamerikastudien der Freien Universitat Berlin, 1988.

Lipset, Seymour Martin, and Jason M. Lakin. *The Democratic Century*. Norman, OK: University of Oklahoma, 2004.

Moynihan, Daniel Patrick. *Came the Revolution: Argument in the Reagan Era*. San Diego: Harcourt Brace Jovanovich, 1988.

———. *Counting Our Blessings: Reflections on the Future of America*. Boston: Little, Brown, 1980.

Moynihan, Daniel Patrick, et al., eds. *The Future of the Family*. New York: Russell Sage Foundation, 2004.

Muravchik, Joshua. *Exporting Democracy: Fulfilling America's Destiny*. Washington, D.C.: AEI Press, 1991.

Saeger, Richard T. *American Government and Politics: A Neoconservative Approach*. Glenview, IL: Scott Foresman, 1982.

Sindler, Allan P. *America in the Seventies: Problems, Policies, and Politics*. Boston: Little, Brown, 1977.

Steinfels, Peter. *The Neoconservatives: The Men Who Are Changing America's Politics*. New York: Simon and Schuster, 1979.

"Tom Wolfe and the Derrière Guard." *Think Tank with Ben Wattenberg*. 27 December 2007. (Television Transcript.) www.pbs.org/thinktank/transcript1294.html.

United States Census Bureau. *Statistical Abstract of the United States: 2007*. Washington, D.C.: Government Printing Office, 2006.

Valenti, Jack. *A Very Human President*. New York: Norton, 1975.

Wattenberg, Ben J. *The Birth Dearth*. New York: Pharos Books, 1987.

———. *Fewer: How the New Demography of Depopulation Will Shape Our Future*. Chicago: Ivan R. Dee, 2004.

———. *The Good News Is the Bad News Is Wrong*. New York: Simon and Schuster, 1984.

———. *The Real America: A Surprising Examination of the State of the Union.* Garden City, NY: Doubleday, 1974.

———. *Values Matter Most: How Republicans or Democrats or a Third Party Can Win and Renew the American Way of Life.* New York: Free Press, 1995.

Wattenberg, Ben J., et al. *The First Measured Century: An Illustrated Guide to Trends in America, 1900–2000.* Washington, D.C.: AEI Press, 2001.

Wattenberg, Ben J., and Ervin S. Duggan. *Against All Enemies.* Garden City, NY: Doubleday, 1977.

Wattenberg, Ben J., and Richard M. Scammon. *The Real Majority.* New York: Coward-McCann, 1970.

———. *This U.S.A.: An Unexpected Family Portrait of 194,067,296 Americans Drawn from the Census.* Garden City, NY: Doubleday, 1965.

Wattenberg, Ben J., and Richard J. Whalen. *The Wealth Weapon: U.S. Foreign Policy and Multinational Corporations.* New Brunswick, NJ: Transaction Books, 1980.

Wattenberg, Ben J., and Karl Zinsmeister, eds. *Are World Population Trends a Problem?* Washington, D.C.: American Enterprise Institute, 1985.

White, Theodore H. *The Making of the President, 1960.* New York: Atheneum, 1961.

Wilson, James Q. *Thinking About Crime.* New York: Basic Books, 1975.

———. *Two Nations.* Washington, D.C.: AEI Press, 1998.

Winik, Jay. *On the Brink: The Dramatic, Behind-the-Scenes Saga of the Reagan Era and the Men and Women Who Won the Cold War.* New York: Simon and Schuster, 1996.

Index